Richard Strauss

An Intimate Portrait

KURT WILHELM

Richard
Strauss

An Intimate Portrait

Translated by Mary Whittall
Colour photographs by Paul Sessner
With 492 illustrations, 23 in colour

RIZZOLI
NEW YORK

Dedicated to Frau Alice Strauss
in admiration and gratitude

First published in the United States of America in 1989 by
Rizzoli International Publications, Inc.
597 Fifth Avenue, New York, NY 10017

First published in West Germany by Kindler Verlag GmbH as
Richard Strauss persönlich
© 1984 by Kindler Verlag GmbH, München

English translation © 1989 Mary Whittall

Library of Congress Cataloging-in-Publication Data

Wilhelm, Kurt, 1923–
    Richard Strauss: an intimate portrait.

    Translation of: Richard Strauss persönlich.
    Bibliography: p.
    Includes index.
    1. Strauss, Richard, 1864–1949.   2. Composers—Germany—
    Biography.   3. Strauss, Richard, 1864–1949—Pictorial works.
    I. Title.
ML410.S93W5413   1989   780′.92′4   [B]   88–43285
ISBN 0–8478–1021–6

Printed and bound in the German Democratic Republic

CONTENTS

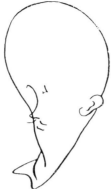

Erst 'ne Birne,   Dann 'ne Stirne,   Haare kraus — Richard Strauß.

Preface

A Beginner's Guide to Drawing Richard Strauss
First a pear | Then the brows | Lots of hair – Richard Strauss.

We know a lot about Wagner, Beethoven, Chopin, Brahms and most of the other great composers. We know how they got on with the rest of the world, how they lived, what they suffered, what aroused their wrath and what lightened their hearts.

Strauss was talked about a lot in his lifetime. For instance, it was said:

'He's a well-to-do bourgeois, who plays skat incessantly and loses his temper if he loses. A native of Munich, thick-skinned, blasé, a millionaire and a miser.'

Yet . . . he paid for the publication of the works of younger composers, Eugen Bodart's first opera *Hirtenlegende*, for example. A gift. No strings. Not an obviously miserly thing to do.

'He's married to a shrew who offends everybody and has him under her thumb.'

Yet . . . the marriage lasted fifty-six years, unblighted by a single infidelity or *affaire*, and he continued to write his wife tender love-letters even when he was an old man.

'He's an opportunist, always protecting his own interests, and collaborated with the Nazis in his old age.'

Yet . . . he had a Jewish daughter-in-law and kept her safe throughout the years of the Third Reich. Under that same régime he composed an opera on a text by a Jew, fought tooth and nail to get it performed and wanted to continue working with the same man. Something there doesn't quite add up.

> 'He is overrated as an opera composer, lets everything be too easy, he ought to write operettas instead of doodling on in that overweight late Romantic idiom. Not one of the great men in the history of music, but only a master of externals, no depth.'

Adrian Leverkühn, the protagonist of Thomas Mann's *Doktor Faustus*, wrote him off as gifted, but as a good skittle player is gifted. Yet his symphonic poems have been unfailingly popular in the concert halls for a hundred years, and his operas have been part of the standard repertory for nearly eighty years. If it's a fad, it's taking its time to pass.

Books about him by the professors and the professional writers about music began to appear in his thirty-seventh year, because his music was so frightfully modern that it was a kindness to the confused public to have the symphonic poems ('an inferior artistic genre') explained and the operas elucidated, so that they should understand the thing that made their ears ache. So the scholars analysed structure and content, took the pieces to pieces, in order to show by the parts how the whole functioned.

They had little to say about the works' creator. There was no immortal beloved in his life, his life was not threatened by consumption, no princes treated him like a lackey, he never seized fate by the throat. Occasionally he expressed a robust opinion, sometimes he lost his temper in public – and of course there was that terrifying wife. Nothing there for a serious commentator to get his teeth into.

Richard Strauss the man 'stayed at a distance, as if behind a veil of smoke'. He always asserted that his music was a self-portrait, that he depicted himself, his nature and his world, painting them in notes as a painter does in oils.

How did he live? What did he experience, what did he believe, think, say, do? What did he think of the people he worked with, the rest of society, the times he lived through, from the establishment of the Wilhelmine Empire to the division of Germany? Did he approve of the unstoppable advance of science and technology? What were his political opinions? The rest of society had no way of finding out.

He lived as if behind a wall, over which no one was allowed to peep. He did not engage in public controversies or indulge in self-explication. He did not formulate artistic theories (unlike Pfitzner, for example). His admirers were left with no other course but to burn incense, while his opponents could only raise a splenetic din, and accuse the admirers of bad taste.

How should we approach him? His genius, his composing are inaccessible and cannot be described in words in any case. But the man is reflected in his everyday life and in exceptional situations, and these can be written about.

In 1951 I was allowed to go through the archives in Garmisch and start a catalogue of the tens of thousands of letters. I found myself among a thousand mirrors, each reflecting a different facet of the characteristics of the man. Then Dr Franz Strauss and his wife, Frau Alice, gave me permission to publish their private photographs, of which there were about a thousand. Was I to use this opportunity for nothing more than a book of pictures with brief captions?

There was no question of my attempting a comprehensive analysis of the life and the music. Much has already been published on his work, and he himself had appointed an official biographer in Dr Willi Schuh.

There did not yet exist, however, a book about the personality, the character: about Strauss the man. So I collected together photos, caricatures, and verbal pictures as well: quotations, anecdotes, reminiscences, even newspaper cuttings; and from these tesserae I began to form a picture in mosaic, an intimate portrait of Richard Strauss.

Unhappily only a few of his contemporaries wrote about him so vividly as Max Steinitzer, Romain Rolland or Elisabeth Schumann. Most of them offer only unreflecting clichés about his reticence, the wall of apparent phlegm and cool sociability that was erected by himself and was hard to penetrate. In the service of my mosaic, therefore, I put together all the snapshots and the spotlit moments that I thought characteristic, so that readers can compile the portrait for themselves. The abundance of material led me to adopt a succinct style, sometimes verging on the telegraphic, but always seeking to convey the necessary facts and information at each stage.

Many domestic and family details were revealed to me by Frau Alice and Dr Franz Strauss, their sons Richard and Christian and Anni Nitzl. The recollections of Clemens Krauss, Viorica Ursuleac, Rudolf Hartmann, Hans Hotter, Franz Klarwein and other distinguished Straussians added to the picture. Dr Willi Schuh and Dr Franz Trenner came to my aid with additional information, criticism and advice. My warm thanks to them all for their trouble and their help.

It is my hope that, having reached the end of this depiction of a life, the reader will be able to say: 'Ah, that's what it was like, that's what he was like, that's what his life, his times, his way of life were like. I feel that I've met him, I've come to know –

Kurt Wilhelm
Strasslach, September 1983

Munich, the city of Strauss's birth, seen from the Maximilianeum, with the Court Opera in the middle, c. 1865.

Munich 1864

Bavaria looks back on fourteen hundred years of history. In 1864 its capital city had a population of 150,000 and occupied an area of some thirteen square miles. There were forty-one churches and seventeen theatres. The foundation stone of a new theatre had just been laid when Richard Strauss was born. This was the Theater am Gärtnerplatz, paid for by public subscription, and destined to be a home of comedy and light opera; it was there, in 1949, during the celebrations surrounding his eighty-fifth birthday, that Strauss paid his last visit to a theatre, for a performance of Hugo von Hofmannsthal's version of *Le bourgeois gentilhomme*, with incidental music by himself.

Bavaria is a land of peasant farmers, born into families who have held on to their land for countless generations, each a monarch on his own soil. The people are frugal – often to the point of miserliness – tenacious, stubborn, and given to greeting anything new, or not Bavarian, with tolerant scepticism. Nor do they hold with making any show of what they have. The Strausses and the Pschorrs were thus true Bavarians. Their illustrious scion, Richard Strauss, was to enlarge his property in Garmisch like any farming forebear, by prudent purchases of the land adjoining his, giving himself space, privacy and freedom from interference.

Its people have decorated Bavaria more richly perhaps than any other part of Germany, in great houses, monasteries and Baroque churches, and in every humble nook and cranny. There is a centuries-old tradition of folk art, of ordinary people painting, carving, writing poetry and songs, dancing and playing musical instruments for the love of it, not to make money. Bavarians made beautiful things because, if a thing was necessary, then it was also necessary that it should be beautiful. They thought of themselves as craftsmen, and of most professional artists as drones. The great Baroque architects – the Dientzenhofers, the Asams, Fischer – were craftsmen. Richard Strauss was a craftsman, supporting his family by his own practical skills.

Genius and greatness have seldom been acclaimed, and Bavaria's contribution to the outstanding achievements in world art has been small. Rather, the omnipresent folk art has fostered an appreciation of modest, average ability. Any genius born in Bavaria has been well-advised to look outside his homeland for recognition – and Strauss was no exception.

The Wittelsbachs, as dukes and Electors of the Holy Roman Empire, had been on the throne for seven hundred years. In 1806 Napoleon made Bavaria a kingdom, a buffer state in the middle of the continent, and the largest in area of all the German states. The portly and popular King Max I Joseph built himself a big new opera house, which would be famous in the history of music for the first performances of several of Wagner's works. For many years Franz Strauss played first horn in its orchestra, and his son Richard, having suffered there the frustrations of a junior conductor, was to return in triumph as an old man.

King Ludwig I (1825–48) loved art, above all that of classical Greece, and he rebuilt Munich as a new Athens. The Romantic era was leavened by a strong classicist bias in Bavaria, because the Bavarian sense of irony will not stomach too much Romanticism. Old, narrow, Gothic streets were levelled to make room for broad processional ways. Museums and propylaea were built with Greek façades, and what might have been built as a belvedere in another place became a 'monopteros' in Munich. A 'Valhalla' was built at Regensburg on the banks of the Danube, but it was a Greek temple, dedicated to German heroes in politics, the arts and learning (a bust of Richard Strauss was unveiled there on 14 July 1973).

Ludwig's son, Max II, drew university men and poets to Munich from other parts of Germany, including Paul Heyse, winner of the Nobel Prize for Literature in 1910, and Emanuel Geibel. Young Richard Strauss would set poems by 'northerners' such as these to music.

Any claim Munich may have to be a Mecca of the arts is no greater, and no less, than that of many other cities. The arts prospered during the nineteenth century, but patronage was no longer the preserve of the church and the monarchy. Increasingly, artists had to please a wider, general public, yet at the same time a gulf began to open between popular art and a more élitist 'artists' art'.

Strauss grew up during the reign of King Ludwig II, of whom it cannot be said with certainty whether his ambition was to establish a kingdom

The hub of Bavaria, the Marienplatz. On the column, the statue of the Virgin Mary as Patrona Bavariae. The young Richard used to hear open-air concerts here. Neuhauser Strasse, in the background, leads to the Pschorr House, where he was born.

11

dedicated to the Muses, as Ludwig I's grandson well might, or merely to live out his life in a dream world. He was popular with his subjects but grew increasingly hostile to human society, and had no talent for politics. Bavaria's influence in German affairs diminished under his rule, and while his country was caught up in the wars of 1866 and 1870 he concerned himself primarily with castle-building and the arts. In 1886 he was deposed and sent under guard to his castle on Lake Starnberg, where he drowned the very next day in mysterious circumstances.

Ludwig was Franz Strauss's employer for over twenty years, recognizing his services with the title of 'Kammermusiker' ('Musician of the Chamber' – an honour still awarded to meritorious musicians by the modern, republican state of Bavaria) and, in 1879, the Ludwig Medal for Learning and the Arts. As a member of the Court Orchestra, Franz Strauss took part in the notorious private performances in the Court Theatre given to an audience of one, Ludwig himself. On 19 June 1886 the dead king was interred in the crypt of the Michaelskirche, across the road from the Pschorr House, where the Strauss family occupied a flat on the upper floor. Lily Bamberger-Reiff, a childhood friend of Richard Strauss, was among the guests invited to watch the procession from the windows, and she recalled that Richard, his friend Ludwig Thuille and other young members of the Pschorr clan were supremely unimpressed by the ceremonial in the street, but munched cake, joked and laughed. To them the funeral was just a spectacle. Certainly Richard Strauss never displayed an interest in the 'dream king', and never once mentioned him in letters or memoirs. His only significance for Strauss lay in his patronage of Wagner, which had made Bayreuth possible. Nothing else counted. There are many who would agree that the fruits of royal patronage – the buildings, the pictures, the poems and the music – are more durable than military or political achievements.

Politics and the kingdom – later the Free State – of Bavaria, were matters of comparative indifference to Strauss for seventy years, until the day came when even he could not escape the tentacles of a relentless political force.

Ancestors

At some date in the seventeenth century a brewer and postmaster named Helfenrieder, from the small town of Weilheim in the lake-studded plains lying between Munich and the Alps, married Maria Agathe Bayerlacher, an innkeeper's daughter from the even smaller town of Uffing on the Staffelsee. Their descendants in the nineteenth century included a number of people of prominence in Bavarian life, and some, indeed, of more than a purely local reputation: the poet Ludwig Thoma, the Biedermeier painter Carl Spitzweg, an admiral in the German navy who took part in the Battle of Jutland in 1916, and a whole family of woodcarvers in Oberammergau, one of whom, Anton Lang, played the role of Christ in the Passion Play in 1900, 1910 and 1912. Another branch of this spreading family tree, many of whose members displayed an interest in, and aptitude for, the fine or the applied arts, was the Pschorr family, one of the Munich brewing dynasties. Richard Strauss's mother was a Pschorr.

The Pschorr family business was established by Joseph Pschorr (1770–1841), who married the heiress of another brewing family, the Hackers. Thenceforth the two commercial empires grew side by side.

His son Georg was good-natured, but growing prosperity did not prevent him from often wearing his underwear about the house, to save his good clothes. Thrift was a matter of principle. At meals, he was always the first to be served, until it came to the cheese, which he did not care for. Then he would grumble at the maid: 'Don't you know the proper way to do things, Kathi? Guests come first in our house.' Georg's wife was a brisk, bustling woman who, as they say, wore the trousers. The patriarch also took a robust attitude to his parental function, saying: 'The boys are beaten every Saturday, whether they've done anything or not – they always deserve it.'

The Neo-Gothic Neues Rathaus on the Marienplatz as it looked c. 1874. The big house next to it was built in 1834 by Joseph Pschorr, the founder of the brewery. He kept his coffin in the house and had it revarnished from time to time.

Strauss's maternal grandparents: Georg Pschorr (1798–1867) and Juliana Pschorr, née Rieg, from Landsberg in Upper Bavaria (1809–62). His paternal grandparents were poor folk and no photographs of them have survived.

A strong sense of familial propriety ensured that their son-in-law Franz Strauss (Richard's father), whose orchestral salary was less than munificent, was given financial help when necessary. The whole extended family of uncles, aunts and cousins loved to get together regularly, to gossip and laugh, speak their minds and render each other support and comfort when needed. Most of them possessed some degree of artistic talent. Richard's Uncle Georg, under whose management the brewery went from strength to strength, was a gifted painter. In 1910, Strauss was to dedicate *Der Rosenkavalier* to his 'beloved kinfolk in the Pschorr family' – which is not to say he loved them all equally.

His mother Josepha Strauss, *née* Pschorr (born 10 April 1838 in Munich, where she died 15 April 1910), was one of five sisters, which meant that her own children had a horde of cousins. She was quiet, shy and the soul of goodness; inevitably she was overshadowed by the somewhat volatile temperament of her husband. Better than anything else, she liked (as Aminta claims of herself in *Die schweigsame Frau*) to sit quietly doing her needlework. She had little propensity for asserting herself. As she grew older she became mentally unstable: nervous breakdowns, allied to an overpowering sense of inferiority, led to periods of treatment in institutions at a time when psychiatry was in its infancy. One of her doctors was Dr Gudden, who was assigned to treat Ludwig II and drowned with him.

During one of her attacks, in 1899, her daughter Johanna wrote to Richard that 'it wasn't so very bad, but her anxiety grew worse and worse, she talked about "standing in our way", and of removing herself from the scene, so as not to damage Otto's career'. (Johanna's husband, Otto Rauchenberger, was an army officer.) Pauline Strauss wrote to her husband on a later occasion: 'Your dear mother was in a truly sorry condition, looked very weak and much aged when they took her to Eglfing [a clinic near Munich]. The doctor out there said she had left the clinic this spring much too soon.' (5 December 1906)

Her son did not inherit her instability but certainly he had something of her hypersensitivity and tendency to overexcitement. The strength with which he controlled his emotions came from his father. It was with reference to his mother's connection with the brewery trade that he would sometimes claim that he himself sprang from 'the dregs of the population' – a piece of mock humility, because the word 'dregs' in that particular metaphor is also the word for 'yeast'.

Franz Strauss came from the Upper Palatinate, that – even today – remote, north-eastern corner of Bavaria bordering Bohemia. Much of the population is of the same racial stock as that of Bohemia and the area has been a rich breeding-ground for musicians; Gluck and Reger both came from the Upper Palatinate. The Walter family, to which Franz Strauss's mother belonged, had been active for many generations as schoolteachers, parish musicians and tower-masters: this last post combined the duties of nightwatchman and director of the parish band. Maria Walter's brothers carried on the family tradition.

Johann Urban Strauss (born 20 December 1800) was the son of an usher employed by the district court in Rothenstadt. At the age of twenty-two he was living out of wedlock with Maria Walter (born 24 April 1800) in Parkstein. They had two children, but Urban Strauss remained dependent on his parents, was unable to support them properly, and abandoned Maria and the children after five years. At the time of the first child's birth he was doing military service and it is possible that he was refused leave to marry. Maria Walter brought up her children with the help of her own family. Urban gave them his surname and then disappeared from their lives. The reason for his going is unknown: poverty and despair can destroy a relationship as easily as fecklessness. He spent the rest of his life as a court usher and constable in various small townships in the Upper Palatinate; he married, fathered another seven children and died in 1859.

Maria Walter died alone and unmarried in Parkstein in 1870, by which date her grandson Richard was six years old and her son a much respected member of the Court Orchestra in Munich.

Franz Joseph Strauss (born 26 February 1822 in Parkstein, died 11 May 1905 in Munich) was recalled by his son in the following terms: 'With his high forehead and his aquiline nose rather reminiscent of a Circassian chieftain, my father may well, in my opinion, have been of Bohemian stock. He was what they call a character. He would have considered it dishonourable ever to revise an artistic opinion and would never listen to me until very late in his life.'

His early life was hard. He was five years old when his father left home, and he was brought up in the care of his mother's brothers. For a number of years he lived in Nabburg, where his uncle Franz Michael Walter was tower-master. This much respected man was a strict guardian, who taught his nephew to play horn, guitar, violin, trumpet and dulcimer. While still no more than a child, Franz played at any number of local festivities – weddings, holidays – in the region, as well as singing in the church choir. He also had to take his turn fire-watching at night from the church tower in Nabburg. The first turning-point in his life came when he was fifteen, and two of his uncles went to Munich to join the private orchestra of Duke Max, the King's cousin (and father of Elisabeth, the future Empress of Austria). The duke was a genial *bon viveur*, a lover of music, poetry, horses, women and

Richard's mother, Josepha Strauss as a young woman.

Richard at the ages of one, two and three years.

Richard's father, Franz Joseph Strauss.

Elise Seiff, his first wife.

a little learning. In his private orchestra, the Walter brothers and, in time, young Franz played before the cream of Munich society. They also formed a trio and toured, giving concerts as far away as Switzerland. Franz was a highly expert and competent musician on all his many instruments, and no less at home with music of a more popular nature. He also composed a little, and some of this music was published.

He was twenty-five when he joined the Court Orchestra, where he was to remain for forty-two years, as hornist and viola-player, serving Ludwig I, Max II, Ludwig II and the regent Prince Luitpold, and proving a thorn in the flesh to Richard Wagner.

Franz Strauss was a strict, inflexible and sometimes bitter man. He never forgot his early life, which stamped his character and his opinions indelibly. He never mentioned it to his children but was unceasing in his efforts to impress upon them the virtues of thrift, order and prudence. At the age of twenty-nine he married Elise Seiff, the daughter of a military bandmaster. Their first child, a boy, died of tuberculosis when only ten months old, in 1854; a yet heavier blow fell on Franz Strauss after three years of marriage, when both his wife and their infant daughter died of cholera. At thirty-two he was a widower.

He made the acquaintance of the wealthy brewer's daughter Josepha Pschorr two years later. With a salary of only 42 gulden a month, it took him seven years to pluck up the courage to propose to her. At the time of the wedding, he was forty-two and his bride twenty-five. Her father allowed the newly-weds to live in a small apartment in the Pschorr House, above the beerhall, with a separate entrance on Altheimer Eck. There Richard Georg Strauss was born on 11 June 1864.

His sister, Berta Johanna Strauss, was born on 9 June 1867, two days before Richard's third birthday; as a result they celebrated their birthdays together. She was as lively and excitable as her brother, and the pair were inseparable partners in crime. When Johanna was small the family lived in

Children's party at carnival-time, 1870. The first picture of Strauss wielding a conductor's baton (back row, right). Though not yet a Wagnerian, he is dressed as a minnesinger.

Beware! The ears of art-lovers who come to see the commemorative plaque are blasted by the strains of Elektra *and* Salome!

The courtyard of the Pschorr House, where Strauss was born and brought up, and where his parents ended their days. The bustle of the brewery on the ground floor did not disturb the family. In 1914, when Strauss was fifty, a commemorative plaque was fixed to the front of the building. The plaque survived when the house was bombed in 1944. After a concrete department store was built on the site, a Richard Strauss fountain, designed by the sculptor Hans Wimmer, was put up in the street outside.

Richard and his sister must be about 12 and 9 years old in these pictures. He had already composed some 30 works: 13 songs, 11 piano pieces, 2 chamber works and an overture for orchestra.

a slightly larger flat on Sonnenstrasse, where the children busied themselves in such enthralling games as squashing little sister against the mirror on the wall, climbing out of the second-storey window and balancing on the sill, crawling about on the sideboard till it fell over, to the detriment of the china: in short, they were entirely normal children.

Richard was an affectionate and gallant brother, regularly bringing Johanna little presents when he returned from excursions long or short; they went to dancing classes together, partnered each other at the fancy-dress parties given at carnival time by the Wilde Gung'l (of which more later), and occasionally made music together, though it was then usually a matter of 'Oh, let *me* do it, you don't do it right'. Later, Johanna's first grown-up ball-dress was a gift from her brother.

Family Life

My mother tells of my earliest childhood that I used to react with a smile to the sound of the horn and with loud crying to the sound of a violin.

RICHARD STRAUSS

In 1869 the Strauss family moved back into another apartment in the Pschorr House, with an entrance on Neuhauser Strasse. It was a simple, modest dwelling, lit by oil and acetylene lamps. There was no such thing as electric light in those days, and no water supply above the ground floor of the building: it had to be drawn up in pails by means of a pulley under the eaves.

Pride of place in the main room went to the Blüthner grand piano, bought with money left to Josepha Strauss by her grandmother. There was a modest amount of cherry-wood Biedermeier furniture; a few rugs lay on the floor and family portraits hung on the walls. Josepha Strauss's sewing table stood in one corner. The windows overlooked the bustle of Neuhauser Strasse, which was always loud with the wheels of carts and carriages, the clatter of feet on the cobbles, and the street cries sung by hawkers of flowers, fruit, vegetables, firewood and eggs. Father Strauss's sanctum, whence he could be heard practising, overlooked the courtyard at the back. The children and the maid each had their own small rooms. Wood was the fuel burned on the huge, old kitchen range.

The family watchword was thrift: plain food (chocolate was strictly a Christmas treat), Shanks's pony rather than the horse-tram, no extravagance in dress, no expensive hobbies. Everyone in the household worked from morning till night: thus young Richard learned economy and good housekeeping by example.

For entertainment, there was the Changing of the Guard to watch at midday on the Marienplatz, to the accompaniment of a military band. In summer they went out for long walks, when Richard risked his neck climbing everything in sight. In winter there were skating, snowball fights, and sliding on the ice. During the school term there was gymnastics twice a week. And there was always some new prank: throwing pebbles at people from a hiding place, knocking over a heap of beer-barrels . . .

The great holiday of the year was Corpus Christi, when a procession wound through the streets, passing the house of Uncle Knözinger (a Munich 'character'), whose windows gave all seven branches of the Pschorr clan a grandstand view, before they started on the traditional party with beer and sausages.

Grandmother's legacy of 5000 marks paid – in addition to the grand piano – for a trip to Italy for the parents, and eight successive summer holidays in Sillian in the Tyrol, where the pure mountain air eased Father Strauss's asthma – the horn-player's curse. Richard played organ sonatas by Mendelssohn in the village church, fished in the river, climbed, was allowed to drive the one-horse chaise, and succeeded in tipping the whole family into a ditch one day when the reins became tangled round the chestnut's legs. There were also holidays spent nearer home, with relatives who lived in small towns all over Bavaria and Franconia. Other people

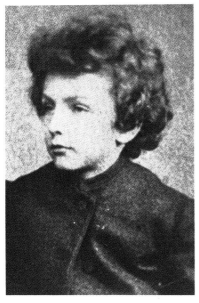

Richard, aged eight.

18

travelled from far and wide to spend their holidays in Bavaria: why should Bavarians go anywhere else? True, away from home, Richard missed his familiar room, his piano and his desk, but he was always happy to be closer to nature. His life-long love of the Alps was born in these years, and would lead him to set up his home in Garmisch in his mid-forties.

Once, when they were staying at Murnau, Richard, aged fourteen, set off with a party to climb the Heimgarten. They left at 2 a.m., in an open waggon, and climbed for five hours. They got lost, and spent three hours more clambering down. A thunderstorm broke, and they got soaked to the skin. After twelve hours on their feet, wet and hungry, they took refuge for the night in a peasant's hut. To Richard, it was not an ordeal but 'interesting and made a change. The next day I depicted our excursion on the piano. Naturally with colossal tone-painting and clangour, *à la* Wagner.' Thirty-four years later, in the Alpine Symphony, he depicted it again, with more philosophical resonances.

The seven families of Pschorr cousins and their friends were constantly in and out of each other's homes, and went together to concerts, the theatre and the opera, whenever they could lay their hands on cheap tickets. Entertainment in the home was frugal: whoever was host paid for beer, but the food was a Dutch treat, the guests each ordering what they wanted from the menu of the nearest restaurant, which the maid would then be despatched to fetch. This was all they could afford, and no one grumbled.

Everyone in the family played an instrument or sang, and domestic concerts were regular events. They worked their way through the classics,

The Odeonssaal (opened 1828), where Munich's young musical enthusiasts made the acquaintance of the orchestral repertory.

giving Richard, who played violin and piano, a foundation in the chamber-music repertory. They argued about such thorny points as whether enharmonic changes in notation, for example Weber's writing E flat instead of D sharp, were permissible. They discussed works they heard at concerts, agreeing that Rubinstein's D minor Concerto was boring, while Spohr's Violin Concerto no. 8 was much more fun.

On birthdays and other holidays they gave each other their own compositions as presents, and ceremonially performed them. Aunt Johanna Pschorr had a mezzo-soprano voice and musical talent which would have graced the operatic stage, had she been so minded: her nephew composed no fewer than twenty-five songs for her, some very difficult. In his chamber music, he took the technical limitations of his various relatives into account, and gave himself the most difficult part. He was learning his future trade, and music was already the centre of his existence.

The music-making was usually followed by laughter and joking, by party games and forfeits. When Richard was alone, he read a lot. Organized games like football hardly registered in those days, and there does not appear to have been much interest in politics in the Pschorr/Strauss circle. The people of Munich turned out on to the streets to welcome the Bavarian troops returning from the Franco-Prussian War in 1870. Richard was seven then, and there is no mention of the occasion in any of the Strauss family papers, or of any other political question. The encroachment on Bavaria's sovereignty – as Ludwig II bowed to pressure from Bismarck, acknowledged the King of Prussia as German Emperor and accepted the fusion of the independent states in one giant empire – was never discussed. One was a Bavarian and now one was a German as well, and that was all there was to it. Politics was for politicians. Work – and music – were much more interesting.

Christmas Song, *the second composition*.

Later, Strauss would grumble about Munich as a 'petty bourgeois nest' and seek to spread his wings in a wider world: that too was a consequence of the times. After a few years of enthusiasm for the idea of German unity, experience of the reality induced a sense of disillusionment in the smaller states. Much that had been long established and taken for granted was suddenly sacrificed to the centralist policies of the imperial government in Berlin. The wind of change blowing through Germany caused many of the country's inhabitants, not just the Bavarians, to batten down the hatches and cling tightly to all that threatened to be swept away. A pervasive spirit of conservatism filled the air, and to a young firebrand, intent on breaking new artistic ground, it was stifling.

An Education

At the age of four-and-a-half, Richard began piano lessons with a colleague of his father's, the harpist August Tombo. He made rapid progress, coming up with some audacious fingering in his eagerness to get a grasp on a piece as a whole, rather than attending to correctness in detail. He liked operatic melodies best, and sight-reading came easily to him. At the age of five he started to compose, without anyone allowing him to get the idea that he was a prodigy. His first work was called *Tailor's Polka* (*Schneiderpolka*), the second *Christmas Song* (*Weihnachtslied*); his mother had to add the words to the latter manuscript, for the six-year-old composer could not yet write his letters, even though writing music in three parts held no terrors for him, and he could bring off a modulation from E major to G sharp minor (in bar 7) with aplomb. He wrote a series of six more songs, then two more piano pieces. One of these, the *Panzenburg Polka* ('Panzenburg' or 'Paunch Castle' is what they call a pile of empty beer barrels in Bavaria), was orchestrated by his father, who performed it with an amateur band he conducted. Richard's mother was away from home at the time, and her husband wrote to tell her about it: 'They were all amazed and said they didn't believe that it was all his own work. . . . It really is very nice and sounds well. He asked me this morning if the gentlemen had liked it, and when I assured him that they had, his eyes shone.' By the age of eight Richard was ready to tackle orchestration for himself, producing a 33-page overture to a Singspiel, *Highland Loyalty* (*Hochlands Treue*), with double woodwind and brass.

At seven he entered the Cathedral School in Munich, and he also went to the opera for the first time and heard *Der Freischütz*. In the following year he started the violin, taking lessons from his cousin Benno Walter, the leader of the Court Orchestra, who was to give the first performance of Strauss's Violin Concerto in Vienna in 1882. At ten Richard entered the Ludwig Grammar School. The curriculum had a conventional bias to the classics – Latin, Greek, also French, and Maths, which he detested. He found other boys in his class who shared his interest in music, including two of his future biographers, Max Steinitzer and Arthur Seidl.

Learn, my son! Whether your talent will last has yet to be seen. Many a good musician has a struggle to earn a crust. You might be better off as a cobbler or a tailor!

FRANZ STRAUSS

Strauss's cousin, and violin teacher, Benno Walter.

A sketch of the Violin Concerto, 1878, done in a maths exercise book. Richard did some of his early composing during lessons at school, on the sheets of manuscript paper which his mother sometimes used to wrap his books in.

An advertisement for the concert at which the D minor Symphony was performed in 1881. The composer was seventeen. The conductor was Hermann Levi, but conductors' names did not appear on posters or in programmes in those days.

A new piano teacher, Carl Niest, put a stop to his splashy fingering when he was eleven: from now on he was to take it seriously. He also began lessons in composition with one of the conductors of the Court Orchestra, Hofkapellmeister Friedrich Wilhelm Meyer, who was successful in channelling his pupil's superabundance of energy. The Serenade for wind op. 7 is dedicated to him 'in gratitude'. Posterity has reason to be grateful to him too, for giving Strauss such a formidable technical foundation.

A report written by his form-master Karl Welzhofer when he was eleven shows that his school work did not suffer in spite of his three types of music lessons:

There can be few pupils in whom a sense of duty, talent and liveliness are united to the degree that they are in this boy. His enthusiasm is huge, he enjoys learning and it comes easily to him. Pleasure in each new accomplishment spurs him on to work yet harder. He pays close attention in class, nothing escapes him. And yet he is incapable of sitting still for a moment, his bench is a torment to him. Unclouded merriment and high spirits sparkle in his blue eyes day after day; candour and good nature are written on his face. His work is good, very good. No teacher could help but like such a boy, indeed, it is rather hard not to betray favouritism. Strauss is a promising musical talent.

The boy was father to the man. In maturity, self-discipline taught him to conceal the overflowing restlessness of his temperament, but the sense of duty spurring him on to use his talents and energies fruitfully, the keen attentiveness, the pleasure in the outcome of hard work which encouraged him to move straight on to something new: these characteristics never left him. In his life, as in his music, he never sat still.

By the age of thirteen, Richard was tackling Czerny, *The Well-Tempered Clavier* (Bach was not much played in those days) and Mendelssohn's D minor Concerto on the piano, duos by Viotti and études by Kreutzer on the violin, and double counterpoint as a composer. The amateur Wilde Gung'l orchestra played his G major Serenade, after his proud father had insisted on copying out all the parts himself.

His composition lessons ceased when he was sixteen. He took part in school concerts and the like, both as a pianist and in chamber-music groups, sometimes performing his own works. By the time he left school at eighteen, he was the composer of some 140 pieces: 59 Lieder, 45 pieces for piano, 1 Mass, 6 overtures, 4 pieces for horn, 5 for orchestra, 6 trios and quartets, 5 choruses, 3 orchestral Lieder, 1 symphony, 2 pieces for wind, 2 for cello, 1 for flute and 8 four-part unaccompanied songs, as well as countless composition exercises and thirty other pieces abandoned unfinished.

'I composed too much, too early, and so squandered a lot of spontaneity and energy as well', he commented in 1910. In his will he directed that his juvenilia were to be neither published nor performed, as they had no bearing on his later development. They show talent but little originality, remaining in the classical mainstream and full of reminiscences of the great – and lesser – masters of the past. But Strauss had learnt his craft in writing them, and from then onwards he was to make a radical change of course, as Wagner, Liszt, Hans von Bülow and Alexander Ritter showed him the way to his true self. Of his childhood idols, only Mozart endured; at the age of eighty he dedicated his Sonatina no. 2 for wind to 'the shade of the immortal Mozart, at the end of a life filled with thanksgiving'.

Strauss grew up with Mozart, Beethoven, Schubert, Mendelssohn and Spohr, rather less with Schumann and Chopin. Chopin's chromaticism greatly appealed to him, but gave him technical problems. He scarcely got to know Bach or Handel. This was still the Romantic age in music, and large tracts of the Classical repertory, let alone the pre-Classical, were neglected: only three or four of Mozart's piano concertos were ever played, for instance. As a teenager, Strauss's taste echoed his father's: in opera, for example, he praised the second-act finale of *La dame blanche* by Boieldieu, an aria from Saint-Saëns' *Samson et Dalila*, and Auber's *La muette de Portici*; he adored *Fidelio* and Mozart's operas, but he took a dim view of the *Ring*. The profound musicality and versatility of Father Strauss lent him authority in the eyes of many others besides his son. He was endowed with an incredible seriousness and sense of responsibility. When he was due to play a demanding solo passage in a concert or an opera, he was ill from nervousness all day, shut himself up in his room and would speak to nobody. He was not at all a rich man, but he never accepted payment from his numerous pupils. It was a matter of simple duty for him to give what assistance he could to impecunious talents, and he was too proud to take money from the wealthy.

From 1875 to 1896, Franz Strauss was the conductor of the Wilde Gung'l, an amateur orchestra founded in the year of Richard's birth by a group of thirty doctors, lawyers, businessmen and public officials. It was named after the Gung'l orchestra, a professional band brought to Munich by its founder Joseph Gung'l, a one-time military bandmaster and a successful and prolific composer of marches and waltzes. Again, Franz Strauss took no fee for directing the Wilde Gung'l, but ruled it with a rod of iron. They rehearsed in a Munich tavern, the Drei Rosen, and gave both public concerts and private ones for their families and friends. Richard joined the orchestra as a schoolboy, in 1882, and stayed with it for three years, until he got his first job. He was popular with the older members, and caused them some amusement when he deliberately provoked his father's wrath, perhaps by tuning his violin pizzicato after a call for silence, his eyes resting guilelessly the while upon the conductor.

The Wilde Gung'l still exists. It is the owner of several of Strauss's autograph scores, including two festive marches and the D minor Symphony, and enjoys the exclusive right to perform them. The experience he gained while a player in it was invaluable to him in his career, as both conductor and master of orchestration.

Lover of the Classical masters that he was, Franz Strauss's loathing for Wagner knew no bounds. He vehemently condemned both the music and the man. As a member of the Munich Court Orchestra, and notably as its first horn-player, he was deeply involved in the premieres of *Tristan*, *Die Meistersinger*, *Das Rheingold* and *Die Walküre*. Though he acquitted himself

Eduard Hanslick, the most feared of the Viennese critics. His review of the Violin Concerto was the only benevolent notice he ever gave Strauss.

23

Richard and Cosima Wagner in Bayreuth.

dutifully in performance, his dislike was often vented at rehearsals. The theme played by the brass chorus during the riot at the end of Act II of *Die Meistersinger* so offended him that he once let fly with a *fortissimo* rendering of the popular song 'O du lieber Augustin' instead, to the fury of Hans von Bülow, the conductor.

Bülow was not popular with the Bavarians in the orchestra, in any case, with his clipped North German accent and his habit of sometimes stamping the beat with his foot. On one occasion, when the rehearsal had started at 9 a.m., he asked for a particularly tricky horn solo at 4 in the afternoon. Strauss: 'I can't do any more.' Bülow: 'Then go and draw your pension.' Strauss put his horn in its case, rose, went straight to the Intendant, Baron Perfall, and asked to be pensioned off immediately, on the instructions of 'Herr von Büloff'.

In Franz Strauss's opinion Wagner's horn parts were clarinet parts, technically speaking. To prevent him objecting that particularly difficult passages were unplayable, Wagner used to get his friend Hans Richter to try them first. Wagner found Strauss 'intolerable, but when he plays you simply cannot be angry with him'. For Strauss, Wagner was a Mephistopheles, the destroyer of everything that he valued. Nevertheless, he played conscientiously, even faultlessly, when he had to, even when he was obliged to go to Bayreuth for the premiere of *Parsifal*. Quite apart from their irreconcilable musical differences, he could never have been anything but antipathetical towards the effervescent Saxon who said of himself: 'My normal condition is exaltation'. From Bayreuth in 1882 the horn-player wrote that Wagner 'is ill with immeasurable megalomania and delirium. . . . He is always drunk. Recently he was so intoxicated at a rehearsal that he almost fell into the pit.' When the news of Wagner's death was announced to the Munich Court Orchestra during a rehearsal, all the players rose in respect – except Franz Strauss.

It is hardly surprising, then, to find the fourteen-year-old Richard Strauss deriding Wagner like a street-urchin. The principal recipient of his views in those days was Ludwig Thuille, an orphaned boy from the South Tyrol with great musical gifts, who was a protégé of Richard's aunt, while his musical training was taken in hand by Franz Strauss. From 1877 onwards, when Richard was thirteen and Ludwig sixteen, they wrote each other immensely long letters, always about the all-important subject of music. In 1878, Richard wrote to Ludwig as follows:

Dear Ludwig,
I went to *Siegfried* recently, and I tell you I was bored to tears, I was horrendously, dreadfully bored, I can't begin to tell you how bored I was. 'Ah, but it was beautiful, fantastically beautiful, the richness of the melodies, the tension of the drama, the refinement of the orchestration, and it was witty and inventive, really beautiful!' Now, you will say to yourself, he's got a screw loose somewhere, so I'll set the record straight again without further ado and tell you: it was appalling. The introduction is one long drumroll, with bass tuba and bassoons mooing away at the bottom of the register, which sounds so silly that I laughed

out loud. All at once it stops dead and then comes the horn quite alone:

Renewed murky drumroll with bass tuba and spuds, er, bassoon: and so it goes growling on and on until the curtain rises, and then it goes:

and that goes on in sequences, quite hellishly. When Siegfried comes on, it really gets exciting:

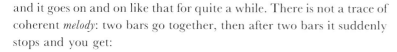

Strauss as a school-leaver.

and it goes on and on like that for quite a while. There is not a trace of coherent *melody*: two bars go together, then after two bars it suddenly stops and you get:

You get that, or the first growling again, I tell you it's chaos. You can't have the remotest notion what it's like. I also heard:

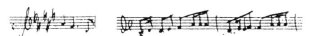

Ludwig Thuille.

from *Rheingold*. Then there's a horrendous passage in the first act consisting of lots of sequences (Wagner is altogether very fond of sequences) of diminished and augmented triads and seventh chords. This passage would kill a cat, it would turn rocks to scrambled eggs from sheer terror at the sound of all those appalling dissonances. The violins wear themselves out in incessant tremolos, and Wagner has used the *brass* and *string passagework*, and even the trumpet mute solely in order to make everything as appalling and infamous as possible. My ears buzzed at all these misshapen chords, if they can even be called that; and the last act is so boring you just want to sn*ff it. The scene between Siegfried and Brünnhilde is one long Adagio; isn't there ever going to be any Allegro, I asked myself; no, there's only this atrocious howling and whining from a seventh down to a ninth, and then up again, like this:

and so it goes on and on; this last scene is. . . . I just cannot find the words to tell you how ghastly it all was; and when you've heard the first scene of the first act, then you've heard the whole boiling, because it all gets repeated. The one thing that was at least *in tune* was the song of the woodbird. The third act begins with a din fit to burst your eardrums. Brass as follows: 4 horns, 4 trumpets, 4 trombones, 4 tubas, 4 bass tubas, and with strings and woodwind that makes a horrendous noise. The whole . . . could be set out in 100 bars, then the same again, and the same again, and the same again, and the same again, and just as boring, and just as boring, and just as bor

The rest of the letter is a hymn in praise of Auber, and the juvenile critic signs off with a flowery protestation of eternal affection. To his dying day, Strauss was to repent of this effusion of schoolboy wit.

However little he enjoyed that first hearing of *Siegfried*, he stood through all five hours of it, as he did through most of his evenings in the opera house. Two years later he wrote: 'You can be quite sure that in ten years' time nobody will have heard of Richard Wagner.' On 9 November 1880 he went to *Tristan*. Wagner himself was present. Richard took no notice of the man he was to idolize before very long.

Thuille soon became an adherent of the 'new music', and his influence told on his younger friend, whom he surpassed in ability at first. Richard was not slow to overhaul him technically, and he quite overshadowed him in imaginative power. The friends hauled themselves upwards, so to speak, by climbing on each other's shoulders. When Richard struck off in a completely new direction, Ludwig stayed where he was. In his first conducting post, at Meiningen, Richard conducted the first performance of a symphony by Thuille. Later, in Berlin, he gave a concert performance of Act III of the opera *Gugeline*, and throughout his life did not stint his efforts to persuade opera houses to stage this or Thuille's other opera, *Lobetanz*: but to no avail.

Thuille soon moved to live in Munich. In due course he became professor at the Munich Conservatory, and established a reputation as a formidable music theorist. In 1904, Strauss consulted him about the double fugue in the *Symphonia domestica*, where he particularly wished to avoid any musical solecisms. Thuille also made the piano reductions of several of Strauss's works. There were misunderstandings, leading to an occasional cooling of their relationship; their wives did not get on together; but the old friendship always recovered in the end. Thuille died without warning, of a heart attack, in 1907 when he was only forty-five.

After hearing a performance of *Tannhäuser*, Richard petulantly picked up the vocal score to confirm his impression of the harmonic and contrapuntal failings of the music marking the transition from the Venusberg to the Wartburg in Act I. But 'botched' though it was, something about the work began to fascinate him. During the winter of 1880–81 he studied the score of *Tristan*, in secret, usually in the evenings so that his father would not know. The sweet poison began to work, though it would be some time before Saul took the road to Damascus. One afternoon he was playing something from *Tristan* to a friend on the piano, quietly, but his father heard the accursèd tones and stormed into the room with his horn under his arm to put a stop to it. It is not the Bavarian way to express differences of opinion diffidently and decorously; people say what they have to say loudly and clearly – especially in a household like the Strausses, bursting with temperament (as we can all witness in the *Symphonia domestica*). Usually a short row clears the air, like a thunderstorm, but not on this occasion: Richard stood his ground and his father, horrified, went off to work and told his colleagues that his son was going badly astray.

After studying the score of *Die Walküre*, the young Strauss was bitterly disappointed by a performance in the opera house. It dawned on him that current performance practices were simply not adequate to the genius of what lay in the score; the older generation could not meet the challenge, and it would be up to the rising generation to do Wagner justice. At this stage, he was still far from Wagnerolatry; he still had to go through a phase of admiring Brahms and other contemporary conservatives before Alexander Ritter, in Meiningen, was able to show him where his heart really lay.

Besides the opera house, the teenager spent many evenings in the main concert hall in Munich, the Odeonssaal. (In a speech on his eighty-fifth birthday, he spoke sadly of the beloved and beautiful hall, destroyed in the war. When the site was redeveloped, years later, an interior courtyard was constructed where the auditorium had been, with the former groundplan outlined. It is no longer a temple to the Muses, however, but the Bavarian ministry for internal affairs.) Here, while occupying his regular standing place beside the first column on the left-hand side ('schoolboys didn't get seats in those days'), he heard his D minor Symphony directed by Hermann Levi, principal conductor of the Court Orchestra and Wagner-devotee. He was seventeen. His father, having copied all the parts himself, was sick with nerves as he sat in the orchestra, but there was thunderous applause at the end, in which Levi joined. Richard went to school the next morning as if nothing had happened, yet he had just accomplished something that was roughly equivalent then to winning an Olympic gold medal today. Later he put his placid behaviour down to Bavarian phlegm. 'No such thing as nerves, only a lack of self-discipline.'

His grateful father asked Levi how he could possibly repay his generous patronage of his son. Quick as a flash, Levi asked him to play at the Bayreuth festival in the following summer, in the premiere performances of *Parsifal*. Strauss was trapped and had to consent. Only his family was allowed to see what it cost him (though Levi probably had a good idea). Richard went to Bayreuth with him, as a school-leaving treat, and heard the dress rehearsal. At this stage the work impressed him less than *Tristan*. From a distance, he saw Wagner, who now had only months to live, but it would have been impossible for the son of Franz Strauss to approach the composer. It would be a number of years before he set foot in Wahnfried, at the invitation of Frau Cosima.

He embarked briefly on a course of studies at Munich University, attending lectures on the history of philosophy, aesthetics, art history,

The seventy-year-old Strauss conducting in the Odeonssaal, where he received many of his earliest musical impressions.

Shakespeare, Schopenhauer, but concluded after a few months that lectures were not for him. He preferred to read about the things that interested him, and many things did: all his life he was hungry for philosophy, history and literature, and expected the same of his son and his grandsons. Above all, he revered the Greek and German classics and completely failed to understand how his grandsons could prefer Karl May's novels about the Wild West to Homer and Goethe.

But his career, he knew, was to be in music. His father advised him to lay a prudent foundation of useful acquaintances, and sent him off to Dresden, Berlin and Vienna in the winter after he left school, exhorting him not to be shy about telling people what he could do and playing them the music he had already written. Richard acted on this good advice, unlike many of his colleagues. By writing letters and paying personal calls on the people to whom his father was able to procure him an introduction, he made himself known, and performances followed. Too many artists are content to die in obscurity and allow posterity to discover them.

In the autumn of 1883, Strauss travelled to Dresden, where his father had friends. He spent several weeks there, as the guest of Ferdinand Böckmann, the principal cellist of the Dresden opera, and his wife. Frau Böckmann recalled the visit sixty years later. 'He went with my husband to the opera, sat in on rehearsals, and accompanied him to the Musical Association. He gave the first performance of his Cello Sonata op. 6 there, to great applause.' (In fact the first performance had been given ten days earlier in Nuremberg, by Hans Wihan, to whom the sonata was dedicated, but Richard allowed the Böckmanns to enjoy the belief that the honour was theirs.) 'He took one of my large wooden knitting needles to practise conducting with, imitating our celebrated von Schuch. My husband was currently embroiled in exhausting rehearsals for Wagner – he took the needle away from him. "Dear Richard, just give over. I've had Schuch bumbling about under my nose for three solid hours today and enough is enough!" I had to close the grand piano on several occasions, too, he used to give it such a hammering. Ten years ago, one of my husband's colleagues told me that Strauss looked sadly at my late husband's place in the pit and said "That's where good old Böckmann used to sit – I had such wonderful times in his house, with his family". And then he told them all the story about the knitting needle, to cheer them up.'

Strauss composed his little Romance *for his uncle Hörburger. The piano part has been thought prophetic of Rosenkavelier*

Dora Wihan-Weis.

Hans (Hanuš) Wihan, the dedicatee of the Cello Sonata op. 6, was a Czech (Dvořák wrote his Cello Concerto for him). In the early 1880s, he was a member of the Munich Court Orchestra. His wife, Dora, came from Dresden, where her father was a respected citizen and Peruvian Consul. She was five years younger than her husband and four years older than Richard Strauss, with whose sister Johanna she became very friendly. In 1947, Johanna Strauss recorded a lengthy memoir of her brother's early life, including this reminiscence of Dora Wihan-Weis in those days: 'She was like one of the family. Herr Wihan was insanely jealous over his pretty and already rather coquettish wife. I often witnessed scenes. For instance, she often asked me to spend the night with her, when her husband came in late from the opera, and sometimes had had a drop to drink, so that she wasn't alone all evening. And when Richard was with us, we used to make music. She was very musical and an excellent piano-player.'

The marriage lasted four years. Mother Strauss was fond of Dora and lent her a hat and veil to wear in court during the divorce hearing. Perhaps she would have welcomed her as a daughter-in-law.

The hot-tempered, suspicious and spendthrift Wihan left Munich for Prague, where he became a professor at the Conservatory and eventually a member of the celebrated Czech Quartet. Dora remained in Munich for the time being. Her relationship with Richard appears to have been one of deep understanding and whole-hearted liking from the time they first met, and there can be no doubt that they were in love for some years. His picture,

Hans Wihan.

inscribed 'To his beloved and only one, R.', stood on her piano until her death. They wrote each other countless letters, over a period of years. Dora left instructions, which were carried out, that his to her should be destroyed when she died. He, who preserved every insignificant postcard, destroyed hers to him at an earlier date. He kept his private life and his private feelings to himself. Neither he nor Dora could tolerate the idea of their letters being read by a third person, however intimate a friend. And in his case – perhaps an even more important consideration – there was a jealous wife.

There was a lot of gossip about Dora in Munich, which was not only unpleasant for her but, in those days, also dangerous. A year after the divorce, Richard was in Meiningen, making himself agreeable to local society, when he had a letter from his father, lecturing him on the need for a young artist, with his way to make in the world, to preserve a spotless reputation: 'Don't forget how people here talked about you and Dora W.'

Dora went to America and then took a position in Greece. At one point they made plans to meet in Italy, but appear not to have done so. They continued to write, but meanwhile Richard had met Pauline de Ahna whom he was to marry.

In 1911 Richard and Dora saw each other again in Dresden, in embarrassing circumstances. Dora was working as co-repetiteur at the opera, where the premiere of *Der Rosenkavalier* was about to take place. Strauss gave her a copy of the vocal score with a cordial inscription. His sister, delighted at having come across her old friend again, invited her to a family dinner. Pauline was furious and treated Dora like a rival. Richard, as always, took his wife's part, and there was no further contact between them.

Dora had friends in Garmisch whom she visited quite often, but she never paid a call at the Strauss villa. Pauline knew, or suspected, the understanding that continued to exist between her husband and Dora. Dora maintained her friendship with Johanna till her death, on 31 January 1938, but she dropped out of Richard's life altogether. One of his letters to her, which she had given away, survives. He wrote then, in 1889: 'The fact is that your letter, putting off the prospect of seeing you again, my sweet Dora, for the foreseeable future, has upset and distressed me deeply. God, what wooden expressions those are for what I really feel. . . . Strauss the artist is doing very well! But may no happiness be complete?!'

We left the nineteen-year-old Strauss in Dresden, in the autumn of 1883. Just before Christmas he moved on to Berlin, where he stayed for three months. He rented a furnished third-floor room on the corner of Leipziger Strasse and Charlotten Strasse, at the intersection of six horse-tram routes. A girls' boarding-school occupied part of the building, so a great deal of squealing and giggling was to be heard. After small, phlegmatic Munich, Strauss plunged delightedly into the bustle of the metropolis. He made new acquaintances daily: in the musical world, Joseph Joachim, the virtuoso of the violin, Philipp Spitta, the biographer of Bach, the conductor Robert Radecke, the Wagnerian Karl Klindworth, the soprano Désirée Artôt de Padilla, the agent and impresario Hermann Wolff, the music publisher Bock, and Baron von Hülsen, Intendant of the Berlin Court Opera. He also met painters and writers; the novelist Friedrich

Spielhagen had three daughters who made a great impression on the young man from Munich by their cosmopolitan self-assurance and wit, and one seems to have been quite willing to flirt with him.

While he may have kept his counsel about Dora Weis, he cheerfully recounted his Berlin adventures to other friends. According to Frau Böckmann he 'composed some lovely songs' literally at the feet of 'the beautiful Frau Begas', the wife of a sculptor, 'with the manuscript paper resting on her knees'. That was clearly gossip, but he was certainly susceptible to older women. His wife was to be older than him, and so was Dora Weis. Pretty young things usually bored him. A 'Marschallin' evidently moved him more than a 'Sophie'. Soubrettes are rare in his operas, and all his great female roles are interesting, resourceful women, who are governed by their will or their passions.

He made his mark in Berlin society, played the piano in many a drawing-room, chattered and sometimes talked about far-away Munich. Politely but persistently he promoted himself. His father reminded him not to let his tongue run away with him. He had little money, but Intendants and impresarios were generous with free tickets. He saw operas and plays, heard concerts and sent home detailed accounts of performances which had dazzled or disappointed him.

The painter Anton von Werner took a special liking to him. During Strauss's stay in Berlin Werner put on an artists' ball, at which he wanted to have some *tableaux vivants*. His original idea was for the young composer, who by then stood six foot one and a half inches in his socks, to represent a girl offering a laurel wreath to Germania. Fortunately he came to his senses and instead the boy was seen posing as 'an angel of peace in a Greek tunic'.

He scraped together the 15 marks admission to a grand subscription ball, where he was agog at the splendid scene and the women's dresses. He saw the aged Kaiser Wilhelm I there, unsteady on his feet, stiff, with dead eyes; he saw Crown Prince Friedrich, who would be emperor for only a hundred days in 1888; he saw the Crown Prince's 'rather ugly' daughter-in-law; and he saw Prince Wilhelm, his future employer and future Kaiser Wilhelm II.

In the midst of the social whirl, the parties and the establishment of useful acquaintanceships, he wrote his F minor Symphony op. 12, and some of the op. 9 piano pieces. Work was already, as it would remain, his greatest pleasure.

There was one alarming incident: the Meiningen Court Orchestra was coming to Berlin, with its conductor Hans von Bülow, no less. They were due to play Richard Strauss's Serenade for wind op. 7. Then, without warning, it was performed – twice and badly to boot – by one Benjamin Bilse with his private orchestra. Was it to spite Bülow? Would that peppery man now refuse to do the work? Strauss was on tenterhooks, because Bülow's patronage could make a crucial difference to a young man hoping to make an international name. He must have cursed Bilse's intervention. But Hans von Bülow had a noble and magnanimous heart behind his crotchety exterior, and was capable of overlooking his old quarrels with the father when it came to recognizing the merits of the son. Richard was introduced to him, and he received him kindly. He conducted the Serenade himself at a rehearsal (though not in the evening's concert) and led the players in a round of applause afterwards.

Strauss could be well-pleased when he set off home to Munich at the end of March 1884. The imperial capital knew his name; Hans von Bülow had formed a favourable opinion of him; he was on course.

The first opinion that Bülow had formed of him had not been so favourable. In October 1881, when the publisher Eugen Spitzweg had sent him some of Strauss's piano pieces, he wrote back: 'Do not care for the piano pieces by R.S. in the least – immature and precocious. . . . Fail to find any signs of youth in his invention. Not a genius in my most sincere opinion, but at best a talent, with 60% aimed to shock.' Two years later, however, he warmly recommended Spitzweg to go on publishing Strauss. He greatly liked the F minor Symphony: '. . . very significant indeed, original, formally mature'. And yet later: 'It is much more to my taste than his most recent symphonic poems. *De coloribus et gustibus non est disputandibus.* . . . The orchestra is his domain. Nobody, including himself, will dispute that.' He was not pleased by Strauss's move towards the 'music of expression'. When *Aus Italien* was dedicated to him, he mused:

> As a whole, as in much of its detail, the work has made a powerful impression on me – but – is age making such a reactionary of me? The author is a genius, but I find he has gone to the utmost limit of what is musically possible (within the bounds of beauty), and has often, indeed, gone beyond the limit, without any really pressing need to do so. A wonderful, enviable mistake, the prodigality of the ideas, the abundance of associations, only . . . well, I look forward to its performance under the composer's direction. What I deplore more than anything are the colossal difficulties for the performers. Absolutely no question of doing it with the usual rundown theatre orchestra.

A Job

Strauss – homme d'or. His playing and conducting début positively dazzling

HANS VON BÜLOW

Twenty years after his turbulent spell in Munich as King Ludwig II's Hofkapellmeister, in which he conducted the first performance of *Tristan und Isolde* and lost his wife to Richard Wagner, Hans von Bülow was world-famous, the first 'star' conductor in the history of music (while his compositions were neglected). Whimsical, ironic and an often bitter jester, he could probably have had any conducting post he wanted, and chose the Court Orchestra of the tiny Grand Duchy of Meiningen; but when he took it on tour, it gave a sensational demonstration of what a world-class conductor can do to create a great orchestra.

He liked Strauss's Serenade op. 7 so much (its composer dismissed it in 1909 as 'nothing more than a decent composition student's work'), that he asked for another piece for the same forces. Thrilled, Strauss produced the four movements of the Suite for wind op. 4 ('the wonderful days of one's youth, when one could write to order'). The Meiningen orchestra came to Munich to give a concert, including the Suite, in the Odeon on 18 November 1884, and Bülow decreed that Strauss should conduct his work himself. The orchestra had no time for rehearsals on tour, and he had never conducted in public before. 'I conducted in something of a haze, and all I can remember now is that I didn't make a complete mess of it.' Bülow did not even listen from the hall, but nevertheless pronounced the début first class, and Strauss a born conductor. When Franz Strauss made an attempt to thank his old enemy, Bülow rounded on him. 'You have nothing to thank me for. I haven't forgotten the way you treated me, here in this god-forsaken city. I did what I did today because your son has talent, not for your sweet sake!!' Franz Strauss crept away, without uttering a word.

Two years later, Bülow repented and asked Richard, then in Meiningen, if he thought his father would like it if he paid a social call on him. Richard, though taken aback, assured him that he would, and wrote to his father, begging him to behave himself. When Bülow arrived, however, he found only Johanna at home: Father had gone out. (That, at all events, is the story as told by Edith Wolff. Strauss's letter to his father is lost, but the tale could well be true: it certainly fits what we know of the characters of both men.)

Bülow's praise of Strauss's conducting début was sincere, and within a matter of months he had arranged his appointment as his assistant in Meiningen. For the twenty-one-year-old Strauss it was the first stage in a career as a conductor, as which he was to be really even better known than as a composer, certainly for the next thirty years. He always described himself as a 'Kapellmeister' in hotel registers. He directed every major orchestra in the world, and many people thought him the most interesting interpreter of his time. From the first, he modelled himself on Bülow, marking his study scores of Beethoven's symphonies with an exact record of Bülow's interpretations, which he thenceforth treasured. He was so moved by a performance of the *Eroica* that he burst into tears afterwards in the instrument room. Bülow, who was a very emotional man, put his arms round him and kissed him. His father commented that he was 'completely unused to such enthusiasm in you . . .'.

Of course Strauss's most important activity in Meiningen was taking the orchestra in rehearsals and some concerts. He did much of this conducting at sight, for large tracts of the orchestral repertory were new to him and he never had the time to study the scores properly beforehand. But he also appeared with the orchestra as a concerto soloist, and while Strauss was modest about his piano technique, Bülow remarked that he would make a good player 'if you weren't something better'. Other duties were as much social as professional. Giving out his age as twenty-two, so as to have more authority, he conducted the Choral Society, composed of eighty ladies and fifty men. The latter tended to play truant at rehearsals, and sometimes Strauss had to make door-to-door calls to summon them. He also gave piano lessons to the Duke's sister, Princess Marie ('not pretty, but amiable

Hans von Bülow.

and intelligent'), played for her, and danced with her at her weekly *thé dansant*. She became an admirer: 'He's certainly a change from the old man we used to have.' He took an active part in the social life of the little city, going to balls, paying calls, practising the art of conversation. There were letters to write to family and friends and somehow he had to find the time to help with the administration of the orchestra as well.

Brahms visited Meiningen while Strauss was working there and conducted his Third Symphony and Academic Festival Overture. For the occasion, the forty-nine-strong orchestra was augmented by two percussion players: Bülow and Strauss,

> which led to the wondrous spectacle of neither of us having any idea how to count rests. In rehearsal I was already out by bar 4, and I placed the full score on my music stand. Bülow would count vigorously for eight bars and then give up. He was forever asking the trumpet: 'What letter have we reached?' and then he'd start again: 'one, two, three, four'. I don't believe the percussion ever perpetrated so many wrong entries as on the evening when the two Kapellmeisters took part.

Strauss 'developed so much enthusiasm on the cymbals that you would think he was playing a concerto'. He sometimes joined the orchestra to play with the second violins when Bülow was conducting.

He composed more songs in Meiningen, and the *Burleske* for solo piano and orchestra, a piece in which the main melody is given to the timpani. Bülow didn't like it – the piano part was too difficult for his small hands – and the first performance was given by Eugen d'Albert. Strauss found relaxation in the company of other artists, especially that of young actresses. Meiningen was a centre of theatre art in those days. The Grand Duke himself, Georg II, was renowned for pioneering a new style of naturalism in production for the stage. Strauss enjoyed many a memorable evening in the theatre, and when he went to take his leave of the Duke, the Duke's wife, a former actress, praised him for being 'the best *claqueur* we have ever had'.

No doubt the Munich Sunday newspaper *Isaria* had its reasons for reprinting another paper's review of a concert by the Meiningen orchestra.

> Dr Bülow perambulated about the stage and surveyed the auditorium. A pale, long-haired youth is to conduct the overture. He looks as though for the last fortnight he has eaten nought but newborn lambs and drunk nought but Karlsbad water. The duke and his wife enter the little ducal box and the orchestra strikes up. Herr von Bülow works away at Swedish drill, swinging the upper part of his body vigorously to and fro, and the long-haired youth seems from his gestures to be seasick.

Strauss thought this account was 'heavenly'.

In the spring of 1886, Bülow left Meiningen, and Strauss was invited to take his place, with a salary of 2000 marks instead of the 1500 he had been getting. But with the loss of Bülow's name to draw audiences, the orchestra was going to be cut to thirty-nine, so Strauss politely declined the offer. The

Duke Georg II of Saxe-Meiningen.

Some snapshots of Meiningen that Strauss kept. The empty streets are a reminder that the world's population was smaller in those days, and spent less of its time travelling from A to B. Top right, the Court Theatre; bottom left, the Duke's palace.

This cartoon shows the eternal triangle that set Munich's tongues wagging in 1865: Hans von Bülow trials behind his wife and Richard Wagner, while the pages of 'King Mark's Lament' slip out of the score of Tristan *under his arm. It was an open secret that Wagner was the father of Cosima's daughter Isolde, and public indignation at the scandal forced King Ludwig to send Wagner away from Munich.*

Johannes Brahms in 1894. In 1935 Strauss set Goethe's poem Zugemessene Rhythmen *which comments on 'talent' and 'genius'. To illustrate the concepts, he used quotations from, respectively, the finale of Brahm's First Symphony and Wagner's* Die Meistersinger.

Hans von Bülow drawn after his death in Cairo, 12 February 1894.

Grand Duke bestowed the Cross of Merit on him, his highest award for artists, worn by only ten other people. It pleased Strauss enormously.

It was also during this season in Meiningen that Strauss received the news that he had been awarded first prize (300 marks) in a competition, for his Piano Quartet op. 13. Clara Schumann sent her heartfelt congratulations. His F minor Symphony was performed in New York, and he began to earn a little money from publishing his works. He decided to travel abroad for the first time and chose Italy, on the advice of Brahms.

Brahms came to Meiningen in October 1885, and conducted his *Variations on the St Antony Chorale*, the Violin Concerto, the Third Symphony, and the newly completed Fourth, which Strauss compared to Beethoven. He travelled to Weimar in Brahms's company, saw the town, but waited in an anteroom when Brahms went to call on the aged Franz Liszt. Thus Strauss missed the opportunity to meet Liszt personally, presumably because he had no interest in doing so. Brahms also heard Strauss's F minor Symphony and Wind Suite, and looked at the scores; he advised the young composer to take a leaf out of Schubert's book and practise the invention of simple, eight-bar melodies, avoiding counterpoint for its own sake: there was no merit in piling up a large number of themes on one triad, when there was only rhythmic contrast between them. 'That was when I realized', Strauss wrote some years later, 'that counterpoint is only justified when there is a poetic necessity compelling two or more themes to unite for a time' – which is not exactly what Brahms had in mind.

The 'poetic idea' gradually became a dominant factor in Strauss's thinking about composition. Beethoven, he reflected, could not have written either *Les adieux* or the late quartets without such an idea. The idea which a piece of music transmits can have had a non-musical origin. As in Beethoven's *Pastoral* Symphony, music can express feelings and events. Such was the creed which Strauss eventually formulated. For the time being, Brahms remained a hero. The *Burleske* (in a minor key, in spite of its title) is a Brahmsian work.

They do not appear to have been drawn to each other in any close personal way during that visit to Meiningen. Did Brahms perhaps envy Strauss's youth, vitality and popularity with the ladies? He grew more ironic by the day, would refer only to 'your young Strauss' when talking to Bülow, and made it sound like a jeer.

'I never found Brahms sympathetic. He was irredeemably petty bourgeois, stolid, unforthcoming, crude in his treatment of Bülow, who was so elegant and graceful, who I had so much to thank for, and who debased himself in being of service to Brahms.' And: 'Brahms is not a great figure, he is an epigone like Rheinberger and Raff. His music is worthy and well made, melancholic, grey and broody. Berlioz did much more for music, Liszt was more inventive. Brahms is a foothill, like Schumann. The peaks are Beethoven, Wagner, Bach and Mozart!' It was a pretty sweeping condemnation. To the end of his days, Strauss called Brahms 'leathery Johannes'.

Although Bülow was disturbed by the direction Strauss took in his composition in the next decade, he kept his more waspish comments for the publisher Spitzweg, and remonstrated with Strauss himself more in sorrow than in anger. He had a very high opinion of Strauss's musicianship, from the very start of his professional career. 'You are one of those exceptional musicians who do not need to serve in the ranks first but have the right stuff to take on a higher command straightaway', he told him. On another occasion: 'The very sight of your handwriting is all it takes to put me in a good mood. You always say something worth saying, whether on the stave or in words. You always know the right paths along which to direct your pen, namely, *not* out into the steppes and deserts.'

Bülow suffered appalling headaches for many years, for which the medical profession could give him no relief. In 1894 the doctors suggested that a warm climate might help, and sent him to Cairo. He died shortly after arriving, of tumours on the brain. With hindsight, it is possible to see that this condition may have been at least partly responsible for his violent fluctuations of mood.

Johann Strauss the younger, 1894. He was a close friend of Brahms and, of the two, Richard Strauss respected him more as a composer.

The loss of his mentor caused Strauss great distress. He was invited to conduct a memorial concert in Hamburg, but choosing the programme for the occasion became a subject of controversy. Many took the view that Wagner's music would be quite unthinkable, even though Bülow himself had the greatness of spirit to continue performing it, in spite of all the personal suffering Wagner had caused him. Strauss stipulated: 'Serious music, therefore no Brahms.' There had been a rift between Brahms and Bülow, too. But Strauss's suggestion of Liszt's *Héroïde funèbre* was not a happy one for, of all Liszt's symphonic poems, that was the one Bülow could least abide. The attempt to change Strauss's mind only led to his refusal to conduct at all. In the end it was Gustav Mahler who directed a chorus by Schubert and the 'Devout Song of Thanksgiving to the Deity', the 'chorale' in the Lydian mode from Beethoven's A minor Quartet op. 132, arranged for male-voice choir, with a text by the chairman of the Hamburg Philharmonia, Dr Hermann Behn. One wonders what Bülow would have thought of that.

The concept of the 'poetic idea' was eagerly discussed in Meiningen and elsewhere: the aesthetic question of the day was whether the innermost secret of music was not, after all, the expression of emotions, events and dramatic situations; and if that was so, must not the poetic content of a piece determine its form? Writing symphonies after Beethoven led to epigonalism. If it was to develop, music's role was to portray emotions and compose poetry, to explore a dimension of inner expressiveness which no other art could reach.

On the way to discovering his own world, Strauss embraced the idea with the fervour of a convert. His incessant harping on 'expression' got on many people's nerves, but Cosima Wagner's habit, a little later, of beginning letters to him with the words 'My dear Expression' was a token of approval.

The fact is that, in Meiningen, Strauss met the full force of a tempest called Alexander Ritter. Born in Estonia in 1833, he was the son of that Frau Julie Ritter who supported Wagner financially for a number of years. Like his brother Karl, he came under Wagner's spell, and strengthened the bond

Alexander Ritter in his forties.

by marrying Wagner's niece Franziska in 1854. He had grown up with Bülow in Dresden, and the two had received their musical education together. In 1856 Ritter went to Weimar, to study under Liszt, which was the equivalent of joining a sect. For a time he was director of music at the city theatre in Stettin, but with no great success: he was not the only musician to lack the stomach for life in the theatre. For twenty years he scraped a living, running a music shop in Würzburg for a time, then joined the Meiningen Court Orchestra as deputy leader, under his old friend Bülow and – in time – 'wee Strauss'. Ritter overwhelmed the young conductor with friendship, advice and help. Proclaiming the philosophy of Schopenhauer and the musico-aesthetic theories of Wagner and Liszt, he was a fanatical prophet of the new music, and brought to the mission all the force of his idiosyncratic and imposing personality.

With both Bülow and Strauss gone from Meiningen, he followed the latter to Munich in 1886. Failing to find a position as a violinist, he tried teaching. A circle of disciples formed around him, including his future son-in-law, the composer Siegmund von Hausegger, and Ludwig Thuille. To outsiders, they must have looked like a clique of loonies: the avant-garde always does.

The symphonic poem looked to be the medium in which Strauss could best work out his lifelong fascination with drama and poetry. Ritter insisted: he should write poetry in music; he was already a master of Classical forms, and he should embody his poetic ideas in expanded sonata forms, in the rondo, in the theme and variations.

Macbeth: no actors possessed the expressive power needed to characterize the thane and his wife, as music could. What better than the modern symphony orchestra as the means to depict the insatiable passions of Don Juan? And music can express humour, too, as *Till Eulenspiegel* demonstrates.

The inimitable musical language of the colossus Wagner had gone to the very limits of expression. To imitate him was to remain stationary. To compose operas after him meant finding a way over an immense mountainous massif. The alternative was to go round the outside, by the path pioneered by Liszt: that of the symphonic poem, an opera in miniature and without the human voice. This was the form on which Strauss concentrated over the next decade or so. Brilliant in themselves, the works foreshadow the production of the future music dramatist. He learnt to live out his fantasies, to convert his emotions and reactions convincingly into musical terms. It was Alexander Ritter who showed him how to do it. A master of musical declamation, he taught Strauss how singing can issue out of the speech-melody, if the declamation suits the sense.

Strauss was devoted to his mentor's operas. Scarcely had he taken up his post in Weimar, when he put on Ritter's *Wem die Krone?* and *Der faule Hans*. They did not cause a sensation, but a few other houses performed them. As director of the Vienna Opera, and still in old age, he was indefatigable in urging theatres to do Ritter's operas, and it can surely not have been solely for reasons of gratitude and piety.

After Meiningen, and before taking up his next job in Munich, Strauss went to Italy for two months in 1886, following the advice of Brahms, but with his head full of the injunctions of Ritter. He visited Mantua, Bologna, Florence, Rome, Naples, Sorrento and Pompeii. He survived a stormy crossing to Capri. He experienced with excitement the artistic unity of nature and the works of man, stood entranced in churches and before great paintings. Raphael made the strongest impression on him, and he was moved to tears by the *Saint Cecilia* in Bologna. His guide in Rome was the painter Franz von Lenbach, with whom he established an excellent rapport, and whose knowledge and taste in art he greatly admired. He was thrilled by Rome, and by the elegance and beauty of Roman women. He travelled by donkey and by boat, wandered through the bustling streets of Naples, and was robbed left and right. 'The Italians that the foreigner gets to see are the most fearsome, unbearable chorus of revenge . . .'. At that date he did not speak Italian, only schoolboy French.

Max Bruch.

He was happy in Italy, and suddenly felt inspired by external impressions and the experience of nature. He had never believed in such a thing before, but now ideas flooded in for a four-movement symphonic fantasy, *Aus Italien* op. 16. But it was not Baedeker set to music. He filled the Classical form of the symphony with poetic expression and the depiction of his feelings. The ruins of classical Rome evoke melancholy. On the beach at Sorrento, we hear the waves sighing in the orchestra. In the final movement, Strauss unleashes all his virtuosity: the street-life of Naples flows and surges across the sections of the orchestra, and weaving through it we hear a popular song, *Funiculi, funicula*, a hymn in praise of the local funicular railway. The orchestra burst out laughing at the first rehearsal. When it was hissed in Munich on 2 March 1887, the composer sat on the table in the green room, swinging his legs. 'There has never been a great artist yet, who thousands of people didn't think was mad.'

The pianist Joseph Giehrl declared that you could tell from the finale that Strauss had been in Naples directly after a cholera epidemic. The Viennese newspaper *Neue Freie Presse* thought it doubtful if anyone would want to visit Italy after hearing this musical depiction of it, and clearly felt that Mignon would not have recognized the land where lemon trees flower.

Aus Italien was not received with markedly greater comprehension in Breslau in 1889, according to the account of the performance which the conductor, Max Bruch, sent to Strauss.

The first movement was judged by its merits and received very well. The second movement made scarcely any impression, because the audience could obviously see no connection between the content of the music and the heading 'In the ruins of Rome', and equally the many fortissimos failed to evoke the idea of a vision. The third movement ('The Beach at Sorrento') gained a grateful hearing again. The last, alas, was not allowed to finish without some rowdy objections.

As an honest man, I will not conceal from you that I find it impossible to like certain details; I would give you the full grounds for my opinion if we were able to meet to talk about it, although I do not expect you to attach any importance to the judgment of an older artist who adheres to a different direction from you.

Strauss, who was still less than half Bruch's age, wrote against this: 'He is absolutely right there.' Twenty-five years later, in the *Alpine* Symphony, he used a theme which is very similar to a subject in Bruch's celebrated Violin Concerto. ('Why not? It's beautiful.') At a rehearsal he asked the orchestra ironically, 'please, from the Bruch concerto again!' They knew exactly where to start.

A Young Revolutionary

'Bei der Musik von Richard Strauss findet man schwer die Strichart raus' (*'When it comes to the music of Richard Strauss The bowing makes the fiddler grouse'*)

ANON.

His reputation was beginning to spread; he conducted in Milan, in Berlin and in Hamburg. Now, in what was surely any twenty-two-year-old's dream, he was on the conducting staff of the Court Opera in his own home town. His father was in the orchestra under his direction, he had his friends near at hand, and he was working under the famous Hermann Levi, who had encouraged him when still a schoolboy, was an outstanding interpreter of Wagner, and had even turned his hand to the production of some very decent German versions of Mozart's Italian librettos.

The reality did not live up to the dream, alas. The three years were three years of disappointment, and accepting the post was the first bad professional mistake. He should have listened to Bülow, who had warned him he would be better off as the only conductor somewhere else, rather than as the third in the Munich hierarchy.

Accustomed to success, filled with enthusiasm and energy, and a recent convert to Wagner and the New Music to boot, Strauss found himself expected to conduct the most routine end of the repertory: Rheinberger, Auber, Delibes, Boieldieu. The orchestra knew all these works backwards, were sceptical about his innovations in the matter of tempo, and did not let the instances of the novice's lack of theatrical experience pass without comment. At a certain point in the third act of Lortzing's *Zar und Zimmermann*, he once began to beat two in a bar, where they were used to four: in the ensuing disorder, he had to stop the music, make a new start and bear the public disgrace. He relived the incident in his dreams for years afterwards.

He was asked to prepare a production of Wagner's earliest completed opera, *Die Feen*. Overjoyed, he worked on it for three months, and then learnt that he was not to conduct the performances: that distinction, according to the laws of seniority, fell to the No. 2 Kapellmeister, fat Franz Fischer, 'one of the least talented musicians I have ever encountered, a real malefactor in the pit'. Levi, too, was a disappointment; his health was failing in those years, and he showed less trust and confidence than Strauss felt he had a right to expect. The Intendant, Baron Perfall, was a civil servant to whom regulations were more important than results. Strauss felt

he was being wasted, and not learning anything worthwhile. He longed to escape from the 'beery swamp'.

Yet not everything was a cause for despondency. The three years' experience backstage in the theatre, that refuge of neurotics and egotists, was not wasted. He had the chance to meet with Alexander Ritter and his circle as often as he wanted to. They would assemble every evening, between 6 and 7, in Leibenfrost's Wine Parlour, and set the musical world to rights. Sometimes, grumbling a little, Franz Strauss joined them, too. And he had an outlet for his energies. Lily Bamberger-Reiff recalled the occasion when he was conducting Lortzing's *Der Wildschütz* and she saw him momentarily check his beat and lower his head. She asked him in the interval if he had felt unwell. 'No – I was composing. A nice little tune suddenly occurred to me, and they can manage without me for a short period.' These years saw the start of the series of symphonic poems.

Macbeth came first, though its opus number, 23, puts it after *Don Juan*. The first version, finished early in 1888, ended with a march celebrating the triumph of Macduff, but Hans von Bülow expostulated that that destroyed the poetic unity of a piece called *Macbeth*. Strauss bowed to this literary judgment and to his own theories, wrote a new, quieter ending and later stripped the instrumentation of 'excess fat' as well. It is a gloomy, austere piece, like the heart of Shakespeare's play, and it was not a success. Hugo Wolf thought it made 'the blood run cold', and Bronsart, the Intendant at Weimar, where it had its first performance, thought the same. The composer sighed: 'If only I could root out that damned consonance!' – by which he meant the music of the past.

The final version of *Macbeth* pleased Bülow much more, and made a great impression when Strauss conducted it in Berlin in February 1892. After the public rehearsal Bülow wrote to Eugen Spitzweg: '*Macbeth's* success this morning was *colossal*. The audience roared for Strauss to take a bow four times. The work really sounded overwhelming. The composer's never had such a reception here before.'

These studio photographs show Strauss
with the expansive gestures that he seems to
have used when conducting in those days.
In later years he was far less ostentatious.
The prints reproduced here were given to
Engelbert Humperdinck, and in the
handwritten notes Strauss explains that
three of them show him conducting works
by his friend. On the third from the left,
tongue firmly in cheek, he claims
'enthusiasm at fever pitch' in conducting
Meyerbeer's Robert le Diable.

Don Juan op. 20 followed the same year. Strauss noted the first ideas for
it in the cloisters of San Antonio in Padua. It is the first piece written fully
and entirely in Strauss's own musical idiom, which from thenceforth is
unmistakable and unique. Nothing and nobody is imitated, not even
Wagner. No one else could have written this piece. Theory has become
practice, the poetic idea has given birth to the form. It is made up of
episodes, and yet forms a united whole in which the changing moods run
riot. No other music of the period burns so fircely, sighs so tenderly or flows
so elegantly. No one before Strauss knew how to mix instrumental colours
like this, or how to make the orchestra sparkle, languish and exult in such a
way. If *Aus Italien* is the apprentice work, *Don Juan* is the first masterpiece. It
aroused a furore, at once and everywhere. Strauss wrote to his father from
Dresden in January 1890:

> I sat in the stalls next to two gentlemen who did not know me and who
> conducted a frightfully funny (for me) conversation about *Don Juan*.
> One of them thought he'd had quite enough of that sort of thing, and
> that I'd had a thorough rummage in the composers' kitbag. The other
> said he admired the colours, thought I had a lot of original ideas, and
> that the rushing about and especially the disgust had been rendered
> superbly. Finally they both spotted the composer sitting in the first row
> in the circle, and I sat beside them and had to exert frightful self-control
> not to burst out laughing.

Tod und Verklärung (*Death and Transfiguration*) op. 24, 1888–9, has a
poetic idea which was Strauss's own. Though he had never been seriously ill
himself, he depicts a dying man who remembers his youth and his ideals; a
conviction steals upon him with ever-growing strength, and in his death-
agony the ideals which it was impossible to realize in life rise up before him
out of the darkness, transfigured. The theme representing transfiguration
does not appear until well into the work, but forms the basis of the final,
culminatory section. Once again, the poetic idea determines the form and

structure of the work. It had the effect, as well, of contributing to the revival of Bülow's faith in the composer. He thought it 'very significant, refreshing too, in spite of all kinds of dross'.

After the three years in Munich, Strauss moved in the autumn of 1889 to Weimar as second Kapellmeister to the Grand Duke of Saxe-Weimar-Eisenach. Weimar is not as large a place as Munich, but it has a very special position in German cultural life, for its associations with Goethe, Schiller and Liszt. When Strauss went there the Intendant was Hans von Bronsart, a pupil of Liszt. All the omens were favourable, even if the salary – 2100 marks in the first months, rising to 3000 marks in 1890 – was low. But he was still only twenty-five, and a lot of energy had been pent up in Munich. He hurled himself eagerly upon the little theatre in Weimar, with its small orchestra and staff, its old-fashioned equipment and its oil-lighting. The repertory was what Strauss wanted to modernize, and he was not altogether unsuccessful, in spite of his habit of charging every obstacle head-first. In accordance with Wagner's practice, he got the orchestral pit lowered, but this was not a good idea, making the violins sound 'dry and salty', and the decision was reversed.

Eduard Lassen, the Hofkapellmeister whom Strauss liked.

His superior was the likeable, long-serving Hofkapellmeister Eduard von Lassen (1830–1904). It was at his and Bülow's instigation that Strauss had been invited to Weimar. He pronounced himself 'ancient' at the age of fifty-nine, and generously allowed Strauss to conduct four concerts a year and all the German operas in the Weimar repertory except *Fidelio*, *Der fliegende Holländer*, *Die Meistersinger* and the *Ring*.

Lassen and Strauss got on well together on the whole (they shared a passion for skat), even if youthful impatience sometimes made Strauss call Lassen an old fool. Explosions of that kind are commonplace in the theatre, Armageddon is a daily occurrence, exuberance plunges into despair at a moment's notice – and the show goes on.

Erfurter Strasse 19, where Strauss lived in Weimar. A plaque above the middle groundfloor window records his time of residence.

Strauss lost no time in Weimar in atoning for his father's sins against Wagner. He founded a branch of the Wagner Society and gave talks with illustrations on the piano. He stood to conduct Wagner's music and sat for that of other composers. He set to work to perform Wagner as authentically as he could and advice was heaped upon him by Cosima Wagner. It was virtually unheard-of for a small provincial theatre to give Wagner uncut but that was Strauss's ambition with *Lohengrin*, *Tannhäuser* and *Tristan*. He was able to report to Frau Wagner on his first performance of *Lohengrin* on 9 October 1889: 'Preparations on a scale quite unprecedented for this place with two five-hour orchestral rehearsals, one blocking rehearsal, and a whole series of piano rehearsals on stage for soloists and chorus. The dress rehearsal was immensely successful, while the performance itself gave me only partial satisfaction.' In the matter of acting, Elsa and King Henry had fallen back into their old habits.

> I had succeeded in making them understand that Ortrud stays seated all through Telramund's scene, that after 'Elsa, ich liebe dich' Lohengrin leads her straight to the King rather than promenading round the stage, that at the end he jumps promptly into the boat, etc. But on the night, none of the entrances went right, they sang out into the audience, ignored the Master's stage directions! The stage director is a totally incompetent, elderly, bass-singing, theatrical hack!

Certainly, Strauss was very conscious of his responsibilities to Wagner.

The first performance of *Lohengrin* had been given in Weimar in 1850. The one-hundredth performance there was scheduled for 1891. Strauss wanted new sets and costumes to replace the old, shabby ones which were quite unworthy of such an important event. Told that he could not have them, he offered the court treasury 1000 marks from his own pocket. In fact, he could not afford such a sum, even though his works were now in demand and *Aus Italien* was on the way to becoming part of the standard orchestral repertory. In the end, the Duke heard his prayer and authorized the expenditure. Frau Cosima came and was impressed.

Giving the premiere of *Lohengrin* was only the most spectacular of Franz Liszt's musical good deeds. Throughout much of his career, and with particular effectiveness during his years in Weimar, he worked selflessly and tirelessly to promote the music of other musicians less successful than himself: Smetana, Cornelius, Schumann, Berlioz, Chopin, as well as his future son-in-law Wagner. He included their works in his recitals, in his own transcriptions, urged them on impresarios, introduced them to publishers. Strauss was fired to follow this excellent example and in Weimar he championed Thuille, Ritter, Humperdinck and Mahler. In later life, any musician of real talent could be sure of his practical help or a word in the right ear, even figures as different from himself as Schreker or Schoenberg. Later still he sighed, 'I don't recommend people any more, it only harms them'.

Following the premieres of Ritter's operas, the theatre in Weimar saw the first performance, on 25 December 1893, under Strauss's baton, of another opera, this time one which was to prove an instant and enduring success: *Hänsel und Gretel* by Engelbert Humperdinck.

There were not many cronies in Strauss's life, not many with whom he used the intimate 'Du': his publisher Spitzweg, Siegfried Wagner, Thuille, Arthur Seidl and other friends of his boyhood, Felix von Weingartner, Philipp Wolfrum, Daniela Thode (a daughter of Cosima and Hans von Bülow), Felix Mottl – and Humperdinck. *Hänsel und Gretel*, Strauss wrote, is

Engelbert Humperdinck, one of Strauss's few close friends at this period.

Pauline de Ahna as Hänsel.

> truly a masterpiece of the first class . . . after a very long time, it's something that really impresses me. Such heart-refreshing humour, such deliciously naive melodies, such art and refinement in the orchestration . . . such resplendent polyphony, and it's all new, original and so authentically German. My dear friend, you are a great master, and you've given the Germans a work they scarcely deserve, but let us hope all the same that they will very soon learn how to appreciate it fully. . . . I implore you to insist on me conducting it – that old simpleton Lassen must not be allowed near it! And young Hänsel is devilishly difficult!

The part of Hänsel was sung in most of the performances by a pupil of Strauss's, Pauline de Ahna, but she missed the premiere because she jumped about so strenuously in rehearsal that she sprained an ankle.

The letters he wrote from Weimar to his family, his friends and various young ladies are a chronicle of everything that interested him at the time. He gives long accounts of concerts, operas, interpretation and performers. He discourses on the work of Wagner, Brahms, the classics, but also on ephemera and the bread-and-butter repertory. Every letter concludes with lists of friends and relations to whom he wishes his greetings to be conveyed, and he finds room for jokes, anecdotes and his state of health. It is informative, too, to observe the many topics that these letters do not mention: politics, industrialism, new inventions, social questions, his feelings, anxiety, discontent, love, boredom, lyrical impulses, questioning of the status quo, creative difficulties, doubt about his own powers, despondency, complaints about over-work, complaints about being misunderstood, complaints of any kind.

A clear picture can be formed of his character in these years: good-natured and temperamental, mocking and ironic, angered by the obduracy of others and quickly restored to humour. The purity of art is the one yardstick. Incompetence in that area infuriates him. He is resigned to weaknesses, but stupidity and backstage intrigue provoke him to tempestuous outbreaks of rage. He can show the patience of a seraph in rehearsal, but insubordination unleashes the thunderbolts. When a Wolfram wanted to observe the unhallowed custom of leaving the stage during Elisabeth's prayer in Act III of *Tannhäuser*, Strauss threatened to have the curtain brought down. He also vowed to throw his baton at the chorus if they did not manage an entry better in performance.

He was not troubled by the failure to understand his works, but cuts in his scores, like cuts in Wagner's, stirred him to incandescent fury. His career

Adolf von Schack.

Felix Dahn.

was of primary and negligible importance to him: primary, in that he spared no effort to acquaint conductors, managers and performers with his music, and performed it untiringly himself; negligible, because everything he did created a sensation without any further effort on his part. He radiated fascination, he was detested, adored, dismissed, admired. Nobody remained indifferent to him. He pursued his career shrewdly while, creatively, trying to avoid developments that led him nowhere and to refuse all compromise. In practice this last was almost impossible: his music was difficult to play when it was new.

Up to his op. 25, the opera *Guntram*, he had composed seventy songs, including the unpublished ones. This is an indicator of the amount he read, for it was often a long search before he found a poem which struck a spark. Composing songs was evidently a necessary act for him: his first compositions as a child were songs, and he never abandoned the practice. There was a constant demand for new songs in the late nineteenth century, for both professional performance in the concert hall and amateur performance in the domestic circle. Most of Strauss's songs, admittedly, were too difficult for the amateur.

The quality of the literary text does not appear to have been a primary concern when he made his choice of a poem. Between nineteen and twenty-nine, he showed less interest in Goethe and Heine than in minor figures whose reputations scarcely lasted beyond their lifetimes, like Adolf von Schack (1815–94), a member of the Munich school of poets and a well-known collector of paintings, seventeen of whose poems were set by Strauss, and Emanuel Geibel (1815–84), a leading figure in the Munich school and perhaps best known as the translator, with Paul Heyse, of the poems Hugo Wolf set in the *Spanisches Liederbuch*; Strauss set nine of his original poems, but none of these songs have opus numbers. Hermann von Gilm zu Rosenegg (1812–64), eight of whose poems Strauss set in 1885 as his op. 10, was an Austrian civil servant, while Felix Dahn (1834–1912), though a professor of the history of law, was known to a wider public as the author of historical novels. Dahn's verse provided Strauss with texts for two collections of songs, his opp. 22 and 23, and they corresponded about an idea for an opera on the subject of the German resistance to Rome in the first century AD. This work, which was provisionally entitled 'The sublime suffering of kings', fortunately never got beyond a scenario, and Strauss developed an interest in more up-to-date writers like Oscar Wilde and the socialist poet Karl Henckell.

He tried to explain how he wrote his songs to the composer Friedrich von Hausegger in 1893. First there was a musical idea which – God alone knew how – prepared itself within him. Once the bowl, so to speak, was brim-full, a song would come of it in no time at all, once he had found a poem with the kind of content he wanted. If he could not find the right text at the crucial moment, he had to use another poem, in order to satisfy the creative urge which had built up in him, 'but then it goes slowly, because the musical substance of the creative moment has to be remodelled, reinterpreted, if it is to take shape at all. A lot of artifice has to go into it, the melody flows dourly, I have to summon up all my technical skill in order to produce something which will stand up to my own severe self-criticism.' No doubt, then, already, as to the only answer Strauss had for the question he explored in *Capriccio*: 'Prima la musica, dopo le parole?' Music first, every time!

Hans von Bronsart, the Intendant in charge of the Grand Ducal Theatre in Weimar had occasion to write to his impetuous and impatient second Kapellmeister in the early 1890s, trying to temper his radicalism with some consideration for the experience of older people, without damping the fire within. One of his problems was countering the influence of Cosima Wagner, who found Strauss an eager disciple in those days.

Hans von Bronsart, who tried to restrain Strauss for his own good.

> There can be no question of the producer being subordinate to the conductor! Some modification of your ultra-radical ideas will be necessary. . . . Every good musician who had a close association with Wagner knows more [about Wagner's intentions] than his unmusical widow. . . . You, my dear Strauss, select tempos (the end of the *Tannhäuser* overture and many other examples) which contradict Wagner's known intentions! . . . You must learn to control yourself at least enough . . . to stop using at every moment turns of phrase which you would condemn severely in the mouth of another. You must learn sufficient respect for the artists . . . to acknowledge their right to a certain amount of independent judgment, and you must not call it 'style-less' every time somebody feels differently from you about a matter. . . . In the long run you will be impossible in situations which rest on subordination. . . . Do not wear yourself out spiritually and physically before your time. Preserve for the good of us all an artistic ability more promising than any I have ever dared to dream of. (8 July 1890)

Strauss naturally included works of his own in the concerts he conducted. A horn player, pouring with sweat after a rehearsal of *Don Juan*, was heard to wail: 'Dear God, what sin have we committed, for you to send us this rod for our backs? And we shan't be rid of it in a hurry!'

There were some moments of relaxation. Strauss belonged to an artists' club in Weimar, which gave a costume ball. The composers of the town wrote songs for the occasion, for male-voice choir. Strauss's contribution was a parody of a popular war-horse of the day, Victor Nessler's *Der Trompeter von Säckingen*, using the text from a Swedish matchbox: 'Utan svafvel och fosfor' – 'Made of sulphur and phosphorus'. He attended the ball dressed as a negro bonbon-seller.

The local composers were also expected to provide a musical accompaniment for the *tableaux vivants* mounted at the gala held in celebration of the Grand Duke's golden wedding anniversary. Strauss's offering bore away the palm. Military bands played excerpts from it for ages afterwards – more often than they did any of his more substantial works in those days. Strauss was awarded his second order: the Knight's Cross, second class, of the Grand Ducal Household Order of Vigilance, otherwise known as the White Falcon.

As if he did not have enough work to do in Weimar, he took on other engagements. In the course of one week in March 1892, for example, he conducted a performance of *Tristan* in Weimar on a Tuesday evening, and caught a late train to Leipzig. After a four-and-a-half-hour orchestral rehearsal for a Liszt Society concert, he returned to Weimar by train on the Wednesday evening. On the Thursday he went to Eisenach to conduct *Lohengrin*, then straight on to Leipzig, arriving at 1 a.m. There were two three-hour rehearsals on the Friday. The final rehearsal was at 10 a.m. on the Saturday, and the concert took place the same evening. The programme included Liszt's *Die Ideale* and *Mazeppa*, the Liszt–Schubert *Wanderer* Fantasy, piano solos and *Tod und Verklärung*. The Leipzig Gewandhaus Orchestra was forbidden to play for Liszt Society concerts, so an augmented military band was used. An enthusiastic audience accompanied Strauss to the station, one kissed his hand, they all cheered as the train drew out. The next day it was work as usual in Weimar.

'I was born to fight battles like this!' he wrote to his father. After the overnight train journeys and a rehearsal schedule which would give a modern musician a heart attack, Strauss still found the time to write long letters home. He gave no thought to the danger of burning the candle at both ends. Later in life, the economy with which he husbanded his strength was much admired, but it was something he learnt to do only after the inevitable collapse.

In Munich he had lacked the power to fight any theatrical battles. In Weimar, he was responsible for everything that went wrong. Apathy, slovenliness and tradition gradually drove him to the condition we now call stress. In May 1891 he caught a bad cold which he could not shake off; before long he was in hospital with pneumonia, and his recovery was slow. He had hoped to conduct at Bayreuth that summer, but this was not allowed. He wrote pathetic letters to Frau Cosima from his uncle's house in Feldafing, pleading with her, but in vain. Diseases of the lungs were no joke. Everyone wanted him to make a complete recovery: Bülow wrote to Spitzweg, thanking God that his life had been spared. 'He has a great future, he deserves to live!' The enforced idleness and the well-meaning injunctions only made him feel worse.

He returned to work in Weimar during the autumn, but he was far from fully recovered. In the following spring he succumbed to severe bronchitis and a renewed inflammation of the lungs. Back to hospital, this time with pleurisy. It was feared that he could contract tuberculosis, against which there were no drugs in those days. The only course of action the doctors could recommend was a prolonged stay in a dry, warm climate: he ought to spend the winter in Egypt.

The family met in conclave. His mother's brother Georg Pschorr (husband of Aunt Johanna of the beautiful voice) came up with the money for the trip: with tickets, accommodation and the carriage of baggage, and an allowance of 15 marks a day for incidental expenses, tips and so on, the final cost was 5502 marks, 10 pfennigs (at a date when two chickens cost one mark).

The grateful nephew left.

Time for Reflection

He was away from Germany from November 1892 to June 1893, visiting Italy, Greece, Egypt, Sicily and Italy again, and Switzerland. Italy had already inspired him musically. Now, in the Greek world that his upbringing in Ludwig I's 'Athens on the Isar' and his schooling at the Ludwig Grammar School had long prepared him for, his spiritual horizons widened again: in the last years of his life, he believed he could justly call himself 'the Grecian German'. In Egypt he discovered the colour he would need for *Salome* and Act II of *Die ägyptische Helena*, a colour which owes nothing to the usual clichés of the operatic Orient.

But the most important experience he gained from those eight months was that of being on his own, with the time to reflect, read philosophy, and arrive at a philosophy that was all his own. Like John the Baptist, he went into the desert to find himself, and returned transformed.

He packed the text of his opera and a lot of books: not literature for relaxation or entertainment, although he enjoyed reading Tolstoy, Dostoyevsky and Ibsen, but Schopenhauer, Nietzsche, Aeschylus, Plato, Sophocles and *Wilhelm Meister*. His letters of the period show how his thoughts were shaping. 'True happiness exists only in the isolation of creating at one's desk, or in the reception of the works of our geniuses.' 'I no longer know what nerves are.' 'The pain of eternally unfulfilled wishes? Artistic creativity, the representation of ideas, is free of wishes, is in itself a source of happiness; the prospect of success as well is a completely secondary matter compared to the joy of creation.' 'The goal of the will is – consciousness of willing: *I affirm consciously, that is my happiness.*'

Strauss with other tourists at Aswan and (right) with a little Egyptian boy called Hassan. A note on the back of the print remarks that Hassan was taught the art of washing his face by some American ladies.

Arthur Schopenhauer, the philosopher of a reasoned pessimism.

Friedrich Nietzsche, the author of Also sprach Zarathustra, *Strauss's choice of which, as the subject of a tone-poem, shocked the musical world.*

Strauss in his twenties.

This is not the pessimism of Schopenhauer, nor the ruthlessness of Nietzsche; it is the purely artistic solipsism of a man who feels he can create something which will mean a lot to a lot of people. From this time forward, he was committed, unconditionally, to this artistic egotism.

His itinerary took him to Corfu, Olympia, Athens, Syracuse (where Brahms was also staying at the same time: neither of them felt any urge to seek the other out), Alexandria, Cairo, Heliopolis, Asyut, Luxor, Aswan. An assiduous sightseer, he visited bazaars, museums, architectural monuments (the Greek made a greater impression on him than the Egyptian). He was on his own ('known by nobody – alone, an indifferent zero'). Interest and enthusiasm helped him to get used to the universal scent of garlic in Greece. He went to the theatre and the opera ('frightful'), saw a display of Egyptian dancing ('boring abdominal gymnastics, which looks hideous') at which only the musical accompaniment interested him: strong rhythms, original, a sustained F providing a bass and incomprehensible quarter and eighth tones above it. Then he went back to his hotel, where *Guntram* lay waiting on the table. He composed (without a piano), altered and orchestrated, with a happiness and concentration he seldom enjoyed in the throes of creation. At the end of the short score he wrote: 'Cairo. Christmas 1892, 24 December, 3 p.m. Deo (and Saint Wagner) gratias. Duration 57 minutes.' He wrote to his friend and publisher Spitzweg from Luxor, a month later: ' . . . for the last three weeks I have been scoring the first act, thirty pages of which have already been spattered with highly neat and dainty little notes. If all goes well, the whole opera may be finished by Christmas!'

He was confident that he had found a Wagner–Strauss synthesis, in an opera packed with philosophy and melody, a masterpiece of tunefulness and contrapuntalism, dazzlingly orchestrated, fresh, bright, serious and intoxicating. He was nearly thirty, at the height of his symphonic powers, and he felt he was in his prime. By the time he got home in June 1893, he had finished scoring the second act. He was fit and well – and would remain so for the next fifty-six years – and he was a new man. He had grown up.

> Best of all, I would like to stay here for good, in this glorious land of palm trees, roses, acacias, beneath a sun which has very little in common with that fixed star which purports now and again to shine on us in Germany; luxuriating in these glorious lighting effects, surrounded by simultaneous spring, summer and autumn; among these charming, highly amusing "savages", quite alone in the solitude of the glorious desert with the Christian God who is so little heard in Germany nowadays, and I'd compose one opera after another, unconcerned with what folk back in Europe would make of the poor thing. (From Cairo, 19 December 1892)

His isolation on his travels was not so very extreme. He made a lot of agreeable new acquaintances: two English painters, whose pictures he sold to the other guests in the hotel, pretending for the fun of it that he was a picture dealer by trade; some ladies, the young wife of an elderly landowner from Eastern Pomerania; on his return journey, he stayed with a daughter of Cosima Wagner, Blandine Gravina, in Sicily, where he went out on horseback, without knowing how to ride ('trotting was distinctly alarming . . . more tomorrow . . . in the winter I will learn how to do it properly'); in Pisa he had a row with a shameless cab-driver, which would have ended in blows but for politice intervention. He was certainly not a timid tourist, but an enterprising, self-confident young man, seeing enough of the world to whet his appetitite to see more.

His friends looked forward to his return to Germany. Hans von Bülow, now seriously ill himself, wrote to Spitzweg that Strauss had, 'after Brahms, by far the most personal, richest [musical] personality! All honour to you for having really discovered it, having been the first to recognize it! May God guard his *physis*, then all will be well with his *psyche*.'

While he was in Sicily, he received letters proposing new conducting posts. Karlsruhe, Hamburg, Berlin were all possibilities. Hermann Levi met him in Florence, anxious to mend fences, and offered him a good position in Munich. The prospect of returning to the 'petty bourgeois nest' did not appeal very strongly. The idea of committing himself to stay anywhere at all for any length of time was altogether unattractive. He would rather go to India or China. He never got to either country, but the urge to travel never left him.

For the time being, however, he went back to Weimar for one more year: his first concern was *Guntram* – or perhaps it was the guest artist Pauline de Ahna. Strauss had been acquainted with the soprano for some years, but it was in the spring of 1894 that they entered into a secret engagement. First, however, we must take a look at the opera in the rehearsals of which Pauline played such a colourful part.

'Guntram'

After Wagner, any self-respecting composer had to write his own libretto. At the age of twenty-three, Strauss found a subject and a period – the world of the minnesingers – and set foot on the thorny road. He wrote and wrestled with it from autumn 1887 to March 1888. The text circulated among family and friends. Alexander Ritter, Fritz Brandt, the theatre producer at Weimar, Friedrich Rösch all wrote him long letters about it. Professional writers, poets and dramaturges expressed the greater reservations. Alexander Ritter went through the ethical content and the moral conclusions with a fine-tooth comb, without improving the quality of the text, which already testifies to Strauss's instinct for the stage, even if it still needed development. Ritter was never reconciled to the ending.

In a country groaning under an oppressive tyranny, Guntram strikes dead the cruel Duke, who is also the husband of Freihild, the woman Guntram loves. He has taken vows in an order dedicated to opposing war and violence but, recognizing that his motives for the killing were anger and

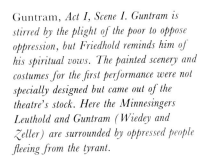

Pauline de Ahna in one of her stage roles. For her Strauss wrote the part of Freiheld.

Guntram, *Act I, Scene I. Guntram is stirred by the plight of the poor to oppose oppression, but Friedhold reminds him of his spiritual vows. The painted scenery and costumes for the first performance were not specially designed but came out of the theatre's stock. Here the Minnesingers Leuthold and Guntram (Wiedey and Zeller) are surrounded by oppressed people fleeing from the tyrant.*

jealousy, he refuses to stand trial before the court of the pacifist order. 'No court can condemn me or absolve me. I carry my law in my own heart, I am my own judge, and I determine my own expiation.' Ritter strove for months to talk Strauss out of this proud defiance of collectivist wisdom. Disagreement came close to a complete breach. From Palermo, where he was orchestrating Act II, Strauss wrote to Ludwig Thuille that Ritter 'still finds my third act horrifying, but he assures me of his love. Loss of Ritter's friendship – I don't know if that dashed chatterbox Guntram would be worth that!' In old age he recalled:

> I owe it to Ritter that he discovered my dramatic vocation. I, alas, felt no 'poetic' gifts within me. Early projects – including an 'Eulenspiegel' and a 'Burghers of Schilda' – did not make any headway.
> The opera was to be staged in Weimar, where the orchestra boasted six first violins and five second, four violas, three cellos and three double basses!! *Guntram* – a testimony to my hair-raising naivety in those days – was studied and put into rehearsal, my poor valiant pupil Heinrich

Zeller went through agonies with his insanely demanding role – at the time somebody calculated that the part had more bars than Tristan – each rehearsal made him hoarser and hoarser, and he had a struggle to get through to the end of the first performance. My fiancée knew her part faultlessly and her performance was vocally and dramatically outstanding. The audience applauded her tumultuously, and it was the same story at the later, disastrous performance in Munich. At one of the last rehearsals, at which I had to rap with my baton to stop Zeller countless times, we at last came to Pauline's scene in Act III which she knew perfectly well. All the same she felt unsure of herself and apparently envied Zeller his frequent 'repeats'. Suddenly she stopped singing and asked me: 'Why don't you stop me?' I: 'Because you know your part.' Whereupon, with the words 'I want to be stopped!' she threw the vocal score at me. To general hilarity, however, it landed on the desk of the second violin Gutheil.

The third act, he thought, when he was starting to score it, was 'hyper-Tristan-ish, [but] it's the most advanced in the precision of expression, the richest and most impressive in the melodic invention and altogether by far the best thing I've ever written. . . . Hold tight to your seats, my friends! The motivikins come so fast and furious, your heads will spin! Metaphorically speaking!' The 'motivikins' often sound like Wagner, and there is a lot of pomposity, hothouse emotion and self-indulgent histrionics – though there is also a lot that sounds like nobody except Richard Strauss. At rehearsals, there was one passage that always caused the cellos difficulty. As Strauss fumed, one of the cellists tried to soothe him: 'We can never get this bit right in *Tristan* either.'

After the first rehearsal with the full orchestra, he wrote to his parents in great excitement: 'I am in heaven. You should just hear my orchestra now, by Jove! It will really make you sit up. But it's hard. Hui!'

He had already found his own voice in the symphonic poem and the song. In opera it would take him another ten years. His would-be Wagnerian text was another liability. The subject of non-violent resistance to tyranny has been a popular one in the past century, but the rightness of the cause is severely hampered here by naivety and cliché. The work also lacks any theatrical excitement or spectacle. Spitzweg nevertheless bravely ventured 5000 marks on its publication, and lost almost every pfennig.

Eleven years after Wagner's death, his mature music dramas were still an immense obstacle in the path of other composers of opera, especially the Germans. Some tried to sidestep the obstacle by taking up the thread of earlier, Romantic opera *à la* Weber. Hans Pfitzner's first opera, *Der arme Heinrich*, taking its subject from medieval German epic poetry, imitated Wagner more directly. In Italy, the 'naturalism' of *verismo* offered an alternative route. Only Verdi, it seemed, as he gave the world *Falstaff*, was aloof from the problem. In France, Debussy fought hard to escape from the spell of Wagner and the dramatics of German, contrapuntalist, high seriousness, and moved towards a new musical language in *L'après-midi d'un faune*.

Pauline de Ahna as Freihild and Heinrich Zeller as Guntram. Both singers had studied with Strauss in Munich; Zeller was already engaged at the Weimar opera when Strauss went there, and Fräulein de Ahna followed.

Photos of the Weimar production of Guntram, *as displayed outside the theatre.*

An enthusiast's depiction of Strauss's departure from Weimar in 1894. Pegasus's head is sunk in sorrow but his wings are spread. The Muse's features are supposed to be those of Pauline.

Act I of Guntram *in the single Munich performance. Scenery came out of the theatre's stock.*

Act II of Guntram *in the Munich production.*

Edith Stargardt-Wolff, the daughter of the Berlin concert agent Hermann Wolff, was still a schoolgirl in 1894, when she went to Weimar with her parents to attend the premiere of *Guntram*. In her memoirs she told a strange tale:

> After the dress rehearsal, as we sat drinking afternoon coffee in the house of the baritone Franz Schwarz, the tenor Hans Giessen was announced. 'Show him in', said Schwarz, but the tenor would not enter the room. 'What's the matter with him?' asked Schwarz, going out to see him. There was Giessen, in a frock-coat and top-hat as if he was going to a funeral, and said, in a stiff and dignified fashion, 'Herr Schwarz, I am the bearer of a challenge from Herr Kapellmeister Strauss, to call you out to a duel with pistols. You have insulted his fiancée.' Schwarz could not believe his ears. 'I didn't even know he was engaged, I don't know his fiancée!' Giessen: 'It is Fräulein de Ahna, and you have insulted her. Pistols!' Even as he said it, he looked very unsure of himself and quite uncomfortable.

What had happened? We have already heard Strauss's version of Pauline's outburst at the rehearsal. Schwarz is said to have upbraided her for talking to the composer like that, when he had been working so hard and had only just recovered from a serious illness. She had told him to mind his own business; she was a general's daughter, when all was said and done, and he was being offensive. It was after this quarrel, according to Edith Wolff, that Strauss and Pauline became engaged, and that meant, according to the strict rules of honour, that he had to challenge Schwarz to a duel. (In fact, it must all have been an elaborate backstage joke, which poor Giessen did not understand.) According to this version, Bronsart intervened and the matter ended in laughter. Schwarz assured Wolff that he would never put a bullet through their Kapellmeister, or do him any other kind of damage. Wolff wondered sceptically if the bride-to-be would be equally considerate in the long run.

Some things about this story do not hold water: for one thing, if the alleged incident took place at a dress rehearsal preceding the premiere of *Guntram*, which took place on 10 May, then this was some seven weeks after their secret engagement. The official announcement of the engagement was actually made on the day of the premiere.

Eighteen months after the Weimar premiere, *Guntram* was staged in Munich. The sets and costumes came from stock, and there was only one, dreadful performance. Experiences like this taught Strauss to supervise later premieres closely, and to make them model performances, as far as possible.

Some of the singers refused to take part. The Guntram, Max Mikorey, demanded an increase in his pension. The orchestra, headed by their leader Benno Walter – the composer's cousin and erstwhile violin teacher, implored the Intendant to rid them of 'this scourge of God'! The local press weighed in, gleefully recounting tales such as this, and publishing a verse lampoon, after Schiller, accusing Strauss of assassinating music.

Fifteen years on, in the garden of the Garmisch villa, Strauss erected a memorial to Guntram, in the style of a wayside shrine. 'Cruelly slain by his progenitor's symphonic orchestra. Peace be with his ashes'.

Among other things, this premiere, or rather dernière, cost Strauss the friendship of Siegfried Wagner, who accused him of betraying his father's artistic principles: the worst thing anyone could have said to Strauss. Frau Cosima, too, found the music empty and the minnesingers ineffective in their vacuum. 'It is unbelievable, how *Guntram* has made me enemies. Alack, one writes as one's heart dictates.'

Many years later, in 1940, *Guntram* was given a single performance in Weimar, in a version cut by Strauss himself and for which he pared down the instrumentation. The conductor was Robert Heger, whom he wrote to thank for sponsoring this 'premature infant'. 'I am perfectly agreeable, if you want to amputate a few little superfluous limbs. I myself cut a few Wagnerian orchestral interludes when it was first done in Weimar.' This must be the only occasion on which Strauss sanctioned cuts in his work: usually he fought tooth and nail to prevent them. He always refused to make changes, too; once a thing was written, it was complete, in his view.

Ein Heldenleben quotes a few bars of *Guntram*: the expansive melody for violin in the 'works of peace' section, where a number of quotations from other works are combined contrapuntally (figs 89–92). And the protagonist's memories of his youth in *Tod und Verklärung* (solo violin) are identical with a passage in Act I of the opera, expressing a similar mood: another self-quotation.

Pauline Maria de Ahna

In the lives of the great composers, the roles played by their wives (if they had them) have been too evenly spaced out along the spectrum from harridan to muse to permit any general conclusions to be drawn. But Strauss's marriage with Pauline de Ahna was exceptional by any standards, and cannot be compared with any other in musical history. Whatever one may think of Pauline Strauss, without her Richard Strauss would not have become what he was.

She was born in Ingolstadt on 4 February 1863. Her father, though he rose to the rank of general in the Bavarian army, was not a very military man in his manner or his predilections. He loved the arts, and music in particular, for which he showed talent; for example, he studied the role of Hans Sachs in the Act III scene with Walther, and used to perform in public. The de Ahnas were typical of their class in Bavaria, in their mixture of *grandezza* and *bonhomie*; art, and the love of art, were things they took for granted. The military caste did not take itself very seriously in Bavaria; its members moved in court circles and were influenced by Ludwig II's artistic ideals.

With this background, Pauline thought of herself all her life as an aristocrat. She wanted to study singing, but her father did not like the idea of her attending the academy in Munich, and had her taught privately. She had drama lessons from Alexander Ritter's wife, Franziska, and for a while she studied operatic roles with Max Steinitzer, who suggested Strauss to her when he himself no longer had the time.

In 1887 . . . she had already spent some months studying at the Munich School of Music, and with the courage of a complete amateur she had naively stormed her way through the aria from *Freischütz* at an examination-recital in the Odeon, to the thunderous applause of her military admirers. . . . She possessed good breath-control, a perfectly even tone and poetic understanding.

They met in 1887, in late August, when Strauss was holidaying with Uncle Georg and Aunt Johanna Pschorr in Feldafing on Lake Starnberg, where the de Ahnas were neighbours. The Pschorrs entertained many guests from the artistic world: even Cosima Wagner dined with them, and strolled in the garden with her old enemy Franz Strauss in perfect amity. Feldafing was a popular resort in summertime. Many well-to-do people from Munich had villas there, with views of the lake, and with flower-gardens and orchards, which provided a respite from the dust and heat of the city during the admittedly few warm days of the Bavarian summer. Even in those days, Strauss composed only in the warmth and light of the summer months.

Pauline Strauss's parents: Adolf de Ahna and Maria de Ahna-Huber.

He was twenty-three, and she twenty-four, when he began to coach the general's daughter with the generous voice. It is hardly possible to speak of love at first sight: it was seven years before they announced their engagement, and even when the marriage contract was being drawn up they were still addressing each other by the formal 'Sie'.

When he went to Weimar she presented herself there too and became a guest artist at the Court Theatre in 1890. Before long her fresh, well-trained voice attracted the attention of other theatres, including Bayreuth, where she sang Elisabeth, a Rhinemaiden and a Flowermaiden.

She had enough temperament for three. It was her habit to say what she thought, uninhibitedly and with disarming directness. 'She gingered me up', as Storch exclaims in *Intermezzo*. 'I must have life and temperament about me!' There was certainly no shortage of those commodities. After two years working together in Weimar he was forced to expostulate with her:

Most respected Fräulein,
By all appearances you are now so set on going your own way that my presence and the influence it inevitably exercises could only seem a burden to you; I regret therefore that I must gratefully decline your kind invitation both today and in the future, and I remain with best wishes, yours most sincerely, Richard Strauss (2 April 1891)

Ten months later, during another altercation, Franz Strauss was obliged to intervene:

> General de Ahna has just called on us in a state of some agitation . . . his daughter has written to tell him that you had had a very forceful conversation with her, and had formally terminated your friendship. He is extraordinarily sorry to learn about this and wishes most ardently that the two of you will be reconciled. To please me, put things straight again. . . . Fräulein de Ahna seems to be rather given to over-exciting herself, and a man of good breeding can always allow some latitude to a lady of that kind, without lowering himself. Also I am sure she is the singer who will come closest to realizing your intentions.

After the wedding, the tables were turned, and it was Strauss who called upon his parents to make allowances for Pauline's temperament:

I would be happy if my unceasing efforts to bring about a good understanding between my wife and my family were not crowned with so little success. If I assure you that she is making a sincere effort to correct her small and in part really quite harmless faults (which she and I know better than anyone else), then the fact that the miserable fabrications of gossiping old women (like the tale which led you to make such serious complaints to Pauline this morning) suffice . . . to destroy forthwith any loving forbearance and understanding of Pauline's unthinking, excited, over-boisterous, but essentially goodhearted, childlike and naive manner, makes me ask myself if it would not be better if communication between you and Pauline ceased altogether. . . . She has sincere love and respect for you in the heart of her jealous heart. I cannot play forever the unhappily unsuccessful explainer of the various characteristics of my wife, whom I chose after very mature deliberation, and love and honour in spite of her faults.

It was after Strauss's return from Egypt, when they had been apart for nearly a year, that he proposed to her. She was thirty-one, he not yet thirty. After acceptance, she clearly felt doubtful, and there is a letter whch is typical of what Strauss found fascinating about her in its impetuosity and veering from one preoccupation to another:

My dear Herr Strauss,
It's all suddenly descending on me like a shower bath; I beg you for God's sake not to rejoice so excessively, you know better than anyone how many faults I have, and I tell you in all honesty that in spite of the happiness I feel, I am sometimes terribly afraid. Will I be capable of being what you want and what you deserve? May I not first fulfil my guest engagement in Hamburg, so that I shall at least have a triumph to show off proudly to my respected teacher? Unfortunately nothing is to come of the Monday Elisabeth.

You should not overestimate me, and your parents and Hanna know my moods too; O God, and now I am suddenly supposed to turn into a model housewife, so that you do not feel disappointed. Dear friend, I am afraid that it will fail, and the more everyone rejoices the more oppressed I feel. It's not nice of Papa to say that he has been worried about me and my theatrical career; I don't understand him; up till now everything has gone smoothly and would continue to do so.

Won't all the conducting you will be doing this summer be too much of a strain for you? O God, I am so worried and concerned. Will your parents like me, and Hanna, if she knew how I have tried to dissuade you from everything. My dear friend, we really don't need to marry so soon; if each of us could first get accustomed to finding all the happiness we can in our careers; you in Munich and I in Hamburg; please bring my contract with you; forgive this letter but the two feelings – my happiness and my fear of a new life – weigh on me so that I am only half capable of reasoning. Please allow me at least to sing a lot more parts

The title page of the Four Songs, op. 27, which Strauss gave his 'beloved Pauline' as a wedding present. Many of his songs in these years were written for her, and it can hardly be coincidence that after she gave up her career as a singer he wrote very few more.

From left: the bride's father, three guests, the bride, Franz Strauss, the bridegroom, Tante Johanna.

here; that will help me to get over some of my difficulties. I am being uncommonly diligent studying Freihild with Klatte and Gutheil; the greatest happiness is our art, dear friend, do not forget that. I can't write any more today. Please do not hold any of it against me.

My most sincere greeting to your dear family; I kiss the hand of your honoured Mama and ask them all to have patience with me.

Farewell and be as happy as you deserve to be.

Sincerely yours, Pauline de Ahna.

Please permit a postscript, since it is about Freihild. In Act II: '(Rising to her full height) "Entweiche Tod vor Freihilds Jubel"' lies very, very high; could it be pointed; then I would certainly be better able to bring off the great vocal effect that is intended; I spend almost the whole day working on it, *difficult* but beautiful!!!

Exactly four months after the official announcement of their engagement, they were married, on 10 September, in Marquartstein in the mountains south-east of Munich, where the de Ahnas had a summer villa. The wedding ceremony was Catholic, although the groom had no connection with the church. They spent their honeymoon in Italy, travelling from Bellagio, where it was cold and wet, via Pegli to Venice, where they had a beautiful month.

In Munich, where Strauss was taking up another appointment with the Court Opera, they moved first into an apartment in Hildegardstrasse and then into one in Herzog-Rudolf-Strasse, both in what was then the idyllic suburb of Schwabing, very popular with writers and painters, and not the tourist attraction it is today.

During the first year of the marriage, Strauss composed *Till Eulenspiegel*, and the sketches for the work have some fascinating annotations in Pauline's handwriting: not to be taken very seriously, but perhaps suggesting that composition took up too much of his time, in her view. Against the passage headed 'Trial' she wrote 'mad', then 'awful', 'dreadful mess' and 'horrid composing'; these remarks, in turn, were annotated by Strauss: 'comments by my lady wife'.

Till Eulenspiegel is unique among the symphonic poems, with its combination of great technical sophistication (it all springs from two brief phrases), rapid variations of mood and vivid, immediate depiction of events. Anton Bruckner heard it in Vienna in 1896, the year of his death, at a concert at which his own Fourth Symphony was also played. While Eduard Hanslick wrote Strauss off as a 'virtuoso of the specious', Bruckner (who was no longer able to walk) returned for the repeat performance because he found the piece 'uncommonly interesting, and probably had not understood it properly' the first time. Strauss met Bruckner ('half genius, half simpleton' according to Bülow) several times, and often performed his symphonies, which he characterized as the 'stammerings of a Cyclops'.

Not content with scribbling on Strauss's manuscripts, Pauline left her mark in the engagement calendars he kept for decades, using them also as notebooks and sometimes as diaries. She inscribed the first page of the 1895 volume 'My dear Richard! I like you very much, although you are not my "baa-lamb"! But therefore more than that.'

One precious document in her handwriting looks like a list of things to be packed before a conducting trip: 'Richard for Berlin. 4 stiff shirts. 1 nightshirt. 2 underpants. 2 undervests. 4 pairs socks. 18 handkerchiefs. 8 collars. 4 pairs cuffs. Sponge bag. Dressing gown, slippers, ties, food, wine, travelling cushion.' He liked travelling, she did not. She was often enough attracted by the idea of going with him but when it came to the point she usually found excuses and reasons for staying at home. In the first twenty years of their married life he was often away, as an internationally famous conductor of the first rank. He wrote to her every day, because 'I need to have a chat with you, even if it has to be at a distance'. Here is a long letter he wrote her from Moscow, some eighteen months after their wedding. His descriptions are so graphic that she must have felt as if she was there too.

The manuscript score of Till Eulenspiegel *with Pauline's annotations. Over the episode of Till's trial she wrote 'mad' and 'dreadful'. Other comments include 'rotten garbage' and 'lousy composition'.*

Pauline Strauss-de Ahna in 1900.

My dearest Pauxerl,

Here I am, safe and sound. The journey was very pleasant, everything went smoothly at the frontier at 1.30 at night, the Russian sleeper from Warsaw was extremely comfortable and warm with the double windows, no coal dust as it's all heated by wood, a very cosy restaurant car on the train, excellent cuisine, the scenery – which is completely uniform: forests and plains, fields and forests – was free of snow yesterday, solid white today from Smolensk onwards, yesterday was minus 1, today minus 6 degrees Réaumur, the villages which you catch sight of from time to time look like collections of snow-covered haystacks – in other words the scenery was uncommonly restful. I passed the time royally, eating, sleeping, reading and composing, and so I was completely fresh and lively when I bowled into holy Moscow at 7, where I was met surprisingly at the station by my friend, the piano teacher Pohl, packed at once into an open sleigh and conveyed to this grand hotel. Thank goodness, it was only minus 6 degrees. There are no hansom cabs. Everyone – even ladies going to concerts in décolleté – drives around in open sleighs, no bells, no lights, a free-for-all, the one-horse sleighs are no higher off the ground than our toboggans, you are liable to get a horse's nose in your neck at every moment, Moscow makes an extraordinary impression with its immense streets and one-storey houses. After we had eaten (marvellous caviar with schnaps) we went out again to look at the Kremlin, which, so far as I could see at night, appears to be something quite superb and marvellous. There are these crazy churches, one beside another, all the cannon taken in 1812 (or found in the snow) in front of the barracks, the huge, cracked bell in the courtyard where it fell, the magnificent view of the river way below you, Ivan the Terrible's place of execution, it has all got – colour, and strikes me as being well scored. First rehearsal tomorrow at 10, concerts begin at 9 in the evening here. Well, I shall have a lot to tell you.

Next time I hope I'll be able to take you with me. As I said, I'm as fit as a fiddle, so far as that is possible without you, my dearest darling, don't worry about me, I am extremely careful in those open sleighs, and otherwise everything is as right as rain! Midnight, and the bells are ringing: they're beautifully tuned. Adieu! I hope all is very well with you too. A thousand good wishes and kisses, your R.

Moscow, 18 March 1896

He kept up the daily letter-writing throughout his life, not least because he disliked the telephone. He travelled by express train, at a later date sometimes in his chauffeur-driven car, once by aeroplane, in 1947. When Pauline went with him on concert tours, she sang his songs more beautifully than any other singer and thus did a great deal for his reputation. She always made an imposing entrance, magnificently dressed, whereas he, according to some reviewers, usually sat at the piano with the air of someone who had nothing to do with what was happening around him. She did not like the long preludes or postludes that some of the songs had, and sometimes a little battle of wills ensued, when she would bow as a way of cutting short a postlude before it was finished.

In 1897 he went to Spain without her, and was to meet her on the return journey. He sent her a letter full of affectionate advice, drawn from his own greater experience.

You leave on Monday at 11.30 and you get to Brussels at 6 in the evening. Don't forget the music and *Tannhäuser* etc. Bring one dress and one hat too many rather than too few, so that you are quite smart and dashing, only bring immaculate boots and buy everything else you need (gloves etc.), because things are dearer in Brussels than in Munich. When you arrive in Brussels, ask about the hotel omnibus, and if one isn't there take a hansom to the hotel, where I have just booked a room with heating. I am looking forward to seeing you enormously, and to our splendid joint enterprise. Do be sensible, don't catch cold, have coffee, rolls and everything else brought to you in the compartment by the sleeping-car attendant (tip 2 marks) because the constant chopping and changing between the compartment and cool air is just the thing to give you a cold.
(27 November 1897)

He took care of domestic decisions, plans and dispositions, and he paid the bills. When he was away for weeks at a time she had to bear the burden alone, and although he used to send advice in his letters, the responsibility, for which she had no experience to prepare her, often infuriated her. One important decision had to be made in 1906 when they had to part with the beloved de Ahna family house at Marquartstein, where Strauss had spent so many summers composing, because their new villa in Garmisch was nearly ready for them. Strauss was away, once again, and Pauline was distraught. He wrote from Turin, the day after Christmas, to comfort her.

I will bring you nothing but chocolate, smuggled, naturally, and myself (not much, you will probably think, but a rascal who gives away more than he owns). If you want to keep Marquartstein, then we'll keep it, that's all. I do everything in my power, so long as I see you just a little more contented and so long as you don't demand the impossible. Are you looking forward to seeing me just a little bit? . . . Come February, and I'll throw my work in a corner and we'll go to the mountains! Farewell both of you, love me a little bit and receive a thousand hugs and kisses from your ever-faithful R.

Out for a walk, Garmisch, 1909.

Marquartstein was sold.

Pauline was the subject of endless talk. When a character in *Intermezzo* calls Frau Storch 'einfach ferchterlich' – 'simply frightful' – Strauss knew he was quoting a commonly held opinion of his wife. Many found her unfathomable, and she did not make it easy for them. But it all pales into insignificance beside the fact that this was a truly happy marriage, right to the end. The relationship and the life of the family were completely stable,

All Strausses are doglovers, and Pauline had a soft spot for cats too. Here with a friend, Dora Breisach.

there were no extramarital affairs, no liaisons, no crises of identity, no rifts. Without Pauline, moreover, Strauss would almost certainly have been less productive than he was: she gave his self-discipline its backbone. What did it matter, then, if she offended or alarmed other people, if strangers shook their heads? She was the perfect complement to him. We can only guess how necessary her whims and unpredictability were to his very existence, and we must respect it.

If a few of the anecdotes about Pauline Strauss are recounted at this juncture, it is because they are entertaining in themselves, not because of any wish to belittle her. But they only illuminate the surface, not the core.

— *While Strauss was working on the closing trio of* Der Rosenkavalier, *he was improvising at the piano one evening, searching for the right conclusion to the scene. Pauline was sewing in the next room, and called through to him: 'Go on! Go on!' 'Do you think so? Isn't it getting too insistent?' 'No! Go on, go on!'*

It would seem, then, that the ebb and flow of this masterpiece, the way it breathes, owe something to the taste and enthusiasm of its first hearer and her wish for more.

— *Vienna has always been stony ground for modern art. In 1901, the ultra-modern Strauss was still regarded with grave suspicion. Much hung, therefore, on a song recital with Pauline. At noon on the day in question, she sent a message to the impresario Gutmann: 'Am ill. Cold and fever. Must cancel!' Gutmann rushed round to the Hotel Bristol and found her to be the very picture of suffering. Resigning himself, he left and met Strauss on the stairs. 'Nice of you to pay a call on my wife.' 'Don't you know? The poor creature – we must cancel, it is terrible.' 'Cancel? Just a moment.' He vanished into the sickroom, came out a few minutes later looking thoughtful, and said, 'The poor thing is really stricken – but – can you recommend a good jeweller?'*

Gutmann took him to Köchert's (the jeweller whose daughter played such an important role in Hugo Wolf's life), where Strauss bought a very pretty ring, as a judicious way of comforting his wife. Lo and behold, it cured her too. The recital was a success: which, as said above, was important for Strauss at the time – and for Vienna.

— *At a large social gathering, she made the acquaintance of Baldur von Schirach, by then high up in the Nazi hierarchy. He proved to be an agreeable and amusing conversationalist, so that eventually Pauline was moved to ask, in a loud voice, overheard by all the other guests, 'Tell me the truth, you're not a Nazi, are you?' On numerous public occasions, she had her husband quaking in his shoes. On his account she was actually accorded some of the liberty of a court jester.*

— *Well-bred North Germans often have difficulty in understanding the South German temperament and the Bavarian point of view. The fact that in 1871 Bavaria was absorbed into a federation under Prussian hegemony, while their Austrian cousins remained outside, and that this unhappy union continued even after the First World War, is one of the subjects on which many Bavarians hold a different opinion from North Germans. Count Harry von Kessler, diplomat, aesthete and friend of Hugo von Hofmannsthal, described a dinner party in Berlin, on 19 January 1926.*

At table Pauline showed herself at her best and her worst. Motherly concern that all her guests should have enough to eat, especially Max [Reinhardt] who sat next to her and whose plate she kept on cramming.... Yet at the same time she was disagreeable and tactless ... Woyzeck (Büchner's play, not the opera) she spurns because she really cannot preoccupy herself with the troubled soul of a squalid non-commissioned officer [sic].... Carmen is also the story of a non-commissioned officer, I observe. Yes, but romantic, Spanish, and a Mérimée creation, protests Pauline.... People do say, and Pauline bends forward to whisper it stealthily, that Count Kessler has become quite a Red. Oh no, I answer, I am just a simple democrat. Pauline: A democrat, you, who are a Count? In that case you are fouling your own nest ...

Strauss was becoming more and more uncomfortable. Now he intervened and, by declaring that his wife knows nothing about politics and I should take no notice of her remarks, tried to put a stop to the talk. Later Pauline, aware that she had gone too far ... [said that] she is a general's daughter, and aristocrat (all this in broadest Bavarian): in Southern Germany they hate the North Germans, the Prussians: they want a South German state, Bavaria and Austria together ...

She seemed to anticipate that the brilliance of these concepts (which, she assured me, enjoy the full blessing of the Bavarian Royal Family) would propitiate me.

I am a North German, I replied. All the same I do not want the South Germans to starve ... Before such sentimental amalgamations are discussed, the United States of Europe must be brought into existence. She acquiesced delightedly in European unity.

The close-by beloved.

(But did Kessler really believe that Bavaria would starve without Prussia? The state, with a population of eight million, had been independent for 1400 years, and in the course of its history had often helped to feed other states – including Prussia.)

— *They were in a horse-drawn cab in Garmisch once, when Pauline was giving her husband yet another fiery curtain lecture. Strauss, as always, remained calm. Suddenly the driver turned round: 'Are you going to stand for that? Throw the cow out!' They all had to laugh. Pauline herself circulated this story.*

— *Strauss avoided social gatherings, and went out as little as possible. His own house was always spotlessly clean. Pauline's passion for the duster was legendary. She felt no embarrassment at sending dinner guests to wash their hands or at making callers wipe their feet, because she saw no reason why they should bring dirt in from the street, which would only have to be swept out again. Wiping shoes with a damp cloth was Strauss's idea.*

When they went on concert tours, they often stayed with friends. That was no problem in those days, when the people they knew had large houses with guest rooms and domestic staff. Even in someone else's house, Pauline had no inhibitions about carrying out an inspection to see if the place had been properly dusted, running her finger over the furniture, opening drawers, looking under beds and asking to see the servants' hands. The embarrassed hosts could do nothing but stand looking on with a fixed smile. She even made an inspection when she had been invited for nothing more than coffee. It is understandable that she should keep her own house clean, but why she felt such a compulsion to run other people's lives is a mystery.

— *She never forgot that Richard's lungs were at risk since Weimar. Her prescription was lots of fresh air. His letters frequently refer to the good Garmisch air. Pauline was a passionate opener of windows, while he declared that sometimes he could hardly endure to stay in his room, there was such a draught. Twice a day, an hour before lunch and an hour before dinner, she fetched him from his work, to go for a walk. The daily walks became a necessity to him, and he kept up the habit even when he was away from home on his own. If something suddenly occurred to her when they were about to leave, she would run off to instruct the cook or make a telephone call, and leave him waiting for her. Strauss never wasted a moment of time, so he would scribble a postcard – or write a song.* Traum durch die Dämmerung *was written during one such ten-minute wait, after a brief argument and some banging of doors. Pauline came back and demanded: 'Well, now what? I'm ready', and he replied: 'So am I'. (Later he commented: 'A congruence between words and music such as exists in this song is not achieved very often.')*

— *Viorica Ursuleac recalled a performance of* Elektra *in Berlin in the 1930s, in which she sang Chrysothemis. The conductor was Wilhelm Furtwängler, and the evening was an outstanding success. Pleased and grateful, Strauss invited her to join him and Pauline for supper in their suite in the hotel. Was it that the presence of the beautiful blonde singer upset his wife in some way? At all events, she suddenly began to rave about Furtwängler: what an attractive man he was, the enchanting curly hair, the hands, the charm, etc. Strauss became so angry that he sprang to his feet, threw down his napkin, uttered a Bavarian oath and left the room. Thereupon she began to sob: 'I only wanted to make him jealous.'*
  The next morning Ursuleac saw them again in the hotel lobby. Strauss rolled his eyes: 'She's always playacting – and I always fall for it.'

— *In later years, she seldom went to performances or discussed his works. Some people formed the opinion that she was indifferent to them. In 1948 they were living in Switzerland, uprooted and depressed. She was eighty-five. He was in hospital in Lausanne after his second major operation. He and Ernst Roth, his publisher, had both been unable to remember the title of the song that begins 'Du sollst nicht weinen', and Roth mentioned it that evening to Pauline. At once she said: 'It's called* Befreit. *A lovely song' – and sang it quietly, as if to herself, in a voice that was still beautiful. 'Half a century is a long time to keep something in your head, if you don't think anything of it', was Roth's comment.*

— *A family friend, Manfred Mautner-Markhof, related what happened once when he called at the villa in Garmisch for tea:*
  Strauss was working on something in the next room, and we were talking about Elektra. *I said that for me the recognition scene with Orestes was one of the greatest scenes in all opera. 'Yes!' said Pauline, 'only the Electras usually act it wrongly. They fall on their brother's neck, like a girl in love finding her lover again. I'll show you how it ought to be.' She jumped up. 'You be Orestes, and I'll be Electra.' I was rather shocked and embarrassed. 'Well, what shall I do?' 'Nothing at all. Just stand still.' She moved away and then started to come towards me slowly, humming the melody. When she reached me, she put her arms round me cautiously, let herself sink against me and was embracing my knees by*

A group photo in Bad Kissingen. Baron and Baroness Thüngen and the other guests are ready: Pauline is not, and her husband has something to say about it.

That's better! Smile please!

Pauline detested being photographed: on this occasion, in the loggia of the house in Garmisch, she evidently did not know it was happening.

the end of the scene. She was seventy-nine years old at the time. I helped her up and saw that tears were running down her cheeks, so moved was she by her husband's great art.

Everyone who knew her closely said that she loved her husband above all else, and did all in her power to further his well-being and enable him to concentrate on his work.

Nobody explained her character as well as he did, in *Intermezzo*. Her temperament was as necessary to him as the air he breathed. When he was working, he did not shut himself away, like Mahler and many others. He liked to hear what was going on in the house. And when Pauline was chatting to somebody in the next room and had a question, she would go across herself or send the maid, and Richard would answer.

Quietly, without fuss, he would repair fences, whenever she had said something that shocked people, and he was probably privately amused by her manifold incautiousness. It is very interesting to discover that, in his private notebooks, he remarked on a similarity between her character and that of Hans von Bülow; evidently he was both delighted and stimulated by unconventional and original personalities such as theirs, who took honesty to the point of rudeness.

Today, we might say her concern with her image, or with her place in the 'pecking order' was neurotic. She wanted to uphold her claim to consideration as a person in her own right. She eventually gave up her own career, and when she saw court being paid to successful singers, she felt overlooked. She liked to be the centre of attention, and to that end would do whatever came into her head. She hauled her successful, eminent husband down from the pedestal where others placed him by derogatory remarks about his ancestry (the brewers, the court usher, the petty bourgeoisie – whereas she was the daughter of a general). They were unusual weapons to employ in the struggle for equal recognition, but then, there were few gaps in his armour. The man who had no equal in the composition of music for and about women, in giving musical expression to sensuality and love, or to the act of love itself, and who loved the company of women – that man was irreproachably faithful. He knew only one all-embracing love, enjoyed complete trust, complete harmony with the woman who was his other self: Pauline.

At the end of the First World War, when the world they had known lay in ruins and a new one had to be built, he wrote:

Dearest Paula,
You are so clever and wise in all things, that you always come up with what is right and can always be sure that I will agree before you even ask me. Only in direct contact with other people am I, I believe, more practised. You are too sensitive and distrustful. If I could, I would gladly give you some of my coolness and phlegm, which makes it so easy to get on with all sorts . . . (1 May 1919)

After thirty-six years of marriage, in 1930, between remarks about the weather and some performances he had attended, he wrote: 'I don't know if it's the same for you – my inner belonging to you grows greater all the time, I think of you and the children all day long. I am wholly happy only with you. With our family!' Two days later, from Brussels, he wrote: 'The director of the Conservatoire still remembers exactly how beautifully you sang my songs here – and how you argued my own view, that Bavaria and Austria are the most beautiful places to be, and nowhere is the air so good as in Garmisch, and nowhere is so beautiful as in my own house with my beloved Pauxerl, who is now most tenderly embraced by her ever faithful – R.'

Travelling by car, aged seventy-two, he wrote from Dijon: 'I look forward to my letter to you every evening, and hope you miss me a little bit too, and that *mes lettres* afford you some small diversion.' (11 March 1936)

Munich Again

The musical world hardly noticed the successes scored by both Strauss and Pauline at Bayreuth in 1894, when he conducted *Tannhäuser* and she sang the role of Elisabeth. Cosima Wagner was pleased, though there is a little mischief in her remark 'Fancy, so modern, and yet he conducts *Tannhäuser* so well'. Then the newly married pair went to Munich to take up a four-year contract at the Court Opera that, on paper at least, promised great opportunities. In Weimar, Strauss had had considerable freedom of action, but had been constrained by the very limited circumstances of the small duchy. Far greater resources were to hand in Munich but, as during his previous term of office, he was hemmed in by bureaucracy and bad habits.

Hermann Levi was old and sick and hardly ever wielded the baton. He left the orchestra to its own devices, rarely held rehearsals and when he did, there were always absentees. Demands for anything unusual were resisted, Strauss's success as a composer earned him envy, and there was open derision of his championship of the new music. ('Let him concern himself with the Opera, and give up the dissemination of his own imbecile works!')

Throughout the four years 1894–8, the several talents of both the Strausses were undervalued and underused, even after Levi's retirement in 1896 which meant that Strauss became nominally the principal conductor. In the second year he noted:

Ernst von Possart (1841–1921) as Shylock.

> Possart's knavery is becoming more and more blatant. After he promised to put on *Guntram* once a month *whatever* the circumstances, he doesn't schedule the work, in spite of the fact that Mikorey has declared himself ready for the last five weeks. He had promised my wife a guest contract from 1 January 1896 (6000 marks, 40 appearances guaranteed), doesn't lift a finger, steadfastly ignores her and sets the press on us, to make us docile. A second Perfall. Munich, good night!

Ernst von Possart had arrived in Munich in 1864, by way of Breslau, Berne and Hamburg. He was a popular character actor, and was General Intendant of the court theatres from 1895 to 1905. Beside his indisputable merits – he oversaw the building of the Prinzregententheater and, in partnership with Levi, began the series of festivals which led to a Mozart renaissance – his Thespian vanity was the source of some amusement. (Once a fly settled on his nose. He brushed it off and intoned 'Must be mad!')

Ever the pragmatist, Strauss tried to establish a working relationship with Possart. To flatter his dramatic aspirations, he toured with him, performing a programme of melodramas, including Tennyson's *Enoch Arden* in a setting by Strauss himself. Possart declaimed the verse frenziedly, rolling his 'Rs', while Strauss accompanied at the piano. Privately describing his *Enoch Arden* as 'the worst sort of occasional rubbish', he dedicated it to Possart. Melodrama was very fashionable at the time, but it had no appeal for Strauss; nevertheless, for the sake of popularity, he composed another, Uhland's *Schloss am Meer*, in four days in 1899.

On 22 December 1896, on Levi's retirement, the new principal Hofkapellmeister had an audience of the Prince Regent, Prince Luitpold. By now nearly eighty years old, the prince had held office for ten years, on behalf of his nephew King Otto, Ludwig II's younger brother, who was insane. Graciously, he enquired of Strauss whether, and how closely, he was related to the Viennese Strausses. Naturally Richard concealed his feelings, as he explained to his employer that he was a native of Munich, and that his father had been a member of the Regent's own orchestra these forty years, but the question was indicative of the lack of interest Munich in general showed for the young genius who already had an international reputation.

Not that time cured the condition: when the city honoured Strauss with a banquet in 1939, on the occasion of his seventy-fifth birthday, Oberbürgermeister Fiehler apostrophized him as follows: 'You, Doctor Strauss, as a native of Vienna . . .'

Like every true musician, Strauss had the highest esteem for Johann Strauss II, and regarded *Die Fledermaus* as 'thoroughly wholesome fare'. They met only once, in the Hotel Vier Jahreszeiten in Munich, but, as Richard Strauss wrote in 1925, he really made the acquaintance of his namesake in Meiningen 'when Bülow played me his waltzes throughout one evening. To me alone, for one whole, unforgettable evening of waltzes. And I readily admit that on occasion I have enjoyed myself more conducting *Perpetuum mobile*, say, than certain four-movement symphonies. And in the waltzes in *Rosenkavalier*, how could I *not* have thought of the laughing genius of Vienna?'

Strauss soldiered on in Munich for the four years of his contract. Contemporaries testified to marvellous performances of Mozart's operas. The way Strauss accompanied the recitatives on the harpsichord was new and amazing. Instead of playing chords alone he created bridge passages, by sketching in brief quotations, with variations, of melodies associated with the characters. By this means he coloured in their emotions so that the dramatic flow continued at full flood. He conducted 121 performances of

The Bavarian Prince Regent, Prince Luitpold.

Mozart and Wagner, and only twenty-four of operas by other composers, but a high proportion of those were new works by composers of his own way of thinking, and they did not go down very well with the old-fashioned, provincial Munich audiences. As a conductor of concerts he was highly regarded, but not the programmes he chose from the repertory of the 'newest music', such as Liszt's *Faust* Symphony (already forty years old).

He would not have any difficulty in moving on from Munich: the only problem was choosing between the various offers. Should he reign alone in Mannheim? Or would it be preferable to be the first in the hierarchy in the larger house in Hamburg?' Pauline nobly offered to give up her own prospects of a permanent contract in Munich, and implored him to consider only his own wishes:

> If you want to go to Hamburg because of the way they try to hold you back in Munich – darling – then go to Hamburg . . . and if I find that the climate, the circumstances, your domestic comfort are sufficient to make it possible for me to resume my artistic career, then, when we have both settled down there, it will be time enough to think of me. My most heartfelt blessings and good wishes on you in this matter!!
>
> I myself am in a very sorrowful mood, I cried all day today, without any reason really, I am just taking everything very hard and my nerves leave much to be desired, dearest good Richard. You and Bubi are all my happiness; may it long be mine and let us take care to earn a lot of money, so that you can soon live your own life. You will be here on the 10th, I am so looking forward to it, I weep for sheer longing for you, oh, it's often so heavy, so heavy in my heart that everyone wishes to comfort me. For now a good, good night, my Richard! I hug you with the utmost love. Paula.
>
> (1 September 1897)

What did her husband always say of her? 'A sensitive soul, who hid herself behind the prickles of a hedgehog.'

> My beloved, sweet, charming wife,
> Your letter was so enchanting that I don't know how to thank you for it. It gave me real support in the worries that I have to keep on going over in my mind in the present crisis. . . . You are a dear good wonderful wife and the man who calls you his has a prop and a comforter for life, and has no need to fear whatever the future may hold.
>
> You must not cry any more, and you must not be sad, because I think everything is taking a turn for the better, and our little Bubi and his dear mother will flourish with me and lead a good life. He and you are my all, and I love *you* more than I can say; I think you already know that, so words are in any case superfluous.

In spite of all his problems, Strauss composed songs, choral works and more symphonic poems during these years in Munich. Study of the scores left Franz Strauss in no further doubt that his beloved classics had been left

Autograph sketch of the beginning of Also
sprach Zarathustra, with annotations.
'The sun rises. The individual enters the
world, or the world enters the individual.'

far behind in his son's development. One of the twenty-one songs dating
from the period was published in the new arts periodical *Jugend*. This was
Wenn . . ., on a text by Carl Busse which justified a change of key in the last
few bars so that, having started in D flat major, it ended in D major. It was,
of course, an infringement of the classical rules, and Strauss appended a
footnote: 'The composer advises singers who intend to perform this work in
public before the end of the nineteenth century to sing it transposed down
by one note, in D flat major, from this point onwards, so as to finish in the
key in which the piece began.' The Intendant of the Court Opera, Baron
Perfall, sent for Strauss and issued a rebuke: a royal Bavarian
Hofkapellmeister was not to make fun of the general public in that fashion.

The tone poem *Also sprach Zarathustra* op. 30 caused many in the musical
world to shake their heads. They did not even know of the work's original
sub-title: 'Symphonic optimism in *fin de siècle* form, dedicated to the
twentieth century'. The bogey of the bourgeoisie, Nietzsche, was still alive
in 1896, his mind irretrievably clouded, and did not die until 1900. Once he
too had composed music which Bülow described as a 'rape of Euterpe'.
Strauss's symphonic poem depicts the division between nature and man,
and the attempt to liberate the individual through laughter. 'I affirm
consciously, that is my happiness!'

Composed in 1896, *Also sprach Zarathustra* uses twelve-note material
fourteen years before Schoenberg: the Science Fugue has a theme which
uses all twelve notes of the chromatic scale and treats it correspondingly.
The work elaborates, according to Strauss, the 'alternation of the two
remotest keys (the second)': C major (nature) and B major (humanity). At
the end the two keys are heard simultaneously!

The choice of key was a subtle expression of Strauss's frame of mind and
was always a first consideration for him. In *Zarathustra* D minor character-
izes despair, B minor longing, and the 'Passion' theme stated by the brass is
in A flat major – a key which Strauss associated with both passion and 'dark
blue', according to a memo. An outline has been drawn up of the symbolic
associations keys seem to have had for Strauss: D flat major and ceremony;
A minor and destiny; E minor and disgust; E flat minor and death; C minor
and heroic defiance; F sharp minor and anguish; E major and (erotic)
excitement; F major and carefree exuberance; and G major symbolizes the
childlike naivety characteristic of Sophie in *Rosenkavalier*.

Eugen Spitzweg, Strauss's first publisher.

Autograph sketch of the end of Zarathustra, *with weather report.* 'When? When? When? . . . Never, never, never, will the weather improve.'

Hanslick didn't like *Zarathustra*, and was able to quote Nietzsche to make his point: 'Oh, Zarathustra! Do not lash about so fearsomely with your whip. You know that noise murders thought!'

Eighty years later, Stanley Kubrick's use of the opening bars of *Also sprach Zarathustra* in his film *2001, a Space Odyssey* made the music a cult with the beat and pop generation. Those bars have been heard in every conceivable context since then, in television commercials and accompanying the tricks of killer whales in a Miami aquarium. Whales could hardly have been further from Strauss's thoughts. On the sketch he wrote in the margin: 'The sun rises. The individual enters the world, or the world enters the individual.'

Béla Bartók first heard *Zarathustra* in 1902. 'My creativity was in stagnation at the time. Freed from Brahms, I could not find the way past Wagner and Liszt. I was aroused as by a flash of lightning by the first Budapest performance of *Also sprach Zarathustra*. . . . At last I saw a way that would lead me to something new. I threw myself into a study of Strauss's scores and began to compose again.'

Hugo Wolf commented that 'with his crazy posing, he achieved only an addition to public merriment, so far as connoisseurs were concerned, that is, for the darling multitude naturally cheered him to the echo. For the latter it was a sensation of the sort the kindly Viennese will always buy.'

Spitzweg paid Strauss 3200 marks; for *Till Eulenspiegel* a year earlier he had only been able to afford 1000 marks, after his heavy loss on *Guntram*.

In the middle of composing *Zarathustra*, Strauss made a joke about the raw Bavarian climate in a letter to Max von Schillings: Man (in B major) asks 'When? When?' and Nature (in C major) answers from the depths 'Never, never, never will the weather improve!' (7 June 1896)

Don Quixote op. 35 is uncommonly hard for the orchestra; Strauss himself sighed over it in rehearsals. It marks a pinnacle in the musical depiction of psychological states, while its formidable technical mastery is no impediment to its unique charm. For sixteen bars it conveys the impression of a herd of sheep seen through a heat haze: this so shocked people that they heard nothing of the rest, nothing of the great art embodied in the piece. ('It's always the same. You get used to it.') Spitzweg paid a record – and valedictory – fee of 5000 marks.

Béla Bartók, who admired Strauss.

Ein Heldenleben op. 40 is 'an *Eroica* without a funeral march, but in E flat major, with very many horns'. It was written as a companion piece to *Don Quixote*. At one point the hero it portrays is a pitiable dreamer, at another a man who rebuilds his life in defiance of the mockery of a hostile world, who finds fulfilment only through a woman and withdrawal from the world. This hero is resigned rather than triumphant, a defeated victor.

Both *Don Quixote* and *Ein Heldenleben* contain much of Strauss's personality and feelings. The French writer Romain Rolland (1866–1944), professor of the history of music at the Sorbonne, advocate of popular theatre, author of that great novel about a musician's life *Jean Christophe* (in which there is a pen portrait of Strauss), humanist and anti-war campaigner, got to know Strauss well in the period around the turn of the century.

> If this music still glows today, you can imagine how it seethed when it was fresh from the oven. The tongue peeled, the breath scorched, the marrow shook at trumpet calls which fanned the fires, deep abysses opened, threatening to engulf the musical idea, but time and again it leapt up again with unbelievable elasticity. It was like dancing upon a sword-edge. The well-bred public was beside itself and came near to whistling, orchestral musicians fell about laughing. It's true that the mediocre melodic writing scarcely surpassed Mendelssohn, but the harmonic and rhythmic invention, the instrumental thunder, the dramatic intelligence, the will were gigantic. Strauss never shot the arrow of life higher in the air than then.
>
> I question him about the Hero's wife (in *Ein Heldenleben*) which so greatly intrigued the audience – some considering her a depraved woman, others a flirt, etc. He says: 'Neither the one nor the other. It's my wife I wanted to portray. She is very complex, very much a woman, a little depraved, something of a flirt, never twice alike, every minute different to what she was the minute before. At the beginning, the Hero follows her, goes into the key in which she has just sung; but she always flies further away. Then, at the end, he says: "No, I'm staying here." He stays in his thoughts, in his own key. Then she comes to him.' In any case this very long, very developed section serves as a foil, an intermediary, between the two outbursts at the beginning and at the battle.

It was the first musical portrait of Pauline. There would be more and fuller ones. She became his favourite model.

A composer called Gottlieb Noren wrote a piece called *Kaleidoskop* which made respectful use of themes from *Ein Heldenleben*. Strauss had sent his permission on a postcard; however, he did not get the publishers' approval, and they spent years suing him for plagiarism. The case eventually went to the Imperial High Court, where a bench of judges ruled that the theme representing the Man 'lacks the integration to make a rounded whole, and the development to form an independent, complete musical structure; it is a melodic phrase, but not a melody'. Hence there had been no breach of copyright.

Hofkapellmeister in Berlin

The end of the old century coincided with the end of a musical era. One generation moved into history: Bruckner, Giordano and Clara Schumann died in 1896, Brahms in 1897, Johann Strauss in 1899, Verdi in 1901, Hugo Wolf in 1903, Dvořák and Hanslick in 1904. In the year 1900, Mahler was forty, Richard Strauss, Pfitzner and Debussy were in their thirties, Schoenberg, Reger, Ravel and Rakhmaninov in their twenties, Stravinsky, Berg and Webern in their teens.

Inventions and discoveries were laying the foundations of the twentieth century. Wilhelm II ruled all Germany to his own satisfaction. The military were held in high respect, by order. Industrial achievements made Germany mighty: not as mighty as the Kaiser believed, but all over the world 'Made in Germany' signified quality.

The arts flourished. More important poets, painters, sculptors, architects and musicians were working in Europe than at any previous period in history. Cultural matters engaged the interest of people from every level of society. The lot of the working class was improving. The under-privileged could look forward to a better future – until the First World War destroyed their hopes, as it destroyed everything else.

German music held a commanding position, which neither the Italians, the French nor the Russians seriously challenged. German conductors were sought after by orchestras in every land, and German singers propagated the new music: Wagner, Liszt – and Strauss.

The most successful composer of the day went to Berlin as Hofkapellmeister in 1898. He was pleased to make the move. His father warned him that there was no artistic talent to be found north of the Main, and Strauss agreed that that was right ('*cum grano salis*'); nevertheless, the imperial capital, now a centre of the musical world, was ready to fulfil all his wishes. Berlin was a young, sprawling city, ringed by lakes, rich in green open spaces and in broad, elegant streets lined by trees. Architects of the Neoclassical school had stamped the face of the city centre in the earlier

Kaiser Wilhelm's Berlin. The station of the elevated railway at Nollendorf Platz.

76

nineteenth century. Since the establishment of the German Empire in 1871, the city had attracted go-ahead, entrepreneurial characters from all the German states. It was said that the genuine Berliner came from Breslau. The population doubled in thirty years. The vitality, the bustle, the eager interest in everything new provided the strongest possible contrast to stick-in-the-mud Munich and dreamy Weimar.

Bülow had injected life into concerts in the city, but the Court Opera was a different matter. It was under two directors, both laymen and bureaucrats: 'Count Hochberg lines up the repertory, and Pierson knocks it down again.' Conductors had no influence. Their names did not appear on posters or programmes, but they were obliged to conduct the performances of works for which they had coached and rehearsed the performers; crying off was allowed only in exceptional circumstances.

The repertory was unadventurous, aimed primarily at pleasing the court, flattering its dignity and respecting its politics. Over a period of seventy years, from 1850 to 1918, only three works had their world premieres on the stage of the Berlin Court Opera. On Weingartner's retirement, the fact that his replacement, at the side of the conservative disciplinarian Karl Muck, was the modernist Beelzebub Richard Strauss promised to let some fresh air in. He had already attracted attention and acclamation with the concerts he had given in Berlin. Now he made his operatic début there with *Tristan*.

> I'm happy and very highly satisfied. I like Berlin with its splendid transport facilities, my apartment in its wonderful position, every domestic convenience, the servant problem solved satisfactorily.... My work to date has been very agreeable. I have conducted to date, without rehearsal in every case, *Carmen*, *Hänsel*, *The Merry Widow*, *Fidelio*, *Rienzi* and, with one orchestral rehearsal, *La muette de Portici*.... The orchestra has excellent discipline. I am treated with the greatest respect. A real blessing after Munich. (From a letter to his father)

The orchestra appreciated his professionalism. Only once, when they were slipshod, did he threaten 'I'll send for Dr Muck!'

The Bavarian's love of Berlin did not prevent him from repeating the well-known jibe: 'Why is a Berliner like a stork? Both are black and white, both have a big beak, and when they have nothing to eat up there, they both move south.' (To Hermann Bahr, 18 August 1916)

Ultimately, Strauss was the employee of the Kaiser. In his own estimation, Wilhelm II was musical, and he published one of his own compositions (*Sang an Ägir* for male-voice choir). Although he did not like Strauss's music, he recognized his worth and allowed him excellent terms of employment and generous leave. He did not like Verdi's *Falstaff* either; in attempting to defend the work to him, Strauss mentioned that it was the work of a eighty-year-old. 'I hope when you're eighty you'll write something better than that!' was the reply.

The Kaiser loved marches and in 1906, following the success of *Salome*, wanted to know why his Hofkapellmeister hadn't written any. Strauss

Georg von Hülsen-Haeseler, Intendant of the Prussian Court Opera, Strauss's sympathetic superior.

politely evaded a direct answer and confessed that he was not well acquainted with the genre. The very next day, on the Kaiser's orders, two military bands were paraded in the palace courtyard and Strauss was forced to listen to marches for three hours without a break. Stunned, and with his ears ringing, he sat down and composed two military marches, his op. 57, which received their premieres under his direction at a small concert at court; he was rewarded with the Crown Order third class.

Strauss was given a nickname: 'serpent in the court bosom'. He told Pauline about it in a letter he wrote from Kassel (25 May 1899).

Dear Pauxerl,

I am sitting up on the judges' rostrum in the Sängerhalle before an audience of 10,000 people, with writing materials on the table in front of me which I am using to write to you during this deadly boring concert. Dr Beier is conducting. The imperial box is near at hand. I am sitting between [Ernst von] Schuch and [Franz] Wüllner. I am writing and it looks as though I'm making significant notes. We have already heard *adagio* the *Meistersinger* prelude and a Mendelssohn chorus. Now a dreadful *a cappella* chorus is trickling out. I was presented to the Kaiser before the concert. He said to Schuch: 'You know, this is an appalling man, he is utterly modern, I have nurtured a fine serpent in my bosom.' – The choruses are over. – I was met at the station by my colonel, who seems to have a well-lined pocket, I was also given a very good meal. I then took part in the first session of the judging at five o'clock. The singing heats begin at ten tomorrow – that will be fun. On Friday at midday there will be a large lunch, given by the press, in the afternoon the caterwauling will continue, in the evening a gala performance of Spohr's *Kreuzfahrer* at the theatre, and a singsong at ten. On Saturday the final heat for the Kaiser Prize will be run, in the evening a bean-feast. It's an unbelievable waste of time. The natural scenery seems very fine, the air very bracing, the town a pokey little place, which looks even sillier swathed in bunting for His Majesty. I am dying of thirst and the concert looks like going on for at least another $\frac{3}{4}$ hour. Schuch has just started to write letters too. The music is too dreadful. At the moment Fräulein Diermeier is wheezing her way through a contralto solo. Farewell! The concert still isn't over.

The Empress did not like Strauss's music any more than her husband did. She thought *Feuersnot* was not quite proper. 'After giving birth to seven children, she probably didn't have a very high opinion of "Fa-la-la"', commented the librettist, Ernst von Wolzogen. After seven performances, she got the production withdrawn. The Intendant, Bolko von Hochberg, resigned in protest, and was replaced by Georg von Hülsen-Haeseler, the son of the previous incumbent, Botho von Hülsen. *Feuersnot* was later revived in response to general demand, but the text of *Rosenkavalier* in turn displeased the Empress and Hülsen had to bowdlerize it.

Even before he left Munich a number of writers had approached Strauss with ideas for operas and ballets. But the time of Strauss the dramatist had

Wilhelm II and his prudish wife, Empress Augusta Victoria.

'King Frederick's Temple to Apollo and the Muses': the Court Opera, Berlin.

The Imperial Kapellmeister taking tea with his wife and son in their flat on Knesebeckstrasse. They led a busy social life, and there were guests to dinner or lunch almost every day. Mostly artists: military and commercial circles kept their distance, but poets came, Franz recalled.

A signed picture of the emperor, presented to Strauss. Wilhelm did not like his Kapellmeister's music, but recognized his professional reputation and abilities, and was generous in the matter of pay and leave.

Hofkonzert.

Im weißen Saal. Der Hofmarschall ruft einen Lakaien heran und sagt ihm leise: „Majestät haben die Entdeckung gemacht, daß sich unter den Musikern ein anscheinend Verrückter befindet. Der Mann soll sofort entfernt werden." Nach wenigen Minuten meldet der Lakai dem Haushofmeister: „Zu Befehl, Exzellenz —

— bestens besorgt!

A concert at court. The Marshall beckons a footman and whispers: 'His Majesty has noticed a person among the musicians who looks like a lunatic. See that he is removed at once.' After a few minutes the footman reports back: 'Your Excellency, your instructions have been carried out!'

not yet come and he remained with the symphonic poem for a while yet. After *Guntram*, it is true, he had written a series of prose sketches and scenarios for operas: *Ekke und Schnittlein*, a kind of medieval Spanish *Threepenny Opera*, and *Eulenspiegel in Schilda*, another satire on municipal complacency and stupidity. But though he wrote a draft libretto in verse for the latter, he did not set any of it to music. He no longer trusted his ability as a poet. 'I need help with the words.' 'In a métier that one has not been master of since the age of fifteen, one is an amateur', he told Hermann Bahr during the work on *Intermezzo*. Mastery at fifteen is a proud claim to make. His literary sense was very acute and he made very high demands, which he felt he could not satisfy himself. At the same time, his instinct for dramatic construction was more sensitive than that of some literary men, as his interventions in librettos by Hofmannsthal and Gregor and the genesis of *Capriccio* demonstrate.

It should be noted, finally, that he invented the scenarios enacted in his symphonic poems. The flow of the musical episodes in *Macbeth*, *Don Juan*, *Don Quixote* and *Zarathustra* derives from their literary sources, but *Tod und Verklärung*, *Ein Heldenleben* and the *Domestic* and *Alpine* Symphonies are the products of his own dramatic imagination.

Each of the symphonic poems takes an overall musical form appropriate to it and for which sub-titles like 'Rondeau' for *Till Eulenspiegel* and 'Fantastic Variations on a Theme' for *Don Quixote* are really too modest as designations. Each work has its own distinct dramatic construction. No one composing symphonic poems before Strauss had constructed drama of quite the same power from the confrontation or union of the tensions in the original poetic idea.

Few listeners grasp the dramatic function of changes of tonality in these works, or the way Strauss moulds his thematic material to the psychological and emotional significance of the moment. As a poet creates mood by the choice of words, Strauss uses sound and timbre to poetic and dramatic ends. 'The modern orchestra paints, explains, recalls – but that is not all: it expresses the essence, the innermost truth itself, it reveals the original image.' Where Wagner's orchestra seldom depicts rapid transformations in a state of soul or mind, but dwells luxuriantly on the description of one emotion, Strauss is quicker on his feet, more pliable, more elegant and more human. A phrase was coined for it: 'a contrapuntalism of the nerves'.

Five years after his disappointment with *Guntram*, Strauss ventured on a one-act opera, in a spirit of mordant frivolity. The plot of *Feuersnot* (*Fire Famine*), which Ernst von Wolzogen adapted from an old Flemish legend, sets the opera, uniquely, in Munich, in the period of the Renaissance. It concerns a young magician with the power to extinguish every fire in the city when the girl of his choice rejects his love, and to rekindle them when his love is requited. The opera displays many of Strauss's strengths, even though he had clearly not yet achieved his mature mastery of dramatic structure, in the creation of tension or larger dramatic shapes. Yet it is still effective in the theatre, full of life, and makes some skilful points in its juxtaposition of late medieval setting and modern musical language. The humour appealed to Strauss, and his imagination was kindled by the

opportunity to be ironic and satirical at the expense of Munich, which had failed to understand both Wagner and himself. By the moral conventions of the time of its composition, the text was salacious, the action coarse. The polemic makes its points with a flail rather than a rapier.

The music was written in two months, orchestrated in a further four. The first performance was given under Ernst von Schuch in Dresden on 21 November 1901. It unleashed a storm of derision and delight. Wolzogen took his bow with a huge white daisy in his button-hole. Two weeks later Strauss himself conducted his 'little non-opera' in Frankfurt, Mahler did it in Vienna very shortly afterwards, and thirty more theatres followed suit. This eighty-five-minute 'intermezzo against the theatre, spurred by personal motives and reaping a small revenge on my beloved native city', earned more than a *succès d'estime*. The waltzes, the lyrical duets, the quotations from folk songs, the caricatures of solid citizenry, the children's choruses, the ensembles for large adult chorus, all add up to a living theatrical experience.

Eduard Hanslick, in his review of *Feuersnot*, used much the same terms as he had applied to *Das Rheingold* thirty-two years before: 'little buds of melody drowned in floods of modulation', where 'orchestral arts are no substitute for soul', and 'the ear is not a magnet, and melodies are not iron filings'.

Wolzogen made further proposals to Strauss, with an emphasis on the grotesque and material perhaps better suited to the cabaret which he had just established in Berlin. He also tried to get some money from the composer – in vain. Strauss was now very keen to write more operas, but theatres paid poorly. 1500 marks for a world premiere? 'Would you like me to throw in something else as well? Perhaps a fire-engine, to extinguish the "Fire (Money) Emergency"? I will change my name to Riccardo Straussini and be published by Sonzogno, and then you will grant my every wish!' He

The view from the flat at Kaiserdamm 39. The mod cons, proudly reported back to Munich, included the telephone ('Wilhelm' exchange), running hot water and electric light. There was a veranda, much use in the mild climate, with geraniums, a wild vine and a tree-frog.

Ernst von Wolzogen (1855–1934), philosopher, founder of the Überbrettl cabaret, and librettist of Feuersnot.

was overflowing with irony, vitality and aggressive energy, an *enfant terrible* carried along on a wave of public curiosity, acclaim and notoriety.

An example of a working day in Strauss's life has him rehearsing *Don Giovanni* from 11 till 2, and Bruckner's Third Symphony from 3 till 6, then back to the opera house for a performance of *Tristan* in the evening. The amount of work he accomplished in these years borders on the supernatural. Besides composing, he was conducting in the opera house – sometimes five times a week – and conscientiously coaching singers and orchestra in a large number of new additions to the repertory. Before long, Berlin, too, was talking of his performances of Mozart and his harpsichord recitative accompaniments.

Weingartner conducted when the opera orchestra gave concerts, and the Berlin Philharmonic had Nikisch, so Strauss took on another orchestra, the Berliner Tonkünstler, on top of his other work, and with them performed exclusively modern music: Bruckner, Liszt, Schillings, Pfitzner, Mahler, Wolf, Reznicek and dozens of others whose names are now forgotten. One of them was a certain Schirach, whose son, as Gauleiter of Vienna forty years later, did not forget Strauss's promotion of his father's music.

Strauss's motto was 'Great music and kitsch will make their own way. Masters of the second rank need promoting. What I perform must please not me alone but also the public. Let time be the judge. Better to overestimate twenty than bar the way to one. With me, nobody had better try to subscribe to conservatism.'

He travelled widely with the Tonkünstler Orchestra during his first years in Berlin, all over Germany and further afield, from Edinburgh to Barcelona. (He still went always by train and horse-drawn cab. Amazement was mingled with scepticism when he saw the electric automobile of the banker Edgar Speyer in London, and he was badly bruised when knocked over by an electric tram in Berlin in 1903.) Most often the journeys were not tours taking him on from one town to the next, but return trips to one at a time. Often that meant travelling overnight, a rehearsal and a concert the next day, and straight back to Berlin the same night. On his first visit to a town, the hall was often half empty: next time, word of his quality would have spread. In some places he was not appreciated, in others overwhelmed with plaudits and enthusiasm. 'An orchestral *Tusch*, laurels and everything else the heart – does not desire', he wrote to his father. Father was in despair: 'We're very unhappy to see the way you assault your health . . . in order to earn enough money to be able to live from your savings later, so as to do nothing but compose. Do you imagine that anyone can create anything of the spirit when the body is enfeebled?' Richard retorted that hard work never killed anyone, if his way of life was in other respects sober and sensible – as his was. But he did do too much. In addition to composing, conducting and travelling, he edited the magazine *Monat* for three months; edited a series of books on music, *Die Musik*, which ran to thirty-two volumes; wrote at least ten business letters a day, longhand; worked for the establishment of a school of music in Berlin; occupied a leading position in the Allgemeiner Deutscher Musikverein (General

German Music Association); founded and was first president of the Genossenschaft Deutscher Tonsetzer (German Composers' League); assisted annually in the organization of major music festivals in Germany and abroad, where, as ever, he fostered the cause of contemporary music. In May 1907 he collapsed in Cologne, and myocardial insufficiency was diagnosed. He recovered in the spa of Bad Nauheim, and thereafter he gave up some of his lesser commitments and took on fewer new ones. He had in any case one outstanding task, which caused him travail enough: the battle against bureaucracy for composers' copyrights.

The Composer's Rights

At the turn of the century, the legal protection for composers' copyrights was sadly restricted, and their royalties depended on the clout they had with their publishers. Even a 'successful' composer needed a regular job if he was to support a wife and child in reasonable style. As Strauss wrote to Pauline on one occasion, 'for the time being we won't starve, and there's even enough for a new dress for you, but one can never know how long one will remain fashionable, or when one will be overtaken and knocked out of the running by someone luckier or more gifted'. He never forgot the deprivations of his father's early life, or the modesty of his circumstances even at the peak of his profession. Nor did he forget the social humiliation of Haydn at Esterházy, the paupers' deaths of Mozart, Schubert and Lortzing, or Weber's and Wagner's struggles with their creditors.

There was a time when the church, royalty and noblemen commissioned and paid for compositions. From about 1820 onwards, composers wrote music at their own risk, and sold it, along with all the rights in it, to theatres or impresarios for a single lump-sum payment. If a work was a success, it was the entrepreneur who made a profit – its creator had had his money. During the nineteenth century many countries in Europe introduced legislation which gave 'authors' – primarily writers, but also composers and artists – some measure of protection for their work. The German copyright act of 1870 provided for copyright to extend throughout an author's lifetime and for thirty years after death. But there were many grey areas, particularly with regard to music, and Strauss lent himself to the struggle to improve matters on behalf of German composers in general.

He was one of a triumvirate: Friedrich Rösch (another Bavarian, born in 1862) was someone he had known since schooldays. Rösch distinguished himself as a school-leaver, finishing among the thirty best candidates in the *Abitur* examination in all Bavaria. He studied law on a scholarship, but he was also a musician, a member of the circle of Thuille and Ritter, and the composer of orchestral songs and 'witty oratorios'. He was unable to gain

If I had learnt any other trade, God knows, I would switch horses to get away from this bunch!

(STRAUSS)

Friedrich Rösch, lawyer, composer and 'truest friend'.

Hans Sommer.

regular employment as a musician, but in 1919 he became president of the Allgemeiner Deutscher Musikverein. When Rösch died in 1925, Strauss, who never attended funerals as a rule, spoke at his graveside: 'He was my truest friend and adviser. With his acute mind, his productive criticism, his artistic and human gifts, he helped me more than anyone I have ever known. He sacrificed his worldly goods and his life for the well-being of German composers.'

The third member of the team was 'Hans Sommer' (his real name was Zincke), whom Strauss had got to know in Weimar, where he lived as a composer of songs and operas on subjects from fairytales. Born in 1837, he had trained as a physicist and taught at the Technical College in Brunswick for twenty-five years before abandoning science for music; he also had some understanding of the law.

In July 1898 the three sent a circular letter to some 160 composers, setting out their intention to fight for reform of the out-of-date copyright laws, and asking for support. By the end of three weeks they had received 119 affirmatory responses, and they drafted a memorandum for submission to the Reichstag. At a conference convened in Leipzig in September 1898, their proposals were approved unanimously by a number of well-known musicians. The time for almsgiving was over, the composer was no longer content to play the role of the unrealistic dreamer, starving in a garret in order to make touching copy for posterity.

Publishers, theatres and managements threatened a boycott. Strauss was decried as 'money-grubbing'; it was a charge that was to cling to him for a long time. A lifelong campaign began, with 160 composers ranged against 100,000 in the ranks of the publishers, the entrepreneurs and governments. Strauss expended time and energy, producing hundreds of letters and interviews. He even hardened his heart against his old friend Spitzweg, and wrote to him in November 1898 (six weeks after the Leipzig conference) as follows:

> Dear friend,
> It is with regret that I learn of your refusal to take *Heldenleben*, because, as I have said before, it is absolutely impossible for me to give the performance rights of my works to the publisher in future. That is the cardinal point in our whole movement, and as instigator I cannot set a bad example. Publishing rights to the publisher, author's rights to the author. There's no other way from this day forwards!
>
> You have written a long screed about the percentages that we want to claim all for ourselves. I can assure you, not for the first time, that we composers are not claiming percentages for ourselves at all, and we even dispute the right of publishers to claim percentages for works of which they have not expressly bought the performance rights.

A new law came into force in 1901, but the protection of composers' interests remained a lifelong concern of Strauss's.

The interests of musicians in Germany had been represented since 1861 by the Allgemeiner Deutscher Musikverein, founded by Franz Liszt. Over the years the association organized sixty-seven festivals, held in a large number of different towns. It administered grants and bursaries, instigated the first complete edition of the works of Liszt, and played a very important role as a sponsor of first performances and a discussion forum. Strauss was president in 1901, and his friends Siegmund von Hausegger and Max von Schillings also served terms. The association was dissolved in 1937. The Third Reich organized its own festivals and conferences, and private institutions were not wanted.

The Leipzig conference gave birth to the Genossenschaft deutscher Tonsetzer (GDT: League of German Composers), and this in turn established a performing rights institute in 1903 (Anstalt für musikalische Aufführungsrechte: AFMA). In 1915 AFMA gave way to an institution which supervised the rights both of performance and of mechanical reproduction (and, most importantly, collected the fees): this was GEMA (Gesellschaft für musikalische Aufführungs- und mechanische Vervielfältigungsrechte), which came through the Third Reich (under the acronym STAGMA) and survives to the present day. In the early years it was a struggle to persuade composers to surrender the rights they had only just acquired, to allow AFMA to act on their behalf, but when the money began to flow, their resistance ebbed. There were occasions when Strauss thought of abandoning his 'serious' colleagues to their fate!

The formal organization of creative artists is a hazardous undertaking. They must be monomaniacs, each must be his own measure of all things. Their apprehension of the currents of their own time is osmotic, and they express themselves according to temperament and talent. The achievements of confrères can be a spur, if only to outdoing them. The success of one artist will be interpreted by another as an example of modishness or of the unreliability of public taste. Genuine friendships such as existed between Haydn and Mozart, Brahms and Dvořák, are by no means commonplace in the history of music.

Strauss's musical idols were all figures of the past. Contemporaries did not influence him, although he noted their contributions – especially those who worked in the higher reaches of entertainment and film music. Mahler and Humperdinck were close to him. He recommended the unknown Max Reger to Spitzweg (who promptly published twenty-five of his works) but he often scoffed at the 'latterday manufacturer of études and variations, who has not advanced very far beyond musical craftsmanship, for whom Bach is the beginning *and the end* of all music'. He recoiled from Reger's capacity for liquor and his acid humour. Reger in turn, while admiring Strauss's technical ability and imagination, had no time for programme music, lavish orchestration or *Salome*. When the two of them were celebrated in the same concert, Strauss murmured softly on the podium, 'There, we're classics now'.

Hugo Wolf was vexed by Strauss's 'mastery in composing without ideas'. Strauss thought Wolf was a 'pure dilettante, sick from the very first'. The success of each of Eugen d'Albert's twenty-one operas was ephemeral, and Strauss thought that that was the best that they deserved, but he regarded d'Albert the pianist as 'phenomenal'. Ernst von Reznicek

Eugen d'Albert, prolific opera composer and 'phenomenal' pianist.

(remembered today almost solely as the composer of *Donna Diana*, of which most of us know only the overture) occasionally stayed in the villa in Garmisch, but Strauss was as silent on the subject of his music as on that of Schreker, Grieg (who sent him an enthusiastic telegram after hearing *Tod und Verklärung*) or Sinding. He had time for Sibelius, with whom he was acquainted, but he took no interest in his Hungarian admirers Bartók and Kodály.

He admired Russian literature and drama, but not Russian music. Tchaikovsky, visiting Berlin in 1888, heard Strauss's F minor Symphony, and thought that it combined 'an astonishing lack of talent' with 'unprecedented presumption'. They met, but Tchaikovsky had nothing to say to Strauss although the next day he remarked that perhaps he had simply failed to understand the music. Strauss wrote to Dvořák in 1884 about his Violin Concerto, and Dvořák recommended him to the violinist Ondriczek. Smetana was the only Slav Strauss esteemed; he often conducted *The Bartered Bride*, though he thought it 'not well orchestrated', and *Vltava*, which actually inhibited him when, late in life, he thought of writing a 'Danube'.

Of the French, he honoured Lully, Couperin, Bizet (for the operas) and Berlioz. From youth up, too, he admired Auber and astonishingly included five of his works in his ideal operatic repertory.

He attended Debussy's *Pelléas* in the company of Romain Rolland, with whom he discussed the opera at length, both in the intervals and afterwards. He complained that 'there is not enough music in this work' and concluded that: 'Debussy is more of a great artist than a musician.'

Debussy wrote of Strauss in 1903:

> He definitely thinks in coloured images. . . . It is difficult to admire certain incongruities [in *Ein Heldenleben*] that are almost banal, and some worn-out Italianisms. [But] it's a book of images, even cinematography . . . Strauss has the frank, confident manner of those great explorers who walk among savage tribes with a carefree smile. . . . I can assure you there is plenty of sun in the music of R. Strauss, but one came away convinced that the majority of the public does not like this kind of sun. There is no resisting the overwhelming domination of this man!

When Rolland introduced them to each other, they found little to say.

Strauss was equally indifferent to Ravel, who did not like him personally, although he admired *Salome* 'in spite of the bad taste that prevails in it'. Ravel took the view that 'except for Strauss, there are none but second-class composers in Germany'.

Most of Strauss's French contemporaries dismissed him, but not Paul Dukas, whose respect for Strauss was reciprocated, and not Charpentier, whose *Louise* delighted Mahler, Debussy and Strauss alike. Rolland recorded that at the premiere Strauss was suffering from a stomach-ache, but once the performance started he forgot it so completely that he laughed, muttered to himself and even licked his lips for sheer pleasure.

Strauss went to the first performance of Hans Pfitzner's *Palestrina* in 1917, and afterwards said something pleasant to the composer about the wonderful atmosphere in the first and third acts. Pfitzner confided that he had found the second act very difficult, and it was in rejoinder to that that Strauss is reported to have asked the famous, ironic question which cut Pfitzner to the quick, 'Why did you write it, then, if you found it so difficult?' It may have been to pay Strauss back in kind, therefore, that Pfitzner remarked to him, so it is said, directly after a performance of the *Alpine Symphony*, 'very impressive, only you came dangerously near to breaking a bone as you reached the top'. Many years later, Pfitzner saw Mikorey's bust of Strauss, in the sculptor's studio, and growled, 'Extraordinary, how well developed the fellow's teeth are'.

Hans Pfitzner.

Both Strauss and Pfitzner revered Wagner, which to some extent created a bond between them. Each respected the music of the other, without greatly admiring it. It was the indefatigable bands of admirers who gathered around each of them who made them out to be enemies: a repeat showing of the Wagner–Brahms story, in fact. Strauss recommended Pfitzner for the appointment that took him to Strasbourg, where, as director of the symphony orchestra, he conducted a lot of Strauss and, as director of the opera from 1910, he also prepared a production of *Rosenkavalier*. Strauss in turn included Pfitzner's work in his concert programmes, and introduced Pfitzner's operas into the repertory when he was director of the Vienna State Opera.

The good fellow is so prickly and so idealistic. We want to do everything we can for him and for his works, but not have him in the vicinity. Why do people always say Strauss *and* Pfitzner? They could say Pfitzner all on his own, so far as I'm concerned – greatest composer of all time – since Beethoven, that is. What little I am, I want to be alone, not in company. The eternal labelling by the press: modernism. For my part, I want to have nothing to do with it. If only they would leave me alone, unshorn, away from the herd. (From a letter to Franz Schalk, 7 March 1919)

The beginning of the rivalry can be precisely dated: 19 March 1900, when the society for the Promotion of the Arts put on a concert in Berlin at which the prelude to Pfitzner's new opera *Die Rose vom Liebesgarten* was heard between *Tod und Verklärung* and *Ein Heldenleben*, conducted by the composer. Strauss scored, while Pfitzner pleased neither the general public nor the critics. It never ceased to rankle. Humorous, ironic and sarcastic as Pfitzner was, he could not tolerate the least disparagement of his godgiven talent. Strauss was unremittingly self-critical, did not allow even his wildest successes to turn his head, but could joke at his own expense. This attitude became him as a figure of international stature in the musical world, whereas Pfitzner's reputation was confined to Germany. The label of an 'introspective, German, late Romantic' stuck to him. His patriotism earned him the reputation of a nationalist, but he made savage remarks about Hitler, the 'German *proletarius*', and his nationalism.

Hans Pfitzner and Max von Schillings.

His health was always poor, he was small and thin, choleric, nervy and egocentric; he craved acclaim and approval, especially from women. Alma Mahler, collector of geniuses, laid a highly indiscreet testimony about him in this respect. There is little ardour or eroticism in his music, unlike that of Strauss, who always kept women and venerators at a distance.

Pfitzner's adherents proclaimed him a musical national hero after *Palestrina*. Thomas Mann, who (perhaps simply because he came from Lübeck in the far north) had small regard for Strauss, founded a Pfitzner Society and wrote warmly about him. In 1933, however, Pfitzner and Strauss, along with many other artists, both signed a strongly worded protest against Mann's Wagner anniversary lecture, which they felt was too dilettante and provocative. Unhappily, this protest was a factor in driving Mann out of Germany.

Pfitzner was a professor of composition and, like Strauss, received an honorary doctorate. However, his works were rarely performed and, when they were, some disaster always seemed to befall, so that he came to be spoken of as jinxed.

In spite of the polemical campaign that he and his supporters maintained against Hugo von Hofmannsthal's librettos for Strauss, he tried to persuade Hofmannsthal to write one for him.

> The following will amuse you: a Munich personality has pursued me for the past two years saying that I must make an opera for Pfitzner, that I am the only one, exactly what he wants and so on, and has tried for all he is worth to bring about a meeting at Salzburg. I replied politely, but very firmly that I cannot spare the time for a meeting and, if I did have an idea for an opera, I would write it for you. (Hofmannsthal to Strauss, 29 September 1927)

Silhouette by W. Bithorn. The signature still lacks the 'Dr' that became customary after Strauss received his first honorary doctorate in 1903.

Strauss pointed out ironically: 'You couldn't wish for a finer recognition than Pfitzner's application for a libretto!'

Pfitzner lost everything he possessed in the Second World War and after some peregrinations found himself, in 1945, with a broken arm, in a military hospital in Garmisch, in a dismal room with an iron bed and a wardrobe. He did not make his proximity known to Strauss; though he remarked a few times that he would be glad to see his old rival once again, he was too proud to seek him out. Strauss presently left for Switzerland. Pfitzner moved to an old people's home in Munich, but was in Salzburg when he died, a few months before Strauss. Vienna buried him in the Central Cemetery, in the Grove of Honour, in the company of such German artists as Beethoven and Brahms. Strauss, by then an Austrian citizen, was buried in Garmisch. The rivalry survives in anecdotes and in musical history, to which both of them added a chapter.

The Younger Franz

Six weeks before the birth, after two-and-a-half years of marriage, the doctor told the father-to-be that Pauline was undoubtedly carrying twins. In fact there was only one baby, but he was born late, already weighing over 8 pounds and measuring 15 inches round the head. He was born in Munich in Holy Week, on 12 April 1897, while his father was away in Stuttgart with Ernst von Possart and *Enoch Arden*. The Hotel Marquart, where Chopin wrote his *Revolutionary* Study, and where Cabinet Secretary Pfistermeister tracked down Wagner for his master King Ludwig II, was where an anxiously and eagerly waiting Strauss at last received the telegram announcing the birth of a 'giant boy'. The mother was well: they had both been in great danger, because of the baby's size, and he had received emergency baptism in the name of 'Richard'. On the arrival home of his proud Papa three days later, he was given the names Franz (after one grandfather) Robert Alexander (after other relatives) Adolf (after the other grandfather).

Young Franz, aged one, with his Mama.

In the *Symphonia domestica* of 1903, the portrait of his family life, Strauss recorded some of his hopes and impressions of his son, some of them clarified with verbal annotations in the score: thus the 'Dream' sequence has the note 'The mother's dreams about the child: will he be like his father (F major) or like his mother (B major)? Answers come from the Aunts (trumpets, quoting the husband's theme) 'Just like Papa!' and from the Uncles (trombones, quoting the wife's theme) 'Just like Mama!'

On the cover of the sketch book for the *Domestica* (started on 2 May 1902) he wrote 'Idea for a domestic scherzo with a double fugue on three subjects: "My Home" (a symphonic self- and family-portrait)'; then a short verse, promising 'a little equanimity and a lot of humour'. The three 'subjects' are identified as 'F major: Papa, returns from travel, weary', 'B major: Mama', and 'D major: Bubi [Baby], a mixture, but more like his Papa'. The 'programme' is outlined: a country walk for all three, cosy family supper. Mama puts Bubi to bed. Papa et Maman seuls: scène d'amour. Le matin: Bubi yells, joyful waking.' There are other notes in the sketch itself, such as 'Richard spends all afternoon working on a melody which was finally finished in the scene in the evening (doing and watching).' It is all there for those who have ears to hear, or who read the score.

The first performance unleashed a pack of cultural critics, baying their indignation at the narcissism of a musical self-portrait. (These same people would stand for minutes at a time, nodding gravely and deeply moved by the artistry and truth of a self-portrait painted in oils on canvas.) A Viennese critic remarked that the work served 'the wit, rather than the spirit of music'. Some were shocked by what the portrait revealed: an orchestral player from Saxony described it as 'the piece where the little kid throws cannon balls at his parents', while Alexander Moszkowski, brother

The 'uncles' and 'aunts' in the score of Symphonia domestica.

Page from Sketchbook 19, in which he jotted down themes over the years. This is a sketch for 'Piano Sonatina, for Bubi', about 1906.

Strauss liked England ('They have such clean beds'), and England was sympathetic to his music and helped to promote his reputation world-wide. This notebook, kept by him while staying on the Isle of Wight in 1902 and 1903 contains ideas which eventually developed into waltz tunes in Rosenkavelier, Arabella *and* Capriccio.

Three generations of Strausses at Altenmarkt, during the summer holidays, 1904. Pauline reads (bottom left) not realizing that she is in the picture.

When Franz was ill, it caused his parents great distress

Paul Wittgenstein, the pianist, a cousin of the philosopher Ludwig Wittgenstein. He lost his right arm as a soldier in the First World War.

of the composer and editor of *Lustige Blätter*, was moved to verse by a performance he attended 'for the first and last time', ending with a gleeful pun on the word 'Fuge', which means both 'fugue' and 'joint': 'This is what Richard Strauss meant by his fugue: his marriage is out of joint!'

As the *Symphonia domestica* suggests, young Franz did not grow up in a house where the occupants moved around on tiptoe out of reverence for the great artistic genius it harboured: far from it. Father joined in discussions of mundane matters, all spoke their minds, and maintained, with no little heat, their various opinions. Temperament clashed against temperament. Each tolerated the other's opinion, even if he didn't share it and was sure of being in the right. Most of the arguments were about trivia, all of them passed over as quickly as a thunderstorm in Rossini, leaving the air clear again. Grudges were not borne, offence not taken.

Franz grew up to be a quiet, placid, good-natured person, sensitive and easily hurt, with an intuitive understanding of human nature. He would certainly have made more of his life, if the overpowering love of his parents had not been stronger than his own will. As it was, his doting father would scarcely let him out of his sight when they were travelling or attending concerts or other official events together. In due course, Franz gained a doctorate in law with a dissertation on the Genossenschaft deutscher Tonsetzer, and from then onwards he was always at his father's side when contracts and other business were under discussion.

Only during the 1930s and '40s did politics cause some more profound differences and – although Franz spent most of his life in his father's house – the time he spent studying medicine in Vienna, while the parents remained in Garmisch, did allow some relaxation of the nervous tension thus generated. His son Richard recalls that 'during the war, when politics had us all by the throat, there were such violent arguments between Grandfather and my father that I sometimes feared that they would both have strokes, and I thought "Then I shall be Mandryka – 'I and no other'"'.

But they meant too much to each other for even politics to come between them for long. The Strausses can never have bored each other, but lived in a state of perpetual excitement, as well as fervent interest in a wide range of subjects. There was no danger of differences of opinion leading to offended silences, followed by eventual departures from home. That was not the way in any branch of the Strauss–Pschorr clan, and outsiders have often found it hard to understand.

The love of his family eventually inspired Richard Strauss to write a *Parergon* to the *Symphonia domestica*, op. 73. In 1924, during his honeymoon in Egypt, Franz fell ill with typhus, and for a time his life was in danger. His father's anxiety came out in music he sketched at the time, in which the child's themes from the symphony are reworked in passages of a heart-breaking despair, alternating with the idyllic recall of the past. Tragedy is never far away, until the danger is banished at the end. The harmonic writing in the *Parergon* goes as close to polytonality and atonality as *Elektra*, and rarely did Strauss express such desperation. The final form of the piece, completed in 1925, is a concerto for piano, left hand, one of the many works commissioned by Paul Wittgenstein from the leading composers of the day.

Father and son, aged 3. Small Franz was a railway enthusiast, and his father was pressed into service as a steam-engine three times a day.

Strauss also wrote his op. 74, *Panathenäenzug*, for Wittgenstein; both works should also be transcribed for two hands.

Summer holidays were regularly spent in the house of Pauline Strauss's parents in Marquartstein. It was a paradisal spot between mountains, close to Rosenheim and Chiemsee, and at the foot of the Hochgern. The song *Traum durch die Dämmerung* portrays the 'meadows outspread in the grey of dusk'. Strauss wrote much music there.

The rooms in the de Ahna villa were small, the living room too small when the whole family was there. An upright piano was put into the so-called 'ironing room' on the ground floor, and there Strauss could work undisturbed and without disturbing others. It was in that little room, with that upright, that he began *Salome* on 27 July 1903, with 'How beautiful Princess Salome is tonight . . .'. By 9 August he had reached Salome's demand for the head of John the Baptist, and by 12 August the 'white peacock', whose shriek is heard in the orchestra. But he did not work consistently through the text from beginning to end: Jochanaan's curse, the

The de Ahna villa at Marquartstein.

end of the previous scene, was not composed until 6 September. It was all written on the table used for ironing, which today is in Dresden.

The conductor Philipp Wolfrum, an old friend, was behind the conferment of an honorary doctorate on Strauss in 1903, by the Philosophy Faculty at the University of Heidelberg. Strauss was very proud of his degree and thenceforth always preceded his beautifully written signature with a 'Dr' just as beautiful. He was always addressed as 'Herr Doktor' too, and people in Garmisch today still use the forms 'Herr Doktor Richard' and 'Herr Doktor Franz' to distinguish between father and son.

One reason for Strauss's pleasure in the Heidelberg honour was that he was aware of the refusal of the Prussian Royal Academy to elect him a member, when a few progressives had put his name forward three years previously. Committees seldom appreciate the exceptional, and the Prussian Academy was true to form in its reluctance even to consider painters, writers or composers, however famous, if they were not blessed with either mediocrity or years. In 1900 Strauss was still an *enfant terrible*, whose popularity with the general public was difficult for academicians to understand. In 1909 he was proposed again, at the same time as Puccini and the Norwegian composer Christian Sinding. Strauss scoffed when he heard the news: 'There must be some mistake, unless, without my noticing it, all my disreputable fifths have turned overnight into meritorious sixths.' Then the official notice of his election arrived from the Academy, to his complete surprise. 'Please be kind enough to forget the bad joke in my last letter, for as an academician one must cease making jokes and conduct oneself with the dignity and decorum befitting that high distinction. I shall devote the entire summer to the study of proper behaviour.'

The USA

Concert-giving in the United States of America at the turn of the century was still dominated by Europeans. Conductors such as Theodore Thomas, Damrosch, Bergmann, Eisfeld, Neuendorff and Conried had settled there; Bülow, Nikisch, Muck and many others visited. Virtuosos like Anton Rubinstein, Paderewski and Eugène Ysaÿe had huge followings. Concerts and the opera were generously sponsored and patronized by European immigrants, many of them Jewish, who had grown rich in America. Dvořák spent three years teaching in New York City, Offenbach and Johann Strauss gave concerts, Gustav Mahler held an appointment at the Metropolitan Opera. It is hardly surprising, therefore, to find Strauss undertaking several tours in order to make himself and his works better known in the new world.

Theodore Thomas, champion of Strauss's music in the USA.

His fame had gone before him, thanks to the conductor Theodore Thomas, born in East Friesland in 1835, but a resident of the United States since the age of ten. After a visit to Franz Strauss in Munich in 1883, he took the score of Richard's F minor Symphony away with him, and gave the work its first performance, in New York, where it was thought to be 'a work of considerable beauty', but 'of [no] very great originality of thought'. Subsequently, Thomas conducted all Strauss's works for orchestra, usually in the year of their first performances, so American audiences had been able to follow the composer's progress. He visited the American continent himself in 1904, 1920, 1921–2 and 1923.

Pauline accompanied her husband in 1904, and Lieder recitals were included among the thirty-five concerts he gave in various cities. 'His better half performed his songs so vitally that one could believe she had composed them herself, while he sat over-bored at the piano.' Pauline reported smugly that Richard was annoyed by that review.

The Atlantic crossing, on the liner *Moltke*, took eleven days.

Rather boring. The eternal motion of the ship, the noise of the water are so irritating that it is impossible to read or work. One can get a massage in the gymnasium, or ride a horse or camel, all electric, very interesting. Also the Marconi Telegraph Station, which works without wires, with electric waves out of the air. The waves were often up as high as a house round the ship, the sea was ice-blue like the grottoes in a glacier, snow-storms, a magnificent spectacle. I run about on the promenade deck like a demented flying fish, to keep my feet warm. A section of the Steinway family is also on board.

Pauline asks you to take special care that Bubi is not covered too warmly at night so that he sweats, that he is always dressed according to the season, and doesn't run about with holes in his boots, and works hard and behaves himself.

The letters recounting the couple's adventures went from hand to hand back in Bavaria.

Richard and Pauline (centre) at Niagara Falls, 22 April 1904.

The menu at a dinner given in Strauss's honour.

Wanamaker's department store in New York, c. 1880, where one of the first performances of Symphonia domestica *was given.*

The reviews are part good, part middling, but at all events appreciative. My first concert, magnificent reception with a *Tusch* from the orchestra, excellent *Zarathustra* under Wetzler, *Heldenleben* under me. I was called back tempestuously five or six times. Carnegie Hall is a splendid, gigantic hall for four thousand people, but good acoustics so that Pauline's voice was able to fill the entire hall beautifully. To the concert in Brooklyn by electric automobile (40 marks), through savage New York and its wretchedly made roads, over the magnificent Hudson Bridge, an hour's ride. Tomorrow a 'reception' at the top millionaires Cutting, Morgan, Havemeyer the sugar-king. Everywhere we go receptions, parties, banquets, the people are charming, and will cut off their right arm to please you or honour you.

Apart from that, the entire country makes a quite magnificent impression, but a bit wild. Hotels, railway stations, the railways, commerce and industry are on a grandiose scale, all practical installations dazzling, the twenty-storey giant buildings sometimes

make a beautiful and magnificent effect, even in my eyes, because of their felicitous proportions.

For Pauline, there were too many occasions when she had to dress up, which she found tiring. On the ship, her eyes suffered in the salty sea-air, and she had to contend with seasickness as well. But her hair-dresser had done well by her, she usually did the packing herself, her *toilettes* on the concert platform looked wonderful and were discussed in the newspapers. One evening she was given a bouquet of roses with stems a yard long, said to have cost a hundred marks.

She eats oysters every day, served up in every imaginable way, for they are wonderfully fresh here and a portion of eight costs only 1 mark. Dear, kind Levin from Berlin gave her a basket of flowers at the concert yesterday which was so big and so heavy that, to the delight of the audience, *I* could not lift it.

The *Symphonia domestica* received its first performance during the American tour of 1904. Strauss, having held fifteen rehearsals with a 'band of anarchists', was well pleased. It was such a success in the concert hall that the Wanamaker department store proposed two repeat performances four weeks later. The blood froze in the veins of those for whom art was a sacred

Someone must have said: 'It's high time we had some decent photos taken.' These studio portraits date from 1905. It would be hard to guess that the cool character in tweeds is the genius who has recently finished the headily erotic, modernistic Salome. His wife is every inch the general's daughter. Their son stands up straight, but his gaze is sceptical.

97

calling, when the news reached Europe: the principal conductor at the Prussian court directing the world premiere of one of his works in a department store! But it was not a world premiere, it was two repeat performances, and Wanamaker's cleared a whole floor and turned it into a proper concert hall. Concerts and orchestras are supported by private finance in America, and patrons like Wanamaker's are the source. At that date, moreover, there were few concert halls in New York. It was on this occasion that Strauss made the remark that aroused so much disgust and contempt: 'Earning money for his wife and child is no disgrace, even for an artist!' The public did not, and does not, want to believe that such things are true.

He earned other things on his American tour besides money, of course. He had the pleasure of finding one of the best orchestras in the world in Boston. He was made a freeman of Morgantown, where he was given a glass sword of honour and the militia turned out to receive him at the gates of the university. In Cleveland he was given a valuable silver goblet and was serenaded by the glee club.

And all the time he was working on *Salome*.

The 'Salome' Sensation

It was the Viennese poet Anton Lindner, whose *Hochzeitlich Lied* Strauss had set in 1898 (op. 37 no. 6), who drew Oscar Wilde's play *Salome* to his attention and first tried to write a libretto in verse himself. But when Strauss read it, in Wilde's original French, he recognized that it already made a libretto as it stood, so he took the translation by Hedwig Lachmann and cut what he found uninspiring, shortening the whole by about a third. Then he went straight in, without an overture, to set 'How beautiful Princess Salome is tonight . . .'. The psychological world of the subject-matter is absorbed into the music, rendered in exotic harmonies and disturbing cadences, shimmering like shot silk. He wrote in two keys simultaneously to underline the contrast between Herod and Jochanaan, depicted Salome's moan while waiting for the execution with the squeezed high B flat of the double basses (the Intendant of the Dresden Court Opera was afraid it would make the audience laugh), and allowed the heroine to sing a hymn of heartfelt love before her death.

'Much too hard!' protested some of the singers in Dresden, at the first rehearsals with the piano, and wanted to hand back their scores, but they were put to shame by the Czech tenor Karl Burian, singing Herod, who said *he* already knew his part by heart. (Strauss said: 'My vocal style has the tempo of the spoken drama, and often comes into conflict with the orchestral figuration and polyphony.')

his expressionistic photograph was taken in America by Edward Steichen. Perhaps the pose reflects thoughts of Herod – Salome was aring completion.

'*Aunt' Marie Wittich, the first Salome.*

Oscar Wilde.

Later the oboist spoke up: 'Herr Doktor, maybe this passage works on the piano, but it doesn't on the oboes.' 'Take heart, man, it doesn't work on the piano either.' (It was one of those passages where precision was not so important to him as an impression.)

The conductor Ernst von Schuch had unshakable faith in the work, even though people cut him in the street and tittered behind his back, prophesying a disastrous failure. The first performance, on 9 December 1905, was a revolutionary event, such as Wagner used to occasion. A new chapter had to be written in the history of Modernism.

At the dress rehearsal the first six rows were empty as usual, except for the composer, who sat directly behind Schuch. After the last chord there was a deathly silence. The house lights came up. Strauss turned round and said: 'Well, I enjoyed that.' It broke the spell, and there was a storm of applause.

Opinions of the opera varied wildly. Cosima Wagner thought it was 'madness!' and an example of Strauss's passion for exoticism. One Dresden critic declared that the Court Opera had not experienced a sensation of such significance since the early performances of Wagner's later works. Father Strauss, who died a few months before the first performance, said, when his son played him scenes from the opera on the piano, 'Such nervous music. I feel as if cockchafers were running around inside my trousers!' Max Reger stated that the work was 'not a turning point, nor the starting-point of any new direction. Strauss is as much himself here as in all his previous works. For the rest, I find the subject very distasteful, and the sensational enthusiasm is a modish modernity.' Felix von Weingartner regretted only that he had been unable to take in the beautiful words of the text.

Maria Wittich, who took the part of Salome in the first performance, thought the whole thing improper, and refused point-blank to perform some of the stage movements suggested to her: 'I'll do no such thing. I'm a decent woman!' A ballerina stood in for her in the Dance of the Seven Veils. In Strauss's opinion 'Aunty' Wittich sang very well but her acting was stiff and matronly. 'During the summer she has put on a fine stomach. It doesn't matter: voice, Horatio, the rest is – tummy.'

Karl Kraus wrote in 1907: 'Music washes the shores of thought. Only those who have no terra firma under their feet dwell in the element of music. The banalest of melodies, like the banalest of women, awakens ideas. Those who have no ideas look for them in music and in women. The music of Herr Richard Strauss is a woman who seeks to compensate for her natural deficiencies by mastering Sanskrit.'

Kaiser Wilhelm would not permit the work to be performed in Berlin until Baron Hülsen had the brainwave of having the Star of Bethlehem appear at the end, heralding the approach of the Three Wise Men. This was somewhat abstruse, since Christ is self-evidently already a grown man in the opera. Was it the belief of the Prussian court that the Magi continued to pursue Jesus all his life? The Kaiser did not hear the opera, but made one of his famous comments: 'I'm sorry, I like him otherwise, but with this he will do himself a great deal of harm.' Strauss remarked: 'The harm it did me enabled me to build the villa in Garmisch.'

Conscious of his worth, Strauss asked his new publisher, Fürstner, for 60,000 marks. His father was horrified: 'Do remain modest – at that price the publisher won't make anything from it!' As events soon proved, it was a modest fee to ask. Strauss hit the nerve of the time, and from then on snobbish opponents were able to describe him as 'a kind of musical tailor, who has the knack of supplying next season's fashions'.

Years later Strauss wrote to Stefan Zweig:

> I tried to compose the good Jochanaan more or less as a clown; a preacher in the desert, especially one who feeds on grasshoppers, seems infinitely comical to me. Only because I have already caricatured the five Jews and also poked fun at Father Herodes did I feel that I had to follow the law of contrast and write a pedantic-Philistine motive for four horns to characterize Jochanaan. (5 May 1935)

When conductors lingered over Jochanaan's description of Christ in a boat on the Sea of Galilee, his son Franz said, the composer would get impatient, stamp his foot and tell them to get a move on.

Strauss composed two different versions of the vocal parts, one to fit the German text and one for Wilde's original. As he wrote to Romain Rolland, 'I hope to a certain extent to have opened the way. . . . How the best French operas of Berlioz, Boieldieu suffer in our country from abominable translations!' In those days, German opera houses always performed opera in German, as a matter of course. The audience expected to be able to follow the action. The snobbery surrounding 'original' versions did not start until

A shot of the original production of Salome.

One of Aubrey Beardsley's illustrations to Wilde's Salome.

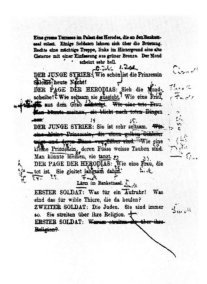

Page of the German text of Wilde's Salome, *used by Strauss in the composition of the opera.*

A cartoonist's view of Wilde and Strauss unveiling Salome.

around 1950. Strauss always said that an audience that did not understand the words went to sleep.

Rolland helped Strauss on matters of intonation and pronunciation (though he was at first amazed that Strauss should 'want to give to poetry by a decadent Anglo-Belgian the realistic declamation of the slang of Montmartre'). The study of Debussy's *Pelléas* showed Strauss that French words could have completely different stresses in different contexts. He worked at it doggedly, Rolland made 191 emendations, and a vocal score including this version was published in 1906. In 1909 another, revised, version was published, in which a good French text was fitted to Strauss's original, German-language, vocal line. This replaced Strauss's well-meant experiment.

In the meantime, his publisher Fürstner was waging war on Strauss's behalf in Paris, where, incredibly, it was customary to calculate fees for operas according to the number of acts! Performance of Strauss's specially composed French-language version aroused amazement and enthusiasm in the French musical world.

After the 'obligatory nonsense from the Press', as Strauss called it, the clergy bestirred themselves. The play by the notorious homosexual had already been judged to be perverse and blasphemous. Now the opera was banned in New York and Chicago. On the command of the Lord Chamberlain's office, the text was bowdlerized in London and the young Thomas Beecham had to fight like a lion to obtain permission to do the work at all. From Vienna, Mahler reported that not even the argument that the Catholic court in Desden had allowed it to be performed was powerful enough for the Austrian court: Archduchess Valerie, the daughter of Emperor Franz Joseph, was against it. (What can have upset that otherwise insignificant lady?)

Graz had the courage that failed Vienna. The production there in May 1906 attracted Puccini, Mahler and his wife, and a large contingent of young people from Vienna, armed with the vocal score and their enthusiasm; they included an out-of-work nobody called Adolf Hitler.

In 1939 zealous National Socialists, cultural vigilantes, got the work banned in Graz. Strauss decided to take no notice. He wrote to his cousin Rudolf Moralt, a conductor at the Vienna State Opera: 'The idea that *Salome* is supposed to be a Jewish ballad is very humorous. The Führer and Reichskanzler himself told my son in Bayreuth that *Salome* was one of his first operatic experiences, and that he raised the money to pay his fare to go to the first performance in Graz by begging from his relatives. Literally!!'

Salome's travails were not over when permission had been obtained for performances to take place. Production brought troubles of its own. The producer Erich Engel received some sound advice from Strauss in 1930:

> The page must be a woman, not a tenor. . . . I would rather not have any dramatics in the dance at all. No flirting with Herod, no playing to Jochanaan's cistern, only a moment's pause beside the cistern on the final trill. The dance should be purely oriental, as serious and measured as possible, and thoroughly decent, as if it was being done on a prayer-

Salome goes on tour.

Salome in London, 1910. 'At the first performance, as we hear, the censor having forbidden the Baptist's head, Madame Akté danced round a plum pudding. This delicate regard for national sensibilities contributed in no small measure to the success of the performance.'

Salome: 'Wait and see, John, they're going to chop your head off!'
John: 'That's not as bad as being made into an opera by Strauss!'

After the ban in New York and Chicago, one cartoonist suggested printing advertisements on each of the seven veils – perhaps that would help.

The hen-pecked husband.

Model: 'Tell me, professor, what made you choose me as the model for Salome?'
Professor: 'Well now do you think a choice like that is left to me?'

The inscription on this photo, in Pauline's handwriting, says 'Richard with a hangover!!! Salome Dresden 1905.' A curiosity, as he was never drunk. The day after the première of Salome *he caught the 10 a.m. train back to Berlin, and played skat throughout the journey.*

On a page of the notebook that Strauss kept about the building of the new house in Garmisch he made a list of places where Salome *was performed in the first years. The numbers refer to the numbers of performances.*

mat. Only with the C sharp minor should there be a pacing movement and the last 2/4 bar should have a slight orgiastic emphasis. I have only once seen the dance done really aristocratically and stylishly, by Frau Gutheil-Schoder.

An Italian company, performing in Amsterdam, had produced its own orchestration, based on the vocal score, in order to save money on royalties (Strauss's copyright was not protected in Holland in 1906). Fürstner's managed to enforce a compromise: Strauss himself should conduct, so as to rescue as much as could be rescued. He arrived, only to find a company 'which would hardly do for a sixth-rate *Trovatore* and scarcely knew their parts, and a tiny beerhall band available for a single rehearsal.' To withdraw would have cost him money for breach of contract. 'It was grisly' – yet a friend of his enjoyed it! 'Was it the suggestive power of my baton, or is the work indestructible? The latter, I think. How many staves of scoring I could have saved myself – but the secret of a forty-stave score is nevertheless greater than the secret of an (Italian) purse.'

He spent the Christmas period of 1906 in Turin, to conduct *Salome*.

In Milan, Toscanini, with the aid of a mercilessly raging orchestra, simply butchered the singers and the drama (à la Mottl). It is a miracle it was nevertheless a success. If I had not got here in good time, and shown the people how the work should look, it could have been lost for Italy for years to come. In Milan, the conductor played a symphony without singers . . . (to Pauline, 26 December 1906).

Some years later, there was an adventure of a different kind, in Rome.

There was nearly a disaster at the premiere, because after Herod's entrance a methylated-spirit(!) torch set light to the scenery, and four dancing girls caught fire, one of them was quite badly hurt. I stayed calm and so did the audience, so there was no panic and after ten minutes, when the fire had been put out with the curtain still up, and the orchestra had restored calm with the *Marcia reale*, the performance was able to proceed to a successful conclusion. My presence of mind stood by me this time, even if at some cost to my nerves. (To his son and daughter-in-law, 6 February 1924)

Gustav Mahler, then principal conductor of the Court Opera in Vienna, spared no effort to overcome the Viennese censor's objections to *Salome*. It was his failure to do so which led to his resignation. He admired the work, and he admired Strauss.

I simply must tell you of the thrilling impression the work made when I read through it recently. It is the high point to date. I would even say that nothing you have done so far can stand comparison with it. You know I don't say things I don't mean – and to you even less than to other people. Every note is spot on! As I've known for a long time: your vocation is to be a dramatist. I confess that through your music you have made me understand for the first time what Wilde's work is about. (11 October 1905)

Strauss had had a great esteem for Mahler ever since 1888, when he had played through his then brand-new First Symphony as a piano duet with Hermann Levi. From then on, he did what he could to promote the work of the Austrian composer, four years his senior. In 1895 Mahler told him 'You are as yet the only one of all my colleagues who takes any notice of what I write.'

In spite of a marked indifference in Vienna, he kept *Feuersnot* in the repertory there. Young people, to be sure, cheered from the standing places but the critics' feathers were ruffled. The difficulty of the choruses for children moved Hanslick to propose a 'society for the prevention of musical cruelty to children'. Alma Mahler said her husband loathed the work, but she has been found an often unreliable witness. She could not abide either Strauss or (especially) Pauline.

Of all Mahler's works, Strauss had a particular liking for the Fifth Symphony: only the Adagietto, which exercises such a strong appeal to the general public, struck him as below the level of the rest. Mahler, for his part, found much that was immature and pretentious in *Guntram*. This kind of informed criticism did nothing to impair their mutual respect. Mahler said: 'We are the opposite poles on the axis of a magnet' and 'We are tunnelling into the same mountain from different sides. Sooner or later we shall meet.' But he could be depressed by Strauss: 'I labour on, with countless rehearsals. He makes do with just a few, and it always sounds right.'

In their personal relations, Mahler was often repelled by Strauss's sangfroid, his boisterous humour, his down-to-earth attitudes and his concern with the commercial side of their profession. Art was Mahler's religion, and he was genuinely shocked when Strauss talked about royalties, cracked jokes, deferred to Pauline and confined the conversation to mundane topics, while Mahler preferred to contemplate higher things. When he and Alma had been moved to tears by an uplifting musical experience, Strauss's detachment offended them.

Mahler and Strauss at the stage door of the Landertheater in Salzburg.

My dear, darling Almschli,
She met me at the door yesterday afternoon with 'Pst! Pst! Richard is asleep', drew me into her (very untidy) boudoir, where her aged Mama was drinking coffeh (not coffee) and poured out on my defenceless head a cloudburst of tittle-tattle about every financial and sexual happening of the last two years, throwing in rapid questions about a thousand and one things, without waiting for any answers, refused to let me take my leave in any circumstances, told me that Richard had held a tiring rehearsal in Leipzig yesterday morning, then travelled back to Berlin, conducted *Götterdämmerung* in the evening, was worn out this morning, went to lie down this afternoon, and she was watching vigilantly over his sleep. I was quite touched. Then she suddenly leapt up: 'Time that lazybones was woken.' There was nothing I could do to prevent her dragging me into his room by main force, where she roared at him, in

Gustav Mahler.

stentorian tones: 'Up you get! Gustav is here!' (I was Gustav for an hour, then all of a sudden it was 'Herr Direktor' again.) Strauss woke with a start, gave a long-suffering smile, and then the animated chatter was resumed between the three of us. Then we had tea, and they drove me back to the hotel in their automobile, after arranging with me to take lunch with them on Saturday.

Salome again made an extraordinary impression on me in the evening! It is entirely a work of genius, very powerful, and decidedly one of the most important things that our age has produced. There is a Vulcan living and working there beneath a spoil-heap, a subterranean fire – not just a firework. I suppose the same thing can be said of Strauss's whole personality. That's what makes it so difficult to separate the wheat from the chaff in him. But I have grown to have an enormous respect for the entire phenomenon, and it has been reconfirmed. I take immense joy in it!

Erotomaniac as she was, Alma Mahler saw herself as a muse, ringed by worshipping, kneeling geniuses. A number of significant artists chose to flatter her (and themselves) by playing the role, but Strauss neither worshipped, knelt nor fell into her toils. In the 1920s, married by then to her third husband, Franz Werfel, she tried to persuade Strauss to make an opera of Werfel's play *Juarez und Maximilian*. The price of his refusal was obloquy in her memoirs: when he read them in 1946, he shook his head repeatedly, and grew increasingly angry for Mahler's sake, for he had thought of him as a true friend.

When Mahler died in 1911, Strauss was unable to work for days and would scarcely speak, his son Franz recalled. In his diary he wrote:

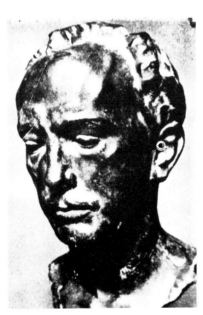

Bust by Hugo Lederer, 1908.

> Gustav Mahler died on 19 May, after grave illness. The death of this aspiring, idealistic, energetic artist is a heavy loss. . . . The Jew Mahler could still be uplifted by Christianity. The hero Richard Wagner descended to it again as an old man, under the influence of Schopenhauer. It is absolutely clear to me that the German nation will only find new strength through liberation from Christianity. Are we really once again as we were at the time of the political union of Charles V and the Pope? Wilhelm II and Pius X?
>
> I will call my *Alpine* Symphony the Antichrist, because in it there is: moral purification by means of one's own strength, liberation through work, worship of glorious, eternal nature.

Are these the thoughts and feelings of an artist who was inspired only by the profit motive? So Alma Mahler would have had us believe. Strauss was a composer who could turn back from tragedy to serenity and the lyric muse and, as Schiller said, 'the world loves to blacken radiance'. There is no symbolic symphonism in the *Alpine* Symphony, by contrast with *Zarathustra* It is a work of pure, undisguised homage to the eternal, glorious nature of the composer's homeland.

Garmisch

Though the position of Hofkapellmeister in Berlin conferred great prestige, though he was acclaimed on all sides, though the work he was engaged to do was worthwhile, Strauss yearned for peace and quiet in which to write music, for 'the good air of my Bavarian homeland', as he frequently called it, for the comforts which, since *Salome*, he could afford. True, he did not feel rich enough to give up the security of his post in Berlin, and Baron von Hülsen lent him a sympathetic ear.

> Your contract, which must be unique in theatrical history, is provisional for this year. Originally you came to me with the request to release you altogether for the entire half year and, *notwithstanding*, to pay you your salary in full. As things were, you could not find the time you needed to collect yourself for your work, and therefore, in the nature of things, a certain anxiety carried over into your official activities. I treated this unusual request as favourably as possible, because I could very well sympathize with your wishes, and regarded it as a *nobile officium* to remove the restraints pressing upon your creative urges. But

Strauss kept his habitual bow-tie on, even for a strenuous mountain walk on a hot day. Pauline has a parasol.

The villa in Garmisch, soon after completion. Today a beautiful wood stands in the field in the foreground.

Strauss's study from the dining-room. Chairs were grouped conversationally beside the piano

In the dining-room with Franz and grandsons Christian and Richard.

The cupboard on the left and the chest of drawers on the right were full of sketchbooks manuscripts. The sofa served for the afternoon nap.

Strauss liked to work in the cool loggia on ho days. He was not the least disturbed by Franz (off the right-hand edge), playing Ni Men's Morris with his cousin.

The Strauss house without dogs is unthinkable. This one was called 'Tuy'. The knickerbockers worn by Master were fashionable, not just for walking.

The house in Garmisch today. The dining
room, with the bay featured in Intermezzo,
is on the right on the ground floor. The
veranda on the left has always been popular
with the family in hot weather. Above it,
Strauss's breakfast room.

On this side the veranda window is to the
right, and beside it the study, where the
desk stands under the window. Above it is
Strauss's bedroom, the room where he died.

The part of the house to the right of the drainpipe was added in the 1920s to make a bedroom and bathroom for Pauline upstairs and an extra room on the ground floor.

The staircase, ground-floor. The pictures are local South German painting on glass, a genre of folk-art which Strauss started to collect long before it became fashionable. The hunting trophies are the contribution of Franz and Alice. Strauss himself went hunting only once, shot a pheasant and decided 'Never again'.

Upper part of the staircase. Strauss's interest in collecting the paintings behind glass which hang on the wall was first stimulated by Mengelberg.

The landing. The trophies of the hunt belonged to Franz and Alice.

The landing.

The upstairs corridor. Strauss's bedroom was on this floor, and it was there that he died.

Strauss with his mentor, Alexander Ritter, painted by Leopold Graf Kalckreuth.

Some of the large collection of works of south German art.

The dining room, with doors leading to the veranda (centre) and study, where the piano stands next to the desk (right).

Left: The curved desk at which all the works were written, from Elektra *onwards. Right: The study seen from the piano stool. The bust of Gluck was a gift from Goebbels. A version of the large painting hangs in the Metropolitan Opera House in New York.*

The door to the left of the piano leads to the little library, where memorabilia are kept in glass cases, such as the many orders.

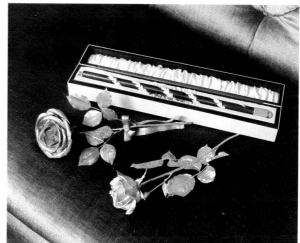

'Oktavians', in every artistic medium, and silver roses galore were heaped upon the composer of Der Rosenkavalier.

In Verehrung und Dank-
barkeit ernennt die Frankfurter
Museums-Gesellschaft
herrn Dr. RICHARD STRAUSS
Den unvergleichlichen Meister der
Tonkunst, ihren treuen Freund
in Würdigung seiner langjährig-
unvergänglichen Verdienste
Durch einstimmigen Beschluß-
des Vorstandes zu ihrem
EHREN-MITGLIED
Frankfurt a.M.17.November 1933
Der Vorstand:

Left: The ceremonial scroll documenting Strauss's appointment as an honorary member of the Museums-Gesellschaft of Frankfurt. Right: A ring presented by the town of Garmisch-Partenkirchen.

The Gobelins tapestry, the carved figures and the piano all came from the house in Vienna. Strauss's death-mask lies on top of the piano.

The grave of Richard, Pauline and Franz Strauss in the cemetery in Garmisch.

*Strauss occasionally rode as a young man,
but not in later life. This photo taken in
Italy records a rare exception.*

*In the loggia, playing with his key-ring.
The pose is very characteristic, according to
the family, and indicates deep thought.*

*In winter Strauss orchestrated his scores,
completing 5–6 pages a day. The short score of
Arabella is on the stand in front of him,
with the orchestration already noted in detail.*

*Enjoying the bracing North Sea breezes at Westerland on Sylt. The three Strausses were accompanied by Emil Tschirch, an actor, who
sometimes performed* Enoch Arden *with the composer. You changed in the bathing-machines, and could leave your books and the picnic
lunch in them; they were drawn up and down the beach, according to the state of the tide.*

Winter in Garmisch. The snowfall is always heavy 720 metres above sea-level.

we have an official establishment to run, and the way things are now being managed has proved both inartistic and impossible. The lack of *artistic* discipline among almost the entire personnel has been, and still is, attributable, first and foremost, to the fact that often no example has been set. I don't need my musical directorate as ornaments, I need them to be serious and dedicated productive artists – conscientious, hard-working coryphaei. You promised me in writing, and *as a personal undertaking, to devote your entire strength* to the Royal Institution in the remaining six months of the year, unreservedly. Your letter now – in a way that touches me in the most painful manner – places your own interests in the forefront again, to such an extent that I must ask you whether you will keep your word and dedicate your entire strength to the much needed betterment of the Royal Institution. By so doing you will enable me to recommend His Majesty to approve, as he has not yet done, your new contract *for the coming year.*

But Strauss knew, egoistic as it may sound, that the works he was going to write next would also redound to the honour of the Berlin Court Opera. In the end Hülsen and the Kaiser were magnanimous, and Strauss was able to proceed with his plan to build the house that would be his home for the rest of his life.

A World Reputation

'*How should a critic judge what an author could do, when he doesn't know what he set out to do? If my works are any good, they will find their place, regardless of criticism and the hateful aspersions cast on my artistic intentions. If they are worthless, then no amount of praise or initial success will keep them alive. The yellow press is welcome to devour them, as they have devoured so many before them.*'

STRAUSS

Strauss received more honours in his life than any composer before him. The Cross of Merit awarded him by the Duke of Saxe-Meiningen in 1886 was only the first in a list that later included many foreign orders as well as German and Austrian ones. Even Bavaria gave him the Maximilian Order for Art and Learning in 1910. Learned societies and institutions awarded him medals and honorary memberships, from the Krefeld Teachers' Choral Society to the Royal Academy of Music in London. The places across the world where he was made an honorary citizen ranged from Cincinnati (1904) to Naxos (1924); Garmisch (1949) was the last – but he had been an honorary member of the Rifle Club since 1909. Already before the First World War his works were performed in cycles, in festivals lasting from three days to two weeks: London in 1903, Wiesbaden in 1908, Dresden in 1909, Frankfurt and Munich in 1910, Vienna, Krefeld and The Hague in 1911. And always he was in demand as a conductor. In one typical year, 1908, he went to Rome and Paris in addition to a tour with the Berlin Philharmonic that took him to France, Spain, Portugal, Italy and southern Germany.

Did all these forms of recognition alter him? He started his career as a model ambitious young man. In Weimar he became a dynamic idealist, an uncompromising champion of art. In another ten years he had calmed down, he was more flexible, relaxed, and incredibly tough. As public adulation and professional demands accumulated, he took on more and more work, because he had the ability to use his time and his energy economically. He worked quickly, after thinking it through first. He planned his life and eliminated everything unimportant. He met the excitement stirred up by each of his works in turn with a relaxed irony, while yet more startling new ideas welled up in him and his ability to fascinate never failed. His personality was unaltered by his fame: he remained modest and clear-sighted, wary of megalomania or any temptation to play The Artist as God. In the midst of the multifarious activities occasioned by his artistic production, he stood cool and collected. The source of his strength was his family – but he was addicted to composition as some people are to drugs.

Karl Henckell, poet and Socialist, an unusual combination at that time.

Symphonic music no longer satisfied him. He needed words – lyric verse or drama – in order to produce his own wholly personal contribution to the ideal of the synthesis of all the arts, in which the text was the equal in quality and imaginative power of the music. He needed a poet.

In the history of the German art-song – *das Kunstlied* – the contributions of Haydn, Mozart and Beethoven are for once not of central significance. The genre's first undisputed master was Franz Schubert; in the eighty years following his death, many composers tried their hands at it, but five names now tower above them all – Schubert himself, Schumann, Brahms, Wolf and Strauss.

Up to 1906 Strauss had composed 141 songs, of which 109 were published. Between 1906 and 1918 there was a pause, of which more will be said later. The poets who stimulated him are an unusual and very personal selection. Of the familiar sources of German Romantic song, he revered Goethe, read him in the complete edition, but set very few of his poems; he set nothing by Mörike, very little by Eichendorff (in contrast to Pfitzner) or Heine; he composed sixteen songs to texts by Rückert, and sixteen more by Uhland, but they are not among his most successful. Like Mahler, he was drawn to *Des Knaben Wunderhorn*, but where Mahler chose songs full of melancholy, despair and longing for a better world beyond this vale of tears, Strauss went for scurrilous humour and the erotic: *Himmelsboten an Liebchens Himmelbett* (op. 32 no. 5), *Für fünfzehn Pfennige* (op. 36 no. 2), *Hat gesagt – bleibt's nicht dabei* (op. 36 no. 3), *Junggesellenschwur* (op. 49 no. 6). He was more interested in his contemporaries, though he never set the poems of either Hugo von Hofmannsthal or Stefan George; instead he was attracted by social and political radicals like the Socialist Karl Henckell, of whom he set love poems such as *Ruhe, meine Seele* (op. 27 no. 1), *Ich trage meine Minne*, *Liebeshymnus* and *O süsser Mai* (op. 32 nos 1, 3 and 4), as well as *Lied des Steinklopfers* op. 49 no. 4 and several others. Henckell published in Zürich, as he was banned from doing so in Germany by anti-Socialist laws. Strauss wrote other love songs to poems by the anarchist John Henry Mackay, a lifelong Berliner of Scottish birth: *Heimliche Aufforderung* and *Morgen!* (op. 27 nos 3 and 4), *Verführung* (op. 33 no. 1) and *In der Campagna* (op. 41 no. 2). Oskar Panizza was in gaol for his published opinions (he was later tried for

Hugo von Hofmannsthal.

Richard Dehmel.

lèse-majesté and transferred to a lunatic asylum) when His Imperial Majesty's Hofkapellmeister set his poem *Sie wissens nicht* (op. 49 no. 5). Richard Dehmel, of whom Strauss set eleven poems, pleaded for the chance to rewrite the text of one of his early poems, *Mein Auge*, so that it would be more worthy of the setting. 'Since we are both past the age for youthful asininities, I don't suppose I need to excuse myself for wanting to do this; you were probably touched by the sincere emotion of the little thing, but that alone is not enough before the tribunal of beauty.' (24 April 1898)

On 23 March 1899, in his house in the Berlin district of Pankow, Dehmel was host to Count Harry Kessler, three poets – Paul Scheerbart, Wilhelm Schäfer and Hugo von Hofmannsthal – and Richard and Pauline Strauss. This was the first meeting of Strauss and Hofmannsthal, in a relationship that, in time, would bear artistic fruit of the very first order. Their second meeting was by chance, in Paris, where they discussed a project for a ballet, *Der Triumph der Zeit*. Hofmannsthal wrote a libretto, but Strauss did not want to set it. He was occupied with *Feuersnot* at the time, and already thinking ahead to *Salome*. (Later, Hofmannsthal told him that the stress in 'Salome' should come on the 'o'; too late, but Strauss got it right in *Die ägyptische Helena*.) Hofmannsthal was thirty-two when he heard *Salome* in Dresden; his remarkable early lyric flow had come to an end, and he was in the process of evolving as a dramatist. He was not musical, but the work aroused a strong emotional response in him.

> A pleasure which it is hard to describe, a violent pleasure which kept up through the entire work, a soaring and uncommon feeling of happiness. One had the sense that there lay yet more beauty beneath a shimmering veil, more than one's senses could manage to take in at such a pace. I have no idea where it ranks as music. It is possible that what we call colour predominates to a dangerous degree, and that the other element which is so hard to denominate, and in which Beethoven is so immense: the inner stirring of the soul, is here relatively underpowered. Perhaps it is music which will not endure, but for the present moment, the moment out of which it was born, it is filled with the power to enchant, and the moment is so important – we must learn to live by moments. (To Helen Nostiz, 1 November 1906)

Before that, Strauss had already seen Hofmannsthal's play *Elektra*, in a production at Max Reinhardt's theatre in Berlin, where he had also improved on his first acquaintance with Wilde's *Salome*. Struck by Hofmannsthal's potential, he first approached him with proposals for a Semiramis, or a 'wild' Renaissance subject: Cesare Borgia or Savonarola.

> To begin with I was deterred by the thought that *Salome* and *Elektra* had many psychological similarities, which made me doubt if I would find a second time the power of intensification necessary if the latter subject was to be treated as exhaustively as the first. But then the wish to set this demonic, ecstatic image of sixth-century Greece up in opposition to the Romanized copies of Winckelmann and the humanism of Goethe

triumphed over my caution, and so *Elektra* turned out to be even more intense in the concentration of its structure, in the violence of its intensification. These two operas stand alone in my life's work, in them I went to the utmost limits of harmony, psychological polyphony (Clytemnestra's dream) and the capacity of today's ears to take in what they hear.

It was in his sense of musico-dramatic structure and his ability to build climaxes of terrifying intensity that Strauss surpassed all his German contemporaries. Since the demise of the number opera and the rise of the through-composed score, composers had to create structure and form anew in each work. Often, too faithful an adherence to the structures of the text led to hours of recitative-like illustration, without a pinch of dramatic spice. Strauss always built forms within a work which, while integrated in themselves, provided the contrast with each other necessary for the intensification of which he speaks above. He seldom lingered for long in one emotion, but switched abruptly into a new mood, according to the demands of the drama, throwing out arcs to span the leap from simple, folksong-like melodies to atonal eruptions.

With *Elektra* he moved forward into unmapped territory, and found the going hard. He wrote three versions of the opening monologue alone. 'People always think something like that succeeds at the first attempt, and that the right style is achieved from the first. Something like that demands to be fought for, and worked at, step by step.'

A month after hearing *Salome*, Hofmannsthal wrote to Helen Nostiz about Strauss's progress with *Elektra*:

Yesterday he played and sang some passages to me, and (although he sings atrociously, of course) it gave me immense joy to hear what I had written in that form, far greater than when spoken by actors. He has been unbelievably successful (so far as I can judge) in contrasting the figures of Electra and her gentler sister. I think it will be very good.

From the time of *Salome* onwards, Strauss was a favourite target of the cartoonists. This is an honour the press reserves for only the really famous and if Wagner holds the world record, Strauss may well be the runner-up. At the time of *Elektra*, one cartoonist showed Sophocles, already 'worked over' by Hofmannsthal, being belaboured by Strauss with a drumstick, while another depicted a victim in the 'Elektric' chair. By the 1950s, the papers no longer published cartoons of composers: only politicians and sportsmen were well enough known, and the musician Ludwig Kusche was probably correct in his claim, in 1953, that after forty years of dodecaphonism, still no caricaturist had tackled Schoenberg.

There is, of course, a crop of anecdotes surrounding the early performances of *Elektra*, the first of which took place in Dresden on 25 January 1909, during a 'Strauss Week'. Strauss himself told one about that first production: 'During one of the early orchestral rehearsals, Schuch, who was very sensitive to draughts, noticed that there was a door left open

At the Lion Gate in Mycenae, the scene of Elektra.

'A dreadful pair. One of them tickles the victim's ivories, and then the other composes him.'

Elektra, *Dresden, 25 January 1909. Strauss with Annie Krull as Electra and Ernestine Schumann-Heinck, an international star, as Clytemnestra. Strauss found the latter wooden; he preferred more spontaneity. A newspaper reported that Strauss had arrived to 'teach the singers all the latest tricks for their difficult roles'. After the première, one critic wrote gleefully 'Flop!!'*

'"Elektricution", by the musical headsman.'

Die „Elektrische" Hinrichtung
durch den musikalischen Scharfrichter.

by a cleaner in the third tier of the empty auditorium. He called up angrily: "What are you looking for?" I was in the stalls and answered: "A triad."'

In Vienna a wonderful clarinettist, an ageing Czech, sat at his desk after rehearsal, polishing his instrument; he was heard to murmur, in a tone of resignation: 'If a Czech had written that!'

In Basle a worthy Swiss was asked how the work had struck him: 'Oh! Quite wonderful!' 'And the music?' 'I didn't hear any music as such.' Strauss commented: 'I much prefer someone like that to a carping dilettante who in the end hasn't understood the music at all.'

The drama critic, playwright and dramaturge Hermann Bahr, husband of the soprano Anna Mildenburg, was present at the premiere of *Elektra*, and left this account of the occasion and of the composer:

All Europe is in Dresden, my hotel porter proudly confided to me. One thinks of Bayreuth: but there the atmosphere is more ceremonial and more contemplative. Everything here is more rushed and hurried, more strident, less hieratic, more like Berlin. Four years ago in Munich, they held that great automobile race in August. It's a little bit like that. These greedy strangers who have come here for the Strauss Week, the poorest of the rich, who would like to experience something for once in one fell swoop; anything else they want, they can buy.

And in the middle of all the tumult created by these hungry over-eaters, quietly getting on with the work, is the magician at whose behest this whole inferno is dancing: Strauss. The splendid thing about him is that he is not at all like his admirers. A durable, weather-proof, remarkably collected man, calm and good-tempered. Gardeners look like this, and people who spend a lot of time looking through microscopes; people who are accustomed to observing things from close to, with a steady eye and painstaking thought, and know what love, patience and fidelity are. He is still quite young, but doesn't even look his forty-four years; the eyes are not yet twenty, so trusting and unclouded is the gaze with which they view the world in innocence, romantic Wanderlust and confidence. Only his mouth does not suit with the rest: a soft, femininely secretive mouth, shadowed by the suggestion of all kinds of malice, sweet nothings, weariness, sorrowfulness, threats of trickery and spite. But when he speaks, it fits the rest of him: the warm, brown, royal-Bavarian timbre of his voice, as he puts in some relaxed but pertinent comment, confirms the steady gaze and the confidence of one's feeling that his roots are firmly in the ground, he is not one to be blown over by a puff of air. No, it is quite true: he is not at all what one would expect from his admirers with their tumultuous, irrational hysteria. His is a unique case: an artist who frightens the cognoscenti with his audacity, but wins the crowd at first hearing.

Hermann Bahr, who in 1916 wrote the scenario for what was to become Intermezzo.

Bahr dedicated a play, *Das Konzert*, to Strauss, who said 'Perhaps my world-famous luck will benefit your play.' It appears to have done so; *Das Konzert*, concerning a conductor for whom Weingartner was the involuntary model, was Bahr's most successful play.

Was Strauss then 'lucky'? He experienced contempt, misunderstanding and obstacles, colleagues intrigued against him, his work was booed, laughed at by orchestras, savaged by critics. His real good luck consisted in the fact that none of this bothered him. His astonishing ideas never failed to win attention. He steadfastly regarded all the activities on the periphery of art as inherently unsatisfactory and devoted himself to art itself. *Ein Heldenleben* eloquently expressed his views on the subject.

The young Strauss had exulted when outraged critics had foamed at the mouth, for they made the public curious. In old age he shook his head over the things they said about him: 'superficiality', 'orchestral illusionism', 'no depth', *Rosenkavalier* was 'saccharine' (T. W. Adorno); he was 'prolific', a 'craftsman of genius', an 'eternal Latin-School boy' (Alfred Einstein); his music was 'garrulous, spurious polyphony', 'cerebral music with smatterings of erudition', 'naive sensuality' (Walter Abendroth).

Artists have no means of defending themselves, and if they try, it only makes things worse. Such was the unhappy experience of the belligerent Hans Pfitzner, on numerous occasions. Strauss withdrew behind a screen of indifference, but in *Ein Heldenleben* he created an outlet for his views of his opponents and his astonishment at incomprehension and hostility. Thin-blooded and venomous, the wind instruments strut and niggle, and from time to time the trombones interject a phrase in open fifths which sounds like 'What a nonsense' or 'Can't abide it'. It could even be 'Doctor Döring' – Theodor Döring of the *Sammler* was an old enemy. When Strauss conducted *Heldenleben* in Munich after the First World War, he muttered to himself in rehearsal, when they reached this passage: 'Another one who's dead now.'

He poured all his technical skill and all the wealth of his imagination into *Elektra*, and thought that after twenty-five years of polemics it was high time for people to rise above their prejudices and concentrate on what he had actually achieved. No chance: hardly anything changed.

With long faces, Siegfried Wagner, Max Reger, Arthur Nikisch, Strauss and Eugen d'Albert listen to the child prodigy Willi Ferrero.

123

The next generation of composers, and the one after next, despised him because he made no further exploration of atonality after *Elektra*, but simply employed everything from simple melodies (though never as simple as Mahler) to cacophony according to what he thought appropriate, rather than follow a principle, such as twelve-tone technique, for principle's sake. 'Me, a renegade? Is that what they say?', he asked as an old man. 'And yet I was one of the first in that business, with *Elektra*.'

There is no need to spend a lot of money on sets and costumes for *Elektra*, and the opera has no interval. When it was put on at reduced admission prices in 1948, Strauss commented sardonically 'The cheap one-acter, and no buffet!'

A Change of Direction

The musical world was waiting for a new onslaught from Strauss, with even more audacious thrills and heady perversities. But after matricide and tragedy, the composer of *Till Eulenspiegel* and *Don Quixote* needed to return to comedy: he was ready to write his *Figaro*.

He and Hofmannsthal had agreed while they were still working on *Elektra* that they would continue their collaboration and Hofmannsthal began the quest for a new subject. There was his comedy *Christinas Heimreise*, but it left Strauss cold. Hofmannsthal turned to Molière, and tried to extract a scenario from one of his plots, while Strauss waited impatiently.

In February 1909, ten days after the first performance of *Elektra*, with the impression of that event still fresh, Hofmannsthal was visiting Harry Kessler in Weimar. Sitting in the garden, he told his friend about his search, and in the course of three more days' conversation the pair had concocted a scenario based on a play Kessler had seen in Paris two years before: *L'Ingenu libertin*. With the list of characters written down on the back of a menu, Hofmannsthal went on to Berlin and outlined the plot of *Der Rosenkavalier* to Strauss, who said 'That's it. Be warned, they will all say that it is, once again, not the long-awaited new comic opera – but we shall enjoy the task.'

They went ahead at a great rate. The text of Act I was written in four weeks, by the middle of March. In another five weeks, by the middle of April, Strauss was going broody, and on 22 May (Wagner's birthday) he wrote the last bars, played the music to his librettist, and was ready for Act II.

Early in July he came to a halt. He was sure that the second act needed more hubbub, more comic business, more twists to the plot. The audience must be made to laugh. He suggested alterations which he thought would be more effective. Hofmannsthal demurred at first, but then they worked out the final version together. Strauss said the music was 'flowing along like

'The Levée' by Hogarth, upon which Act I of Rosenkavelier *was based. On the left, the tenor and flute-player; in the centre 'the Marshallin' with her hairdresser Hippolyte; and on the right the little negro page.*

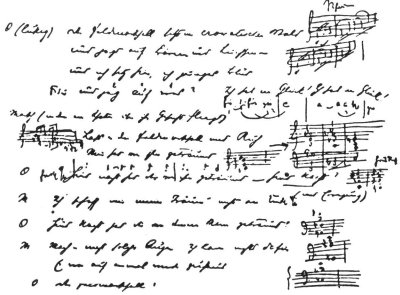

A page of Hofmannsthal's manuscript for Der Rosenkavalier *on which Strauss began to note down his ideas as he read – themes, harmonies, rhythmic patterns, and bar-lines even at this early stage, before picking up his sketchbook.*

Strauss and Hofmannsthal at Garmisch, outside the villa.

the Loisach: I am composing everything – neck and crop', including at least one stage direction and, in his haste, misreading a comma so that what was written as 'The noble father, says propriety, must leave the house' came out as an exhortation by the father to drive out propriety.

For the famous waltz, in which he threw down the gauntlet to the Viennese Strausses, he turned to the sketchbook where once, holidaying on the Isle of Wight, he had jotted down a string of ideas for waltzes, and developed one of them; and if there is a strong whiff of Josef Strauss's *Dynamiden* about the outcome, it is as little fortuitous as the presence of Russian folk-tunes in Stravinsky's *Firebird*, an exact contemporary.

Strauss composed in the summer, and by the autumn of 1909 two acts of the opera had been written, while not a word of the text of Act III existed. During the winter Hofmannsthal worked on that while Strauss scored the first two acts, which, words and music, had taken only six months. Now the pace slackened. Strauss put forward more proposals about the course of the action in the last act. He did not start to compose again until the following spring, by which time Acts I and II had been printed.

He began Act III on 23 April 1910. (He had invented the melody for Sophie and Octavian's final duet in the previous year, on 26 June 1909 to be exact, and Hofmannsthal wrote the words to fit.) The death of his mother interrupted the work after three weeks. There was a pause, a period of grief, then he was up and away again. *Der Rosenkavalier* was finished on 26 September 1910, and the first performance was given exactly four months later.

Both its authors later came to hold the view that they had worked too quickly and that there was something uneven about the opera. In spite of its popularity they were not satisfied with it, and they preferred *Ariadne* and *Die Frau ohne Schatten*. And yet it may be that *Rosenkavalier*'s success is due in part to the very disparity in the character of each of the acts. More integrated pieces, where the unity of text, musical material and structure has been worked for, do not always have the same direct appeal. Uneven works like *The Magic Flute*, Beethoven's Ninth Symphony or Schubert's *Unfinished* seem to exert an attraction all of their own.

At all events, *Der Rosenkavalier* is the first of the operas to exhibit the capacity for love, tenderness and glowing eroticism which Strauss had previously revealed only in songs. It also offers the paradigm of Straussian

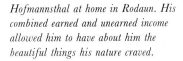

Hofmannsthal at home in Rodaun. His combined earned and unearned income allowed him to have about him the beautiful things his nature craved.

vocal melody as something which is born from the intonations of conversation and elevates speech to the level of music. The words are more than the carriers of a preconceived melody. In Italian and other operas the orchestra often plays the melody that is being sung, but Strauss effects a total separation of singing and accompaniment. The essential musical drama is played out in the orchestra. Feelings, melodies and descriptions have their being in that second musical stratum, while the singing voice floats freely above it. The orchestra is more than an accompaniment; it interprets the moods and emotions of each of the characters, elevates and intensifies the sung speech and melds with it to create a musical whole. To give just one example, from Act I: Ochs raises his voice in argument with the notary, the Italian tenor struggles on bravely with his aria, and the orchestra depicts the emotional tensions underlying this – on one level – comic scene. In no other of Strauss's operas is the symbiotic relationship of music and words so successfully and felicitously represented.

In the libretto, the adulterous Marschallin is discovered in her bed, with a scantily clad young man in the room. Even though the young man is sung by another woman, the Saxon court was shocked. The Intendant of the Dresden Opera, Count Nikolaus von Seebach, poured oil on the waters with a few tactful changes: at the first performance, the princess was not reclining in, but sat beside her bed, already dressed in her morning *toilette*. That was acceptable.

Hülsen in Berlin was against the whole project. 'That's not the text for you! If I had the time, I would write you a genuinely German libretto.' By the hundredth performance he was won over: 'The text is first-rate, too, I agree.' He had also made some alterations, for the sake of the court's finer feelings: 'bed' became 'screen', 'a silly ass' became 'a dull dog', and 'a good dog on a good trail, and doubly keen after every hare' was transformed into 'a good wind for its weather-vane and doubly keen each time it veers' – which makes very little sense of any kind. Baron Ochs's monologue was shorn by two-thirds, and the rest was bowdlerized. In Vienna, London and elsewhere, the beds in the first and third acts had to remain unseen; otherwise the work would have been banned altogether. It is cause for gratitude that the censors were wholly unmusical: if they had had ears, neither *Feuersnot, Salome, Arabella, Der Rosenkavalier, Don Juan* nor the *Symphonia domestica* would ever have been performed at all. But the god Apollo has wrapped a spell of incomprehension around music.

Gone were the days of *Guntram*, when sets and costumes were brought out of store and dusted down. The best was now regarded as fitting for a Strauss premiere, and that was commissioned from the director of the Kunstgewerbeschule in Vienna, Alfred Roller, in whom stylistic flair, taste and imagination were combined with some practical experience of craftsmanship. Stage designs, painted in full colour, often look delightful on the page, but, once built, lose their enchantment and are all too patently made of papier-mâché. Roller had the gift of making his ideas real in the execution. Strauss and Hofmannsthal commissioned a prompt-book from him, with illustrations, diagrams of the sets and pictures of all the costumes. It was printed at Strauss's expense. All productions of *Der Rosenkavalier* were

Alfred Roller.

127

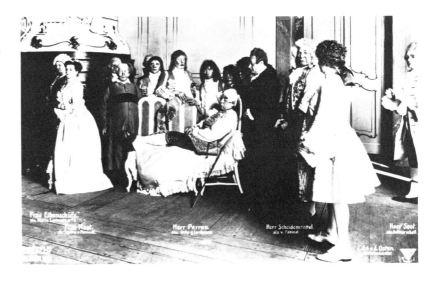

Der Rosenkavalier: A tableau representing a scene in Act II – although Sophie and Octavian have no business to be on stage as Ochs nurses his wound.

obliged to make use of Roller's designs, a condition intended to ensure quality and tie the hands of minnow talents. Art first: an opera ought to be produced as its creators intended.

The opera went into production in Dresden and it was quickly apparent that the whole enterprise was at risk from the inability of the chief resident producer, the worthy Professor Ernst Toller, to grasp what was required. Everything looked stiff and provincial. Strauss and Hofmannsthal had foreseen this possibility, and weeks earlier they had persuaded Max Reinhardt to hold himself in readiness. Due to an indiscretion, this reached the newspapers. Their backs to the wall, the authors insisted that Reinhardt, with his flair for comedy, must be engaged, while the Intendant, Seebach, was adamant in his defence of Toller. Finally, after Reinhardt had promised to work in secret and for no fee, he was permitted to come but with the proviso that he should not actually set foot on the stage.

At least Strauss was allowed on the stage, and so rehearsals were resumed with him doing his best to act out his idea of how scenes should be

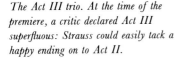

The Act III trio. At the time of the premiere, a critic declared Act III superfluous: Strauss could easily tack a happy ending on to Act II.

played. (It was something he liked doing, whenever he had the opportunity.) Reinhardt sat and watched, took individual singers aside and spoke to them in whispers. The next day, it was as if they had all been transformed. The magic had worked, as the Intendant was ready to admit. For three days, the doors of the theatre were locked, while Reinhardt rehearsed the cast intensively, and the comedy began to blossom. Nevertheless, Reinhardt's name did not appear on posters: that of the deeply offended Toller did.

The day of the premiere dawned, 26 January 1911. In the morning, Schuch was closeted with Strauss, discussing the performance, when Pauline sailed in, fired with the conviction that, at the fifty-ninth minute of the eleventh hour, nothing more would be achieved by discussion. 'You've talked enough, Richardl, come along with me to Prager Strasse, I must have something to put on my head.' Strauss rose without a word of protest, and went with his wife to Dresden's main shopping thoroughfare to give her the benefit of his advice. That evening she wore a spectacular gold turban: a victor's crown, in every sense.

Schuch ('a greatly talented conductor, but in other respects a very modest subaltern of a Kapellmeister', Strauss told Franz Schalk, 28 September 1921) was a victim, like many another conductor, of a mania for making cuts. There is an old theatrical saying: 'If it's cut, it can't fail.' (The composer Felix Draeseke had his own answer. As he once told Strauss: 'I've finished my new opera. All I have left to do is compose the cuts.') Schuch once went so far as to cut an entire act of d'Albert's *Tiefland*. His overriding motive was a concern for theatrical effectiveness. If an aria, however beautiful, held up the flow of the action, he would raise his voice from the pit and demand to know 'What's going on up there?'

Scarcely had Strauss left Dresden after the premiere when Schuch began to wield the scissors, meeting the composer's protests with the excuse that it was 'only eight minutes'. Angrily and contemptuously, Strauss asked him to consider cutting the eight minutes of the Act III trio, from 'Ich weiss nix – gar nix' ('I know nothing – nothing at all') to the beginning of the final duet. The trio, he pointed out, did absolutely nothing to advance the action, and a cut there would save time and bring the happy ending sooner. Schuch took umbrage. Abandoning the attempt to be jocular about the matter, Strauss turned to Count von Seebach, and complained bitterly about the damage caused by cuts in Ochs's narration in Act I and the ensuing trio, to choruses in Act II, and elsewhere. 'When I agreed to a few cuts after the premiere, I never imagined for one moment that anyone would undertake such totally impossible, absolutely unmusical amputation, involving the wholesale destruction of integrated musical structures. Yes indeed – amputation!' Seebach's stuffy, official answer made him even angrier. 'If he tries to mitigate artistic requirements with references to high box-office returns and substantial royalties, he only succeeds in revealing his utter lack of understanding of honourable artistic requirements.'

Like all artists, however, he would experience contempt and misunderstanding time and again. Perhaps Seebach's snub had some influence on the decision not to entrust the next opera, *Ariadne*, to Dresden.

The obscene new opera was not yet allowed to be seen in Berlin, so Berliners had to travel to Dresden for it. They went in such numbers that the Imperial Railways put on special trains. During the journey the opera-lovers studied the score with mounting horror. It's hard to imagine special trains being run for a new-music even nowadays.

Mounted on the ostrich ('Strauss' in German) is Ernst von Schuch.

'The Rosenkavaliers.' Hofmannsthal weaves the garland, and ducats pour out of Strauss's violin. The cartoonist appears to have disapproved of anyone earning money from their art.

Adolph Fürstner, Strauss's publisher.

The directors of theatres have little vision and prefer to put on works they know and such as they have observed to be successes elsewhere. If an artist does not keep on nagging them until they agree to meet his demands for the sake of peace, nothing will happen. Strauss therefore made it a condition that when a theatre wanted a new opera of his the others must also be revived. All his life he waged war against apathy with regard to the less popular works, pleading and bullying, so that *Die Frau ohne Schatten*, *Intermezzo* and *Helena* should not be forgotten in the shadow of *Der Rosenkavalier*. Repeatedly, he heard the same excuses: 'We haven't got a tenor, we haven't the soprano', and then he would have to make suggestions, and persevere in his bullying and pleading.

Those who sneered at 'money-grubbing Strauss' could see nothing more in this action than a determination to rake in even higher profits. They would not believe that no other course was open to him, that some works – and *Die Frau ohne Schatten* is a prime example – have to grow on the public: damned as unplayable and incomprehensible, such pieces need to be performed, and performed again, until understanding dawns.

The campaign mounted against Strauss in the press, encouraged by theatre managements and publishers, accused him of being insatiable in his greed for power and money. Hitherto contracts had covered only the publisher's fee for the hire of the parts, the standard ten per cent of box office receipts for the author(s), and the date of the first performance. Strauss wanted to be able to insist on a number of further provisions: a guarantee of a cast of singers of the first rank, at revivals as well as the premiere; a guarantee of high standards in design and production; a guarantee that a successful piece would not simply be exploited while it was new, not put on forty times in its first year, but – preferably – four times a year for ten years; the maintenance of standards in revivals, for the sake of young people just beginning to visit the theatre; a guarantee that problematical works would stay in the repertory for ten years, as well as the big successes. Arguably, all of these conditions were in the long-term interest of the theatre managements as well as the composer, but Strauss had to fight for every one against shortsightedness and lethargy. The model contracts he managed to get drawn up were eventually accepted even by the most recalcitrant and blinkered managements, and benefited all composers.

Until the 1940s, Strauss's publisher for many years had been the firm of Fürstner. The association went back to October 1890, when he had ordered a copy of *Rienzi* directly from them, and had received in return not only that but an enquiry from Adolph Fürstner about the possibility of publishing something of his. Strauss let him have the songs *Mädchenblumen* op. 22, for 800 marks, and before long Fürstner was his regular publisher. In time, he even bought the rights to those earlier works which had originally been issued under Eugen Spitzweg's imprint of Joseph Aibl. When Adolph Fürstner died in 1908, his son Otto took over the firm.

In 1930, in the world economic crisis, Fürstner could not afford to publish *Arabella*. Strauss published it himself, but allowed Fürstner to handle it on commission. He could have found another publisher – he was under no contractual obligation – but he preferred to stand by Fürstner.

Otto Fürstner had to emigrate, leaving Johannes Oertel and Strauss as assignees of his German business, a duty they conscientiously carried out. With the erasure of the Fürstner company from the German trade register during the Second World War, Otto sold what he could rescue to Boosey & Hawkes, where Strauss's affairs came into the hands of Dr Ernst Roth, another émigré. Roth had joined Boosey & Hawkes in 1938 and had commercial and personal dealings with Strauss in his last years.

'*The Rosenkavalier:* "*If my two lady-loves are not invited, then I shan't go either!*"'

> It was said that his commercial acumen far exceeded his musical genius. As his publisher I know more about it. Strauss had no business sense at all. His contracts were drafted by his lawyers and he trusted their advice implicitly. In investing his money he relied on the counsel of experts, which was not always good. His houses in Garmisch and Vienna were not speculative investments; he built them for himself and never parted with them.
>
> Since *Salome* he . . . sold his publishing rights for large sums and retained the performing and mechanical rights for himself, though not without allowing his publisher the usual share. . . . He did not bargain. 'If it is too much for you, don't do it and we shall remain good friends,' he used to say.
>
> He was invariably correct and reliable in all his dealings and had absolute confidence in his partners. It would never have crossed his mind to check accounts or to have them checked by accountants.

But, as Roth also reported, Strauss was far from naive:

The Press Ball, Munich, 1934. A 'statuette' of Oktavian, brought to life by the strains of the Rosenkavalier *Waltz, presents the silver rose to the conductor, Strauss.*

> In circumstances which [Strauss] had helped to create, his music earned big money for concert-promoters, opera-houses, conductors, producers and singers. His were box-office successes, and Strauss, who was no hypocrite, felt entitled to his fair share, said so and demanded it.

Thomas Mann knew Strauss. They had no particular sympathy towards each other. At one time Strauss had been a welcome guest at the house of Professor and Frau Pringsheim, whose daughter Katja married Mann in 1905. In his *Doktor Faustus* Mann described Strauss as the sort of person you might encounter at a skittle alley, who also happened to have talent. For his part, Strauss found Mann a 'boring patrician'.

Der Rosenkavalier was received so well in Berlin that even Wilhelm II was moved to go to it. He sent Strauss a message of congratulation, but is also reported to have said 'That's no music for me!' It was the only opera by Strauss that he ever heard.

After the Munich premiere of *Rosenkavalier*, Mann wrote to Hofmannsthal:

Strauss as the 'Cavalier of the Rose', a silhouette by W. Bitthorn.

> I read the published version of the text beforehand, with the most sincere delight in so much grace and delicacy. But what, in God's name, do you really feel about the way Strauss has loaded and stretched your

airy structure? A charming joke weighed down by four hours of din! Would that that were the only stylistic misapprehension! Where is Vienna, where is the eighteenth century in this music? Hardly in the waltzes. They are anachronistic, and put the stamp of operetta on the entire work. Would that it were one. But it is the most pretentious type of music drama – and, as Strauss has not the slightest understanding of Wagner's skill at not burying the declamation in the gigantic orchestra, not a word can be heard. All the thousand and one verbal delights and curiosities of the book are suppressed and swallowed up, and that is just as well as it turns out, because they are in clamant stylistic opposition to the sophisticated noise in which they are submerged, and which ought to have been twice as sophisticated, and only a fraction as loud. In short, I was thoroughly put out, and feel that Strauss has not treated your work as an artist should. Still, the success here was as colossal as it has been elsewhere. At the very end, after a full quarter of an hour's applause, when Strauss had taken perhaps a dozen bows, one enthusiastic student's voice was heard in the background calling 'Hofmannsthal!' *Where were you!* (5 February 1911)

It has to be said, as part of the explanation for Mann's reaction, that the performance was conducted by Mottl. That meant, as so often in the case of Toscanini, that the orchestra was loud enough to swamp the singers. But the inability of the two men to get on with each other only increased; in 1933 Strauss was one of those who signed the document protesting against Mann's address discussing Wagner in Freudian terms, because he was opposed to the psychological interpretation of Wagner.

Rosenkavalier's success was reflected in that year's carnival in Munich: nineteen Knights of the Rose, clad in silver silk, rode in the procession, followed by the two wailing figures of Salome and Electra, with, towering above them all, a weeping Richard Wagner, shaking his papier-mâché head over the new monarch of the operatic stage. In later years, *Rosenkavalier* brands of cigarettes and champagne went on sale. And theatres everywhere were eager to stage the work and profit from its sensational success.

Only a creative artist knows the concentration, the euphoria of invention, the persistent torment and the indescribable joy of creation. As for inspiration, it is beyond comprehension. Strauss, like most composers, was repeatedly asked about it, and he did his best to give an answer.

Where do the indescribable melodies of the great classical masters come from, for which there are no models? The sweeping, infinite melodies of Mozart. . . . You think it must be at an end, yet it continues on and on for ever! What is the immediate inspiration in such a case, and what has been worked out by the mind? It all appears to be one unmediated inspiration.

Melody is one of the most sublime gifts that an invisible Godhead has bestowed on mankind. The melodic idea which suddenly assails me, crops up without any external, sensual stimulus, or any internal emotion being present; it appears directly, unmediated, in my imagination, unawares, without the influence of the conscious mind.

Is the imagination perhaps an intensification of the conscious mind, the highest flowering of the soul? Is it seated in the brain? Does it work only after special impregnation by the blood? In my experience, the artistic imagination becomes especially active at times of great excitement, anger or annoyance – and not, as is often supposed, after receiving some sensual impression, from the beauty of nature, or in moods of great solemnity. On those occasions the translation into sound images is more likely to be worked out by the mind, that is, to be transferred, not immediate.

I am inclined almost to believe that there are chemical elements in the blood, which pass through certain nerves, or join up with certain parts of the brain, so as to produce the highest possible intensification in the activity of the spirit. There is ground for this belief in the fact that melodic ideas very often come in the morning at the moment of waking, when the brain, which has drained during the night, refills with fresh blood. Has my imagination been working independently in the night, without my consciousness knowing of it? Without being linked to a 'reminiscence' (Plato)? When I am composing in the evening and stick at a particular spot, and however much I rack my brains I cannot come upon any feasible way to continue, I shut my piano and my sketchbook, go to bed, and in the morning the continuation is there! What can the spiritual or physical process have been?

Unmediated, an idea for a motive, or a phrase two to four bars long, occurs to me. I put it down on paper, and go straight on to expand it into a phrase eight, sixteen or thirty-two bars in length, which of course does not remain unchanged. I work at this melodic shape for a long time.

How to shape melody is not taught with the requisite thoroughness at conservatories. In my view, it is the most important thing of all. The motive is a matter of inspiration, and most people are satisfied with that. But the way the initial idea unfolds is where true art is first revealed. How a melody begins is not what matters, but how it continues. Meyerbeer had brilliant opening bars, but then the brilliance fades. It's the same with Brahms: his melodies are not worked through to the end, but allow their wings to droop after the first bold flight.

Admittedly, if people do not feel the difference between melodies by Mozart and by Rossini, Schubert and Gounod, Johann Strauss and Lehár, if their spirits do not comprehend it, there is no way by which the 'problem' can be explained to them.

Building melodies is one of the hardest technical problems. I let them lie and wait until my imagination is ready to serve me further. It can take a long, or a very long, time. A melody that appears to have been born of the moment is almost always the product of wearisome labour, of long thinking during periods of idleness, or assisted by some excitement. Sometimes production flows very slowly, sometimes inspiration is there in a moment. It came in a moment when I was reading Arnim's poem *Der Stern*, and I wrote the song there and then.

I work in the summer, very coolly, without hurrying, without emotion, and slowly. Invention takes time, if it is to lead to something new and exciting. The greatest art in the inventive process is the art of waiting. Materials take shape the way beings do: slowly. I compose everywhere, taking a walk, driving, during meals, at home or in noisy hotels, in my garden, in railway carriages. My sketchbook never leaves me.

Thus Strauss strove to describe the genesis of the melodic nucleus. He did not attempt to analyse how he developed the musical variety, the metamorphosis of the themes, the variations, the great accumulations; he did not analyse the techniques of his work. That he left to others.

A young conductor told him that he had taken a year's leave to write his opera. 'What for?' cried Strauss. 'The day has 24 hours, 12 for one's duties, 8 for sleep, 2 for meals. That leaves you 2 hours every day for composition. With so much free time, why do you need any leave?'

Was composition really not work for him at all, but a pleasure for his free time? Between 1885 and 1911 he held full-time posts, as well as travelling a great deal to fulfil conducting engagements: in that period he nevertheless got as far as op. 59, including five operas. From 1911 he was a free agent, but had to go back under the yoke in 1918. Not until he was well over sixty could he live for his creative work alone, and go on to register op. 86.

For years he said, and Pauline repeated it in her own way, 'I shall conduct until I have one or two million put by, then I shall cry a halt'. The world about him shuddered. Alma and Gustav Mahler were incensed. Siegfried Wagner turned spiteful. 'There he goes again, nothing but money!'

'I should like to retire – to Italy, to Ceylon. I need warmth and the sun to compose!' That is a prayer which would be echoed by every person with something to give to the world: to be able to immerse oneself in one's work, in a warm climate, free of material worries, free of distractions, duties and interruptions. For Strauss it remained a prayer: during his final years as Kapellmeister in Berlin he was able to shed some of his routine duties; in 1911 he signed a new contract whereby he ceased to be director of the Court Opera, and became a guest conductor instead; but the volume of distractions remained the same. He had more conducting engagements involving him in more travel, and more socializing. War, revolution, inflation, the hectic pace of life in the 1920s, all took their toll. His dramatic *alter ego*, Hofmannsthal, died. And then came the Third Reich, presenting problems of a kind he had never experienced before, and putting his creativity in a straitjacket. If financial matters had long ceased to be a cause for concern, the world changed so much that the dream of living in the warm south, and devoting himself exclusively to composition was never realized.

'Ariadne'

Hofmannsthal often found Strauss's personality and his music less than wholly enchanting. After the successful launching of *Elektra* in 1909, he wrote to Harry Kessler:

> I hope I shall be able to exert a certain influence on him. In this unusual relationship, it is certainly my duty to guide him in a certain sense. For I have more understanding of art than he has, or perhaps it is a question of a more elevated, a better taste. He may well be my superior in energy or in actual talent, but that is beside the point.

After Strauss had played the first act of *Rosenkavalier* to him, he expressed his annoyance with the *fortissimo* accompanying Ochs's boast that the girls on his farm come to no harm – so long as there is some hay for them to fall back on when he grabs them ('Muss halt ein Heu in der Nähe dabei sein').

> Strauss is such an incredibly unrefined person, he has such a frightful bent towards triviality and kitsch. Everywhere else, the first act has much that is charming, witty and tuneful. An extraordinarily mixed character, but vulgarity rises as easily in him as ground-water. He's not going to kill it stone-dead, but it is going to be as far from Beardsley as a Bavarian cow is from dancing minuets.

While they were working on Act II, Strauss suggested a number of changes in the action:

> I was dismayed at first, but then I came more and more to accept them. The act has certainly gained a great deal from them, not just in the sense of theatrical effectiveness, but in every respect. I am very grateful to Strauss for this. Strauss seems to be extremely pleased with the new version and, given the accuracy of his instinct, I can be sure that it is essentially right.

Hofmannsthal's aesthetic reservations slowly weakened. Yet the two were too different ever to grow close. Much of their collaboration was conducted in letters. On his rare visits to Garmisch, Hofmannsthal did not stay in the villa as a rule, but in a hotel, and they met to discuss the work in hand at agreed times.

For all his pleasure at the success of the operas, Hofmannsthal never regarded the librettos as his chief literary achievement. He was aware that they made possible the happiest example of symbiosis between words and music in the entire history of music, but that was less important to him than his plays. Posterity has good reason to be grateful for the distance he and Strauss preserved, since their correspondence gives a fascinating and comprehensive picture of the collaboration. (And in 1945 Strauss admitted that 'he educated my often not wholly unexceptionable taste'.)

A talented cartoonist, one Enrico Caruso, depicted Strauss with Salome and Electra dangling at his waist and bearing a Rosenkavalier on a silver salver.

Max Reinhardt.

In 1911 the immediate question was: what should they do after *Rosenkavalier*? While the envious hoped for a flop, and admirers for some new surprise, neither party can have expected what they got: a chamber opera. It was Hofmannsthal, desiring to express gratitude to Max Reinhardt for his productions of his plays, who had the idea of creating the operatic divertissement which is ordered by Monsieur Jourdain in *Le bourgeois gentilhomme*, so that it could actually be inserted in a production of Molière's play.

Strauss hankered after another big opera: the idea of *Die Frau ohne Schatten* had already been conceived, and he had long been badgering Hofmannsthal for a text based on Calderón's *Semiramis*. (He never abandoned this idea, but neither Hofmannsthal nor, later, Josef Gregor gave him what he wanted.) But he agreed to do 'the little Molière piece'. 'Don't forget: I've still no work for the summer. Writing symphonies doesn't amuse me at all any longer.' (To be exact, the *Alpine* Symphony: 17 March 1911)

Hofmannsthal set himself to wrestle with questions of style, form, the effectuation of the transition from play to opera. He looked to Strauss for moral support: 'What's the matter with you? I get quite anxious when I do not hear from my *alter ego* for such a long time.' (27 June 1911) Strauss's reply was more bracing than tactful: 'Dear Poet. You are funny. You want to hear something from me! But I want to read something from you, and only then will you be able to "hear" something from me. Go write your poetry, please, and wait!' Hofmannsthal was hurt: 'Was I really so funny? Was it so hard for you to understand that I was waiting for some sign of life, for a simple word that you were back at Garmisch . . . that *you* – not just an empty writing desk – were there, ready and able to welcome what had been produced for you alone!' (5 July 1911)

It was not a good year for Hofmannsthal. He had to suffer incessant petty criticism of the 'immorality' of the text of *Rosenkavalier*, even Hermann Bahr failed to find it funny, and in every theatre where it was staged, it was disfigured by cuts. When the completed text of *Ariadne* reached Strauss, he showed it to friends who found it boring, and he hurt the poet's feelings by his own cool reaction. Nevertheless, he got on quickly with the composition while Hofmannsthal wrote him long letters endeavouring to put the text in a broader context. The music was finished by mid-December: the twenty minute intermezzo had grown into a ninety-minute one-act opera.

Pauline was strongly opposed to the idea that the work should have its premiere in Max Reinhardt's theatre in Berlin. In her view Reinhardt needed Strauss more than Strauss needed Reinhardt. 'Your things demand the best, the very best, people at every level, an elegant theatre with room to breathe in it, and good resources for sets and costumes. Producing this little opera in his place is mad. It's good enough for a Busoni, but not for Richard Strauss. Please listen to me, you will be grateful. I have always given you good advice!!'

Reinhardt's theatre was too small to accommodate an orchestra of thirty-six. The Cuvilliés-Theater in Munich was considered and rejected. Reinhardt had had bad experiences there with a 'band of evil businessmen and Strauss was against the very idea of a premiere in the city ('bloodthirsty critics, lukewarm public'). A new theatre had just been built in Stuttgart: was there a possibility of opening it with a guest production by the celebrated Reinhardt? Accompanied by his own company, his staff, and imported musicians and singers? The house was just the right size, and it went without saying that it would be a gala occasion. Strauss's old friend Max von Schillings was Intendant there, the King of Württemberg was delighted with the idea, so Stuttgart it was.

Famous singers can make the difference between the success and failure of a first performance of a new work, so they must be flattered and cajoled to undertake the labour of learning a new part. The thicker the butter is laid on, the better. Strauss wrote to Emmy Destinn:

Emmy Destinn, deaf to Strauss's eloquence.

Dear and honoured Fräulein!
Unforgettable, unsurpassable Salome!
I have written a new little opera, *Ariadne auf Naxos*, with a small chamber orchestra accompaniment. Duration one hour. Will you create Ariadne for us? A short, beautiful, lyrical role, only one big scene and aria, plus a beautiful, purely lyrical love-duet. Two performances, second half of October, before you go to America: the choice of the exact dates, between 10 and 25 October, is entirely yours. Eight days of rehearsals will suffice, the whole affair a matter of about ten days. You will learn the part in three. It is for you to command what fee you will! May I count upon you? I will not use flattery, but perhaps you already know that you've never had a greater admirer of your art than me. To hear you in a new role would be the fulfilment of my most sincere desires. (27 January 1912)

Alas, Destinn was deaf to his pleading, and the role was created by Maria Jeritza from Bohemia, then at the beginning of her international career, and still known by the good Austrian form of Maria: Mizzi. Her voice and her stage personality rapidly made her one of the outstanding interpreters of Straussian roles. She also sang the title parts at the first performances of both *Die Frau ohne Schatten* and *Die ägyptische Helena*. As Ariadne she was 'splendid. Unfortunately the woman has too beautiful a voice and too much talent. She hadn't the technique for the part, either musically or vocally, or in the phrasing.' (To Franz Schalk, 7 June 1916)

Departing from his usual practice, Strauss decided to conduct the premiere himself. Early in June he set off across country to Stuttgart, in his own car, with his chauffeur. 'Wonderful journey, no dust, magnificent roads, especially in Württemberg. During the drive I composed a march.' (To Pauline, 6 June 1912) Everything in Stuttgart pleased him: the theatre, the orchestra, the first rehearsals. 'It sounds splendid, beyond my expectations, more beautiful than anything I have written so far. A completely new style and new sound-worlds. . . . Am blissfully happy.'

Later on, the rehearsals turned into a theatrical nightmare of intrigue, noncooperation and discord. The Stuttgart actors and singers were offended by the number of stars imported from Berlin, leaving only minor

Maria Jeritza and Hermann Jadlowker as Ariadne and Bacchus.

One of Olaf Gulbransson's many caricatures of Strauss.

parts for the home company. The Swabian wardrobe and workshops were offended by the quantity of sets, props and costumes Reinhardt brought with him. Since the small orchestra required a player of soloist calibre at every desk, five strangers from Berlin sat among thirty-one Stuttgart players. They were all at loggerheads.

Schillings, who had been thought to be a friend, arranged for the dress rehearsal to take place at the same time as a performance of *Undine* in the adjoining main theatre, which meant that key figures – stage managers, technicians – were absent. Everything went wrong, chaos set in. Strauss flew into a rage and then had to apologize publicly to Schillings.

The premiere took place on 25 October 1912. In a bold theatrical experiment *Ariadne* was preceded by Molière's *Le bourgeois gentilhomme*, for which Strauss had also written incidental music, and which itself played for almost three hours. As Strauss recalled in 1949: 'Everything took rather a long time at the first performance. In addition, the dear King of Württemberg held a reception during the interval which went on for three quarters of an hour – while everyone was waiting for the opera by Strauss.' The evening lasted a full six hours.

The anti-Strauss camp declared that it was no *Rosenkavalier*. The doyen of the critics, Alfred Kerr, wrote:

An extraordinary evening. Just what this manifestation of Hofmannsthal's weaknesses amounts to, I am still unable to decide. As soon as
Molière ceases to speak and he begins, as soon as Ariadne begins to
operate, boredom sprouts all over the house; something horrendous.
This mixture of serious matter which is not serious with comic matter
which is not comic . . . esoteric and incompetent. Unmitigated disaster.
Meanwhile, in another part of the wood, a score by Richard Strauss

Ariadne auf Naxos in Munich. The 'commedia dell'arte' troupe, with Hermine Bosetti as Zerbinetta.

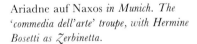

138

goes its own way, whispering, rattling, skipping, whistling, cajoling, humming, shrieking, smiling and wailing like – like something by a Mozart who has studied the warp and woof of *Meistersinger* – and Leo Fall [the composer of *The Dollar Princess*].

There was no disguising the fact: in this form, *Ariadne* was a failure. It made the audience yawn. The authors had not appreciated two things: the opera-going public is not interested in Molière, or in a literary idea like the transition from prose to the heights of music; further, theatres which are both opera houses and playhouses have to involve all their forces in the one performance, and employ both teams in return for only one lot of ticket sales, while opera houses have to go to the expense of engaging actors. It is simply impracticable, it has rarely been given and only with many cuts.

Ariadne (Mizzi Jeritza) and Zerbinetta (Margarethe Siems). These singers created the roles in Stuttgart in 1912.

With heavy hearts (Strauss, for one, never liked going back to a work he considered finished) the authors decided to separate the two elements: the play was to be provided with music, and the opera should be a full-scale opera for the opera house. The prologue for the new version already existed in prose. In the revision, Hofmannsthal made more of the figure of the idealistic composer who is driven to despair as he learns of the ways of the theatre. Strauss's friend, and colleague at the Berlin Opera, Leo Blech, thought that it was surely another breeches-role, and Strauss exulted at the prospect of a new Oktavian. Hofmannsthal had doubts, but allowed himself to be persuaded by the consideration that the tenor and leading baritone were already needed for Bacchus and Harlequin, while every theatre had a good mezzo-soprano, for whom there was as yet no part written. What Strauss did not explain to him was that no tenor could embody, with so little corporeality, the poetic unreality of this idealistic and ideal figure with his credo of music as the sacred art.

The revised *Ariadne* was composed in 1916. The new Prologue was a masterpiece of humour, irony, poetry and feeling. Many connoisseurs regard it as the finest thing Strauss ever wrote. He wrote to Franz Schalk in June 1916 'It includes that *secco* recitative in strict rhythm that has been so much feared since *Lohengrin*, and that no King Henry in the world has ever learned to sing properly. Donkey that I am, I am giving it a second try. In the first place to revenge Wagner, and in the second place, probably, to fret myself half to death over it in my turn.' In the opera proper, as it now follows the Prologue, substantial passages from the original version were discarded. The revised version of Zerbinetta's aria is certainly more integrated; the first version was more original, a whole tone higher in some places, and more difficult. (Hofmannsthal never learned to like this number, regarding it as a bravura exhibition which threatened to disrupt the unity of the work.) The long ensemble before Bacchus's entrance had provided a hymnic preparation for the awakening of love in Ariadne. The revision, with some cutting, leaves the rhythmically turbulent B flat major passage (at Fig. 274), hanging motivically in the air. Previously the motivic material had returned several times, and more identifiably each time, like the principal theme in *Tod und Verklärung*. The ironic conclusion led back to the prologue, and it was more original than the ecstatic hymn we now have.

An Ostrich, misquoting 'Töne, töne, süsse Stimme', lays an egg, from which Zerbinetta emerges. It is a mystery why it was seen fit to give the title 'Noise Contest' to a cartoon about Strauss's quietest opera.

The new version of *Ariadne*, first performed in Vienna on 4 October 1916, was a success, and it remains so. In 1937 a new production was put on in the Cuvilliés-Theater in Munich, and Strauss attended the dress rehearsal. Hans Hotter recalls that when it was over, 'I saw him come out of the box. Not realizing that anyone was watching him, he stretched, shook his head and said to himself: "To think I once wrote like that . . .". I don't know how he meant it. Ironically? Pleased?'

Der Bürger als Edelmann, Hofmannsthal's adaptation of Molière's play with the suite of short, graceful pieces which Strauss wrote for it, is a *bonbonnière* of artistic delights, but has never been as successful as the two-act *Ariadne*. At the end, instead of the opera, there is an ironic 'Turkish ceremony', and Strauss did it proud.

> I worked into it themes by Lully, who wrote the original music for *Le bourgeois gentilhomme*. The play can always make me laugh. When Jourdain says ' "Nicole, bring me my slippers", what is that?' – 'That is prose, Monsieur Jourdain.' – 'Then I have been taking prose all my life, and never knew it!'

He made these remarks in an interview in 1949 (which included the recollections, already quoted, of the first *Ariadne* premiere), not long before he attended a theatre for the last time in his life: for a performance of *Der Bürger als Edelmann* in the Gärtnerplatztheater in Munich.

The End of an Epoch

Berlin played host to royalty from all over Europe in 1913. Complete harmony and understanding reigned among them. The very idea of war was pooh-poohed. Parties all the way across the political spectrum had founded peace organizations. War had been outlawed; but armies and battle-fleets were in an ever-increasing state of readiness.

While *Die Frau ohne Schatten* waited, Strauss and Hofmannsthal undertook another project. Diaghilev and the Ballets Russes were the talk of Europe, introducing new forms of dance, to modern music, with sets and costumes of dazzling artifice and uncompresing modernity. Hofmannsthal and Kessler, aesthetes both, were fascinated recruits to the Diaghilev circle, and in 1912 they wrote a libretto for Strauss: *Die Josephslegende*. Strauss accepted the idea with characteristic laconicism. '*Joseph* is excellent: I'll bite! Have already started sketching it out.' (2 July 1912) Some weeks later: 'The chaste Joseph himself isn't at all up my street, and if a thing bores me I find it difficult to set it to music. This God-seeker Joseph – he's going to be a hell of an effort! Well, maybe there's a pious tune for good boy Joseph lying about in some atavistic recess of my appendix.' (11 September 1912)

One of the brilliant caricatures of Strauss by Olaf Gulbransson, published in Simplicissimus. *Strauss enjoyed reading Munich's famous satirical magazine, but his brother-in-law Otto Rauchenberger, as a military man, strongly disapproved of it.*

Hofmannsthal waxed eloquent for several humourless pages to expound Joseph's character and dramatic function. In an old sketchbook (no. 19) Strauss found something he had given the title 'Dance Legend', and he also discovered that a large quantity of material that he had originally sketched for *Kythere*, a pantomime of his own devising, inspired by the paintings of Watteau and Fragonard, could be put to use in the ballet. He still found it hard work, as he discarded and condensed. When it was finished, Fokine, the choreographer, and the dancers were a little nonplussed by the gigantic score: accustomed to the motoric rhythms and sharply defined orchestrations of Stravinsky, they felt all at sea in the surging billows of Strauss's sound-world.

Hofmannsthal had had Nijinsky in mind for the role of Joseph, but Diaghilev had cast him off in 1913, because of his marriage; in consequence Fokine had given notice, and the company threatened to break up. But Fokine returned after a year and Diaghilev had found a new leading male dancer: Leonide Massine.

Nijinsky went to America and founded his own company. One of the ballets he created, taking the title role himself, was *Till Eulenspiegel*; it is said to have been a most original and skilful realization, but unfortunately the choreography was lost.

Die Josephslegende was performed for the first time in Paris on 14 May 1914, with Massine in the title role and Marie Kuznetsov as Potiphar's Wife. It was a long programme, beginning with *Papillons*, a thirty-minute orchestral version of Schumann's piece, conducted by Monteux. The Strauss followed, conducted by the composer and lasting an hour. The last work was *Sheherazade*, another hour of music, under Monteux. It appears to have been an exhilarating success, with Strauss and Hofmannsthal taking ten curtain calls, although some derisory whistles were heard in the midst of the applause. Gabriele d'Annunzio was among the whistlers: he had sent Strauss an emphatic telegram, offering to write him a libretto, and had received a polite but cool refusal.

The role of Potiphar's Wife attracted singers like Marie Gutheil-Schoder and actresses like Tilla Durieux, the *femme fatale* of Reinhardt's company, as well as dancers. Karsavina danced it in London before 1914 was out:

> After the rehearsal Strauss came to my dressing-room and in great seriousness suggested a change to me; to show me what he meant, he started to sing the music, went over into the corner and shuffled through the passage, coming diagonally across the room towards the sofa, which represented Joseph. But I could see what he wanted, and I did it, to his satisfaction, I think.

The outbreak of war prevented the ballet becoming more widely known, but in the 1920s the public was again ready for music of such a hymnic radiance; there are some magnificent moments in the score, such as the scene in which Joseph sinks into sleep.

Leonid Massine as Joseph.

Tilla Durieux, painted by Renoir in 1914. Her first husband was the painter Eugen Spiro, her second the art-dealer Paul Cassirer, who shot himself on her account. She died in 1972, at the age of 93.

Igor Stravinsky.

First night of *Josephslegende* under Strauss. Enormous, almost unprecedented success. The audience was really *tout Berlin* – the Reichskanzler . . . numerous ministers, the outstanding figures in society, art and literature, Albert Einstein, and so on, and so on. The applause would not stop. We had to appear on the stage again and again. Durieux beyond praise. (Harry Kessler's diary, 4 February 1921)

The relationship between Strauss and Stravinsky, however, was one of mutual antipathy. The latter told Robert Craft:

I would like to admit all Strauss operas to whichever purgatory punishes triumphant banality. Their musical substance is cheap and poor; it cannot interest a musician today. I cannot bear Strauss's six-four chords: *Ariadne* makes me want to scream. Strauss himself? I had the opportunity to observe him closely during Diaghilev's production of his *Legend of Joseph*, more closely than at any other time. . . . He never wanted to talk German with me, though my German was better than his French. He was very tall, bald and energetic, a picture of the *bourgeois allemand*. I watched him at rehearsals and I admired the way he conducted. His manner towards the orchestra was not admirable, however, and the musicians heartily detested him; but every corrective remark he made was exact: his ears and his musicianship were impregnable. At that time his music reminded me of Böcklin and Stuck, and the other painters of what we then called the German Green Horrors. I am glad that young musicians today have come to appreciate the lyric gift in the songs of the composer Strauss despised, and who is more significant in our music than he is: Gustav Mahler. My low esteem for Strauss's operas is somewhat compensated by my admiration of von Hofmannsthal.

Arnold Schoenberg.

During that period in Paris, in 1914, Stravinsky showed Strauss some of his scores. The latter commented: 'Very fine, but why do you put so many wrong notes in? Basically it's all built on simple triads.' That was one remark unlikely to please Stravinsky. Then he heard of the crack attributed to Strauss, concerning *Le sacre du printemps*: 'More like a *sacrilège du printemps*.' A further source of annoyance to him was the homage paid to Strauss on the occasion of the first Donaueschingen Festival in 1923. And there was another matter: Stravinsky was as interested in earning money as Strauss, as his *Autobiography* makes perfectly clear. Strauss was earning much more than Stravinsky, however, and it is not inconceivable that some of Stravinsky's animus stemmed from that fact. In any case, it is far from uncommon for great contemporaries to have a low opinion of each other. 'If he [Stravinsky] finds a public for his efforts,' declared Strauss,

then the best of luck to him! It is perfectly true that mathematics is one of the fundamental elements of music – but it is not the only one, any more than drawing is the only element in painting. But let's not waste breath chattering about theory, the great masters of the past didn't. Let us get on with our work in silence.

Between Strauss and Schoenberg things started well, then deteriorated. Strauss was a generous champion of his colleagues, including those whose artistic opinions he did not share. Schoenberg, his junior by ten years, had had lessons from his brother-in-law Alexander Zemlinsky and early compositions like *Gurrelieder* show him apparently following in the footsteps of Wagner and Strauss. Then he adopted the twelve-note theory, and went beyond the threshold of what the contemporary public could take in aurally. In 1901 Strauss helped him to obtain a post teaching music theory in Berlin.

I called on Direktor Holländer today: he promised me to take the greatest care of you. He will arrange for you to start taking a small class at once, so that you will at least be able to call yourself a teacher at the Stern Conservatory. . . . If you are in serious need, make a written request for support to me, as president of the Allgemeiner Deutscher Musikverein . . . So, best of luck!

In 1903, Schoenberg was once again without paid employment. Mahler helped him, until he had to leave Vienna. In 1909 Schoenberg, by then thirty-five, sent Strauss his Five Orchestral Pieces op. 16, an early example of atonal composition:

I hope you will show these pieces the kindness that you have so often bestowed on me. . . . The usual run of conductors have no idea what to do with them. It has to be the best or nothing. And, abstruse though my things may perhaps appear to someone who does not believe in this style – I hope they will make sufficient impression on you to persuade you to perform them. It would be the utmost help to me. In Vienna, you see, I am at daggers drawn with practically everybody and everything. I can only be pleasant to those I respect, and therefore I have few friends in Vienna.

Strauss had to refuse the request: 'You know that I like to help, and I have the necessary courage. But your pieces are such daring experiments in both content and sound that for the time being I cannot take the risk of presenting them to my ultra-conservative Berlin public.' As well as giving advice, Strauss made a donation of 100 marks to a fund set up to support Schoenberg (at that date a four-course dinner cost 1 mark). Twice, Schoenberg was awarded a Liszt Foundation bursary on Strauss's recommendation, and as a trustee of the Mahler Foundation, Strauss supported the payment of grants to Schoenberg in 1913, 1914 and 1918. It was also Strauss who recommended Maeterlinck's *Pelléas et Mélisande* to him in 1902; Schoenberg cannot have known of Debussy's opera when he began his symphonic poem on the same subject.

Cartoonists never tired of the fact that 'Strauss' means 'ostrich'.

But it was in connection with his Mahler Foundation trusteeship that Strauss was rash enough to express his private opinion of Schoenberg in colourful language. The actual mischief was done by Alma Mahler who, with her customary tactlessness, passed it on to Schoenberg. How he felt about it was revealed when he replied to a newspaper which had invited him to write something on the occasion of Strauss's fiftieth birthday in 1914.

Unhappily I cannot meet your request. Herr Strauss wrote the following about me in a letter to Frau Mahler: 'Only an alienist can help poor Schoenberg now. I think he would do better to shovel snow than scribble on music paper.' I fancy that the view which, after remarks of that nature, not I alone but anybody at all can have of Herr Strauss's personality as a human being (i.e. envy of a 'rival') and as an artist (i.e. the 'song-theme-like' banality) is not appropriate for proclamation to the world in celebration of his fiftieth birthday. It is not my intention to

1914: Strauss in Oxford, where he received an honorary doctorate. The photo is a rarity in that it shows Strauss wearing a long tie.

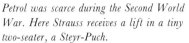

Franz takes the wheel for a family excursion. Richard Strauss drove only once, ending up in a heap of gravel. 'I was thinking of something else.'

Petrol was scarce during the Second World War. Here Strauss receives a lift in a tiny two-seater, a Steyr-Puch.

1939.

cast 'moral' aspersions upon Herr Strauss. As an artist he does not interest me at all nowadays, and as for what I may have learned from him in the past, I thank God that I misunderstood it.

Reconciliation was impossible. Though the differences between Strauss and Schoenberg eventually engendered personal hostility they had no effect whatever on the course of musical history.

Strauss had no interest in technology as such, though he was ready to make use of such practical advantages as it brought: electric lighting, the telephone, central heating. He considered installing a domestic telegraph in the villa in Garmisch. There was a gramophone in the house, although he had no faith in the future of the gramophone record. Radio interested him even less. Occasionally he listened to news bulletins during the war, on a tiny, primitive apparatus. The only time he entered a cinema was to see a film about the 1936 Olympic Games, which featured his *Olympic Hymn*.

He found the motor car convenient for professional travel, and enjoyed rides for pleasure in an open car in good weather. He gave Hofmannsthal a lift to Rome and back in April 1913, which gave them the opportunity to

Die Frau ohne Schatten: *costume designs by Alfred Roller for the Dyer and his wife*.

discuss *Die Frau ohne Schatten* uninterrupted. Owning a car in those days meant employing a chauffeur who was also a competent mechanic and equipping one's own garage as a repair workshop. (Strauss's diary for 1907 has a note concerning a lathe and an anvil for the 'Carrage'.) On journeys, tools and a full range of spare parts had to be carried, spare tyres and cans of petrol were stacked on the running boards, and the luggage was strapped on the back. Some models, still looking back to the horse-drawn carriage, had two sets of coachwork – one for summer, one for winter.

Hofmannsthal had had the first idea for what became *Die Frau ohne Schatten* only one month after the premiere of *Rosenkavalier*, on 26 February 1911, and mentioned it to Strauss in a letter three weeks later with the note that 'for one of the women your wife might well, in all discretion, be taken as a model'. He told him more about it a fortnight later in Vienna, and Strauss lost no time in writing to Pauline in great excitement:

> Hofmannsthal has just left, after disclosing a wonderful new subject, the most beautiful thing imaginable, noble and fantastic. You will be enchanted. He is a wonderful fellow, knows exactly what he wants, what will suit the present day, what I need: head full of poetry and ideas, there's no one to match him! You shall see! There is no need for you to worry about the portrait of yourself: he has adopted a few very general features, culled from fleeting remarks I have passed, with happy results. You have no grounds to fear that anyone will recognize anything of you in it. In any case, your wish is our command. But where else is the poet to seek his inspiration, if not in real life? It is a pure, very noble, fairytale subject with symbolism (at a distance, a little like *Die Zauberflöte*, for which Goethe wrote a sequel, as everyone knows). No direct similarity of course, just the same genre overall, but much more significant and profound. We're on the right path, believe me; Hofmannsthal has learnt an enormous amount from *Rosenkavalier*, and understands me and my needs as no one else does.

Like the Hero's Companion in *Ein Heldenleben*, the earthborn, impetuous yet unselfconfident, and beautiful Dyer's Wife does indeed display, musically, some of the character-traits of Pauline Strauss.

Convinced that the work would only benefit from not being hurried, Hofmannsthal put the project on one side to ripen 'beyond the threshold of consciousness', while he got on with writing the first version of *Ariadne* and the libretto of *Die Josephslegende*, and Strauss with the *Alpine* Symphony; he was confident that '*die FroSch*', as he later called it, would be worth waiting for.

In January 1913 Hofmannsthal felt that the right moment had come, and set to work. Since they both had appointments in Italy in April that year, Strauss suggested that they should seize the opportunity to travel together, in the privacy of his car, and discuss the new opera at length. They made a rendezvous in Verona on 29 March, and drove, via Rimini, Urbino, Perugia and Orvieto, to Rome, where Strauss conducted two concerts, then returned to Garmisch via Parma, Brescia and Trent. They rode with the roof down, wrapped in travelling rugs. Hofmannsthal proved a civilized and considerate companion. The conversations about *Die FroSch* were highly beneficial, and by the time they reached Rome Hofmannsthal had every step in the action planned. It was while driving by moonlight from San Michele to Bolzano that Strauss had the idea of accompanying the world of the mortals with full orchestra, and that of the immortals with the chamber orchestra of *Ariadne*. This beautiful idea was only partly realized.

Hofmannsthal retreated from the world, in order to undergo the travail of mastering his material. It was very nearly a year before the text of Act I was ready, at the beginning of April 1914. The music took three months. Strauss received the text of Act II in the middle of June, and spent another three months, July to October, on that. His son Franz recalled:

> I shared the experience of the composition as a listener, because he wrote a lot of this opera at the piano, and always played every new instalment to us. I can still remember exactly how the Watchmen's call at the end of Act I came into being. It was evening, I was already in bed, and I heard the music rising from below. He played it with such rapt emotion – I have never heard it performed more beautifully since.

Meanwhile, a world war had broken out. Exultantly, Europe prepared to do battle.

World War I

The four weeks following the assassination of Archduke Franz Ferdinand at Sarajevo on 28 June 1914 were marked by diplomatic chaos and the raising of emotions to fever pitch. The several declarations of war between the European nations started on 27 July. Artists and men of letters were fired with enthusiasm and shouted 'Gott straf England' – and the Tsar and the old enemy France – as lustily as anyone. Max Reger was depressed by his unfitness for military service, Thomas Mann wanted to fight, and Hofmannsthal, who had joined the dragoons as a volunteer in 1895, was called up, at the age of forty, even before Austria had declared war and was sent to Pisino in Istria as an officer with the territorial reserves. He wrote Act III of *Die Frau ohne Schatten* in uniform, and was posted to Cracow in 1915, but after two months, poor eyesight was made the excuse for releasing him to become the editor of a series to be called the 'Austrian Library'. Somewhere, somebody had discovered that there was a better use for artists than putting them in the trenches.

The Strauss family were in the Dolomites when Germany joined the war on 1 August, and struggled home to Garmisch over a Brenner Pass

The whole of history is almost entirely an unbroken chain of acts of stupidity and wickedness, every sort of baseness, greed, betrayal, murder and destruction. And how little those who are called to make history have learned from it!

STRAUSS, MEMORANDUM, 1947

The beloved son.

Richard keeps good hold of both his son and Tuy.

The caption in the family album is 'Toothache'.

choked with Austrian troop transports. Strauss did not join in the public patriotic chorus. In private, he wrote at the end of Act I of the short score of *Die Frau ohne Schatten*: 'Completed 20 August 1914, the day of the victory at Saarburg. Hail to our brave troops. Hail to our great German fatherland.' That was all – and the war was then only twenty days old. Richard Specht's claim that Strauss's paean to motherhood in *Die Frau ohne Schatten* was a contribution to the war effort borders on the ridiculous. In any case the composer's attitude soon changed. Writing to Max Reger after fifty-eight days, during which one victory after another had been announced, he wrote:

> Of course it will give me great pleasure to arrange for the first performance of your *Patriotic Overture* to take place under your direction. What Beethoven symphony would you like to share the programme?
>
> To think that the Duke of Meiningen has thrown out his old and famous orchestra on to the street: whoever heard of such a thing – *that* is German vandalism! How are we innocent citizens to summon up enthusiasm for all the fearful sacrifices this war demands of us, if the Kaiser's own sister sets an example like that!

In other words, he was quite happy to promote the performance of heroic music such as Beethoven's symphonies, coupled with an overture which ends by combining 'Deutschland über alles' contrapuntally with *Die Wacht am Rhein*, 'Nun danket alle Gott' and 'Ich hab mich ergeben'. On the other hand he began to wonder if a country which could stand by unmoved while a cultural institution was disbanded was worth fighting for.

At the age of seventeen, Strauss's son Franz volunteered for military service, an idealist eager to serve his country and win, if need be, a hero's death. Strauss suppressed his own feelings about heroic death when he wrote to comfort Franz about the army's rejection of him:

> It is a quite unexpected stroke of luck for you and for us that as a consequence of your slow physical development you will be spared from risking life and limb in this dreadful war – although I know that it is against your honourable and courageous will. Now, it is to be hoped, you will feel a double spur as you strike out along the path which leads by way of scientific study of the fine arts to a noble cultural end, to cultivate yourself ever more diligently and to become an effective labourer of the intellect and the spirit, even if you have been denied the opportunity to render your fatherland the service of the body. (22 November 1915)

It was an attempt to show the young idealist that there was a good side to his rejection, guardedly expressed so as not to offend the boy's sincere patriotic feelings.

There can be no doubt that Strauss, too, honestly loved his country; at the same time his horizons were international. The world of music is international. When he was fêted in other countries he always regarded it a a triumph for German music. When he visited America after the First World War, and London after the Second, and people rose to their feet to applaud him as he entered the concert hall – people to whom only a short time before the 'Hun' had been an enemy – he felt that it signified the triumph of art over politics. He saw himself as an ambassador of the German tradition which had given the world Mozart, Beethoven, Wagner and Bach.

At a time when men were dying in their thousands as huge armies fought backwards and forwards over the same few square miles of ground, and when civilians, too, hundreds of miles from the battle fronts, were suffering shortages of food and other necessities of daily life, Strauss composed the third act of his mythic opera of motherhood and love, of mortals and immortals. '*Die Frau ohne Schatten*, this child of sorrow, was finished during the war amidst cares and worries [which] left their mark on the score, especially towards the middle of the third act, in the form of a certain nervous overexcitedness which finally expressed itself in melodrama.' At the point to which Strauss refers, the Empress ceases to sing and in a speaking voice gives expression to the remorse and desperation she feels at the sight of her husband, who has been turned to stone, while the orchestral accompaniment answers her. Singers and conductors do not like it and always cut as much of the passage as they can, for their appreciation of dramatic construction and stylistic effect is seldom as strong as their sense of vocal beauty. It is seldom, too, that they do justice to the sensitivity of Strauss's rapid, rhythmically meticulous *secco* recitative, accompanied by solo instruments, in the Nurse's *scena*, for example. Such passages are all too often bawled.

The full score was finished in June 1917, though the autograph is undated. There was no prospect of a performance while the war continued. Too many musicians were at the front, and resources could not have been diverted to the provision of the sets and costumes of what was Strauss's biggest and most difficult opera to date.

The theatres kept open, however, and concerts were still given. Strauss travelled about Germany and to such neutral countries as Holland and Switzerland. Travel was not as pleasant as it had been before the war, of course.

My darling! What a grind! I'm not one to complain, but eight hours from Berlin to Bielefeld [about 250 miles] in an unheated train – that came close to getting even me down. No restaurant car, nothing hot to eat or drink. There is only one train from Cologne to Aachen on a Sunday: packed, of course, and 1½ hours late. What made it worse is that the war is so eerily close along that stretch of line. Trains full of the wounded, trains loaded with whole fleets of aircraft or with ambulances that have been shot to pieces – appalling! I hope the war will be over soon: enormous numbers of troops are moving up to the western front, and they say that the French front line is already very 'jittery'. (To Pauline, 9 December 1917)

Outside the Hotel Adlon in Berlin: father and son with Marie Gutheil-Schoder, a celebrated Oktavian.

Even during the war, artists could still travel to neutral countries. The Hague, 8 November 1917: a careworn Strauss with Marie Gutheil-Schoder and the tenor Leo Slezak.

There were domestic problems, too, and he had occasion to write a letter of complaint to the regional government offices in Garmisch:

> My lightning conductor has been removed and replaced by an inferior one on the orders of the regional authority. As must be self-evident, if the state forcibly requisitions the citizen's property in this way, the state should also bear the costs that the citizen incurs as a result. I therefore enclose the bill I have received, to be forwarded, if the regional authority sees fit, to the Imperial Office of Metal Collection, as I have no intention of paying it myself.
> Your obedient servant,
> Dr Richard Strauss,
> Royal Prussian General Musical Director. (6 June 1918)

There is little sign there of any readiness to make sacrifices, or of any enthusiasm for a war that still had five months to run. The requisitioning of materials needed for the war effort, copper in this case, was still almost unknown at that date, which makes Strauss's indignation the more understandable. The matter was referred to Munich, whence came a reply citing Paragraph III, Section 2, of the Ministerial Resolution which had ordained that, in short, even the Royal Prussian General Musical Director had to pay for his inferior new lightning conductor.

Even while he laboured at *Die Frau ohne Schatten*, Strauss was starting to think about his next opera. This one would be worlds away from myth, ancient Greece or heroic drama. It would be concerned with some everyday subject in the modern world, there would be a telephone on the stage, characters would send telegrams and travel in express trains. He yearned for something to lighten the darkness of the times.

It was years since he had written any songs. One reason was that since Pauline's retirement from the concert platform in 1905 he no longer had the incentive of writing for her. There was, however, another reason.

He had not been on the best of terms with the publishing fraternity since his campaign to reform the copyright laws. When he sold the *Symphonia domestica* to Bote & Bock of Berlin in 1903, the contract gave them an option on his next collection of songs. Busy as he was with the composition of operas, Strauss failed to produce any songs, until Bote & Bock began to press him. Strauss tried in vain to get out of the contract: whatever their views on the subject of musical copyrights, Bote & Bock were only too willing to share the rewards of a composer's success.

In the end he thought of a way of extricating himself from that tiresome contract. Alfred Kerr, the most prominent of Berlin's theatre critics, wrote him a set of verses lampooning every music publisher unfortunate enough to possess a name which lent itself to this usage. Knowledge of the circumstances is necessary to an understanding of the texts and all their allusions but although they gave a new meaning to the expression 'occasional pieces' the music Strauss wrote for them is wholly delightful. *Der Krämerspiegel* (*The Shopkeeper's Mirror*) overflows with sparkle, fun, irony

Alfred Kerr.

150

humour and things that are simply impossible by any norms of song-writing. Four lines of text are decked out with piano preludes and postludes by the yard. The Drei-Masken Verlag is honoured with a dry-as-dust fugue which topples over into a skittish polka when its director's name is reached at the end. Much use is made of quotations from Strauss's own and other composers' works. There is one wonderful, lyrical theme to which he returned years later. Great dramatic climaxes swell and swell – and burst into waltzes. The rapid alternation of contrasting moods is as exhilarating as anything he ever wrote. The formal and technical excellence of these songs is as great as their composer's evident glee, and thanks to it their listeners can enjoy the joke as much as he did.

Offered the option of twelve such fine songs, in accordance with a contract that stipulated only six, both Bote and Bock indignantly refused them and proceeded to sue Strauss for breach of contract. The law proved as Prussian and as deficient in a sense of humour as the publishers and, with all the solemnity appropriate to a deal involving millions of marks' worth of cotton, Strauss was ordered to supply 'proper songs'. The case is a monument to the institutions of German justice, continuing in their stately process even as the German Empire crumbled, an epoch in human history ended in flames, and civil war, profiteering, starvation, a continent-wide influenza epidemic and the collapse of civil order lay about on every side.

So Strauss wrote six 'proper songs', his op. 67. The texts he chose were unimpeachable: Ophelia's three songs from *Hamlet*, and three poems from the 'Book of Ill Humour' from Goethe's *West-östlicher Divan*. Each of these last is progressively more stiff-necked in expressing contempt for 'the world' and its invariable failure to appreciate any point of importance. All six are set in a style of outstanding technical virtuosity, harmonically abstruse, tortuous and inaccessible: the direct opposite of the elegance and humour of *Der Krämerspiegel*. Bote & Bock found them hard to sell.

As for *Der Krämerspiegel*, the music-publishing establishment closed ranks and refused to touch it, and would have been happy to see the public prosecutor condemn it as an obscene article. But in 1921 it was accepted by an outsider with a sense of humour, Paul Cassirer, the husband of Tilla Durieux, who ran a private press specializing in contemporary painting and graphic art. He published *Der Krämerspiegel* in a limited edition of 120 numbered and signed copies, printed on handmade paper and illustrated with lithographs by Michael Fingesten. The title page depicts Strauss mounted on a winged horse, crossing a high wire beneath a blazing sun. Monkeys are shown climbing the posts supporting the wire and between them a hand holds up a mirror which reflects a distorted and rather threatening face.

Strauss warned Alfred Kerr to keep the edition a secret, in the interests of allowing it to be sold out before the music publishers could demand its confiscation. Frustrated in that move, the publishers actually succeeded in obtaining an injunction forbidding the songs to be performed in public, and this remained in force until after the Second World War. Alas for the music publishers! After thirty years of fear and trembling at what they conceived as a threat to their reputations, they suddenly discovered that it was a

The title page of the first, private edition of Der Krämerspiegel.

151

1949. Strauss conducts the 'Moonlight' interlude from Capriccio *in the studio of Munich Radio.*

superb advertisement for them. After a radio broadcast of a selection of the songs, some publishers complained because 'their' songs had been omitted.

Clemens Krauss loved *Der Krämerspiegel* and when he was writing the libretto of *Capriccio* he drew Strauss's attention to the marvellous melody in two of the songs ('Von Händlern wird die Kunst bedroht' and. 'O Schröpferschwarm, o Händlerkreis', in which the composer of, respectively, *Tod und Verklärung* and *Till Eulenspiegel* shakes his fist at the 'tradesmen'). Strauss had forgotten the tune: he never looked at finished works. He got the music out and his son Franz supported Krauss: 'Such a beautiful melody, it's a shame to leave it there.' So it was included in the opera, in the noble and lyrical orchestral interlude, a portrayal of moonlight, prefacing the final scene. This interlude was the last piece of music Strauss conducted, in 1949, in the main studio of Munich Radio, for the short film that was made about him in the last months of his life.

That's what happens when a genius makes a joke.

The war drew to its close. Nine days before Kaiser Wilhelm fled to Holland, Strauss was in Coburg to fulfil an engagement.

My best beloved! Things are starting to be really desolate. The war is over, definitely over! But what is to come may be worse.

After a 12-hour journey I had a rehearsal of two acts of *Rosenkavalier* this morning, with new sets. The King of Bulgaria [a refugee by this time] and the Duke were present throughout the entire rehearsal. Afterwards lunch with the Duke: soup, pullets, mashed potatoes and apple sauce! *Rien plus*! Even dukes are having to tighten their belts. It's a scandal that we have to live through times like these. They say we shall all have to diligently learn new ways now. I shall not make the effort to do so until the whole situation has become a little clearer, otherwise there will be too much twisting and turning with every wind that blows. I am still holding my head high, in the belief that Germany is too 'diligent' to fall into such a complete decline – in spite of all the nonsense the worthy government has instituted. Bismarck's dream has suffered a rude awakening, at all events, and 200 years of Prussiandom are at an end. Let's hope that it will be replaced by better times. I don't believe that it will – but there's nothing we can do about historical facts. Please don't upset yourself unnecessarily – it won't do any good. We are going to need all our nerve now to steer our little ship safely on its way. We will think over everything calmly, although I wouldn't know what else to do, even now, other than carry on as usual for as long as possible according to plan, for as long as theatres and concerts keep going and pay fees. If you love me then there isn't much the world can do to harm us. I am in perfect health!

Strauss despised politics and his lifelong interest in history only confirmed his low opinion of politicians. He had other things to think about and better things to do. He had no great interest in the idea that he was witnessing a turning-point of history and the birth of a new social order. He believed that not politics but art and learning are the only human

Kaiser Wilhelm II at the frontier, leaving Germany after his abdication.

achievements which endure: the Pharaohs are commemorated by the Pyramids, not by their conquests; the Punic Wars are in the past, the sculpture of Praxiteles is now. It was an attitude which contributed to the tragedy that overcame him in the last fifteen years of his life.

As the Kaiser abdicated, an armistice was declared and a Soviet Republic was set up in Munich, Strauss stuck to the engagements in his diary, which meant that he had to leave Garmisch for the turmoil of the cities.

A soldier of the government forces, killed by the Spartacists, as the German Communist Party called itself in its early days.

> When I got to the station in Munich yesterday, people were running about, soldiers were loading their guns and I was told, 'There's going to be trouble, the Spartacists are on the march.' It was impossible to leave the station again, so, like everybody else, I ran up the platform to the front of the train and, in the company of a very nice Consul from Bremen, waited for 'things' to happen. But of course, as usual, nothing happened, and so we left on time, three of us in the compartment, and the heating actually working!
>
> Dear old Berlin is much more orderly than crazy Munich. There are officers to be seen, soldiers, all in uniform. . . . This idiocy cannot last much longer. (To Pauline, from Berlin, 1 March 1919)

During the next six days, however, the unrest spread to Berlin:

> I've just come back from the theatre, where it should have been *Fidelio* but wasn't, as the lights went out. There was a lot of shooting today, the government troops won at Alexanderplatz and did a thorough clear-out of the Spartacists.
>
> My contract is being changed to a fixed salary, so it's all one to me, more or less, whether I conduct or not. On Saturday I'm giving an interview to the *Daily News*, no politics. Beecham wants to do *Frau ohne Schatten* next winter already. I wonder if I am really so very necessary as Rösch thinks I am for the organization he is setting up so energetically, to unite the associations of independent artists and the various musicians' bodies, with which the minister expressly wishes to work.
>
> With these matters to think about, which are very important for the future of the arts, it is best to forget the whole idiotic revolution and enjoy the inner satisfaction of working selflessly for a good cause.

The 'good cause' was the continuing effort to improve the economic and social position of musicians, and to rescue as much as possible of what had been achieved since the foundation of the Genossenschaft deutscher Tonsetzer in 1903. This was another reason to stay on in Berlin, in addition to the fact that his dream of retiring from conducting in order to concentrate on composition was further away from realization than ever since the sequestration of his savings, which he had deposited before the war in the Bank of England. (The banker Edgar Speyer had advised him that this was the safest place for them.) As it turned out, the first chance to put the musical profession on a really solid and secure footing appeared to be offered in 1933. By the time the terms of the offer were clear to Strauss it was too late for him to withdraw from a decision he had reason to regret bitterly.

Meanwhile the revolution rumbled on. Franz Strauss was due to travel to Heidelberg to start his university studies. His father sent a frantic letter from Berlin:

> I got a terrible shock yesterday when I heard you both wanted to come to Berlin. I had already hired an airship to fly to Garmisch when Under-Secretary of State for Air Erler urgently advised me not to, and Dr Vogel forbade it, and likewise travel by car! I got the same answer wherever I enquired: travelling without express trains is catastrophic. I spoke to people who had taken 88 hours to get to Berlin, and – although they had 1st-class tickets – had to stand in 4th or ride in the cattle truck. Why on earth did you leave home? Garmisch seems to be quiet still, and now that Starnberg has been 'taken' by the government troops today the danger that the beaten Spartacists would fall back on Garmisch has more or less disappeared. My head often feels as thick as a melon but I won't give in to things. Only worry about my family can get to me, such as overcame me yesterday when I heard about your sudden departure from home. (30 April 1919)

It was only later that he discovered that as the Spartacists were driven out of Munich, with the approval of the bulk of the population, they had drawn up a list of hostages to be shot – and that his name was on it. Gradually the situation grew calmer.

Strauss was not to stay in Berlin much longer. He was invited to be acting director of the erstwhile Court, now State, Opera, but in the end the new committee of management freely and democratically elected Max von Schillings to the post. That suited Strauss: recently he had established a good relationship with the Vienna Opera, and his appointment as director there had been under discussion since the summer of 1918.

Hofmannsthal still showed no inclination to write the satirical libretto he hankered for, so he approached Alfred Kerr for a text appropriate to the times:

> Like Offenbach in his parodies of Grand Opera . . . I should like to play the musical Aristophanes of today's Grand Operetta – known as The Revolution. In *Singspiel* form, like the *opéras comiques* of Auber. On the one hand the state of the theatre today, with workers' soviets and works' committees, prima donnas' plots, tenors' ambitions, General Intendants of the old régime proffering their resignations, could provide the milieu of one plot – and the political operetta: National Assembly, Old Comrades' associations, party politics, while the people starve, a souteneur as Minister of Education and Culture, a burglar as Minister of War, a murderer as Minister of Justice, could form the background of the other comic scene.

Director in Vienna

Vienna welcomes artists from Germany with a certain condescension (rather as Bavaria greets Prussians), and that includes Bavarians, although it was from Bavaria that Austria was first civilized around the year 1100. In the case of the Bavarian Richard Strauss, however, the no-longer-imperial capital found that it could make an exception and treat him at first as half, and eventually as wholly, Austrian.

The Vienna Opera was and is one of the world's leading houses. But as Gustav Mahler discovered, in the process of pulling it up from a trough of routine and slipshod complacency at the turn of the present century, accepting the post of director is like volunteering for a suicide commando. Every operagoer in Vienna is convinced that he could run the place better than the director, however illustrious – and some of them have the influence to make things very difficult for the incumbent. History is littered with the broken reputations and lives of past directors of the Vienna Opera, on many of whom it seems that Alberich's Curse has lighted.

For the first time in Strauss's career, he was not to be anyone's subordinate in the opera house, yet he was still not in sole charge: he was to share the directorship with Franz Schalk, who had been a popular member of the conducting staff at the house since 1901, having previously worked in Graz and at the Berlin Opera in the 1890s. He was on friendly terms with Strauss, who looked forward to collaboration with someone he could rely on to steer the ship while he, Strauss, navigated: that is, he would take responsibility for artistic standards and for engaging singers, and would conduct only what he wanted to.

Before his contract was signed, word got out, and a storm blew up in the press. The press was against Strauss, though no one quite knew why,

A BERLIN ACQUAINTANCE: *'You're going to Vienna? Where the people are so deceitful?'*
STRAUSS: *'People are deceitful everywhere. But in Vienna they're so pleasant about it.'*

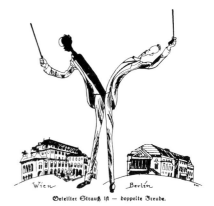

Geteilter Strauß ist — doppelte Freude.

'A Strauss divided between Berlin and Vienna is as good as two Strausses!'

With his co-director Franz Schalk. Schalk, born 1863, was a pupil of Anton Bruckner and hence a devoted Wagnerian. He was a career-conductor: Graz 1884, Berlin Opera 1890, Vienna Opera under Mahler 1901.

155

Vienna held a Strauss festival to celebrate his arrival: 'Flower Maidens' presented a rose; Salome presented a 'Strauss ham' on a silver salver; Electra drove the tram in which he drove in state through the streets.

including the press. It was said that the Opera would become a 'Strauss house', there would be too much egoism, and not enough Puccini. At 80,000 kronen, he was going to be overpaid. Emotion ran high, and no one would have supposed that there was anything else to worry about: the recent loss of a disastrous war, serious shortages of coal, food and clothing. Stage-hands, singers, chorus-members and orchestral players joined in signing a protest against the new régime. The handsome figure of Felix Weingartner, director of the rival house, the Volksoper, was said to be behind it: he had wanted the job himself.

The general public cast their votes on 11 April 1919, at a performance of *Parsifal*. The house lights dimmed, Leopold Reichwein – one of the anti-Strauss faction – came to the podium, and all hell broke loose in the standing-room at the back of the stalls (whence, as all Vienna knows, God speaks): 'Strauss! We want Strauss!'

With that, the fuss was over, and in the autumn Strauss was what the groundlings got. He brought with him, as dowry, the world premiere of *Die Frau ohne Schatten*. Dresden waived its claim, for Vienna disposed of an ideal cast: Karl Oestvig and Maria Jeritza as Emperor and Empress, Richard Mayr and Lotte Lehmann as the Dyer and his wife, Lucie Weidt as the Nurse.

Strauss invited Lotte Lehmann to come and stay in the villa at Garmisch, to study her part there. She had already done some preliminary work when they had their first session together.

Strauss was greatly amazed at my knowing even a single phrase of the work, and time and again expressed his surprise and delight. 'God,' he would cry out, 'that's really a hard bit. I'd never have thought that any singer could learn this.'

There in his home I came to know an altogether different Strauss. . . . No hour was too long, no amount of sunshine could lure him away from the piano, and I felt that although my own life had been hard-working I had never known before what work can really mean for a musician.

He made few suggestions regarding my interpretation of the role; I believe that, for one thing, he liked my own approach. . . . But the phrasing and the divinely inspired music were developed and worked out. At times he seemed to be sitting there with tears in his eyes, but I kept thinking that perhaps my imagination was playing tricks on me; the chill and impersonal Strauss could not possibly . . .?

Lehmann was amazed by the phenomenon that was Pauline, by the almost aseptic cleanliness in the house, by the screams of pain that rang out each day as she allowed herself to be pounded by a masseuse – an ordeal that was quite unnecessary for one with her figure and constitution. Strauss always went out for a walk while it was going on. Pauline talked a lot to Lehmann: if her husband was there, she tried to shake him out of his smiling calm. She called him a peasant and their marriage a *mésalliance*: she could have had a dashing hussar, and his music couldn't compare with that of Massenet. Richard refused to be ruffled. 'I suspect that actually he rather enjoyed it all. "Believe me, Lotte," he said to me the day I was leaving, "the whole world's admiration interests me a great deal less than a single one of Pauline's fits of rage."'

One year in Salzburg Pauline made a hurtful personal remark to Lehmann in the interval which made the singer burst into tears and refuse to sing any more. She resisted all attempts to comfort her. Clemens Krauss knew the only thing to do: he began the next act, Lehmann heard her music, went on stage and, tears or no tears, gave the performance of a lifetime.

The premiere of *Die Frau ohne Schatten*, in Vienna on 10 October 1919, was a success, but thereafter things did not go smoothly, as Strauss recalled in his memoirs, *Betrachtungen und Erinnerungen*:

The opera embarked on a *via dolorosa* through the German theatres. Even in Vienna it was more often cancelled than performed, because of the demanding roles and the difficulties with the sets; in the second theatre to stage it, Dresden, it got off on the wrong foot altogether. It was so ill-prepared scenically – the good Eva van der Osten had seriously harmed her voice in the meantime with heavy dramatic roles – that after the dress rehearsal I had to ask Seebach for a postponement. In spite of the excellent orchestra under Fritz Reiner the evening suffered greatly from the inadequacy of the Dyer's Wife – it was no joy!

It was a bad mistake to allow so many middle-sized and smaller theatres to attempt this opera directly after the war, for it is very hard to cast and makes great scenic demands. Some time later, when I saw the Stuttgart postwar production (on the cheap), I realized that the work would never have much success. Yet in the end it did establish itself, and people with artistic taste, in particular, regard it as my most significant work.

Years later, Strauss took a walk round the Alster in Hamburg with one of the local critics, who made the following admission: 'Ten years ago, I regarded *Die Frau ohne Schatten* as a horror, libretto and music. Yesterday, when you were conducting, I understood the music for the first time.' Strauss replied: 'Wait another ten years – then perhaps you will understand the libretto too.'

Vienna had seen *Salome* for the first time only in the previous year, and had been duly scandalized. Strauss's appointment to the Opera was marked by a 'Strauss Week', and one newspaper cartoonist depicted his triumphal entry into the city, greeted by curtseying flower-sellers and riding on an 'Elektric' tram, while a Salome serves brawn on a silver salver. He set up house at No. 4 Mozartplatz. According to his contract he had to conduct fifty opera performances in four (later five) months: he began with *Fidelio*, *Tristan* and *The Magic Flute*. He threw himself without delay into the tasks of polishing productions that were already in the repertoire, engaging new artists, planning, selecting new works for the repertory. He worked with the speed and concentration he brought to all his activities, and had no time for the weighing of pros and cons: 'That's just a waste of time.

Otto Strasser with a bespectacled Strauss in 1939.

Die Frau ohne Schatten: set design for Act II, Scene 2, the falconer's lodge.

Something that Schalk will spend all day talking about, I can dispose of in ten minutes.'

Otto Strasser joined the Vienna Philharmonic Orchestra in 1922 (rising later to manager):

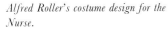

Alfred Roller's costume design for the Nurse.

When I joined the orchestra, Strauss had just prepared a new production of *Der fliegende Holländer*. It is amazing how ahead of the times he was in solving problems which are tackled by technology nowadays. The chorus of ghosts sat underneath a part of the stage that jutted forwards, and without the distortion caused by electroacoustic aids they sounded really ghostly. We had green lights on our desks – which no works committee would permit today – and thus, without any disturbing reflection, the whole scene was truly spooky. The first works that I had the experience of being rehearsed in by Strauss were *Tannhäuser* and *Hänsel und Gretel*, one of his favourite operas. The repertory he conducted was fairly comprehensive, and we have him to thank for the rediscovery of *Così* in all its beauty. It was a delight for us to hear his accompaniment of the recitatives, because every performance was different. It appeared to give him pleasure to direct from the harpsichord, like the old Baroque masters, for he improvised in *Don Giovanni* too, and he joined in with the orchestra to accompany the whole of Don Ottavio's B flat major aria on the pianino which had been there since Mahler's time.

In those days Maria Jeritza was the big star and box-office pull. We musicians were less fond of her, because she used to cut *Salome* in her own very individual way. There were so many cuts in our parts that we seemed to be left with only the torso of the opera. I was curious, therefore, to see what Strauss would say. But he conducted this semi-

Salome with every sign of enthusiasm, and all he had to say to us, as he walked through the pit on the way out, was 'Devil of a woman!' I was disappointed, and even today I think he must have been thinking more of the takings than of his opera.

A mite priggish, perhaps: surely, in the economic crisis of 1922–3, every artist and every other employee of the Vienna State Opera depended on good box-office receipts. The battle for *Salome*, uncut, had been fought and won long before, and it was a time when a capricious star could be indulged if she filled the theatre: especially if, as vocal and dramatic artist alike, she was a 'devil of a woman'.

South America and the USA again

The dollar became the measure of all things in the postwar period, while European currencies melted like snow in August. The word 'precarious' hardly did justice to the state of the Austrian economy. Opera houses swallow subsidies at the best of times, and there are always people who will point to other and better uses for the money. It was to seek out dollars, therefore, that Strauss sailed for South America in the first summer of his Vienna directorship, with Schalk and the Vienna Philharmonic Orchestra. South America had prospered while the rest of the world was at war, and the purpose of the expedition was to arouse interest in European music and in the Vienna State Opera in particular.

The party, which included Franz, were away from August until November 1920. They were at sea for fifteen weary days, stopping to take on coal at the Cape Verde Islands. Strauss sent Pauline an account of the voyage in his letters:

> We lay there for a full fifty-one hours – an appalling time. On both sides of the ship four immense boats carrying coals; the loading was an extremely noisy process, and caused so much dust and dirt that the foredeck had to be rigidly partitioned off with canvas and all doors and windows kept tightly closed. I leave you to imagine the first night in the baking, steaming cabin, on lumpy wool mattresses which smell and get fearfully hot as soon as you lie down on them. . . . We got under way again at last on Sunday at midday, amid general rejoicing. Then began a wholesale swabbing down that it would have done your heart good to see, scrubbing of all the decks, roofs and cabins, spring-cleaning of our persons and changing of clothes. Today all the ladies have fluffy hair after washing it. (20 August 1920)

Richard was never seasick, but Franz was not so lucky. They shared a cabin, and his loving father had to minister to him at three in the morning.

Rio-bound: Richard and Franz in the rigging.

The proud father wrote the caption for this one 'Sempre bello!'

In Rio, with the impresario (right).

For the celebration of Crossing the Line, they came round collecting donations for the lottery. I had the bright idea of giving them a few autographs and so got off cheaply. We were baptized with champagne, shaved and given fishy names: 'Triton' for me and 'Whale-Calf' for Bubi. Then we played all sorts of childish games: it was all very pleasant, harmless and quite charmingly decorous. In the lottery, Bubi won a little inkwell, a silver perfume bottle, some things made from shells by the blacks of St Vincent and – one of my autographs. The Italians ran the lottery and an auction very nicely and wittily. My two autographs fetched 2,700 lire: the high-spot of the evening.

Fernando Island: enchantingly formed mountains, with the Kofel from the Ammergau slap in the middle, quite green. The sojourn on board ship is slowly beginning to impose burdens that even my armour-plated stoicism will be able to endure for only another four days. All the same, being confined on board like this is good for composition: I have already filled a sketchbook with melodies and themes. And Goethe is a true comfort in the midst of these all too harmless contemporaries who keep getting under my feet. (26 August 1920)

The concerts in Rio (with Beethoven, Wagner, Schubert, Weber, Debussy and Strauss himself on the programme) were a great success musically and received ecstatic reviews, but were given to empty concert halls. The rivalry between two impresarios was to blame, one of them having exhausted the relatively small Rio audience for European classical and modern music before the Vienna Philharmonic arrived.

At the time of the visit, Rio was looking forward with feverish excitement to one from King Albert of Belgium:

with an outlay on flags and soldiery such as Wilhelm in his day could not have outdone. At home we are getting rid of that junk, and here the swindle is flourishing. He is to be here for fourteen days, with banquets and excursions on every one of them! You can imagine how much interest there is for art and concert-going in a muse-forsaken coffee town like this. It's a totally uncivilized set-up, which I am studying circumspectly and calmly, and which we will have to thread our way through with the utmost cunning. Up until now, I have managed to win the greatest sympathy for myself on all sides. Today I was given a banquet by the committee of the Brazilian orchestra which is supplying me with extra players, and I received a call from the American Ambassador, who has invited us for Tuesday. Later this week I have an audience with the President and pay a call on the First Mayor, and I shall take the chance to broach the subject of our Vienna project with the greatest delicacy.

By the end of the tour, not only had the audience figures picked up, but the 'project' was also launched with success: the entire Vienna Opera, including orchestra, was to visit Brazil, at Brazilian expense and sailing on a Brazilian steamer, in 1922 with Weingartner, and in 1923 with Strauss. He also succeeded in setting up a fund-raising scheme in aid of the Opera.

Paul Hindemith (right) with his cellist brother.

Back in Vienna, people grumbled at his absenteeism (earlier in the year he had spent four weeks touring Hungary and Romania, where there was a great deal of anti-German feeling), but that did not stop him travelling. In 1921 he attended the first Donaueschingen Festival of contemporary music, as honorary chairman of the founding committee, under the patronage of Max Egon Prince of Fürstenberg. Though a square in the town was renamed 'Richard-Strauss-Platz', for the younger musicians whose work was heard at Donaueschingen Strauss was old-fashioned. One of the works he heard there was Paul Hindemith's Second Quartet, which he found 'cheeky, mad but very talented'. He asked the twenty-six-year-old composer why he wrote in such an atonal style, 'after all, you have talent'. He replied, 'Herr Doktor, do you make your music, and I'll make mine'. In later years, Hindemith's youthful radicalism faded, and he said of his *Harmonie der Welt* in 1957 'I think Richard Strauss would like that, too'. In the summer of 1921, Strauss informed Schalk that he would be doing a concert tour of the United States in the autumn (it was possible to do such things at such short notice in those days). For the first time in their partnership, Schalk remonstrated, and Strauss had to explain himself:

> When I asked at the American Passport Office, who was going over there nowadays for the most part, I was told 'cooks and artists'. *Voilà tout!* I am not going for pleasure! After England confiscated the chief part of my capital, having no pension to look forward to from any quarter, I have only the royalties from my works to fall back on if anything happened to me that stopped me going on conducting. Even operatic successes are unreliable – if the royalties fail, which I hope will not happen for a while yet, I shall be a beggar and shall leave my family in 'poverty and shame'. I must free myself from this worry, if I am to work in peace again. (22 June 1921)

And so he set sail on the *Adriatic* of the White Star Line, on 19 October 1921, to cross the Atlantic for a third time. There were three in the party: Richard and Franz Strauss and the soprano Elisabeth Schumann, who was to play her part among the former wartime enemies in earning money and support for the Vienna Opera and the music of Richard Strauss. She was already married to her second husband, the conductor Carl Alwin. ('A good girl never loses any time in marrying the conductor who studies her

Strauss with Elisabeth Schumann in Paris.

With Elisabeth Schumann outside the Louvre.

roles with her', commented Strauss.) She kept a diary of the tour, not intended for publication. They met at her hotel in Munich, on 15 October:

On the dot of four, Dr Strauss drives up in his car and quickly gives me the Munich–Paris tickets, then rushes off to the station to the Luggage Registration Office, because Bubi's cigarettes have only arrived at the last minute, and he has to stow them in the secret compartment in the trunk. We meet at the Luggage Registration a quarter of an hour later and during the weighing, which takes forever, we talk about America. I moan about how long the journey will take, and he moans about how boring it will be. Then he casts his eyes up to heaven in the old familiar way: 'Well, I've packed some manuscript paper.'

He asks me about Vienna and the Opera, and listens *very* interestedly, grumbles about the rehearsals in Italian – and Schalk. [Strauss thought operas should be sung in German, so that they were understood, and didn't want too many Italian operas in the repertory.] We get on the train, each in our own compartment, next to each other. After five minutes he invites me into his for a chat and we talk about Hempel's fiasco in Vienna, and my engagement at La Scala (at which his eyes light up). . . . Then we both read. Later he goes to the dining car, while I sit in his compartment eating a half chicken that I bought in Munich. Before long he returns and gallantly presents me with a banana. We chat for a little while longer and then I bid him goodnight, dead tired. He is going to sit up until we get to Karlsruhe at twelve, where 'Franzl' is joining the train. I get into bed with my clothes on, because we reach the border at two, and I shall have to go to the luggage compartment. – A knock at the door. – Passports. – I get up and receive a cordial greeting from Franz, who is waiting in the corridor with his father's passport. Nevertheless, they open *his* door, too, and I see the great man in the upper bunk, blinking wearily, and I feel cross because they've wakened him. Then Franz and I pay a quick visit to the luggage compartment, and back to bed. The next morning the three of us breakfast together in the dining car – Strauss talks a lot about the scenery we're travelling through and is very taken by the colours.

When he hears that I intend to stay at the Majestic in Paris, he persuades me to go to the Grand Hotel with him instead. 'We're going to do some sightseeing in Paris, and so we must stick together.' So I go with him. At one we meet again in Prunier's – a wonderful place. Strauss sates himself on oysters, I feast on lobster – we both feel well satisfied – he is wild about Paris – finds *everything* so tasteful and knows of no more beautiful city. I congratulate him on Prunier's and the marvellous lunch and he answers: 'Yes, I'm a good courier, a moderate composer and a rotten theatre director.'

(Schumann's fondness for lobster earned her the nickname 'Elobsterbeth' from Strauss.)

On their arrival in Cherbourg the next day, Strauss again showed his mettle as a courier: their cabins were unsatisfactory, but Strauss discovered

Chaliapin on board and through his influence they were able to move. H.G. Wells was another of the eminent passengers they met. Chaliapin and Strauss played poker during the voyage. Though skat was always his favourite card game, Strauss is said to have been a good poker-player: he was an excellent bluffer.

On the penultimate evening of the voyage, the celebrated musicians on board gave a concert in aid of seamen's widows and orphans. Schumann took part, of course:

Had a great success with three Strauss songs. Chaliapin sang too – marvellous artist, unhappily no longer *quite* at his peak. Then a lady violinist played Strauss's Sonata. He is so charming, and always concerned that I shall be a success. Before the concert he said to me: 'By all means hold on to the high notes a little longer, you needn't always be too precise.' Afterwards, I said, 'Well, did I sing the high notes long enough?' 'Yes', he said, laughing, 'but with a certain inward sense of shame.'

With Mayor Hylan on the steps of City Hall.

On board the Adriatic. *The man in the trilby is Chaliapin.*

163

The photographers and the newsreel cameras were waiting for them on the quayside. Some of the newspapers thought it was the 'Waltz King' and printed pictures of the statue in the Vienna Volkspark. Strauss told Pauline with some amusement that Marshall Foch, the French commander-in-chief, was also touring the country, and that receptions were being given for them by turns. He didn't mention the official reception by the city of New York, but it is there in Schumann's diary:

> 31 October 1921. . . . At twelve midday approximately fifteen cars draw up outside the Hotel St Regis – all have the city coat-of-arms at the back. Strauss goes into the first with three gentlemen, Franz and suite go in the second, I in the third. . . .
>
> The cars are accompanied by policemen to left and right, riding on motor-bicycles and sounding their sirens all the time. That means that we go over every crossroads without stopping, *all* the other cars stand still, people standing to left and to right – of course, they have all read about the reception. Strauss drives through N.Y. 'like a king'.

The pavement outside City Hall was packed with photographers and newsreel-cameramen, and a crowd of guests was waiting inside. Speeches were made, Strauss replied, at first hesitantly and with an apology for speaking German, but growing more confident and fluent. 'I would not wish to be so immodest as to claim this great honour on my own account alone, but I accept it on behalf of great German music. This festive occasion will evoke a joyful and grateful response in my country, and I will take pains to prove myself worthy of it. . . .'

The war had been over for three years, and he was received without a trace of rancour or prejudice, both in the streets and in Carnegie Hall, where, in the first concert of the tour, he conducted the Philadelphia Orchestra in *Don Juan*, *Till Eulenspiegel* and the *Symphonia domestica*. He wrote to Pauline:

> The applause as I entered went on for several minutes, I had to turn round and take a bow four times before I could even start. A storm of applause after each item. The Philadelphia Orchestra of the very first rank and enthusiastic – about my short rehearsals.
>
> Yesterday lunch and a reception at the Women's Club (there's no end to it, I give my same speech everywhere), filthy American food and 1200 worthy provincial ladies all in one room – I let it all flow over me patiently, allow myself to be fêted for the good of our dear country, and am already looking forward to seeing you again, my home, Garmisch and Vienna. Apart from New York, which is really fabulous, staying in the land of universal mechanization is deadly boring. All the hotels are overheated, while the weather remains mild. On Friday (when we leave for Chicago) we give up this expensive St Regis Hotel (38 dollars a day) after having done enough for the publicity, and move into the Wellington Hotel, two bedrooms with bath and sitting room for 9 dollars a day. Bubi has worked out that it will save us the equivalent of the petrol for 500 trips to Munich. . . .

In every town they visited, before every concert, Strauss had to submit to a press conference. He proved himself a diplomat in deflecting questions, designed to catch him out, about American culture or colleagues:

'What is your favourite symphonic poem?'
'Those that show me and my opinions most clearly: Zarathustra – Quixote – Domestica.'
'What is the programme of "Zarathustra"?'
'The relationship of Nature and the Human Will. C major is Nature, Man as a being; B minor (at the end of the work B major) his metaphysical aspiration. Both worlds culminate in a shout of laughter.'
'What do you think of the American school of composers?'
'There aren't any schools; there are only talents and geniuses.'
'What is a genius?'
'Not every talent has genius, but every genius also has talents in him, as part of his abilities.'
'What do you think of jazz?'
'I have already heard some in Europe. Very interesting, especially the rhythms.'
'What do you think of American women?'
'They are all wonderfully beautiful.'
'What is your best song?'
'*Traum durch die Dämmerung*, composed in five minutes, while waiting for my wife.'

The press seemed to like him: they found him equable, lively, youthful in appearance and ready to laugh. A sympathetic southern German, they told their readers, 'a man of no Prussian tendencies'. The critics showed less prejudice, more intelligence and more understanding than their European confrères; they appeared both better informed and more objective, and the sound of axes being ground was not to be heard.

An American jazz musician wrote and asked for permission to perform the song, '*Tram Doo Dee Dam Rung*', which he wanted to turn into a 'Strauss' Rag'. This caused considerable perplexity, until somebody recognized a phonetic spelling of *Traum durch die Dämmerung*.

Already on good terms with Strauss before they left Europe, Elisabeth Schumann's diary shows how she improved on the acquaintance. It is full of well-observed and telling details. Few of his contemporaries left so true and unrefracted a portrait.

On the art of singing: 'You must sing more *legato*, and learn to use facial expression to make good what, for example, the voice does not convey. You often sing too honestly – disguise your weaknesses.' He's quite right.
On his marriage: Strauss brings me Pauline's letter to read – tender lines, quite different from the way she speaks!
On Brahms: During the journey, tired and on edge, he talks about

Brahms with Hubermann [the Polish violinist]. 'I much prefer Spohr. I always get so angry with Brahms – he is so overrated – he doesn't have enough ideas.'

On writing conclusions: 'It's very difficult. Beethoven and Wagner knew how to do it. Only the great composers can do it. I can do it.'

The tour took its toll in nervous strain, and while their hosts did not suspect anything, Franz and Elisabeth (practically one of the family, by now) witnessed Strauss's blacker humours.

10 November 1921. 9 a.m., arrival in Baltimore. Strauss badtempered, takes it all out on Franz – grumbles about *everything*. I say that I don't understand his making the sacrifice this tour represents, and remind him of how the dollar stands to the mark. 'Yes,' he says, 'I only do it so as to be able to live in Italy again one day.' I do not altogether understand why he couldn't do that without dollars. We sit at breakfast – his elbows are working – a bad sign – finally I break the spell and pour ridicule on the whole scene – especially his scolding of Franz – to such good effect that we all start laughing like lunatics. Otherwise it is simply unendurable when he sulks all the time. But the morning is his bad time, I've already noticed that. By midday his mood is brightening – then he too is sorry for his insensitivity – and in the evening he is enchanting. Detroit, 7 December. Day of disaster – trunk left behind. Have to buy dress, shoes, stockings, while the manager runs round the town in search of the music. He cannot find all of it, and we have to put some Schubert in the programme. Strauss as placid as ever, thank God, for I was rather nervous.

We had various Strauss songs, and some he played by heart. He is not a good 'by-heart-player', and something quite wonderful happened with *All mein Gedanken*. Already by the third bar he had quite forgotten the accompaniment and he composed a completely new song. I kept up with him, the words fitted perfectly, nobody in the audience suspected a thing and when we reached the end safe and sound, I looked to the right out of the corner of my eye to see his reaction. All I saw was his mouth stretching from ear to ear in one huge grin – it was really hard for me to muster the calm and serious mood needed for the next song. Later we had another laugh about it in the Artists' Room, and I begged him to write down the new version of *All mein Gedanken*, but he said, 'Oh, I've already totally forgotten it.'

Richardl and Franz have just spent a little while in my sitting room – we are like a family, delightful relationship. Strauss's eyes shine when he looks at me. He is so touching, the day before yesterday he brought me a tablet in my sleeping compartment, and when I couldn't swallow it he ran to fetch a glass of water and handed it to me with a gallant flourish. Our digestion and other discomforts often form the topic of our conversations – it is *so* funny.

The singer closed her diary with a paean of gratitude to Strauss and the fatherly way he had protected and cared for her throughout the exhausting tour. 'I have learned to know you as one of the noblest of men.'

Before they left America, Strauss gave his first concert on the newly invented wireless. Schumann did not want to do it, but he insisted.

The tour was unremitting hard work to the very end. Strauss described to Pauline how he spent New Year's Eve: 'On the 30th and 31st concert rehearsals in the morning, recitals (songs) in the afternoon, and the rest of the day and evening playing the piano or conducting for the gramophone. I was so tired that we just ate a steak alone in the Wellington Hotel, thinking of you, and were in bed by 10.30.' After sixty-seven days of it, and having spent the equivalent of 13 days and 5 hours on trains, he and Franz sailed for Europe on the *America* of the United States Line on 4 January 1922. (Schumann stayed on for another month.) He had accumulated a tidy sum in dollars at concerts in aid of the Vienna Opera.

'After this horrendous and exhausting concert tour, I look forward to rational activity at my desk and some stimulating work in the theatre.' (To Franz Schalk, 12 January 1922)

Laying the foundation stone of a new festival theatre at Salzburg which was never built. The very stone has vanished and no one knows where it was, except that it was near the palace of Heilbronn.

Salzburg – Brazil – Vienna

Salzburg, the city of Mozart's birth, had been the scene of a number of festivals celebrating him since 1877. The institution of a regular, annual festival had already been mooted before the outbreak of the First World War; in 1917 Max Reinhardt sent a proposal to the appropriate office in the Austrian government, but it vanished without trace; in 1918, following an initiative by two Salzburg citizens, Damisch and Schey, an 'artistic advisory council' was set up consisting originally of Strauss, Reinhardt and Schalk, joined in the following year by Hofmannsthal, Roller and others with a professional artistic interest.

Strauss had idolized Mozart since boyhood, and in the 1890s had played an active part, alongside Levi and Possart, in the pioneering performances of his operas in Munich. During his term in Vienna the Redoutensaal in the Hofburg, the former imperial palace, began to be used for performances of Mozart, being a more suitable size for opera of the eighteenth century than the State Opera itself. The idea of Mozart festivals in Salzburg was very dear to his heart.

The directorate of the proposed festival was divided between Vienna and Salzburg, and the two committees, made up of dignitaries, not artists, were at daggers drawn, with the result that neither was capable of producing any useful results at all. Both chose to ignore the existence of the

This snapshot of Strauss and members of the Vienna Philharmonic in Brazil has rarity value: he is tieless and collarless! It is obviously very hot, yet they all wear waistcoats and ankle-high boots.

When Alice von Grab first met Franz Strauss she preferred the company of the boys she met at the dancing classes. But in 1923 she became engaged to him.

'advisory council', and decided to hold a festival in 1921 in accordance with their own ideas, which meant operettas and 'star' guests of no standing. This nonsense was halted when Straus issued an anathema. In 1922 Strauss and Schalk brought the Vienna Opera company to Salzburg, with four productions of Mozart which set the standard of what was desirable and possible. That was the beginning of the international reputation of the summer festivals in Salzburg, although the well-to-do audiences had to run the gauntlet of socialist demonstrations. The marchers threatened festivalgoers with cudgels. No café or restaurant anywhere near the theatre dared to stay open. In hotels, cards were placed on every table asking for money 'for the poor of this city'. Because the festival brought lots of foreign currency into the city, a grateful directorate made Strauss president – that was in 1926, the year in which the festival was cancelled for lack of money.

In the summer of 1923 the Vienna Philharmonic Orchestra and State Opera toured Argentina, Uruguay and Brazil. The economic depression which drove them out of Austria to seek money in the New World had now spread, but the rate of inflation was not so horrendously high in South America as in central Europe, where a loaf of bread cost billions in a degenerate currency. *Elektra* and *Salome* were both successes at the box office in Buenos Aires. Then they all packed into the S.S. *Vestris* to sail to Rio, where they played *Elektra* ten times, and gave concerts featuring Bruckner, Brahms, Mahler, Schillings, Korngold, Reger, Pfitzner and Franz Schmidt: modern music in South America in 1923.

On the way to catch his ship in Naples, Strauss travelled south through Italy with his family and two further car-loads of friends, the Grabs and the Goldsteins. Emanuel von Grab was an industrialist, owning cloth-mills in Prague and Györ; he played skat with Strauss and usually lost. They had known each other since 1907, when Strauss went to Prague for a performance of *Salome* and they were introduced by Leo Blech, a Jew like Grab. Strauss stayed at Grab's house in the country on several occasions before the war and again in 1919, while his new accommodation in Vienna was being made ready. It was during that summer that Franz and Pauline also stayed there, and made the acquaintance of Grab's fifteen-year-old daughter Alice – who had no time then for musicians or their 'frightfully boring' sons. Now, in 1923, on his arrival in Rio, Strauss found a long letter from Franz waiting for him: he and Alice wanted to marry.

Strauss sent a cable of delighted consent. For the wedding on 15 January 1924 he composed an epithalamion, the *Hochzeitspräludium* for two harmoniums, into which he worked themes from the *Symphonia domestica*, the introduction to *Guntram* and the trio from the closing scene of *Der Rosenkavalier*. The marriage was as happy as that of Richard and Pauline and lasted fifty-six years, until Franz's death on 14 February 1980.

Franz's parents took Alice to their hearts. It cannot have been easy for her to find her way in the world of music at first, when it was all new to her and when adapting herself to life with three strong and disparate personalities. She became Strauss's secretary and amanuensis, and before long her diligence, complete reliability, untiring energy and talent for organization made her his most important assistant in the matters of

Franz and Alice.

Strauss and Alice.

Richard, Pauline and Franz, in 1919, at Emanuel von Grab's country house near Vienna, where Strauss was a regular guest.

everyday life. Joking, he said to her: 'It's true, isn't it, Alice? You and I are the only people who do any work in this house.'

After the Second World War, when Strauss and Pauline were living in Switzerland, it was Alice who rescued the archives, carrying them from Vienna to Switzerland in suitcases. Back in Garmisch, she made herself useful in social and charitable work for the numerous refugees in the town, watched over the house in those difficult times, and still looked after her husband and sons.

Following Strauss's death, Alice spent years of work organizing and cataloguing the archives. It was an act of wholly personal gratitude towards her father-in-law, who had lovingly shielded and protected her, a Jewess, under the Third Reich. What she has done for Strauss and his family is beyond praise.

There is an old theatrical saying: 'After a war one must write comedies.' Strauss had gradually come to an interest in ballet, through Diaghilev and the choreographer Heinrich Kröller, for whose appointment Strauss had had to fight at the Vienna Opera, where he raised the ballet to international standards. The composer of *Die Josephslegende* may nevertheless have felt wary of another literary libretto: certainly the one he himself thought up for his next ballet had as flimsy a plot as ever made an excuse for dance.

Frau Alice and her father-in-law from the family album.

On the day of his confirmation, a small boy comes into Demel's, the famous Viennese café and confectioners, where he is allowed to celebrate the occasion by choosing whatever he wants. He eats far too much and begins to feel ill. As he lies on his sickbed, he is surrounded by all kinds of sweets, from the realm of Princess Praliné and the cupboard of liqueurs.

The ballet was called *Schlagobers*, the Viennese word for the whipped cream piled high on the kind of goodies the boy gorges himself on. Although

169

Schlagobers, *9 May 1924. Prince
Coffee (Fräulein Pfundmayer) and
Princess Tee-blossom (Fräulein Losch).*

At the first performance of Schlagobers,
*Vienna, 9 May 1914, the part of the little
boy was taken by Gretl Theimer, who later
became a well-known film actress. Here
'he' is surrounded by 'whipped cream'.*

it inhabits the same world as such popular pieces as *Nutcracker* and *L'enfant et
les sortilèges*, for some reason Strauss's ballet did not have the same success.
Audiences, except in Vienna, were lukewarm. Critics derided this new
departure for the composer of *Elektra*. Someone in Munich wrote, around
this date, 'Strauss, originally destined for the service of music, later turned
to trade.' When *Die Josephslegende* was new, it was rejected for not being
Rosenkavalier. Now *Schlagobers* was dismissed, apparently for not being *Die
Josephslegende*. It is a score full of humour and all Strauss's accustomed
mastery: yet the critics and the regular 'first-nighters' could not accept it for
what it was. Predictably: *Carmen* suffered the same fate in its day.

Schlagobers did enjoy some success with the public in Vienna, to begin
with, but it was not sustained. Yet the score is full of delights: in the first act,
'In the Café Kitchen' (graceful and ironic, with a parodic march
concluding after the manner of the end of Act II of *Siegfried*, of which Strauss
was particularly fond), and 'Dance of the Tea-Blossom' (sensual and sultry
in F sharp major). The big waltz (which goes back to the same page in the
1903 sketchbook where the *Rosenkavalier* Waltz was born) does not strike the
right kind of spark. The second act offers, among other things, a genial
Minuet and a 'slow waltz' which is a veritable Bavarian Ländler, and is
brought back at the end to crown the swirling conclusion of the ballet. Some
of the happiest music Strauss ever wrote is to be found in *Schlagobers*.

A few weeks after the ballet's premiere on 9 May 1924, Strauss had his
sixtieth birthday. He could now be considered an Olympian – and for the
first time in his life he was experiencing inactivity. His directorship of the
Vienna Opera had gone wrong, and he would not accept the fact, or what
Franz and Alice bluntly told him: 'Papa, you underestimate the work
Schalk does. This business can't be directed in an authoritarian manner on
a long rein. You have to get up close and peg away at details.' He believed
that his immense experience would serve to solve every problem, and he did
not appreciate how smallminded some artists could be.

He also resisted the idea of being written off as old-fashioned by the
rising generation, started to talk about the place he was entitled to in the
history of music and at the same time experienced uncertainty as to the
continuance of his creative powers. It was years since he had written
something which had roused real attention. He had now finished the new
opera, *Intermezzo*. Would it prove to be a new stylistic impulse, in an age
which often preferred the primitive to the polished?

His placid self-confidence was shaken, he began to be puzzled and to
brood, silently. From the outside, he seemed to be dozing, showing his age.
Romain Rolland visited Vienna in May 1924 and called on him, to find the
apartment on the Mozartplatz thronged with boring people, the *haute volée*
of Vienna, cultivated by Pauline because she liked to play the society
hostess. Strauss still showed the signs of his concern for Franz, who had been
dangerously ill with typhus in Egypt, and was worried about his financial
position. He was deeply preoccupied by the growth of political fanatic-
ism, and the threat that nationalism posed to European civilization.
He conducted concerts for the workers on May Day that year, so as
to demonstrate what Europe really was.

When Strauss moved to Vienna in 1919, it was understood that he would not be the usual kind of bureaucratic administrator, who would run the Opera as he would a government ministry. He was to compose, conduct throughout the world, and beat the drum for Vienna; his role at the State Opera was to lay down guidelines for repertory and the engagement of singers, ensuring the high standards which would add lustre to the reputation of the house.

By the end of three years there were loud grumbles: 'That foreigner – he's never here, gets paid the earth, thinks of nothing but his own works – and now he's building himself a palace beside the Belvedere!' It was his custom to preserve a cool silence about things that annoyed him, and he met these accusations with exactly that. The groundlings were only provoked. They began to spin intrigues *à la Viennoise*, to agitate in the salons, in the newspapers, in the cafés where the press foregathered, in the opera house and everywhere else where agitation was possible. The counter-agitation of over-eager friends, like Carl Alwin and the stage director Josef Turnau, only did more damage. Ever since opera was invented, the money it takes to run an opera house is a subject guaranteed to bring unmusical people to a white heat of indignation. It was easy to accuse Strauss of extravagance, of bankrupting a poor country.

And his co-director Schalk? Merely the day-to-day running of the opera house was enough to wear out one who hated to make decisions. He wasted his energies on mundane arguments, on the vanity of tenors and the hysteria of ballerinas, on the administration of finances. For the first time in history, opera houses had to contend with unions, works' councils, strikes. In the past, the court, the Emperor himself, had decided everything. Under the new republic there were hundreds of emperors, haggling, quarrelling and insatiable. Schalk tried to be an honest broker, and stood between the two fronts, confused by the intriguing that swirled about him. As the ground grew ever stickier, the public decided that he was a victim of exploitation, and gave him their sympathy.

Strauss pressed on with new ideas and dealt with artists. Schalk carried out the ideas imperfectly, and showed himself ever sceptical and unwilling. Before long they disagreed on the engagement of German artists, whom Schalk, the Viennese, regarded as 'unartistic *boches*'. Premieres failed to take place as planned, performances were cancelled because singers fell ill and there were no covers. More than once Strauss thought of giving it up.

In 1923 it was impossible to fill the house, because of the economic crisis. Strauss offered to absent himself in the next season, so as the save the Opera the cost of his salary. By 1924 he and Schalk were hopelessly alienated from each other. Each objected to everything the other did or said. The archives in Garmisch contain sheaves of letters to and from officials and journalists. All in vain: Vienna wanted the blood of another Opera director.

Schalk demanded new and fuller powers during Strauss's absences; he was granted them, subject to Strauss's consent. Strauss wrote to the ministry, demanding, if he was to stay, that Schalk must be shown the door, and refusing to accept responsibility for the poor quality of productions which had been starved of funds. That was too much for officialdom.

Franz Schalk, a cartoon by Alfred Gerstenbrand.

Strauss's strained relations with Schalk became notorious. This cartoon was published with a doggerel poem:
    The baton belongs to Herr Strauss,
    The toast of each opera house;
    Its beat is so strong it would seem
    To be frothing a bowl of whipped cream.
    But his glory is over, they say,
    And Herr Strauss must be going away.
    Why not stay, and conduct, and be bolder?
    It's Franz Schalk looking over his shoulder.

Richard and Franz Strauss with Max Reinhardt at the opening of the Theater in der Josefstadt in Vienna as the 'Actors' Theatre'.

While Strauss was in Dresden, overseeing the rehearsals for the first performances of *Intermezzo*, a senior Viennese civil servant, Herr Kossak, and Ludwig Karpath, critic and dedicatee of *Schlagobers*, who had been trying to pour oil on the troubled waters for the past two years, travelled to see him. Kossak argued for two days, then said that if Strauss wanted to tender his resignation, he was authorized to accept it. Strauss raised his eyebrows. 'Indeed? Then you can have it at once.' Kossak concealed his satisfaction, Karpath tried to make him unsay the words. Strauss stood his ground, rejoicing to be rid of his burden.

The root causes of the failure of the dual directorship lay in the difficulties of the time. By his own lights, neither Schalk nor Strauss was to blame.

With the architect, Michael Rosenauer. Strauss was so pleased with his work that he was drawn in when a Strauss Festival Theatre in Athens was proposed.

Strauss had a key to the gate admitting him from his own garden into the grounds of the Belvedere palace.

A Palace in Vienna

Strauss liked Vienna and its atmosphere; nearly all of his librettists were Viennese. He had had high hopes of his contract, with its reasonable terms, and he had trusted in his own authority to make it work. He had wanted to spend the rest of his life in the city and help to guide an opera house and an opera company which would serve as models for the whole German-speaking world. For four years he behaved less like a manager than an affectionate adviser, and not once did he attempt to act the dictator. In 1921 he actually referred to himself as the 'ostensible director'. Since then he had started to build himself a house in the Jacquingasse, along the eastern periphery of the gardens of the Belvedere. It was almost finished when he resigned.

The house he had built in Garmisch fifteen years earlier was essentially a summer villa of the type and size usual for the well-to-do before the First World War, when finding servants was no problem. The house in the Jacquingasse was to be the winter residence of the director of the Vienna Opera, and a man who was in his own right a prince in the musical world.

The simple blue exercise books in which Strauss used to write down his thoughts and reminiscences contain the history of the Vienna house. Pauline, in particular, felt penned in after four years in the rather gloomy apartment on Mozartplatz and wanted a house with a garden. They considered a site in Munich, but that was too close to Garmisch and Munich was no metropolis. Strauss spoke to the Austrian Minister of Works about a site in Vienna. Two possibilities in Schönbrunn were turned down because of the time it would take to go to and from the Opera. Then the former private garden of Archduke Franz Ferdinand at the Belvedere was suggested.

The Ministry of Culture let it be known discreetly that Strauss would not be director of the Opera for ever. 'Schalk had already begun to undermine my position.' But Strauss took the optimistic view and started to

During the Second World War, Strauss spent most of the year in Vienna. There were no air-raids before 1944, the streets were lit, the regime was altogether less severe.

The Jacquingasse house from the former private garden of Archduke Franz Ferdinand.

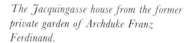

Sitting under the portrait of Pauline, painted in Weimar.

Photographs taken at various dates in and outside the house in Vienna. In 1946 it became the residence of the Dutch Ambassador.

Strauss in the Archduke's garden, at some date in the early 1940s.

build, with the dollars he had earned in America and some help from Emanuel von Grab. Under the terms of the lease, the house and the ground were to belong to Strauss and his heirs for sixty years, at the end of which they would revert to the Austrian state. Strauss paid for the lease in kind: the autograph score of *Rosenkavalier* (valued at $25,000) went to the National Library, and that of *Schlagobers* (valued at $10,000) to the City Library. In the economic climate of the 1920s those were solid securities for a piece of ground which had no other use.

After a few months the new General Intendant of the Opera, Franz Schneiderhan, approached Strauss about the terms on which he would work in the Opera in future. They agreed upon a hundred performances over a period of five years, without fee. In addition Strauss handed over the autograph score of *Die ägyptische Helena* (another $25,000). With that the site was his. By then he had also already paid for the building of the house.

The house was filled with art treasures that Strauss brought home form his conducting tours, and others given him by friends and relatives on special occasions, instead of flowers.

Originally the government had been willing to give him the site, so that he could join the ranks of those great composers – Beethoven, Brahms and many others – who chose to be Viennese. 'While I gratefully acknowledge the generosity of this initial gesture, in the interests of truth it must be stated that in the end, with 60,000 dollars' worth of manuscripts and 200,000 schillings' worth of conducting, I paid handsomely for my building site, indeed, I probably paid *too much*.'

'Intermezzo'

In 1916 Strauss decided that for his next opera, as a change from high drama, higher passions, philosophy and mysteries, he would put everyday life on the stage. He wanted to write a *jeu d'esprit* in which he would go further along the path he had explored in the *Symphonia domestica*. 'For preference I would always compose myself': that is, give organized, musical expression to his reactions to experiences. His music is never abstract. It portrays emotions, events and processes, showing them in greater depth thereby. His intention this time was to find an equivalent to contemporary spoken theatre, render conversations in music, and move still further away from the number opera. But – 'Satan puts counterpoint in the cradle of every German, to make things awkward for us on the operatic stage!'

In 1902, while Strauss was away from home, Pauline, left behind in Berlin, opened a letter which was addressed to him:

Dear Herr Strauss,
I expected to see you yesterday in the Union Bar, but in vain, alas. I am writing therefore to ask if you will be so kind as to let me have a few tickets for Monday and Wednesday of this week.
  With my best thanks in anticipation, yours sincerely,
  Mieze Mücke.
Lüneburgerstrasse 5, ground floor right.

It is hard to see anything improper about this letter, unless it is the reference to the Union Bar. The lady expresses herself politely, and wants tickets for the opera, which is a sign of cultural interests, even if she is impecunious – or thrifty. Mieze was a common enough name in Berlin.

But to Pauline, Fräulein Mücke was self-evidently a Scarlet Woman. After a week of raging silence, she copied the letter in her own hand, sent a telegram signalling their divorce to her husband on the Isle of Wight, and put the matter in the hands of their lawyer, who happened to be their friend Friedrich Rösch. So far as she was concerned, it was an open and shut case of marital infidelity.

Pauline: alone in the garden and with the family.

There is something rather touching about Pauline's assumption that her husband was capable of frequenting bars and carrying on with a clandestine Mieze, when he was on the threshold of forty, snowed under with conducting dates and spent every free moment at home working. She seems never to have realized that her Richard was probably the most faithful husband in musical history. Faced with this 'evidence' to the contrary, she at once determined on divorce and everlasting separation.

In life, as in the opera that resulted from it, *Intermezzo*, the explanation lay in a confusion of names. It was Josef Stransky, a conductor from Prague, visiting Berlin with an Italian touring company, who had gone to the Union Bar with a tenor called De Marchi, and De Marchi's manager, an American called Edgar Strakosch. There they had got into conversation with Mieze, and since the talk was all of opera, the young woman asked for a ticket. De Marchi spoke German with an Italian accent and he was liable to lose the letter 'n', so she understood him to say that 'Herr Strausky' would take care of it. When nothing arrived for her, she looked in the city directory, and, failing to find anyone with the name of 'Strausky', decided that the 'Strauss' dwelling at Joachimsthalerstrasse 17 must be the man she sought. There was actually another conductor, Edmund von Strauss, at the Berlin Opera, who was also often confused with Richard.

While the 'unfaithful' husband was still reeling from the shock, Pauline was taking steps to close the house, including the withdrawal of 2000 marks in gold from the bank; she also returned all his letters unopened.

My dear Pauxerl,
This business with the Mücke woman is so stupid! Now: you get the precious document on Whit Monday, and spend a week harbouring fearful resentment against your adulterous spouse, while I sail off to England, in blissful ignorance of the thunderstorm brewing at my back. You take a whole week to decide what to do about your monster of a husband, and the first act of your revenge is to draw my beautiful money out of the bank. I wish I knew what you intend to do with full 2,000 marks. There were no bills waiting to be paid, and that one dress from Gerson's can hardly cost 1,500 marks. Or is this your way of taking revenge? In that case, I would suggest you wait until you have some reason for revenge, and on this occasion I rather think you have none.

Now: I have never been in the Union Bar, I don't even know where it is, any more than I know who Mücke is. I am not acquainted with Mücke, or any other such. You could have thought that out for yourself, instead of demanding grand statements from me and simultaneously sending back my letters, which really makes it difficult for me. However, as that is you all over, and as you still do not know what you have in me, and *never will know*, I must ask you to seek out the proof and the explanation you want yourself in Berlin, as I am not in a good position to do it on Wight. Now: either precious Madame Mücke has confused me with someone else – after all, Berlin also boasts Edmund von Strauss, Oscar Straus, etc. – or someone has played a stupid and quite unnecessary joke on us. Now: I am asking Rösch to check the address of the said Mücke and to establish first and foremost whether such a being even exists. If she exists, he can ask her who the letter was intended for. If it then emerges that the letter was not meant for me, Rösch can box the lady's ears with it, three times if he will, and send me a short telegram, four words long: Mücke settled and explained.

It's a beautiful afternoon, and it's been quite spoilt for me, instead of going for a stroll in God's wonderful nature. Yesterday I had already begun composing something really nice, and had to waste my time on a letter clearing myself. You really could spare me things like this and go and hunt for your own explanations. I will send the authorization for the 2,000 marks to the bank at once. The best thing would be if you took the money straight back, and left the bills for me, which I can then settle on 11 June (in celebration of my birthday). For today, loving greetings and kisses from the adulterer to yourself and Bubi, who can have no notion of this horrendous business.

Still, for the time being, your Richard. (26 May 1902)

In the end, after much to-ing and fro-ing, the matter was cleared up.

In 1916, after *Frau ohne Schatten*, Strauss wanted to write a more light-hearted opera set in the present. Hofmannsthal refused to write a libretto with a contemporary setting, just as he refused to write something *à la* Scribe, involving a beautiful spy. So Strauss turned to Hermann Bahr and told him the old story of Mieze Mücke. They corresponded on the subject, and Strauss contributed a candid and detailed description of his family life and his relationship with his wife.

He is a lover of order, like her, though it is partly due to her influence that he became so. He plans everything very carefully, can always find time for anything, while in fact he works very hard and yet regards himself as not at all hard-working. She thinks he is a kind of absent-minded professor, remote from the world and always working. That is just her fantasy: she can interrupt his work at any time, he will go for walks and outings with her whenever she wants.

She thinks she is hard at work all day long because, in her very vivid imagination, she attributes to herself all the work done at her command by servants and others (the friends who she likes to send on her errands). She is very pedantic in her love of order and passion for cleanliness. In her heart too, she loves seemliness and purity, and rigorously deplores moral shortcomings in others, unless mitigated by some cause for fellow-feeling: artistic talent, housewifely virtues, a good tourist record in women, physical assets, good manners, good family in men. In such cases she can be very tolerant. Just as he can, with people who play skat well and are not major criminals.

One of the favourite subjects the couple argue about is that she, because of her pedantry, can only ever see one way to reach a goal, whereas he will weigh all the possibilities and choose the most convenient and time-saving. She will not acknowledge the help he gives in his quiet way, because she thinks he is no use in practical matters. He

Pauline and Richard with one of the family dogs.

does everything that needs to be done quietly, efficiently and without haste. She, though she possesses practical gifts, creates confusion because of her superabundant imagination and over-lively temperament. When she is excited and busy, she fails to see the purpose of his actions, and this often drives her to despair. She has the habit often of not listening when people say things to her, and often forgets that she has been asked a question, what it was, or what she answered. In the end, when it comes to the point, and when she has reflected, she does as he suggests.

Her vivid imagination, jumping rapidly from one thing to some other diametrically different thing, often leads her to assume that another person already knows what she is talking about. But she is so fidgety and quick that the other person would have to be a mind-reader to know what she means by 'this doodah' or 'that thingy'. He administers their capital on his own, not unsuccessfully, and would also deal better and more quickly with the small domestic bills, but she won't hear of it. She doesn't trust him not to muddle things, or pay something twice, or allow the tradesmen to take advantage of his good-natured generosity and cheat him left and right. Yet bills and receipts always cause her enormous trouble, and are only mastered after enormous expenditure of effort and with the aid of the honest serving-maid of a good memory. She often thinks he is being extravagant, when he takes the larger and longer view, while she will haggle over 50 pfennigs. On the other hand she has no instinct that tells her if the spending of 10 marks, or 30,000 marks, will give her value for money. She calculates only with small sums, he only with large ones.

The idea that her husband takes up all her time is another thing that exists solely in her imagination. He spends most of his time quietly on his

Richard, Pauline and Franz on a mountain walk.

own, working. Because she has the feeling that she is always doing things for him, she longs to be left on her own, but no sooner has he gone away than she experiences great longing for him.

Bahr wrote a scenario, but was uneasy about the whole project. He was afraid that Pauline would be made very angry, and that he would get small thanks from anybody else. These or similar considerations must have been his reasons for telling Strauss that 'You are the only person who can find the right words for this'.

Strauss had the leisure for it when he spent a few days in a Munich clinic for a check-up. With Bahr's outline of the action to guide him, he began writing at seven in the morning and finished the libretto in a week. The result is dialogue that exactly reproduces the way the family talked among themselves, without poetry and without artificial eloquence. Max Reinhardt declared he would stage it even without the music. As well as reflecting the conversational style and the diction of the Strauss household as clearly as if in a mirror, it also puts into Storch's mouth a number of its author's opinions and favourite expressions: 'I have a talent for dozing and ambling along: I have her to thank for my condition now, especially my health! She gingered me up!' 'No such thing as nervous temperament – lack of self-control.' Even the outbursts of anger are authentic, according to witnesses, and the tight-lipped, ironic use of the formulas 'Please excuse me' and 'I am quite extraordinarily grateful to you!', as in the opera, was evidently enough to strike terror into the unlucky recipients.

Strauss's life was strictly ordered. He experienced and assimilated much as an observer, visitor and sightseer. But he never exposed himself to escapades, adventures, or personal danger. He never knew the abject poverty of Mozart, or the political involvement and amorous intrigues of Wagner and Liszt. His sexual taste was straight. His knowledge was all at second hand, from reading, hearing, seeing, and it was his phenomenal imagination that converted it all into experience. It is no wonder that the trivial episode with Mieze Mücke gave him as much as he needed for a whole opera. The heart of the work feeds on something that was undoubtedly personal: his sense of irony.

Strauss had both wit (which comes from the intelligence) and humour (which is the gift of God). Many of the people who had to do with him did not understand that, and took offence. Hofmannsthal was the worst of all, having no sense of humour and disapproving on principle of jokes about art. But the sight of the earnest faces at a performance of, say, *Till Eulenspiegel*, shows that Hofmannsthal was not alone. When once Strauss had made some self-depreciatory remark like 'The chaste Joseph bores me', or '*Salome* is a scherzo which ends with a fatality', he never succeeded in making people understand thereafter that it had been meant humorously.

Those who have a repertory of jokes which they insist on telling in lieu of conversation have no claim to true humour. Strauss did not like such people, and smut made him angry. He did not like being told jokes, even intelligent ones and, while he drew humour and wit in with the air he breathed, he did not seek the society of wits and humorists. His humour was

Richard and Pauline in 1939, celebrating his 75th birthday with the Vienna Philharmonic Orchestra.

a character trait, his way of looking at life. Clemens Krauss and a few other friends understood that rather better than Pauline and his family did. Pauline took *Intermezzo* very hard indeed.

The part of the callow Baron Lummer, who is taken up and mothered by Frau Storch while her husband is away, is sung by a tenor: a clear sign of what Strauss thought of the character. In Sketchbook no. 46 he wrote: 'Baron – F major. She sees him in D major.' That is, in terms of Strauss's tonal symbolism, she grossly overestimates the Baron, who hasn't a chance against a strong character like hers.

The musical treatment of the everyday prose of the libretto is highly subtle, a psychologically aware, heightened recitative, both *secco* and *accompagnato*. The characters talk in normal prose, and the music provides everything they say with a background. Strauss had adumbrated something of the kind in the Prologue of *Ariadne* and in *Die Frau ohne Schatten*. Here it is the dominant stylistic trait. When humour and lyricism come to the fore, the musician spreads himself – above all in the symphonic interludes during which the audience is usually chattering or eating chocolates.

The game of skat at the beginning of Act II is also full of humour: 'A game of skat like this is something to enjoy. The only recreation after music – this to quotations from the Triumphal March in *Aida* and from *Tristan*

In the closing bars of the entire work Strauss quotes a melody he gave to the Dyer's Wife in Act I of *Die Frau ohne Schatten*, in the scene where the Nurse tempts her with a vision of a handsome youth. This also has a melodic affinity with some of tipsy Mariandel's philosophizing in Act III of *Der Rosenkavalier*, so perhaps there is no reason to read anything confessional into it. The composer wrote according to the dictates of his heart, just as he did in *Guntram*, still intent on extending his phenomenal technique.

It is scarcely credible, but the family insists that Pauline did not know that she was the subject of this musical joke until she was in her seat listening to the first performance of it on 4 November 1924. She had never suspected that her husband had been using her as a psychological model for years. The consequence, naturally enough, was a furious row. She thought the way he had put her and her private life on the stage for all to see was shameless. Many in the audience, then and since, have seen it as a grand declaration of love: but not she. The housemaid, Anna, was also enraged by the stage portrait of herself, and gave Strauss a piece of her mind.

In the hotel, in the lift, Pauline preserved her self-control. To a singer, who enquired, as if butter would not melt in her mouth, 'Did you enjoy it?', she answered, sweetly smiling, 'Better than you did!' The storm broke only in their room, and it was still rolling the next day, as they drove home. Martin, the chauffeur, told of a thunderstorm that raged outside the car, while the other storm burst out again and again inside it. Strauss, it seems, bore both in silence, though at one point he grew so angry himself he nearly jumped out. It was a worse row than the one in the *Symphonia domestica*, but, like that one, ended in reconciliation.

Many years later, admittedly, Pauline said to Rudolf Hartmann: 'Who knows, whether there wasn't something in that Mieze story after all' – and it is not certain if she was joking or not, because she then leant over to Frau Hartmann and said: 'In that respect, all men are scoundrels. And I can tell you this: I would still scratch the eyes out of any hussy who was after my Richard.' She was then eighty years old, and he seventy-nine.

On the set of the Rosenkavalier *film, with Michael Bohnen (Ochs).*

Robert Wiene, director of the film.

For all the interest Strauss took in it, the cinema might as well not have existed. But it was the favourite entertainment of millions, and by the 1920s there was enough money in it to enable more ambitious film-makers to risk films with serious cultural pretensions. Though the film with sound still lay in the future, some cinemas had pits, and large orchestras and conductors were employed to provide live musical accompaniments to films. Now Robert Wiene, the director of *The Cabinet of Dr Caligari*, approached Strauss with a scheme for a film version of *Rosenkavalier*. It would not be the first film based on an opera: *Carmen* and others had already proved successful. Strauss and Hofmannsthal decided to cooperate: the film might attract a new audience into the opera houses, which were fighting for their lives. Hofmannsthal wrote a script, reconstituting the action of the opera in pantomimic terms (which Wiene ignored). Strauss's part was to provide an orchestral score as an accompaniment; with the help of Carl Alwin and Otto Singer a selection of numbers from the opera score were rearranged (in every sense), and Strauss composed a new march as well.

The film was shot in 1925. The part of Baron Ochs was taken by the celebrated bass-baritone Michael Bohnen, but the other roles were played by film actors from half the nations of Europe: Austrians, French, Italians.

Strauss conducting the Barcelona Banda Municipal in an open-air concert, 1925.

Strauss was an aficionado of bull-fighting, which he regarded as the last ancient spectacle to survive in the modern world. He once let a concert start half an hour later than advertized, so that he could see a corrida through to the end.

A slender French boy played Oktavian, so that the special piquancy created by the presence of a young woman swaggering in the part was lost along with the centrality of Strauss's music.

The premiere took place on 10 January 1926, not in a cinema but in the Dresden State Opera House! On that occasion Strauss conducted, and his indifference to the cinema turned thenceforward into an active loathing. The film soon disappeared from the cinemas. Parts of it were found and reconstructed in 1965: it was appalling. The makers' intentions were evidently good, but the execution was botched. The film score was issued as a recording in 1980, played by an ensemble of thirteen instrumentalists, and projects some of the charm and brilliance of the original even in the chamber format.

'Helen' and Dresden

Strauss loved the countries that border the Mediterranean, and they came to return his affection. In 1925 the Banda Municipal in Barcelona ambitiously engaged him to conduct a concert of his own works. *Tod und Verklärung*, *Till Eulenspiegel* and *Don Juan* were arranged for brass and wind orchestra. The band was first-class and rehearsed the pieces well. The big square where they played provided an ideal acoustic, and a huge crowd packed it to hear the concert. Perhaps it reminded Strauss of the military band concerts he used to hear in his childhood in Munich. The success of the occasion was all the more remarkable, in view of the hold that Verdi and Puccini had on southern Europe, where many thought of Strauss as an 'atonal' composer.

Visiting Greece for the first time in 1892, he had been struck powerfully by the harmony reigning between mankind and art in the Greek landscape, by the beauty that lived on even in the ruins. There was no difference, for him, between the artistic ideals embodied in the myths and the drama of

Patti said once, when someone asked her why she was content to take the second place at a formal banquet, 'Where I sit is always the first place'.
STRAUSS TO MARIA JERITZA,
30 DECEMBER 1927

In Athens with Michael Rosenauer and his fiancée, the actress Dora Kaiser. Strauss wanted her to be cast as Sophie in the film version of Der Rosenkavalier, *but she did not get the part.*

There was an obstacle, however, and that was money. Another economic crisis was sweeping the world, and theatres were required to tighten their belts like everyone else. One way in which theatres can save money is to cut back on the fees and salaries paid to artists. The Deutscher Bühnenverein (Association of German Theatres) had fixed the rates that could be paid to singers within Germany, and absolutely no exceptions were allowed. Jeritza, however, who was Austrian, and knew her worth, could be equally intransigent. The rates Germans would work for were nothing to do with her, she argued; if they wanted her, they must pay her fee. Strauss wangled a special fee for her from Dresden, whereupon the Deutscher Bühnenverein threatened a boycott of all his stage works in every theatre in Germany. Jeritza, for her part, refused to back down. Appeals to the paramountcy of artistic considerations were useless. The composer had only one weapon: his right to decide where his work should be staged, and Strauss decided that if Germany could not guarantee the quality he wanted, the honour of the first performance should go to Vienna. Jeritza was already a member of the State Opera company there so there would be no haggling.

A proposal to stage a first performance in Dresden the day after the Viennese world premiere was met with expressions of outrage, and the spectre of a boycott was raised again. By now Strauss had little to lose: Dresden should give the actual world premiere, he proposed, but Vienna would stage *its* first performance, with Jeritza, the next day. Now Jeritza was outraged: if she didn't sing Helen in the world premiere, she would not sing the role at all. Strauss wrote to her, pleading:

> I cannot reconcile myself to the news that you will not sing the part of Helen, your Helen, conceived with you in mind from the very first, and written for you, unless the premiere is given to Vienna. . . . Your standing down is the heaviest blow that could befall my Helen before she has even been born. I perfectly understand your position, and I share your view that you are the one foreordained to create the role. But alas, you see things from afar, and do not know the exasperation I have been caused in the past eight weeks over this tiresome and at bottom utterly stupid question of the premiere. Legally, of course, I am in the right. But do you know what has happened? The Saxon Ministry of Culture got on to the German Ambassador in Vienna, to work on the Austrian ministries to desist from giving the world premiere in Vienna!

Gingerly, patiently, handling the vanity of each side like newlaid eggs, Strauss brought about the eventual compromise. Dresden would give the opera on 6 June 1928, with Elisabeth Rethberg in the title role and Fritz Busch conducting. On 11 June, his birthday, the composer would conduct the Viennese premiere, with Jeritza heading the cast. Jeritza consented to this – then caused him fresh alarm with an interview she gave that March.

> To judge by that utterly remarkable interview, if J. is going back on all previous undertakings and still has not learnt the part of Helen, I think

Outside the Dresden Opera with Fritz Busch, director of that house 1922–33. Busch conducted the first performances of Intermezzo, Helena *and the* Parergon zur Sinfonia Domestica. *He was one of four talented brothers: Willi was a well-known actor, Adolf was a violinist and founder of the Busch Quartet, of which Hermann, a cellist, was also a founder member.*

186

it will be impossible to start rehearsals on 16 April. J. has had the vocal score of Act I in her hands for the past four weeks. She ought to know it by heart by now and be ready to start on Act II. She has nothing more 'to discuss with me', unless she does in fact know the part already, is frightened by it and wants some things made easier or cut. There could be some discussion of that, *but only to a very limited extent*. I have the feeling, after that interview, that she wants to get out of it. (She has probably found some snag, some hair in the soup.) If she claims that she does not

Interior of the Dresden Opera house, designed by Gottfried Semper. Nine of Strauss's operas had their first performances here.

Exterior of the Dresden Opera House.

Strauss with Pauline and others in a box at the premiere of Die ägyptische Helena, *6 June 1928.*

yet know Act I, at least, I am sure she is lying! Please talk to Schneiderhan about it: let Carl Alwin act as musical adviser. What is at stake is having the premiere on my birthday. I have worked out the most precise timetable for the rehearsals, starting on 16 April, and there is no margin! (To Franz, 27 March 1928)

One might think that a composer would not have to worry himself about matters like this, but he does. Others reassured him and praised Jeritza's diligence; he wrote to her again, pleading with her not to be discouraged in her study of the part. Then he had to leave for a concert tour.

Now it was the turn of Jeritza's husband, Baron Popper. He demanded to know why there was so little publicity, and why his wife's 'great-hearted decision' was not being widely acclaimed. There must be posters advertising the event in every express railway train, in all the best hotels, on Atlantic liners. More suspense: would this be made another excuse for her to withdraw at the last moment?

In the end, she turned up trumps. Flattered, caressed, reassured on every side, she worked hard, she sang, she conquered. No one, except Strauss, seems to have noticed Rethberg's vocally better performance in Dresden. The *prima donna assoluta* triumphed alone.

The dress rehearsal went brilliantly, made a great impression, thanks above all to the immense dramatic power of Jeritza. She is particularly thrilling in the second act, which she fills so completely by her performance that we were left breathless with excitement. Vocally and musically too, she was very good. The only place where Rethberg is vocally much her superior is in the aria at the beginning of Act II.

[The Vienna premiere] was perhaps the greatest triumph of my life. After the first act the audience went mad for a full quarter-hour, at the

In Dresden, visiting the grave of Carl Maria von Weber on the centenary of his death, 5 June 1926. Wagner (a prime mover in the removal of Weber's remains from London to Dresden) and Weber had both worked at the Dresden Opera, and both were models for Strauss. He once described the clarinet cantilena in the overture to Der Freischütz as a primal image of descriptive expression: 'the pleading of concerned innocence'.

Dresden, before the première of Helena. From the left, standing: Willy Levin, a very good friend of Strauss, skat-player and legal adviser; Elisabeth Rethberg (Helen); Friedrich Plaschke (Altair; later the first Waldner in Arabella and Morosus in Die schweigsame Frau); Frau and Herr Vogelstrom, the hosts; Strauss; Eva Plaschke-von der Osten, the first Oktavian, but an assistant producer for Helena; Fritz Reiner, principal conductor at the Dresden Opera 1914–21, who came from America for the première. In front, crouching: Leonhard Fanto, designer of sets and costumes, an Austrian whose diplomatic talents made him an invaluable go-between in an opera house.

Crossing the street from the Hotel Bellevue to the Dresden Opera for the première of Intermezzo, 4 November 1924. Baroness Thüngen, Strauss, Pauline, Franz.

Strauss with Dr Paul Adolph who, as Intendant of the Dresden Opera, found himself the buffer between art and politics in 1935, when Die schweigsame Frau *was staged.*

Ernst von Schuch, director of the Dresden Opera from 1873 to his death in 1914. It was thanks to his persistence that Dresden became the regular venue for the premières of Strauss's operas. As a young man, as well as collecting a degree in law, he played in Johann Strauss's orchestra.

end the enthusiasm was beyond bounds, for Jeritza too, whose triumph was undisputed, although (after fainting in her dressing room after the first act) because of the enormous excitement she was not as good in the second act as she was at the dress rehearsal. What a shame you were not here. (To Pauline, 13 July 1928)

Pauline was at home in Garmisch. Though she never ceased to complain about the boredom of country life, she always found some excuse not to travel, felt unwell, or really ran a temperature, until the hour of departure was safely past. She loved big cities – and hardly ever visited one. She went to Dresden for the premiere of *Die ägyptische Helena*, but evidently felt no compulsion to hear the work again in Vienna, even with Jeritza and under her husband's direction. Or perhaps it was an economy measure. Strauss himself, from time to time, would tell his family not to travel: 'Unnecessary and expensive. I don't earn money in order for us to waste it.'

In spite of the initial success, a model performance, and an international star, *Die ägyptische Helena* remained one of the least often performed of Strauss's operas.

Fritz Busch, the conductor of the Dresden premiere, recalled Strauss in his memoirs. He discovered during the rehearsals for *Intermezzo* that:

Strauss spoke very frankly on professional and artistic questions. Not only did he willingly accept my critical objections, but he often asked me for my candid opinion of various details of the composition. . . .

In Garmisch he played me his *Aegyptische Helena*. . . . I did not hesitate to say, amongst other things, that I thought Daud's song was cheap and that he ought to weigh such 'inspirations' more carefully. He in no way disputed this criticism, but actually repeated it with enjoyment to his wife . . . but then added with disdainful cynicism: 'That's what's wanted for the servant girls. Believe me, the general public would not go to *Tannhäuser* if it didn't contain "O du mein holder Abendstern", or to *Die Walküre* without "Winterstürme". Well, well, that's what they want.'

Friends, Adventures, Family

After Germany and Austria, England was the country which gave Strauss the most attentive and receptive hearing. From the time of the English premiere of *Elektra* in 1910, his works were presented thoughtfully and regularly revived. George Bernard Shaw campaigned on his behalf with characteristic ebullience. Ernest Newman brought Shaw's wrath down upon his head in 1910 when, reviewing *Elektra* in *The Nation*, he deplored 'the degeneration of the musician in Strauss from what he was fifteen years ago'. Shaw let out a 'yell of remonstrance': Newman had once been wrong about Wagner and ought by now to have been cured 'of asserting that everything that does not please him is wrong, not only technically but ethically'. Newman issued a sharp retort, Shaw replied, and the polemics went on for weeks.

The readers loved this sort of thing, and the quarrel did Strauss's reputation in England nothing but good. He and Shaw met on frequent occasions during the course of their long lives. In the summer of 1929 they found themselves on the island of Brioni at the same time as the world heavyweight boxing champion, Gene Tunney. 'He was the most sought-after celebrity there,' Strauss related, 'not we two artists.'

There are very few operas which successfully combine the comic with the lyrical. After *Helena*, which both Strauss and Hofmannsthal loved with its blend of fantasy and seriousness, they thought of attempting a second *Rosenkavalier*, full of waltzes, emotion and a touch of the elegiac. On 16 December 1927 Hofmannsthal outlined to Strauss a subject that he had been thinking about for some time, concerning a family of impoverished nobles in Vienna. Because they lack the funds to bring the younger daughter out into society in the style befitting their rank, she masquerades as a boy. The family's fortunes depend on the elder daughter, Arabella, making a good marriage, but she only flirts with her admirers, without having serious feelings for any of them. Then a stranger comes into their lives.

Strauss liked the subject, but he did not find the first act inspiring when he got it four months later. With no great sense of urgency, the pair began to revise it. It was a quiet crisis, and both felt a chill in their relationship, as after years of marriage. Strauss wrote at one point: 'The main thing is that the subject must be fully exploited and the best possible yield squeezed out of it. That requires time and leisure. For the moment I have written enough operas, and a rest will do my imagination good: I shall therefore wait till the autumn – I'll wait until Easter, I'll wait as long as you like.' (8 August 1928).

The text was finished in December 1928, a year after Hofmannsthal first mentioned it, but he held on to it in the belief that further revision might still be needed: changes in motivation, greater concision and more tension. On 29 December he read it to Strauss, who was very pleased with it, but thought that Act I could still do with some reworking. Hofmannsthal agreed with him, and went on with the task until mid-July 1929. At last he sent the final version to Strauss, who despatched an enthusiastic telegram on 14 July: 'First act excellent. Many thanks and congratulations. Sincerely – Richard Strauss.'

Hofmannsthal did not read it. It reached his house at Rodaun on 15 July, the day he died of a stroke, just before the funeral of his son Franz, who had shot himself three days earlier.

Harry Kessler went to the poet's funeral at Rodaun. 'The coffin, altar and altar rail disappeared under a sea of roses. Every rose garden in Vienna must have been pillaged to produce such splendour. The church was cram-full. I sat . . . behind Richard Strauss's son. The absence of Strauss himself and Max Reinhardt was unexpected.' (Kessler's diary, 18 July 1929) The

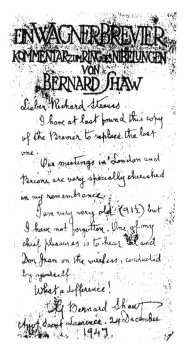

A copy of the German edition of The Perfect Wagnerite, *which Bernard Shaw inscribed to Strauss on Christmas Eve 1947.*

A picture taken in Hugo von Hofmannsthal's study after his death, showing him lying on the sofa where he died.

In some quarters Dada was taken more seriously than it took itself. It was one of many artistic movements that tried to replace the high technical accomplishment of prewar art with a turn to primitivism, in the belief that talent and craftsmanship were not essential to artistic expression.

next day Kessler called on the surviving members of the family, Hugo's wife Gerty and their younger son Raimund. 'Gerty Hofmannsthal . . . believes, and it is a consolation to her, that the death of the son was not the cause of the father's death. The doctors, diagnosing advanced hardening of the arteries, gave up Hugo three years ago.' Raimund 'and his mother think it fortunate that Hugo was spared an awakening to hopeless and protracted suffering. But Gerty is grieved that he never received the letter from Richard Strauss confirming arrival of the the revised version of *Arabella*, Act I, and congratulating him on its success.

'Hugo von Hofmannsthal has died. Thanks be to the noble, unforgettable man!' Strauss wrote in his diary. The next day he went, unannounced, to call on his neighbours, Elisabeth Schumann and Carl Alwin, who had Clemens von Franckenstein as guest in their house (a former pupil of Ludwig Thuille, conductor and composer, Franckenstein was at that date Intendant of the Munich Opera). Strauss read the text of *Arabella* to them, continually overcome by tears. His listeners were deeply moved, understanding that he was attempting to commemorate the poet according to his own rites, in the presence of friends, under the pressure of a great sorrow which he had probably violently suppressed in his own home.

It was a time of rapid change. Cinema screens showed the silent, flickering images of other worlds, newspapers brought people floods of information from far away, the globe seemed to be shrinking. New fashions in art, jazz, contemporary subjects in the theatre, musicals and revues, all displaced older concepts of art as something uplifting, enchanting or cathartic. The heavier the burden of everyday life, the lighter art became: entertainment reigned.

Dada, Expressionism, cabaret, *chansons*, appealed not only to the undemanding public who had always enjoyed operetta and farce, they also sapped the taste of the more cultivated classes, in the face of poverty, unemployment and the increasing politicization of the streets, where factions confronted each other like bands of brigands. In the wake of economic inflation, the golden twenties also brought artistic inflation. Young people adopted new, more material values.

Strauss's musical language had become familiar to people. He was written out, they said, nothing new since *Rosenkavalier*; well, perhaps *Ariadne*, but after that! At sixty-five, he stood for his own monument, a conservative, patriarchal figure. The time when he took the risk of associating himself with a social outcast like Wilde or with political subversives was long past. He remained loyal to himself and his musical principles, still commanded the admiration of many younger, musical people, but anyone with a good conceit of himself dismissed him. His loyalest adherents were his contemporaries, an ageing company. He had another twenty years to live, an Olympian, remote and irrelevant. His style was widely imitated: there was not a piece of 'superior entertainment music' which did not pay homage to him: in the cinema above all.

When Christine Storch, in *Intermezzo*, asked her husband not to travel in the front or rear carriage of the train, she showed some prescience. Twice within a few years of that opera's première Strauss experienced accidents on the railways. The first took place on 17 February 1925. Frau Alice was there:

> Papa was on his way from Paris to Spain with Franz and me. We had already crossed the frontier and were sitting in the dining car when there was a sudden jolt and directly afterwards an almighty bang. The train went off the rails. One of the wheels on the goods van had broken. It derailed three carriages. We were hurled into each other's laps. Beyond that nothing happened to us. The engine-driver's presence of mind prevented anything worse. In gratitude, we passed the hat round for him on the spot. Of course we had to wait beside the track for hours before a relief train arrived.

The second occurred on 5 December 1927. Richard, Pauline and Anna, their maid, were returning from Prague to Vienna. Near the Czech border, at 1.30 a.m., a carriage went off the rails. The Strausses were hurled against the further wall of their compartment but were unhurt. Anna, in the next compartment, hurt her arm and was trapped for several hours. Meanwhile, Franz and Alice were waiting anxiously at the station in Vienna. When he got home, Strauss went to his work, as though nothing had happened.

Photos of the derailed train in Spain.

One day in March 1927 the telephone rang in the house in the Jacquingasse: Strauss was seriously ill in Dresden, his life was in danger, he was in hospital. Come quickly! Emanuel von Grab chartered a single-engine aeroplane. Franz and Alice, who was expecting their first child, flew up to Dresden in the frail craft. There stood Leonhard Fanto, the stage designer and longstanding colleague. Ill? Strauss? He had taken the train to Königsberg the previous day. They called Königsberg and were blasted over the phone: 'Are you mad, to fall for a trick like that? Never felt better in my life! What did you spend all that money for, on a wild goose chase? An aeroplane – I don't believe it!' On their way home, the chartered plane had to make an emergency landing in a field of cucumbers: fortunately no one was hurt.

The story became part of the family mythology, and everyone had his or her version of it. It was discovered later that the macabre hoaxer was a madman, who had made similar calls to dozens of other famous people. He called himself 'The Fountain Pen King'.

Everybody knows one 'fact' about every famous person: Schiller got his inspiration from smelling rotten apples; Beethoven moved house every six months; Mozart had a pauper's funeral; Haydn's wife was a shrew; Strauss played skat incessantly, liked to win, and his wife hauled him from the card-table with the command: 'Richardl! Composition!' Every cliché has its grain of truth.

All other occupations transformed themselves into sound impressions for Strauss, so that musical themes incessantly and inevitably developed to the point of oppressing him. But at the card-table he found a respite, a soundless recreation, enabling him to unwind and relax. A well-played game of skat gave him better entertainment than idle conversation or other distractions. He liked winning (who doesn't?) but his was not a gambler's nature. Games of chance did not interest him. The only reason he needed skat was to free himself from the clutches of music. Always on the lookout for the necessary 'third man', he could make a good friend of a good partner.

He had developed a liking for card games while still a schoolboy, when he played with Thuille, Arthur Seidl and his cousins, and he had improved his skat play during the winter he spent in Berlin in 1884. It was still considered quite a new game in those days, having evolved as a variant of another game called 'Sheep's Head' between 1810 and 1820 in Altenburg in Thuringia. Strauss could remember and recite the sequence of play in games that had happened years earlier.

The tenor Franz Klarwein was the son of the people who kept the restaurant at the railway station in Garmisch. The Strausses often ate there, particularly on account of the excellent sausages. After Pauline heard him singing, she told her husband about him, who straightaway recommended him to the Berlin Opera. Klarwein played many a game of skat with Strauss, often with Hans Hotter as well:

He was a very good player, flexible and ready to take risks. Like a mathematical genius, he knew what card the other player had after three or four tricks. He was a master bluffer, and when he bluffed you

Studying his hand. A score card.

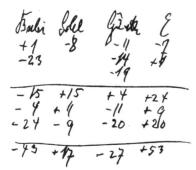

The skat scene in Intermezzo *(from the Dresden première, November 1924). Robert Storch: 'Ah, a game of skat like this is such a pleasure, the only way to unwind after music. [The orchestra quotes* Tristan*] You know I'm very fond of my wife, but when you're playing skat it's nice if there are no ladies in the next room.' Commercial Councillor: 'Every minute one of them puts her head round the door: "Will you be finished soon, gentlemen?" "Very soon, my angel" he says – Devil take you, he thinks.'*

The skat-player. The man in the middle is Manfred Mautner-Markhof.

A hand of skat with Theodor Martin and Franz.

made mistakes. That was his great strength. He often won, even when we had all the trumps. After a double he always redoubled, and usually knew by the third card what had been dealt. We often played for two pfennigs a point in those days, during the war, when the Reichsmark had very little purchasing power.

One evening, the luck was against Strauss and he was losing. Enter Frau Pauline:

Franz Klarwein (the Italian Tenor) and Hans Hotter (Olivier), in costume for Capriccio.

'Once and for all, go home! I don't like these men who play skat with you all the time.' 'But, dear heart, we've got a spinach soufflé, the gentlemen could join us for a bite to eat, and then we could have another little game afterwards.' 'No fear. Their wives are waiting for them. Go home!'

She knew at once he'd lost, however assiduously he denied it. He used to get very angry when he played badly – because of his mistakes, not because of the money. But he got our winnings out of the safe, secretly, so that Pauline shouldn't see. He went with us as far as the garden gate, where he said: 'There's your money, you young rascals – now, be off with you.' We were grown men, but it was like getting a medal to be called 'young rascals', and to have ruffled Strauss's calm.

After the dress rehearsal for the premiere of *Capriccio*, he was very moved, had tears in his eyes, but he invited us straightaway to come and play skat in the hotel. The rehearsal finished at 3, and Hotter and I had to present ourselves at the Vier Jahreszeiten at 4 – and then we played until 11.30 at night. We both wanted to go to bed – after all, we had the premiere the next day! But he liked staying up late and in any case he was losing and didn't want to finish. So we let him win, as otherwise we would never have got to our beds. After losing he was generally a bit grumpy, not on account of the money but because of the blow to his reputation. When that happened a few days would pass before you were asked to play again.

Son Franz was often called upon to play, and so too was Theodor Martin, the family chauffeur: it was only one of the many ways in which he made himself indispensable. Another regular player in later years was the industrialist Manfred Mautner-Markhof, a close family friend, whose father had made Strauss's acquaintance at a race course. The Nazis arrested 'M–M–M' in 1938. Encountering the new Gauleiter of Vienna at the reception for his birthday, Strauss said bluntly that his birthday wish was for the release of Mautner-Markhof. 'The arrest can only be an error, in any case.' At that date a request like that would still be countenanced, and M–M–M was released forthwith.

M–M–M's wife was a Kupelwieser before her marriage, a member of the same family as Schubert's friends. It was for Leopold Kupelwieser's wedding that Schubert composed an impromptu waltz. It is a wonderfully elegiac piece, for Schubert was himself in love with the bride. He never wrote it down, and it survived in the Kupelwieser family, passed down from one generation to the next. Strauss wrote it down, when Frau Mautner-Markhof played it to him.

Strauss became an ancestor on 1 November 1927, when Richard Max Emanuel Hermann Strauss was born in Vienna. Grandmother Pauline sent off a telegram: 'Hurrah, the dynasty is assured. An All Saints baby will be Pope at least. We are superlatively happy.'

In the great majority of photographs, Strauss's facial expression is noncommittal, neutral. The family snapshots of him with his grandsons are an important exception to the rule: his features are expressive, his eyes alert.

Young Richard Strauss with his mother and grandfather.

And young Christian with his grandfather.

Young Richard recalls his grandfather vividly.

He was a perfectly normal grandfather, just what anyone would wish. Of course he didn't play with us as often as my parents, after all he was already quite an elderly man, but we could go in to see him whenever we wanted, even when he was working, without knocking. Sometimes he played ball in the garden with us, football, on the patch under the washing-line. He taught me chess and skat before I could read or write. When we were small we didn't know that he was world-famous, and it wouldn't have interested us if we had known: he was Grandpapa, that was all.

He sometimes told us stories when we were out for walks. The plot of the *Ring*, for instance. Of course, as a little boy I didn't understand it very well, but it was a super story. He was always keen to give us information and educate us in the humanities. A cultivated European must know Latin and Greek, or else he's not a fully qualified human being, he must read philosophy, he must have Goethe on his bedside table, Herder, Wieland, Homer and Sophocles in the original; he must study, get a good education, concentrate, not waste time.

I often fell short of Grandpapa's requirements. If you'd told him a boy should be allowed to find self-fulfilment, he wouldn't have known

197

From the family album, with young Richard the centre of attention.

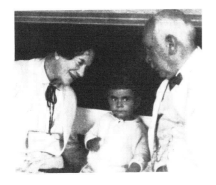

what you were talking about. Lead his own life? Go out with girls? 'My grandson doesn't do that sort of thing.' It would have pleased him best if his son and his grandsons had been at their desks by 8 in the morning, occupying themselves with learned dissertations on literary, aesthetic or musical topics. Research of that kind was what he regarded as the real purpose of life, it was what Goethe meant in *Elective Affinities*. In the early evening, one might have a little recreation, play a game of skat, and then, for the evening's entertainment within the family circle, read a little art history. Why did Fra Lippo Lippi paint gold haloes, and not Fra Angelico? He would probably also have liked to do what Wagner did, and have family play-readings of the classics.

There were some big rows when my father wanted to study medicine: 'My son, doctoring to peasants? Lancing boils and prescribing pills for old biddies?' After they had let off steam in an argument, they would give each other a big hug, and Grandpapa would go back to his work, which preoccupied him without ceasing.

He was implacable in artistic matters. When I was preparing my first production of *Figaro*, working it out on paper, I wrote him a letter referring to 'my *Figaro*'. I got a rocket back: 'How dare you be so arrogant, you young rascal! "My" *Figaro*?!' He would not tolerate anything like that.

There was a time when we shared a dressing room. Grandmama and my parents each had their own, and I was billeted on Grandpapa. He had the washbasin on the left, and I had the one on the right. We always met there in the mornings. In later years I used to shave him, after the war with an electric razor, and rub his back with alcohol. We had long conversations when we were in there, always about culture and education. To my regret. It was the most important thing to him.

He didn't teach me the piano, he could never have stood it. After all, he was already seventy when I started to play '*Hänschen klein*'. Only I was always being told: 'You won't get anywhere if you don't practise, you must be able to sightread.' When I was seven I said I wanted a flute, meaning a recorder – a block flute, that was all. Lo and behold, on my birthday I was given a silver flute and informed that Professor Rezn̆iček of the Vienna Philharmonic had been engaged to give me lessons twice a week, the full drill.

None of us ever felt the least desire for individual privacy within the family. We did everything together. Sometimes Grandpapa sorted the post, sometimes Grandmama. When she did it, she always returned, unopened, anything that looked remotely like an unsolicited opera libretto. At mealtimes we talked about everyday matters, family concerns. Never about professional things. We took our time. We usually took only a little of each of three courses. There was no rush, we waited until everyone had cleared their plates, and then went on to the next course. Nothing was shut away in the house, there was no 'mine' and 'thine', everything was 'ours'. Owning and doing everything together was something I took so much for granted that I simply couldn't conceive of its being different in other families.

He never talked about his work with anybody. With us, he would at most, occasionally, tell us the plot of his latest opera, *Daphne* or *Danae*. When he was writing *Friedenstag*, I was supposed to read Treitschke on the Thirty Years' War, but I was only eleven or twelve and I was more interested in skating and football than in Gustavus Adolphus. I'm sure he was disappointed, but later he said to himself: 'I have always demanded much more of people than they've been able to accomplish. Probably too much.'

What I especially admired was his ability for rational organization. He liked to sleep late, to 8.30 or so. But the fourteen hours of his day were wholly filled. Conducting, two hours for walking, time and leisure for eating and skat – and composing, or scoring four to five pages in winter. I have tried a few times to emulate him, and get through a comparable pensum of written work. It was simply impossible.

1905: helping his son with his lessons.

The personality of Strauss, more than most of the great composers, is such as to provoke a searching examination of the question: 'How likeable can we expect a genius to be?' Broadly speaking, the contemporaries of great people are inclined to treat them with contempt, to attribute despicable motives to them, and to depreciate their stature. Then comes posterity which goes to the other extreme, idolizing and idealizing them. This became especially prevalent during the nineteenth century, when the great composers were assigned to one or other of the two general categories: the sweet-natured, modest darlings of the gods (Mozart, Weber, Lortzing) and the ungovernable, awe-inspiring titans (Beethoven, Wagner, Berlioz). Best of all was the neglected genius, unlucky in love, too timid to press his suit, and pouring out his soul in song, a figure of fantasy embodied in the popular image of Franz Schubert.

Changing fashions in biography have brought out more of the shadow side: most people in the latter part of the twentieth century would admit that none of the above-mentioned was an angel in human form. If 'divine' or 'heavenly' is the word that still springs to the lips to describe the music, the thought that it originated in the brains and hearts of human beings, possessed of all too human weaknesses and characteristics, should lead us to ponder more on the meaning of the word 'human'.

1935: helping the grandsons with their lessons.

All great artists have been egoists and monomaniacs. With the kind of inspirations that they receive, modesty can only be an affectation. They are hyper-nervous, unstable and excitable. No work with the stamp of eternity upon it is an exact reflection of the personality of its creator, or of the frame of mind in which it was produced: rhapsodies can be written in a rage, tragedy in a state of content. The genesis of every work of art is individual, and it issues from the very complexity of its creator. Schubert was indeed unlucky in love – if that is the right term to use of contracting syphilis. Wagner was not *just* a monster. Strauss was not *just* a skat-playing, money-grubbing, *haut bourgeois* opportunist.

Strauss never revealed his inner life to anyone. Outwardly he was cool, rational, logical and devoid of vanity. Orally and in writing, he delivered valid judgments on art, business, philosophy and personalities. His letters

Some musical hints at the piano with his grandson Richard.

and other writings are clearly expressed and avoid bombast or phrase-making. He was helpful and fair. No intrigue or malicious gossip could ever be laid at his door. He was polite and well-mannered, but never 'smooth' or 'nice'. It cannot be said too often: everything in his life centred on his music, his every action or thought was directed towards the goal of creating his works and helping them to prosper. It was inevitable that in the process his opinions and his endeavours sometimes brought him into opposition with the world about him.

His marriage is something of a mystery for outsiders. It is hard to understand his inexhaustible patience and affection towards Pauline and her crotchets, his acceptance of the irritation, his need for the agitation and the emotional tempests (while her prickly tenderness concealed respect for him behind a front of boisterousness and provocation, whimsicality and argumentativeness).

Strauss's own temperament and hypersensitivity found vent sometimes in outbursts of rage and hasty condemnation of persons and incidents. His work-centred egoism was the lodestar of his own life, and he could be as unpredictable and moody as his wife, roundly cursing one day a person who had been his friend the day before. He enjoyed occasional irreverence, too; it purged the brain and the bile, he believed. Expressing his anger soothed him. When enraged, he often had powerful musical ideas.

Nothing fell easily into his lap. He had to wrestle to give every work its proper form, in lonely concentration and creative masochism, but never spoke to anybody else about it. Getting the work performed and better known was the next problem: the constant renewal of the effort to overcome the old obstacles of vanity, indifference, performers' footling objections. Nothing could ever be taken for granted, he had to chase up everything himself, strategist and diplomat in one. He was in fact an entire modern business: manufacturer, packer and despatcher, advertiser, salesman, and quality controller. He had no use for agents, managers, offices or secretaries. He did everything himself, indefatigably, patiently and always under pressure. He was nice to people because he needed to be. Not, therefore, the type of squeaky-clean, likeable genius beloved of the popular imagination. But who is? Or ever was?

The grandsons also learned to play skat: here they are in the loggia at Garmisch, Christian on the left, Richard II on the right.

The Conductor

His conducting shows a strange mixture, peculiar to him, of apathy and masterly directness which is not without an element of suggestion. This style of conducting practically never appears exciting but it can arouse excitement in the hearer. Then there seems to be direct contact with genius.

FRITZ BUSCH

Strauss led a triple life: the composer; the *paterfamilias*; and the conductor. In the last role, he belonged to that élite who were regularly on the move about the world. He performed his own works, to demonstrate by example what could not be written down in the score, and he conducted the masters he revered, with all the great orchestras of the civilized world, in the opera house and in the concert hall. Many of those who heard him had a greater admiration for him as interpreter than as composer.

In 1906, he outlined his preferred repertory to Friedrich Sieger, the Frankfurt lawyer and director of the Museum Concerts series, in whose house he usually stayed when he visited Frankfurt.

> I would much prefer to conduct as little Strauss as possible, because I find that very boring. What I enjoy conducting: all Beethoven (especially the *Eroica* and VII and IX) – Mozart (G Minor, *Jupiter*) and Haydn – Liszt: all the symphonic poems and the *Faust* Symphony – Berlioz and Wagner of course – Brahms IV (authentically, as it was first done in Meiningen, under Brahms and Bülow) – Weber overtures – Elgar's *Variations*, the new symphony by Hermann Bischoff – Bruckner III and IX – Spohr's *Jessonda* overture – overture of Rheinberger's *Widerspenstige* (pretty and harmless) etc. etc.

In 1908 Oscar Bie, Max Reinhardt, Ernst von Reznicek and Strauss were talking about his great success with Beethoven's Fifth. Strauss said:

> In Beethoven, it takes an ictus, temperament and élan to bring out his greatness. The beauty of orchestral tone is less important than this

Generally Strauss found it enough to be vigilant but appear calm and relaxed. After successful rehearsals with the Monte Carlo orchestra, which he found rhythmically very precise, he wrote to Pauline: 'French conductors are not "geniuses", and pieces fare all the better for it; what is played is nothing more and nothing less than exactly what the composer prescribed!'

'If you don't have the score in your head, you will have your head in the score.'

He always acknowledged applause with an inclination and bowing of the head, marked by a courteous grandezza *and slow, calm movements.*

particular fiery spirit. Usually they play it like sugared water. True, his instrumentation doesn't match the grandeur of his intentions, at least, not nowadays, when ears have been spoiled by my orchestra [general mirth]. Effectively, I perspire only in the C Minor Symphony, the Ninth and the *Eroica*. And of course in *Tristan* and Act I of *Walküre*. In everything else, I don't lose my self-command and don't give out too much of myself. If I did, they might as well pack a coffin in my baggage when I do a tour like the one to Spain this year.

He did not rehearse very much, or for very long. In opera, singers had to keep their eye on him: he helped them and followed their breathing. He accomplished everything by projection. A glance to the player in question was the only cue he needed to give. On the rare occasions when he raised his left arm or actually rose from his seat, it caused an immense burst of orchestral sound. He would sometimes stand at the end of *Salome*.

Accidents can happen when rehearsal has been minimal. He was conducting *Daphne* in 1942, in Munich, and came to a passage marked 'three in a bar', where Krauss had the habit of beating four. Strauss beat three, completely throwing out both the orchestra and Franz Klarwein, who was singing Leukippos. Strauss turned the pages of his score, while making signs to get things back on the rails: after twenty bars, they were all together again. At the end he said to Klarwein: 'Franziskus, this time I didn't know myself where I was.'

He told Ernst Roth why he always turned the pages of his score, without reading it: although he knew the music by heart, he did not know the rehearsal numbers. When he was a young conductor in Weimar, during a performance of *Don Giovanni*, the Commendatore had come in fifty-four bars too early. Strauss tried to rescue the situation by making a jump, and shouted 'D minor chord'. The orchestra was not aware of what had happened on the stage, and did not understand what he wanted. So they stopped playing and the curtain had to be brought down. 'Such a thing happens only once in a lifetime and since then I have never conducted without the score in front of me.'

Roth often saw him conduct:

His beat was like the pendulum of a metronome, regular and merciless. From the first note the tempo of every piece was firmly and unmistakably laid down. 'One can conduct the prelude to *Tristan*,' he used to say, 'only if one has the tempo of the last bar exactly in one's ear.' After a rehearsal I heard him say to the conductor, 'You cannot conduct with the baton alone.' Indeed, when conducting his eyes wandered constantly through the orchestra, from one player to the other, and they all felt his magnetic influence. There was nothing loose or casual in his performances.

Strauss made a host of remarks about conducting:

In the course of fifty years' conducting, I have thoroughly tested the

Pictures taken during a rehearsal of Till Eulenspiegel, *Cologne 1936.*
'It's best if the conductor keeps calm. The smaller the movements are, from the wrist, the more precise the execution.'

importance of beating every crotchet and quaver. The crucial thing is a rhythmically precise upbeat, in which the tempo to come is already clearly signalled, followed by a precise downbeat. The second half of the bar is not important, I very often do it alla breve.

Music should be heard with the ears, not the eyes. Orchestral musicians groan if you give them every single crotchet in the alla breves in *Tristan*, or if you ceremoniously beat twelve quavers in every bar of the scene by the brook [in Beethoven's *Pastoral* Symphony] or the second variation in the Adagio of the Ninth, or if you shout 'ssh' or '*piano*' at them while your right hand goes on doing *forte*.

He thought of *forte* tuttis in Mozart and Haydn as columns, framing the more expressive passages, whereas in Beethoven they were explosions of painful despair and defiant energy. He admonished younger colleagues to get broader when a principal subject was reprised, or when a composer had indicated a broader tempo. He pointed out that works often required a uniform tempo to be maintained in the background throughout all modifications, and he never ceased to emphasize the importance of simplicity. He always requested a large complement of string players: 'Up to twelve first violins is still chamber music. Sixteen are the minimum!'

He compiled a list of golden rules for young conductors:

Keep in mind that you are not making music for your own pleasure, but to please your listeners.

You shouldn't perspire when you conduct, it's for the audience to get warm.

Never look encouragingly at the brass. If they're not playing loudly enough for you, bring them down by two notches.

Heinz Tietjen, director of the Berlin Opera, and an invaluable mentor to the young Winifred Wagner at Bayreuth in the 1930s. He did much to shield Alice Strauss during the Third Reich.

On the other hand, never take your eye off the horns or woodwind: if you can so much as hear them, they are already too loud.

It's not enough if you yourself can hear every word of a singer, when you know the text by heart. The audience must be able to follow without the least difficulty. If they can't hear the words, they go to sleep.

Accompany the singer in such a manner that he can sing without straining.

If you think you have reached the utmost *prestissimo*, take it twice as fast.

(He added a rider to that last rule in 1948: 'To conductors of Mozart: half as fast!')

Otto Strasser of the Vienna Philharmonic played under Strauss's direction for the first time in 1922.

The general public never appreciated Strauss the conductor as much as his artistry in this area, too, merited. He was never a popular conductor, because nothing was more alien to him than adopting poses, he did not think a conductor was a public spectacle. Usually conducting with only one hand, his gestures were simple and clear, the baton moved within a small area. Frequent changes of tempo, as in *Salome* and *Elektra* for example, caused him no trouble, and I noticed that he used to turn back the pages of the score to check something while his right hand went on beating with absolute certitude. At rallentandos he used to raise both elbows, a characteristic gesture. His facial expression usually remained relaxed and yet there was an extraordinary tension in his whole demeanour. At climaxes, he would rise to his feet and usually his face got very red, and the visible excitement, as a natural consequence, communicated itself to us. The tempos he gave us were individual, often idiosyncratic; in his own words, music could be anything at all but it must never be boring. He applied this rule to his own works, too, and I

Hans Richter, Hermann Levi and Felix Mottl, three 'star' conductors of the 1890s on whom Strauss modelled himself and who helped him in the early part of his career. For composers of the generation of Strauss, Mahler and Pfitzner, conducting was an inseparable part of a career in music.

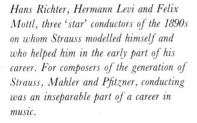

often thought to myself, during performances of *Rosenkavalier*, when other conductors lingered over some beautiful passages, extracting every last drop from them, how much more lightly the composer took them.

As composer, Strauss needed to be on good terms with other conductors. Especially when he was young, it was not always easy. Summoning all his diplomacy, he often dipped his pen deep into the honey pot to maintain friendships, smooth over disagreements and disarm prejudice. Of all his correspondents, other conductors were the most demanding and the most time-consuming. His relationships with Hans von Bülow, his mentor, and Gustav Mahler have been described in earlier chapters. He and Felix Weingartner called each other 'Du', but they detested each other's music (though they conducted it) and more than once found themselves rivals for the same appointment.

Felix Weingartner with his third wife, the American soprano Lucille Marcel. Strauss recommended her to Vienna as an Electra, which is how she met Weingartner.

It was on Strauss's recommendation that he was succeeded as conductor of the Berlin Staatskapelle concerts in 1920 by the then thirty-four-year-old Wilhelm Furtwängler. A year later he told Schalk that Furtwängler was 'a cobbler in the theatre and a thresher in the concert hall', but his esteem for this noble musician grew over the years. In the last year of his life, he asked for Furtwängler to come and visit him when he was in hospital in Lausanne, and the conversation they had on that occasion gave him great pleasure.

Furtwängler, like Strauss, stayed in Germany after 1933. He discovered the draconian nature of the new régime's artistic policies when he tried to perform the banned Hindemith. Strauss did not hold a very high opinion of Hindemith, but nor did he take the ban seriously until experience taught him that Goebbels intended to rule with a rod of iron. Like Furtwängler, he avoided further confrontations.

Wilhelm Furtwängler with Strauss.

Bruno Walter.

Bruno Walter served his conducting apprenticeship under Mahler, in Hamburg and then in Vienna. *Tod und Verklärung* made an immense impression on him as a boy; when he heard Strauss conduct *Tristan*, the performance struck him as displaying a subjective ardour, but too much *rubato*, by comparison with Mahler's interpretation.

Walter became director of the Munich Opera in 1913. During the war Strauss asked him why *Elektra* was not done in Munich: 'When I pointed out to him that the score called for eight clarinets, and that I had not got that number, nor even five, he replied: "Four will do!" I was greatly surprised to see that he was less affected by the idea of the corruption of his most important work than by its absence from the Munich repertory.' (It is curious that Walter should not have appreciated this pragmatic approach.) Walter's first new production in Munich was the original version of *Ariadne auf Naxos*. He went to visit Strauss in Garmisch, where the composer played the opera to him.

I am still conscious of the pleasure the composer's cool and perfect piano performance of the rather artificial but masterly work gave me. His playing was as lucid and objective as his written music on the desk

Herbert von Karajan with Strauss in 1939.

before us, but in spite of its uniform coolness it still left the impression of latent agitation. True, the storm and heat of the dramatically moving scenes impressed me as being ordained by the enthroned power of a weather god rather than by the upsurging of a human emotion. I was strangely affected when I found at the end of the neatly written manuscript the words in his handwriting: 'Finished on Bubi's birthday'. My chilled soul thawed slightly at this indication of a friendly family feeling.

But Walter's relationship with Strauss was not transformed by the revelation. They remained cool towards each other. It should be said that the dismissive remarks about Walter in Strauss's private correspondence were not inspired by anti-semitism: he simply did not like Walter, and Walter did not like him.

A generation of conductors a little further from Strauss in age proved to be at once more respectful and more responsive. Herbert von Karajan was still a student when Strauss returned to the Vienna State Opera to conduct in 1926. He told his biographer, Ernst Haeussermann:

> We admired him very much when he conducted his own works, but also in Mozart, above all. We never ceased to be amazed at the evenness of tempo, the harmonious equilibrium he achieved with such a minimal amount of gesture. I have never felt so drawn to any other interpretations of Mozart that I have heard since his.
>
> Once, with great difficulty, we managed to get into the gallery when he was due to rehearse *Elektra*, which he had not conducted there for a very long time, or perhaps not ever. We were avid for the experience of hearing him take a rehearsal. Strauss arrived, played the opening bars *fortissimo*, and broke off. 'Is there anybody here who doesn't already know the piece?' No. 'In that case, the rehearsal is over.' We were disappointed beyond measure, of course, but felt compensated by the really thrilling performance.
>
> I did not meet him personally until very late, unfortunately, when I conducted a *Salome* in Berlin, in honour of his seventy-fifth birthday. The next day he invited me to breakfast and we discussed some details. At the very end he said: 'You are much closer to it than I am, for whom it's so far in the past. It will be alright as it is.'

Clemens Krauss and Viorica Ursuleac.

Of all the works he has conducted, according to Karajan, *Elektra* is the one that most excited and taxed him.

But the most important conductor in Strauss's life, after Hans von Bülow, was surely Clemens Krauss: not simply because of his exemplary interpretations of Strauss's works (he conducted the premieres of four of the operas, the same number as Ernst von Schuch in Dresden) but also because of his immense knowledge and culture, his versatility and his instinct for the theatre. He was so close to Strauss that he was even allowed to initiate alterations in his works, which the composer never permitted to anyone else.

While Strauss's letters to other conductors are friendly enough, they are essentially business letters; he had a repertory of set phrases with which he made requests, gave advice and lavished praise. Between him and Krauss, on the other hand, the tone is that of a friendship between artists and equals who enjoy the same interests. Krauss had an elegant and allusive sense of humour and the power to stimulate Strauss's imagination, as well as give positive assistance in the theatre. Unlike many of their colleagues, he could talk with Strauss about non-musical topics, too – philosophy, history and the composer's beloved classics.

In an autobiographical memoir, Krauss related:

Clemens Krauss in the uniform of the Hofburg choristers (now best known as the Vienna Boys' Choir).

I was born in Vienna, on Good Friday, 31 March 1893. My beautiful mother was only just seventeen, my father, Hector Baltazzi, was an officer at the court of Emperor Franz Joseph. My mother's parents had been opposed to a marriage, because of the great difference in age – my father was forty-four years old, celebrated among sportsmen as a hard rider to hounds and steeplechaser, and he was an uncle of Baroness Vetsera, the inamorata of Crown Prince Rudolf. After the Mayerling tragedy, he left the country, having sworn to the emperor to preserve a complete silence about everything to do with the affair. In return for his word of honour he was offered whatever he wished – but he wanted nothing for himself. I never knew him. We should have met when he came back from Paris in 1916, but he died suddenly before I could get to Vienna myself. My mother, who became an actress after my birth, came from a very musical Viennese family. Her grandfather, one of the founders of the Viennese Male Choral Society, had actually sung under the direction of Beethoven. One of her aunts was the famous Gabrielle Krauss, prima donna at the Grand Opéra in Paris, and an officer of the Légion d'honneur.

Clemens Krauss

Ursuleac, Krauss and Strauss.

I was brought up in my grandparents' house. My grandfather wanted me to be a diplomat. He was secretary for many years to Prince Metternich, ambassador at the court of Napoleon III. When I was eight I became a chorister in the chapel of the Hofburg – and that sealed my fate! I learnt the old clefs, the church modes, the elements of the theory of harmony. I could read any kind of music, I could even decipher full scores. The songs of Schubert, which I could sing for myself, the masses of Haydn and Mozart, and the piano sonatas of Beethoven, inspired in me a longing to be a musician. At twelve I was determined on it – at nineteen I conducted my first opera performance in Brno. Ten years later, having been discovered by Schalk, I was a staff conductor at the Vienna Opera and a professor at the Academy of Music – director of the school of conducting in succession to Ferdinand Löwe – at twenty-nine.

In the ten years between nineteen and twenty-nine he had worked in Nuremberg, Riga, Szczecin and Graz. After two years in Vienna, in 1924 he moved on to Frankfurt am Main, where he spent five years as Intendant of the opera house. It was there that he formed a production team with the designer Ludwig Sievert and the producer Lothar Wallerstein, who continued to work with him later, and it was there that he caught the eye of Strauss.

In 1928 Vienna wanted blood once more, and it was Franz Schalk's turn to be dismissed from the Opera, despite his vehement and bitter protests. The post was vacant again. Strauss sent a telegram to Krauss in Frankfurt: 'Implore you to accept without delay stop Trust yourself and me stop This is the decisive moment stop Express letter follows – Greetings Strauss.' The express letter exhorted him, 'in the name of the Opera in its dire need, in the name of Vienna, sign the contract and come!' Although as a native of Vienna he knew the facts of life at the Opera, Krauss came for five fruitful and successful years, in which he steered the house through the economic crisis and forged even stronger links with the Salzburg Festival.

Krauss's wife was the soprano Viorica Ursuleac, Romanian by birth and a Yugoslav citizen. She was, for Strauss, the ideal interpreter of all his great female roles, and created four of them: Arabella (1933), Maria in *Friedenstag* (1938; the opera is dedicated to her and Krauss), the Countess in *Capriccio* (1942), and the heroine of *Die Liebe der Danae* at the public dress rehearsal in Salzburg in 1944. After 1933, like other artists resident in Vienna who still took engagements in Germany, Ursuleac was the victim of bureaucratic hounding. She was summoned to official inquisitions and her apartment was searched by the police.

Viorica Ursuleac with Strauss, who orchestrated several of his songs specially for her.

Then a campaign against Krauss began. Suddenly he had a lot of enemies, some of them in unexpected quarters. He had made some attempt to root out the old system of organized claques; now, when he entered the pit he was hissed by the claqueurs, because he threatened their livelihood. The directorate of the federal theatres met in secret session to discuss the problem of how to rid themselves of 'collaborators with Germany'.

Krauss solved it for them by resigning without giving notice. On 1 January 1935 he took up the post of director of the Berlin Opera, where he was able to promote his standards of artistic quality without interference for just two more years before politics again raised its head. Munich beckoned, and there, over the next seven years, he made the Bavarian State Opera one of the leading institutions of the operatic world, until the destruction of the theatre in a bombing raid in 1943. The model productions staged, with first-rate singers, under the Krauss/Rudolf Hartmann/Ludwig Sievert régime, had moved Strauss to raptures of delight: over the ruins he looked back on them as the last flower of three hundred years of artistic history.

For people who had grown up during the nineteenth century, it was very hard to understand that now, almost overnight, everything had its political aspect. In vain they protested that no one had reproached Beethoven for dedicating – or not dedicating – the *Eroica* to Napoleon, or Mozart for composing the subversive *Figaro* on the eve of the French Revolution. No one had paid any attention to what side Brahms, Bülow, Wagner or Liszt had supported in 1866, when Prussia went to war with the German Confederation. And even though politics grew in importance from the end of the First World War onwards, conductors who had once been in the pay of ex-kings and emperors who now lived in exile went on conducting in the new republics.

But in the 1930s even the directors of opera companies came to be regarded as representatives of the totalitarian régimes of the countries where they worked, and willy-nilly guilty by association. In 1945, therefore, all the conductors who had stayed in Germany under the Nazis were forbidden to work until further notice: a brief period in the case of Knappertsbusch, months or even years in those of Böhm, Karajan and Krauss. Sports stars, on the other hand, who had brought just as much glory to their country by gaining prizes in international competitions, were left in peace.

As the systematic investigation continued, there were few artists indeed against whom any charges of committing or even supporting Nazi crimes could be substantiated. No evidence ever emerged of connections between music and politics, and musicians were found, almost without exception, to have remained apolitical.

Thus the bans imposed, however temporarily, on artists hit the general public hardest, the people whose need of art is greater in lean times than at others. Krauss was allowed to work again in 1947, in Vienna, and in the same year conducted in London. After working in South America and living for a time in Rome, he was eventually allowed back to work in Germany, but was not offered another permanent engagement there. At the Salzburg Festival in 1952, he conducted the last premiere of an opera by Strauss, *Die Liebe der Danae*.

His end was tragic. The Vienna Opera was to be rebuilt and he was designated as director; he began preparations for the reopening, drawing up a repertory, engaging singers. All of a sudden, influential politicians declared their wish to have Karl Böhm appointed instead. Industrialists with a love of the arts let it be known that their support for certain parties in politics was contingent on the appointment. Krauss was ditched. He told the author of the present book: 'The post was positively sold.'

The shock and humiliation dealt him a profound blow, and can be said to have broken his heart. He was in Mexico City, 2260 metres above sea-level, on a guest engagement, when he suffered a fatal heart attack on 16 May 1954, at the age of sixty-one. He was buried at his home in Ehrwald, in the Tyrol.

'Arabella'

In October 1930, Strauss went to conduct in Paris and Brussels. He wrote to Franz:

> There had been fears of nationalist demonstrations, but in the end my concert went well, and everyone is being fearfully nice to me. In general, ever since those stupid Hitler elections, the atmosphere here has been grim; people spoke of nothing else but the war that Germany is supposed to want to start at any moment. As soon as Briand is well, Hösch [the German ambassador to France] wants to take me to see him, as he is in deadly earnest about the Paneuropa proposal: having held office sixteen times, he is said to have no further ambitions except to pursue that noble ideal. All the same, because of the Hitler elections, he is going to have some hard tussles in the Chamber of Deputies. Hösch had a session recently in Berlin with the Hitlerian Rosenberg (!), a pipsqueak of twenty-six [actually thirty-seven], who simply hasn't a clue and whose empty phrases about defeatism and pacifism Curtius [the German Foreign Minister] was able to dismiss in a few brusque words! (25 October 1930)

This is the first reference in Strauss's correspondence to the National Socialists. In elections held in September 1930, they had become the second-strongest party in the Reichstag, to the consternation of many inside and outside Germany. It was a nervous France that nonetheless welcomed Strauss. To Pauline: 'As old Clemenceau assured me, I am wholly "*admis*" here, so that's the most important object achieved. My symphonic poems are played at every French concert, so I can take my leave with no further worries.' (29 October) And from Brussels: 'Here, too, the ambassador hailed me as the most effective apostle of peace.' (31 October)

The Paneuropa movement to promote European unity was founded by Count Coudenhove-Kalergi and led to the establishment of the Council of Europe after the end of the Second World War. The count invited Strauss to write an anthem for the movement.

At this time he was at work on *Arabella*. He composed the first act in eight weeks. The second and third acts took much longer. He refused to alter a word of the text, out of a sense of piety towards Hofmannsthal. The full score was not finished until October 1932, thus taking far longer than any previous opera of his. 'There's no hurry. Until folk have got halfway to understanding *Frau ohne Schatten, Intermezzo* and *Helena*, they don't need to hear anything else.'

The score is dedicated to 'My friends Alfred Reucker and Fritz Busch' – Intendant and musical director respectively of the Dresden Opera. The first performance was scheduled for July 1933, in Dresden. But Busch was in trouble: his outspoken, liberal but apolitical style had made enemies of a few of his subordinates, who compiled dossiers of his remarks and instructions, diligently reported his contempt for the National Socialists, and launched a smear campaign. An assistant prompter with a phony doctor's title, a hairdresser and a character actor staged a theatrical scandal. When Busch appeared in the pit, SA members raised the roof, and the next day they got Reucker dismissed. At that Busch handed in his resignation.

Adolf Hitler and Field-Marshall Hindenburg, President of Germany 1932–4.

The press had not been 'brought into line' at that point. The *Deutsche Allgemeine Zeitung* had a banner headline: 'Mediocrity gives itself airs'. The paramilitary SA gave malcontents the chance to put on uniform and claim an authority they did not possess. Busch was accused of associating with Jews, showing bias in favour of Jewish and foreign singers, taking frequent leave, receiving a big salary. But he was an 'Aryan', and held in esteem by prominent National Socialists. Hitler and Goering put a stop to the harassment of Busch, but he would have nothing to do with such people and refused all offers of mediation.

Strauss's immediate reaction to the trouble was to withdraw *Arabella* from Dresden and turn to another theatre, another country, Austria. But there was a performance contract already binding him and Fürstner to Dresden, and the opera could be given its first performance there even against his will. Dresden offered him Krauss as conductor and Josef Gielen as producer: two safe pairs of hands into which to entrust the work. Fritz Busch witnessed his dilemma:

Richard Strauss came to Berlin and we had a conference with Tietjen, the Intendant of the Prussian State Theatres, to discuss the affair of *Arabella*. Tietjen was watching over the interests of his absent colleague and friend, Reucker. Strauss declared it was to be taken for granted that the premiere of this work, dedicated to us both, would only be allowed if produced by Reucker and conducted by me. My remark that he was not to take me into consideration he put aside with derision. If I positively refused to conduct in Dresden then it should be somewhere else. There was no question of any other solution, as far as he was concerned.

When Strauss said this there is no doubt that he was sincere. Many years later common friends assured me that he really tried to keep his word and withdrew the work in due form. Nevertheless, in the end he had to give way to the claims of the contracts he had signed.

Hans Knappertsbusch was eager to have the premiere in Munich, but he could not offer a cast of the same calibre. He was easily offended, and the

211

A pin-up photo of Ursuleac.

Rehearsals for Arabella, *1933. (Right, above) Strauss, the producer Josef Gielen, Karl Albrecht Streib (Elemer), Viorica Ursuleac (Arabelia). (Right, below) Advice for Martin Kremer (Matteo).*

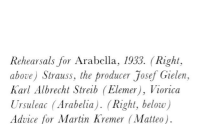

refusal of this offer led him to break with Strauss altogether – to Strauss's sincere regret, for 'Kna' was more to him than a conductor who was willing to perform his works. His attempts at reconciliation ('Kna – how can you be cross with *me?*') seem to have touched Knappertsbusch, but not sufficiently to make him change his stance. (In earlier years, when Strauss was to conduct a performance of *Salome*, he invited Knappertsbusch along to hear how he did it. 'Kna' retorted: 'I'll do no such thing! I'm not going to let you muck up my tempos!' He meant it as a joke, and Strauss laughed, but not very much. In 1948, in Zurich, he stole silently into a box at the back of the theatre to hear Knappertsbusch conduct *Elektra*.)

The premiere of *Arabella* took place in Dresden on 1 July 1933. It was the first Strauss premiere to be broadcast by all the German radio stations, as well as by several foreign ones. As a result, Stefan Zweig, who was to be the librettist of the next opera, was able at least to hear the music from his home in Salzburg, though he did not see the work in the theatre until the following year, when the Dresden Opera, under Krauss, performed it in London.

Confidentially – I was not expecting too much of *Arabella*. I worked hard on it and now this enormous success, hardly less, so far, than that of *Rosenkavalier*. It is strange. The public is inscrutable. Despite all one knows about the art, one knows least what one is really capable of doing. One is in God's hand. Best thing would be not to think at all, and yet one has to consider: Now what?

What suits me best, South German bourgeois that I am, are sentimental jobs; but such bull's eyes as the *Arabella* duet and the *Rosenkavalier* trio don't happen every day. Must one become seventy years old to recognize that one's greatest strength lies in creating kitsch? But, seriously, don't you have some new, warm-hearted little theme for me? (Strauss to Zweig, 21 January 1934)

It would be unwise to take this specimen of South German self-mockery as a serious artistic credo. *Arabella* did not turn out to be a second *Rosenkavalier*. There is a change of gear upon the entrance of the Fiakermilli. Had Hofmannsthal lived, Strauss would surely have insisted on structural improvements. Clemens Krauss had some suggestions on how the unhappy Milli might be amended, and the second act made to flow more smoothly, but Strauss could not bring himself to change anything.

Rudolf Hartmann omitted the last few bars of Act II, and went on without a pause into the introduction of Act III. This was effective theatrically, creating a little more unity. But over the years operagoers have shown themselves tolerant of the work's weaknesses, because the conclusion of Act III is one of the most inspired passages Strauss ever wrote, and everything that has gone before it then falls into place.

Viorica Ursuleac recounted:

When we were making a guest appearance in Amsterdam, Strauss took the conclusion very fast in rehearsal. As we were leaving the theatre, I

A lithograph by Leonhard Fanto, designer at the Dresden Opera and skat-partner.

At the Dresden Opera with the producer, Alois Mora (top), and the Intendant, Alfred Reucker. These men wee Arabella's godfathers, but the christening was spoiled by politics.

Strauss taking a bow from his box, at the end of Act II.

said to him: 'Herr Doktor, if you conduct that scene at the same pac[e] this evening, I shall positively have to gallop down the stairs with m[y] glass of water. It's such a shame when the music is so beautiful!' All h[e] did was growl: 'Oh, those six-four chords!' – and then, in the evening, h[e] took the conclusion with a poetic breadth. The audience cheered to th[e] echo. The next day we went to the Rijksmuseum, to see Rembrandt'[s] *Night Watch*, which had just come back from Petersburg. On the way [I] thanked him for that lovely tempo which had allowed me to sing out t[o] the delight of the audience. 'You've only yourself to blame', he snorte[d]. We were just going past a jeweller's shop. 'Just a minute!' He came bac[k] with a beautiful ring. 'There, that's for your Arabella!'

I think he was embarrassed by his own feelings. He praised me, bu[t] he wouldn't say a word more than he had to. He expressed himself b[y] giving me the ring instead. And it was exactly the same with the close [of] *Arabella*. He was embarrassed by his own feelings.

Bayreuth

In 1933 Arturo Toscanini withdrew from his engagement to conduct at the Bayreuth Festival, in protest at the anti-semitism and dictatorial trend of the new German régime. Politics and *Parsifal* were forced into an incongruous confrontation. Wagner's widow Cosima and their son Siegfried had both died in 1930, and Siegfried's widow Winifred, who could count Adolf Hitler among her friends and admirers, now reigned in Bayreuth. The festival was endangered by Toscanini's decision: Winifred took the step of asking Strauss to conduct *Parsifal*. It was the first invitation he had had for thirty-nine years to return to what was for him (and for thousands of others) holy ground. He accepted without hesitation (and without a fee).

Hermann Levi first drew Frau Cosima's attention to the young Strauss and his enthusiasm for Wagner in 1889. He took part in the festivals of 1890 and 1891 as a musical assistant, but was not given the chance to conduct a performance there until 1894, when he directed *Tannhäuser* with Pauline in the role of Elisabeth. His subsequent breach with Wahnfried (at the very time when he was leaping to world fame as a conductor) resulted in his not performing there for nearly forty years, but that had no effect on his veneration for Wagner. 'I have heard perhaps fifty performances of *Parsifal* and the *Ring* (most of them rehearsed and conducted by myself) and I can never grow tired of the revelations of that orchestra; I am forever discovering new beauties and give thanks each time for new insights.' (1940)

In the early 1890s, he briefly enjoyed a friendship with Cosima that was founded on complete misunderstanding of each other's aesthetic and artistic goals. She appears to have thought he would make the ideal husband for her youngest daughter, Eva, but there were, after all, limits to his love of Wagner. He was proud to call Siegfried Wagner 'Du', until such time as he was forced to recognize that Siegfried was over-confiding and over-reticent by turns, and that in his fondness for gossip he was given to distorting a tale as he passed it on. They began to needle each other. On one occasion, Strauss was in Berlin and staying at the expensive Hotel Adlon. Siegfried: 'Is your business making such good profits, then?' Strauss: 'Oh yes, and it's my own business, not my father's.' A hit, a palpable hit.

After Strauss's appointment as Kapellmeister in Berlin, he told Siegfried 'I'm in fashion at present, I will compose accordingly, make my pile, and retire [from Berlin] in seven years' time. I don't care about anything else.' That was too cynical and too ingenuous for Bayreuth, and Strauss fell into disgrace. On 11 January 1896 he wrote in his diary: 'Momentous conversation with Siegfried Wagner. Unspoken but nonetheless irrevocable separation from Wahnfried–Bayreuth. Only indirectly my fault.'

Siegfried regarded Strauss as a dangerous renegade from the sacred Wagnerian cause. He distanced himself after the failure of *Guntram* in

Cosima Wagner, and her children by Richard Wagner:

Eva. Her mother would have liked her to marry Strauss, but she married Houston Stewart Chamberlain, prophet of 'Aryanism'.

Isolde and Siegfried.

Strauss in Bayreuth, 1933. (Top) With Eva Chamberlain-Wagner. (Top, right) In the garden of Wahnfried, where he stayed as house-guest during the 1933 and 1934 festivals. (Above) With a guest of the festival, King Ferdinand of Bulgaria. (Right) With the young Wieland Wagner, who wears the Nazi party badge in his lapel.

A musical joke for Willi Schuh, combining opening and closing bars of Tristan.

Franz and Richard Strauss with the Führer. It was during this discussion that Strauss suggested financing Bayreuth by levying a 1% royalty on performances of Wagner.

A cartoon by Thomas Theodor Heine, published in the satirical magazine Simplicissimus. *The gesticulating trumpeter is Siegfried Wagner, enraged by the one-man band Strauss, who gets all the public attention.*

Munich. After the success of *Salome*, the breach was complete. Cosima's public condemnation of *Salome* brought the following comment from Strauss: 'What an honour! Saint Wagner, if only you knew how your heirs underrate you.'

In the years between *Guntram* and *Salome*, Strauss had been leading the campaign for the reform of the copyright law as it affected music. A principal pillar in his arguments and appeals for support was the prospect of *Parsifal* being released after 1913 for 'prostitution in every provincial opera house, no matter how small', instead of being reserved for Bayreuth alone, as Wagner himself ardently wished it might be. That particular objective of the campaign was doomed to failure.

In Bayreuth in 1933, Strauss seized the chance of an audience with Hitler to suggest that the new government, which spoke so much of its desire to do things for the arts, should levy a 1% royalty on every performance of Wagner in Germany, and that the money thus raised should go to Bayreuth. Hitler refused, on the grounds that he could find no legal precedent for such an act. The Führer gave a reception in Wahnfried. Alice Strauss wanted to refuse the invitation, but Frau Wagner insisted that she would only make herself a laughing-stock. So Alice went and Hitler kissed her hand when they met, although he knew perfectly well that she was 'non-Aryan'. After the blatant brutality of the fight to attain power, the new government did what it could to project an image of statesmanlike *savoir vivre*.

In token of her gratitude Winifred Wagner sent Strauss a Wagner autograph, a page of sketches for *Lohengrin*. He was overjoyed:

Dear, honoured Frau Winifred!
Your kind letter was a great joy to me, although there was really no need for further thanks: my modest help for Bayreuth was only a respectful

Outside the Festspielhaus at Bayreuth, with two of Cosima Wagner's daughters: Blandine Countess Gravina (left) and Eva Chamberlain.

It was at Bayreuth in the 1890s that Strauss formed his friendship with Engelbert Hunperdinck, seen here at a later festival with his wife. Hunperdinck was one of the copyists when Wagner was preparing the score of Parsifal *(and composed several bars of its music at a late stage of rehearsals, when it was found that more time was needed for the stage machinery to complete a change of scene).*

repayment of the great debt of gratitude stored up in my heart for all that the great master gave to the world and to me in particular. It is really I who should thank you for the opportunity, in the evening of my life, to conduct his sublime work once more, in that sacred place: it was a high honour and satisfaction for me. I came back from Bad Wiessee today, to find the wonderful sketch from the master's hand, fulfilling a long-cherished wish, beyond all expectations. You can scarcely imagine the joy you have given me. I accept it with the most sincere and profound gratitude, and as a sign, too, of the enduring friendship in which I feel myself bound to you in true devotion to the task that is now entrusted to your hands.

With the most sincere respect, your devoted servant,

Dr Richard Strauss (23 September 1933)

Not everyone was prepared to see his alacrity to stand in for Toscanini as the instinctive reaction of a lifelong Wagnerian. It got a bad press abroad. A boycott of his work was considered in Austria. As always, when Alice wanted to cut out things like that from the newspapers to put in the archives, Strauss told her not to blunt her scissors.

Governments come and go – Bayreuth and Wagner endure. In 1934 he conducted *Parsifal* in Bayreuth again.

The Honorary Office

I made music under the Kaiser and under Ebert – I'll survive under this one as well.

STRAUSS TO HIS FAMILY

Unfortunately we still need him, but one day we shall have our own music and then we shall have no further need of this decadent meurotic.

JOSEPH GOEBBELS IN HIS DIARY

Since 1864, Strauss had lived under fifty-eight governments: at first Bavarian, then the German Imperial chancellorships of Bismarck and his successors, several War Cabinets, then seventeen ministries during the fourteen years of the Weimar Republic. None of those cabinets, formed on a party-political basis, had achieved the aims set out in its electoral programme: why should anyone suppose that the eighteenth, the National Socialist government elected in March 1933, would be any more effective?

Strauss was bored by politics, which had little if any bearing on his philosophy or his interests. He had paid no more attention to Hitler's *Mein Kampf* and the aims of the National Socialists than the majority of his contemporaries. He had never experienced life under a dictatorship and had no idea of what it would be like.

In November 1933 the minister (Goebbels) nominated me president [of the Reich Music Chamber] without obtaining my prior agreement. There was also a presidial council, about the membership of which, equally, I was not consulted. I accepted this honorary office because I hoped that I would be able to do some good and prevent worse

Strauss with Joseph Goebbels who proved as slippery as an eel and as dangerous as a cobra.

misfortune, if from now onwards German musical life was going to be, as it was said, 'reorganized' by amateurs and ignorant place-seekers. (Private memorandum, 1935)

His 'superior' in this unsought position was the propaganda minister Dr Joseph Goebbels, whom he soon found to be a dangerous opponent, and would later call a 'Bübchen', a 'pipsqueak'. Goebbels told him: 'The world looks different, Dr Strauss, from the way you imagine it in your study in Garmisch!'

Strauss had been concerned for years to improve the lot of the individual artist, by improving and strengthening the laws of copyright and other rights, and thus strengthening his professional status. Now he thought that a government had given him the chance to crown this life's work. He regarded his new office as carrying the duty to represent the interests of his profession, and believed that his instructions in this area would be heeded. He also believed he had the authority to reprimand party officials and promote the performance of works by Jewish composers.

A cultural warden in Frankfurt has objected to a performance of Debussy's *Nocturnes*. Minister Goebbels told me recently to report directly to him any such instances of a provincial caesar exceeding his powers, but I think that that is scarcely necessary, as you have ultimate responsibility for the concert programmes. Please write and tell Councillor Spiess that nothing stands in the way of a performance of *Nocturnes*, any more than that of any of the symphonies of Mahler, which he has not yet ventured to include in the programmes. Perhaps you would also see to it that this cultural warden is forbidden in future to meddle in programme-making. (To Wilhelm Furtwängler, 13 December 1933)

The official document of Strauss's appointment as president of the Reich Music Chamber.

Reichsmusikkammer

Berlin W 62, Lützowplatz 13 · Fernruf B 2 Lützow 9021

Präsident: Dr. Richard Strauß
Stellvertreter: Generalmusikdirektor ...
Präsidialrat: Dr. h. c. ... Prof. Dr. h. c. Walter
Gmeindl, Prof. Dr. Fritz Stein, Prof. Dr. h. c. Paul Graener,
Geh. Rat Karnbach
Geschäftsführer: Heinz Ihlert
Stellv. Geschäftsführer: Carl ...

A

Berufsstand d. Deutschen Komponisten

Bbds.-Führer: Dr. Richard Strauß
Stellvertreter: Hugo Rasch
Geschäftsführer: Gerd Karnbach
Org.-Rechtsfragen: Dr. Julius Kopsch

Berlin-Charlbg. 9, Adolf Hitler-Platz 7/11
Westend 13, 5518

Führerrat

Max Donisch
Willy Geisler
Prof. Dr. Paul Graener
Prof. Joseph Haas
Geh.-Rat Prof. Dr. v. Hausegger
Prof. Paul Hindemith
Eduard Künneke
Prof. Hans Pfitzner
Prof. E. N. von Reznicek
Prof. Clemens Schmalstich
Prof. Dr. Georg Schumann
Prof. Hermann Unger

Großer Rat

Gau-Obleute

Wertprüfungsausschüsse:
1. für nationale Volksmusik
2. für künstlerische Unterhaltungsmusik
3. für Kunstmusik

Ausschüsse:
1. für personelle Angelegenheiten
2. für mechanische Vervielfältigungsrechte
3. für Tonfilm
4. für Werbung
5. für Arbeitsbeschaffung

Soziale Einrichtungen:
Hilfs- und Pensionskasse
Friedrich-Rösch-Fonds
Mitgliederbestand: 2123

Like every institution set up by bureaucrats, the Reich Music Chamber boasted numerous committees, with co-opted members – including Paul Hindemith for a time.

He proposed founding a newspaper for the 140,000 members of the music profession in Germany, but this was opposed. He wrote to Professor Gustav Havemann of the Music Chamber with other proposals.

> I have long been conscious of the abysmal quality of the programmes given by spa orchestras. There is so much charming entertainment music of the better sort, yet the spa bands play some fearful rubbish. I would like, through the Reich Music Chamber, to exercise an influence, to the end that there should be some supervision of these programmes, and I would like you to draw up a long list of entertainment music of decent quality, for which our German publishing houses should be asked to furnish the performance materials.
>
> 1) I should like, in due course, to see two-thirds of such programmes made up of German and Austrian music, but excluding the worst rubbish from Viennese operetta; I would also like to see a total ban on potpourris compiled from all manner of works, while decent fantasias from just one operatic work should of course be permitted.
>
> 2) It is high time that a stop was put to the murder of pieces like the Funeral March from *Götterdämmerung* in the stuttering performance which is all a band of sixteen can hope to give it. There are charming French and Italian pieces, the numerous divertimentos and serenades of Mozart, and of course the entire oeuvre of Johann and Josef Strauss, Lanner and – naturally – Schubert, from which a decent audience could draw real pleasure. Please have a list made for me on those lines, to be sent to the spa orchestras as the model they should follow, at the same time as we notify the provincial authorities of the need to supervise the compilation of artistic programmes. We get a spa band from the orchestra of the Bamberg Civic Theatre here [Garmisch] and I will be glad to take the trouble of exercising personal supervision over the conductor. (23 February 1934)

(Can he really have hoped that the public would allow itself to be led by the hand, away from *The Land of Smiles* to Mozart divertimentos, from *White Horse Inn* to Schubert?)

A ceremony of the Reich Chamber of Culture, 1934. In the front row, from right to left: Walte Funk – deputy minister of propaganda, Strauss, Wilhelm Furtwängler, Hans Pfitzner, Joseph Goebbels – minister of propaganda, Adolf Hitler, Franz von Papen – foreign minister, Hermann Goering – minister of the interior, Wilhelm Frick – minister of labour.

The first German Composers' conference.
1. Joseph Marx. 2. Wilhelm Kienzl. 3.
Hugo Rasch. 4. Hans Pfitzner. 5.
Clemens Schmalstich. 6. Richard Strauss.
7. Hermann Unger. 8. E.N.v.Reznicek. 9.
Hermann Graener.

He suggested to Goebbels that foreign works had too large a share of the repertory, and wrote on the same theme to Otto Laubinger, the then president of the parallel organization, the Reich Theatre Chamber.

... unless a ukase from above sets a limit on the expansion of indolence. Undoubtedly, for theatre managements and for audiences wanting only superficial enjoyment, the operas of Verdi and Puccini are less trouble and less demanding than our German works, which are significantly more taxing for both performers and listeners. It goes without saying that Germany, with its universality and greatness of heart, affords generous hospitality to meritorious works of art from abroad, but it must be done in proportion, more or less, to the hospitality shown by foreign countries. The operatic repertory abroad offers exclusively Wagner, with the addition, very sporadically, of Mozart and Beethoven, a few of my oldest works and otherwise, apart from *Tiefland* and *Hänsel und Gretel*, not a note by any living German composer. The programmes of German theatres last week yielded the following: Hamburg, 6 operas by Verdi and Puccini within the one week; Berlin State Opera, 5 Italians and 1 Russian; Berlin Reichsoper, 4 Italians and *Le postillon de Longjumeau*. That is not the proper cultural function of theatres in receipt of state and municipal subsidies. The foreign repertory should occupy a third, or perhaps once in a while, as an exception, half the scheduled programme, and that is still a considerably higher percentage than foreign countries afford to us. (12 December 1934)

Only a matter of days before the storm which was to sweep him from office broke, on his seventy-first birthday, he wrote to Bruno von Niessen, stage director and Intendant, and a colleague in the Reich Music Chamber.

After he had resigned as President of the Reich Music Chamber, the bureaucrats required Strauss to fill in a questionnaire to attest his bona fides as a composer. He had the answers typed, except for the names of two known composers who would furnish references of his professionalism. He wrote in: 'Mozart and Richard Wagner'.

Vichy, 1935. Perhaps the most lugubrious photo ever taken of Strauss, but he had a big smile for those receiving him at this function.

Some of the gifts Strauss received for his seventieth birthday.

A conference of the Conseil Permanent pour la Coopération Internationale des Compositeurs, Venice 1934. As president, Strauss sits at the head of the table, opposite Ermanno Wolf-Ferrari (extreme left).

The minister does not have the time to receive you and me, to discuss and carry out the most important reforms. Herr Rosenberg, as ever, preaches the world view; result: new music for *A Midsummer Night's Dream* [which Strauss refused to write]. I will outline for you in writing for the last time what ought to be done: Herr von Niessen to spend half a year visiting every opera house in Germany and establish their individual needs. Size of pit, capacity, technical facilities of the stage, by how much orchestra and chorus ought to be enlarged and the budget increased; in order to match the rise in demands due to film; collaboration between a number of small theatres and one larger, central theatre after very careful investigation.

When the level of the subsidy from the Reich has been established, the means must be obtained, either from radio or from tax (the 'culture groschen'), the latter acknowledged by the Führer and Reichskanzler to be reasonable. Distribution to be accompanied by strict admonitions about the theatre's role in raising cultural standards and the banishing of operetta from the big houses. These must retrench, the foreign repertory must be limited, and the performance of worthwhile, old, forgotten works recommended. Encouragement of contemporary literature. This is my last 'all-highest' proclamation. (11 June 1935)

The new-made freeman signing the Golden Book of the city of Dresden, 1934.

The seventieth birthday of the president of the Reich Music Chamber was celebrated with due ceremony. Dresden made him a Freeman of the City and an honorary member of the Opera, as well as putting on a Strauss cycle with a festival production of *Der Rosenkavalier*. There were Strauss weeks in Berlin, Munich and Vienna. There was a radio cycle, for which he produced a revised version of *Guntram*. President Hindenburg awarded him the 'Eagle Shield of the German Reich'. Goebbels gave him a bust of Gluck: the family at once tried to discover if it had been come by dishonestly, perhaps from a Jewish owner, but no – its purchase through the art trade was perfectly regular.

Another honour Strauss received in 1934 was to be elected president of the Conseil Permanent pour la Coopération Internationale des Compositeurs, founded that year by distinguished composers from many European nations with the aim of breaking down national barriers, to promote the spread and exchange of music: the performance of German, English, Polish music in Italy, French music in Austria, Czech music in Denmark. A festival was arranged, to be held in Vichy in 1935. 'This first French, non-atonal, international festival of music is immensely important. It is the first step towards smoothing the way abroad for those of our composers who have not yet been performed in other countries.' (To Hausegger, New Year's Eve 1934)

Liszt would have heartily approved of Strauss's use of his own fame for the benefit of others. The Vichy festival took place in September 1935. Strauss devoted months of work to the preparations for a festival in which Jewish composers were represented alongside their colleagues.

The idea was floated of establishing a 'moral right' to protect works of art against 'arrangement' and the arranger's subsequent right to make

Strauss in the pit for Ariane et Barbe-bleue *by Paul Dukas, who had died a few months earlier. The* Zweig *affair, which gave Strauss a taste of the deadly earnest of Nazi anti-semitism, was even more recent, but the fact that Dukas was of Jewish origin did not deter him from conducting this festival performance. In a letter he wrote: 'Civilised France was a real rest-cure.'*

money from other people's out-of-copyright inspirations. After the expiry of rights, royalties ought still to be paid, but into a general fund for the benefit of living artists. It was a fine and idealistic notion, but of course it could not be realized. The Conseil Permanent continued in existence until 1945.

'Die schweigsame Frau'

I will not give up on you just because we happen to have an anti-semitic government now. . . . Why now raise unnecessary questions which will have taken care of themselves in two or three years?

STRAUSS TO ZWEIG,
26 FEBRUARY 1935

On 3 July 1935, as the furore caused by his collaboration with the Jewish writer Stefan Zweig reached its crisis, Strauss wrote his own version of the story in a private memorandum. He began by recalling the cruel personal and professional loss that the death of Hugo von Hofmannsthal had meant to himself. 'Attacked and maligned by the press and the profession for thirty years . . . he was a faithful genius and I obstinately stuck with him. Now, after his premature death, he is finally recognized as "my true poet". I had to resign myself to admitting that my period of creating operas had come to a close. . . . I flirted and negotiated with the best German poets . . . but in fifty years I found only the wonderful Hofmannsthal.'

In October 1931 Anton Kippenberg, of the Insel-Verlag publishing house, urged Strauss to talk to Stefan Zweig. A brief conversation was all it took to establish a working relationship. To begin with, Strauss tried to interest Zweig in a subject-field that Hofmannsthal had always adamantly refused to touch: an intrigue *à la* Scribe, with a *grande dame* as spy or confidence trickster. Once again he was disappointed in that hope, but Zweig had a suggestion of his own: Ben Jonson's comedy *Epicoene, or The Silent Woman*.

In spite of repeated invitations, Zweig always refused to stay in the Strauss villa in Garmisch, pleading 'an almost *heathen* bashfulness . . . the feeling that I might disturb would be too oppressive'. He wrote of their first meeting, in a Munich hotel in November 1931, in his autobiography, *The World of Yesterday*.

It was a pleasant surprise to see how quickly, how clear-sightedly Strauss responded to my suggestions. I had not suspected in him so alert an understanding of art, so astounding a knowledge of dramaturgy. While the nature of the material was being explained to him he was already shaping it dramatically and adjusting it astonishingly to the limits of his own abilities of which he was uncannily cognizant. I have met many great artists in my life but never one who knew how to maintain such abstract and unerring objectivity towards himself. Thus Strauss frankly admitted to me in the first hour of our meeting that he well knew that at seventy the composer's musical inspiration no longer possesses its pristine power. He could hardly succeed in composing symphonic works like *Till Eulenspiegel* and *Tod und Verklärung* because pure music requires an extreme measure of creative freshness. But the word could still inspire him . . . hence he had been devoting himself exclusively to the opera in his later years. He knew well indeed, he said, that as an art-form opera was dead. Wagner was so gigantic a peak that nobody could rise higher. 'But,' he added, with a broad, Bavarian grin, 'I solved the problem by making a detour around it . . .

'I am not one to compose long melodies as Mozart did. I can't get beyond short themes. But what I can do, is to utilize such a theme, paraphrase it and extract everything that is in it, and I don't think there's anybody today who can match me at that.' Again I was dumbfounded by this frankness.

Before Zweig could start on the text for the opera he had to finish his *Marie Antoinette*. While he waited Strauss orchestrated *Arabella* (in summertime, his preferred season for composition). Act I of *Die schweigsame Frau* arrived in October 1932, Acts II and III in December and January. There were a few small changes, a tightening of the action in Act II, a discussion of the feasibility of using both recitative and spoken dialogue (Zweig suggested 'dashes of colour from individual instruments . . . the orchestra amuses itself, as it were, with butting in, making brilliant asides while the people talk') – and then Strauss set to work.

During the spring of 1933, as Hitler seized total power, Strauss composed his new opera. Act I took three weeks, Acts II and III flowed equally fast. No cuts, no problems, no alterations. Politics was not allowed to intrude: only the threat to the premiere of *Arabella* disturbed him, and that was not on account of the political issues themselves.

'None of my earlier operas was so easy to compose, or gave me such lighthearted pleasure.' (Memorandum of 3 July 1935)

Pure Bavarian pigheadedness, his family said, kept him true to Zweig. He ignored ethical and dramaturgical weaknesses in the text. Zweig was as faultless as Hofmannsthal, he maintained, and more of a realist, because he ranked theatrical effectiveness above literary profundity.

The work was finished: would it ever be performed? The librettist was an Austrian citizen, but he was a Jew. Since April 1933, Jews had been barred from government employment in Germany; the Nuremberg race laws of September 1935 would forbid marriage between 'Aryans' and Jews. In 1939 Jews would be forbidden to take any part in public or economic life.

It took time for the anti-semitic measures of the National Socialists to gain a hold, and to sink in. Few Jews emigrated in 1933; most stayed in the expectation that the Nazis would bankrupt the country and lose power. Jews who had been decorated during the First World War and those who had attained eminence without any political involvement were left in peace, so far as could be seen. Mozart's operas were played, though da Ponte was a (converted) Jew; *Carmen* too was played, though the libretto was written by Jewish authors. Mendelssohn and Mahler were not performed – but no objections were made to the works of the part-Jewish Hofmannsthal.

Stefan Zweig in Salzburg.

I recently . . . asked Dr Goebbels whether there are any 'political objections' against you, to which the minister answered no. . . . All efforts to relax the stipulation against Jews [the 'Aryan paragraph'] here are frustrated by the answer: impossible as long as the outside world continues its lying propaganda against Hitler. (Strauss to Zweig, 24 May 1934)

There was no one in the National Socialist administration prepared to assume responsibility for giving permission for a performance of *Die schweigsame Frau*. In the summer of 1934, when Strauss was in Bayreuth to conduct *Parsifal* and staying in Wahnfried, Dr Goebbels called on him.

I received him, saying that it was perhaps significant that in the house of the 'great martyr' I too, the smaller man, had to suffer my martyrdom. I told him that I did not wish to embarrass Adolf Hitler and himself by performing my opera, and that I was willing to withdraw *Die schweigsame Frau* altogether and to forgo all showings at home and abroad. Goebbels said later that this talk had 'deeply impressed' him – perhaps because I told him openly that the whole affair was a 'big disgrace'. In parting we agreed to submit the score to the Führer for a final decision. . . .
   Next day Goebbels called up, saying that he had carefully considered my 'case', had also talked with Hitler, and that he wanted me to submit the libretto. Goebbels added that if the book was unobjectionable (other than being authored by an uncomfortably talented Jew), he hoped that there would be no difficulties with the world premiere in Dresden. (Memorandum of 3 July 1935)

Approval was given: after what consideration on Hitler's part is not known. Did he read the libretto in a benevolent frame of mind? Did he have such a high esteem for Strauss's music? Did he want to show the world that it was mistaken in its opinion of National Socialism?

Did I write to you that Dr Goebbels told me the Reich Chancellor approved the performance of *Die schweigsame Frau*? I am now negotiating with Dresden about the necessary guarantees, also on the part of the Saxony government, and about safeguards (so far as possible), such as Dr Goebbels has most readily promised. . . . In the meantime I will finish the score. (To Zweig, 21 September 1934)

The full score was finished on 20 October 1934, leaving only the overture to write, the 'potpourri' which Strauss composed in January 1935.
   Ever since he had finished the short score, he had been asking Zweig for a second opera: a 'Meistersinger' or a one-acter to pair with *Feuersnot*. Each had plenty of ideas, but none were wholly acceptable to the other. Strauss led with Ulrich von Liechtenstein, the medieval German minnesinger; Zweig parried with the Pied Piper of Hamelin. Strauss: did Zweig know *Calandria*, an Italian renaissance comedy? Zweig knew it but thought it would not do; what about Kleist's *Amphitryon*? Kleist was not Strauss's line,

and he suggested the eleventh century and Emperor Henry III instead. Zweig countered with Goldoni's *Mirandolina*, but he had also mentioned his intention to read all the librettos written for Pergolesi by the Abbate Casti. Strauss pricked up his ears at that, but a few months later he suggested the subject of 'Achilles Disguised'. Zweig, meanwhile, had been reflecting on a way of making *The Jewess of Toledo*, by Grillparzer after Lope de Vega, acceptable in the climate of the time.

In the summer of 1934 the government forbade the president of the Reich Music Chamber to conduct at the Salzburg Festival (it had made it virtually impossible for anyone to enter Austria from Germany by levying a tax of 1000 marks on the border-crossing): it was a way of ensuring that he was not seen working with Jews. Eventually he was allowed to attend, as a member of the audience only, and he had a meeting with Zweig at which they discussed a subject, proposed by Zweig, derived from Calderón's *La redención de Breda*, transposed to a fortress under siege in Germany at the end of the Thirty Years' War, and this was the one Strauss accepted. Before the end of August, he received an outline of the action of *Friedenstag* (also known as *1648*).

Zweig's exploration of the oeuvre of the Abbate Casti had also produced a fascinating title, *Prima la musica, poi le parole* (*Music first, then the words*), but a plot was required to suit it. Strauss implored Zweig to write both librettos, but Zweig refused: Strauss could have the ideas as a gift, he would give advice and assistance, but he would not write for him again. As he persisted in his refusal, so Strauss's despair grew until he poured it out in the fateful letter of 17 June 1935.

Strauss's delight when he heard a new work with full orchestra for the first time was an endearing weakness. Probably every composer experiences something of the same emotion, but scarcely any other has ever expressed his joy with such exuberance. Even so, as he now witnessed *Die schweigsame Frau* in rehearsal, it was wholly typical of him that he revealed his pleasure only to those closest to him.

My beloved! The opera is magnificent: both the work and its execution. Böhm and the producer have already done some splendid work, it is already running smoothly both on the stage and in the orchestra. The act finales: first-rate. The text non plus ultra: as I've said before, it is the best comic opera since Beaumarchais. Enthusiasm is the order of the day. I hope Rosenberg and a few others like him will burst. One has to provide one's own compensation for all the nonsense that goes on in the world around one. You have nothing to worry about: nobody can raise any objections to *this* opera. Perhaps it has too much wit and humour for the present age! In that case, there's the twenty-first century to look forward to. It is all of a piece. No dead spots anywhere, furious tempo, not a moment's boredom, yet full of feeling and the three finales are simply phenomenal! It will be a shame if you won't come up before the performance itself. If possible, come to the dress rehearsal. The premiere could be sold out three times over. I am perfectly confident. (To Pauline)

Leaving the hotel for the première of Die schweigsame Frau, *24 June 1935. The Strausses with Leonhard Fanto and (in uniform) Bruno von Niessen, a member of the Reich Music Chamber. The sentry on the hotel steps was not posted to honour the composer, but to guard members of the government. Hitler and Goebbels should have been there, but cancelled the appointment.*

Pauline, who detested being photographed, raises her bag, as if to keep the evening sun out of her eyes.

Two days before the first performance, in the middle of a game of skat, Strauss suddenly demanded to see the poster. The management froze in horror. Zweig's name was not on it, only the attribution 'after Ben Jonson'. Strauss flushed scarlet. 'Do it, if you like, but if you do I shall leave tomorrow morning and you can hold the premiere without me.' Zweig's name was reinstated.

It had been a few days previously that he had received a letter from Zweig which has not survived, but which can be reconstructed from Strauss's reply. Evidently Zweig spelt out in it his reasons for trying to persuade Strauss to accept Joseph Gregor as his new librettist: out of consideration for his fellow Jews, he could not continue publicly to work with someone who held an office under the National Socialists – and it would do Strauss no good to work publicly with a Jew. Even so, Zweig was ready to work for Strauss with Joseph Gregor, so long as everything was published under Gregor's name. He must also have referred for the first time in their association to the two acts of Strauss which had in particular been widely criticized in the foreign press: his conducting in place of Bruno Walter in Berlin in the spring of 1933 and in place of Toscanini in Bayreuth.

Strauss's explosive answer is compounded of exasperation, pride in his own artistic integrity and continuing incomprehension both of Zweig's very real fears and of the mentality of the people who now governed his country. He had no idea that the letters sent to Zweig by himself, a world-famous artist who had done more for Germany's good name than any government had ever done, were intercepted by the Gestapo in the name of German honour.

Dear Herr Zweig,
Your letter of the 15th is driving me to distraction! This Jewish obstinacy! Enough to make an anti-semite of a man! This pride of race, this feeling of solidarity! Do you believe that I am ever, in any of my actions, guided by the thought that I am 'German' (perhaps, *qui le sait*)? Do you believe that Mozart composed as an 'Aryan'? I know only two types of people: those with and those without talent. 'Das Volk' exists for me only at the moment it becomes the audience. Whether they are Chinese, Bavarians, New Zealanders, or Berliners leaves me cold. What matters is that they pay full price for admission. Now please stop plaguing me with that good Gregor. The comedy you sent me is charming and I don't doubt for one moment that it is your idea exclusively. I won't accept it under an assumed name, no more than *1648*. So I urgently ask you again to work out those two one-act plays as soon as possible: name your terms. Just keep the matter a secret on *your* part and let *me* worry about what I will do with the plays. Who told you that I have exposed myself politically? Because I have conducted a concert in place of the greasy rascal Bruno Walter? That I did for the orchestra's sake. Because I substituted for that other 'non-Aryan' Toscanini? That I did for the sake of Bayreuth. That has nothing to do with politics. It is none of my business how the gutter press

interprets what I do, and it should not concern you either. Because I act the part of president of the Reich Music Chamber? That I do only for good purposes and to prevent greater disasters! I would have accepted this troublesome honorary office under any government, but neither Kaiser Wilhelm nor Herr Rathenau offered it to me. So be a good boy, forget Moses and the other apostles for a few weeks, and work on *your* two one-act plays.

Maybe the Mexican text could become a good opera, but not for me. I am not interested in Indians, red or white gods, and Spanish conflicts of conscience. Let Gregor finish that text, but for another composer, who will surely be more appreciative than your well-wishing, equally stubborn

Dr Richard Strauss.

Regards for the well-being of your mother. The show here will be terrific. Everybody is wildly enthusiastic. And with all this you ask me to forgo you? Never ever! (17 June 1935)

The letter never reached Zweig, but was discovered in Gestapo files in 1948. A photocopy of it had been sent directly to Hitler by the National Socialist governor of Saxony.

On 20 June a 'strictly confidential' memorandum was issued by the Office for the Cultivation of Art in Berlin, to all district supervisors of the National Socialist Cultural Unit.

The new opera by Strauss receives its premiere in Dresden on 24 June. Like almost all Strauss's works, it has been published by the Jewish music publisher Fürstner, the text is by the Austrian Jew Stefan Zweig who furthermore, according to the foreign press, has placed his share of the royalties at the disposal of Jewish 'charities'. The vocal score is the work of the Jew Felix Wolfes. The General Intendant of the Dresden State Opera, Councillor Adolph, is married to a woman of wholly Jewish parentage.

It can be supposed that the new opera, like all the earlier works, will be performed in most other German opera houses. The National Socialist Cultural Unit has good cause to distance itself from this work. The local associations will not buy tickets or otherwise deal in them.

But it was years before the work was performed in any other German theatre, and it was withdrawn in Dresden after four performances.

Strauss made further memoranda in his notebooks, perhaps for himself, or perhaps for members of the Nazi hierarchy or even for Hitler, though by this time he had reason to understand that it would be useless.

On 6 July Ministerial Councillor Keudell, on behalf of State Secretary Funk, called on me and demanded that I resign as president of the Reich Music Chamber for reasons of 'ill health'. I did so at once. Herr Keudell pointed several times to a red-marked copy of a personal letter to my friend and, up to now, collaborator Stefan Zweig. Although the full name of the sender appeared on the cover, the letter had apparently been opened by the state police of Saxony, and several (!) government offices in Berlin had been informed (allegedly, Dr Frank [the Minister of Justice] thinks that's a lie). I did not know that I, the president of the Reich Music Chamber, was under direct state police surveillance, and that I, after a life of creating eminent works 'recognized in the entire world', was not considered above criticism as 'a good German'.

He defended the content of his letter to Zweig ('We simply compose, ever since Bach, whatever our talent permits us, and we are Aryans and Germans without being further aware of it. This can hardly be construed as 'treason') and explained his expression of contempt for 'das Volk' ('for me . . . people begin with the upper two million that pay their tickets in full – not those who for 15–30 pfennigs listen to *Meistersinger* or *Tristan*, causing great financial loss to the theatres which then require ever larger subsidies . . . a purely artistic question, not a question of *my* purse').

In other memoranda he reviewed the vanity of his efforts to use his honorary office to improve the quality of musical life in Germany. He was never consulted about the appointment of Intendants or conductors; when he made suggestions, they were disregarded. His plans for the distribution of state subsidies for the theatres were ignored and the money went only to Otto Laubinger's favourites. The central concert organization was riddled with corruption. He had spoken on the radio against the ignorant and inappropriate means adopted by the National Socialists to promote German music, and had warned the Führer that the Hitler Youth's practice of singing as it marched would only ruin its members' young voices, but his words went unheeded.

> My office was never anything more than a meaningless label, bringing me nothing but hostility and abuse from abroad, without giving me the satisfaction of being able to put into effect any decisive measures for the German theatre and German music.
>   All my appeals to the German cultural conscience vanished without trace, they are continually reorganizing, but nothing actually happens.

And in a memorandum which follows directly after that of 10 July 1935 he repeated his defence against the charge of anti-semitism.

> I have been slandered as a servile, selfish anti-semite, whereas in truth I have always stressed at every opportunity that I consider the Streicher–Goebbels Jew baiting as a disgrace to German honour, as evidence of incompetence, the basest weapon of untalented, lazy mediocrity against a higher intelligence and greater talent. I openly testify that I have received so much support, so much self-sacrificing friendship, so much generous help and intellectual inspiration from Jews that it would be a crime not to acknowledge it with all gratitude
>   True, I had adversaries in the Jewish press. . . . But my worst and most malicious enemies were 'Aryans' – I merely need to mention the

Die schweigsame Frau *at the Salzburg festival, 1959.*

names of Perfall, Oscar Merz (*Münchener Neueste Nachrichten*), Theodor Döring (*Der Sammler*), Felix Mottl, Franz Schalk, Weingartner, and the whole party press: *Völkischer Beobachter* and the rest.

What could he have done in addition to resigning? He was seventy-one years old. An old tree cannot be replanted, says the proverb. Should he have given up Germany, Garmisch, house, friends, singers, conductors, the opera houses in Dresden, Munich and Berlin, when he was not in actual urgent need or danger? Should he have allowed his work to vanish from the German theatre or from German concert halls?

Should he have moved permanently to Vienna? The ex-president of the Reich Music Chamber was execrated in Austria. He never seriously considered that it would be possible to speak out against Hitler from Austria, in the interests of the truth and in defence of his own reputation. 'We'll outlive them all', was all he would say.

Zweig's decision was a heavy blow to him. Of course he would have composed librettos written by him secretly, in defiance of Goebbels. But the cultivated, modest and worldly-wise poet would not change his mind. He knew it would be unworthy of Strauss to compose clandestinely. During the year before the premiere of *Die schweigsame Frau* he had put forward the names of several other writers until in despair and desperation, Strauss agreed to the suggestion of Joseph Gregor, a historian of the theatre.

The last letters between Strauss and Zweig, in the autumn of 1935, use the pseudonyms 'Storch' and 'Morosus'. After the 'Anschluss' of Austria into Greater Germany, Zweig joined many other Jews in exile, in England, France, Holland and finally Brazil, where he killed himself in 1942. The cause was not financial difficulty and he could have foreseen an end to the Nazi régime. He died on account of his second wife, and above all, perhaps, because he did not want to live on in the age that was coming. His world was

'the world of yesterday'. He had finished with Germany, and his farewell letter to his first wife was written in English.

Die schweigsame Frau was performed in Graz, Milan, Zurich, Prague and Rome, then vanished for ten years, until 1947. At the Salzburg Festival of 1959, Karl Böhm, who had conducted the world premiere, introduced the work to an international public, with an outstanding cast (including the young Hermann Prey and Fritz Wunderlich). It was done, nevertheless, with some savage cuts, almost fifty minutes' worth. Böhm seems to have inherited Ernst von Schuch's mania for the scissors.

There is some wonderful music in this opera, especially in the first half of Act II. The conversation between Morosus and Aminta and the wedding scene, culminating in the sextet, are among the most felicitous passages Strauss ever composed for the operatic stage. Perhaps the twenty-first century will justify his faith in it.

Snapshots

On a hotel terrace. Strauss, not noticing the photographer, nodded off.

This chapter presents Strauss without his guard up, without the bland, indifferent face he showed photographers when he was conscious of being in the public eye. The snapshots come from the archives at Garmisch, and the anecdotes from the family and close friends.

— *Once, when he and Franz had spent a hot summer day scrambling about on the Schachen (where Ludwig II built a curious Moroccan house), they had developed a mighty thirst and had had little to eat. Richard undertook to guide his son across to the sleeping-hut in the dark, but alcohol made their steps unsteady. Both toppled over a low wall and fell several feet. Their guardian angels (Mozart and Wagner?) were watching over them, however, and neither was hurt on this, the only known occasion when Strauss was the worse for drink.*

— *He gave up cigarettes at the age of seventy-five, after a long campaign on the part of his wife and the doctors ('foul temper as a result'). He had been a chain-smoker when working under pressure. He had his cigarettes specially made at the tobacconist's, Dora Weid, in the Maximilianstrasse in Munich; long thin ones with his favourite blend of tobacco and his name on them. They were also sold to his fans, who smoked then reverently, feeling themselves close to their idol.*

— *In 1907, after conducting a performance of* Die Meistersinger *in Berlin, he caught an overnight train to Cologne, and took a morning rehearsal for a concert. In the afternoon he was suddenly assailed by weakness: it was a warning that he was no longer as young as he had been. He took heed, and thereafter organized his time even more precisely than in the past, had regular medical check-ups, and visited spas boring though he found the 'cure'.*

— *After the Zweig débâcle, he at first retreated to Garmisch, hoping to be left in peace. He reduced his conducting engagements and travelling. For years his daily routine at Garmisch was as follows: he would get up around 9, take a small breakfast in the little room on the first floor, and was at his desk by 9.30. Frau Pauline ensured quiet, because 'if he doesn't compose anything in the morning, the whole day is wasted'.*

Whatever the weather he went for a walk at midday, taking any letters to the post. At 1, lunch with the family, then half an hour's rest on the sofa in his study ('no longer, or I only get tired'). Then back to his desk until the evening, composing or scoring, and writing letters. He would take another walk, often alone in the garden, usually with his sketchbook. His favourite spot was under the yew tree at the top of the garden.

After the evening meal, at which he ate only a little of each course, he would go to his study or the drawing room with Frau Pauline. If she wished, he played the piano: either something she asked for, or, occasionally, something he had just composed. Otherwise they read or talked. Spending so much time together and sharing so many interests, the couple always had plenty to talk about in the fields of domestic and current affairs but rarely discussed professional matters: 'None of you understand them, it's my business, I can look after it.'

He went to bed towards midnight at the latest: playing skat kept him up later than anything else. While he was still a smoker, he would empty the ashtrays and air the room before going upstairs.

Happy.

— *In the years when he travelled a lot, his letters home sounded as if he had only been there as a guest. 'I am so grateful for the wonderful weeks I spent with you. I long for you and feel homesick. I'm curious to know what you will decide about [something or other].'*

But of course he wanted to take care of everything himself. When his grandsons, as is the way with small boys, had turned their rooms into pigsties, he picked up the clothes and other objects lying on the floor and threw them out on the landing in a heap, to teach them a lesson. If some job needed to be done about the house or garden – laying a new path, felling trees – he hired the labour, planned the work and supervised it. His notebooks contain recipes, for pickled cabbage, say, or Pauline's method of frying liver. Of course, frozen and convenience foods were unheard-of; tinned foods existed, but were despised. Nearly everything they ate was prepared at home, and from fresh ingredients in their proper season. The archives preserve a note addressed to Anni Nitzl, who was only a girl when she first went to work for them in 1940. 'Annie. There are chestnuts. Frau Bierling is to bring some, or whatever else there is. Annie is requested to bake a vanilla loaf and a double batch of plätzchen *for the children. If Martin has the time, ask him to come to Frau Doktor.' Frau Doktor was Pauline.* Plätzchen *are yeasty biscuits – and children are not the only people who are fond of them.*

In high good humour in the theatre in Dresden . . .

. . . and in a less formal environment.

— *Everybody in the family liked the vanilla-flavoured* plätzchen, *and it was Pauline's practice to lock them away in the cupboard and carry the keys about with her. Grandson Richard: 'Grandmama was small and very quick. Essentially, she had only two modes of walking – scurrying and rushing. She ran into the open door of the dresser once, and gave herself a bad blow on the head, because she would*

Gallantry in Garmisch: Strauss chats with a family friend, Frau Irene Hellmann. She was the dedicatee of the song Schlechtes Wetter *op. 69 no. 5.*

Waiting during a film break.

With Xaver Markwalder, proprietor of the Verenahof hotel in Baden bei Zürich. The uniquely Bavarian word for the emotion expressed by Strauss's face is 'Grant' (pronounced 'grunt').

usually not wear her glasses. Everything about her was temperamental. She was always in a hurry.'

She rationed the plätzchen. *Once during the war, when sweet things were in short supply, Strauss got up in the middle of the night and without putting the light on crept down in his nightshirt to raid the dining-room cupboard.*

His heart nearly stopped: a large, white, ghostly figure was moving about in the dark room! It was Franz, also in his nightshirt, tormented by the same desire and equally startled by his father's unexpected appearance. They had a good laugh – quietly, so as not to disturb Mama – then sat down, still giggling, to eat the whole baking.

— Rudolf Hartmann, the stage director, recalls:
He was always exquisitely polite to women, regarded them as beings to be treated with deference, took care that they were comfortably seated, served, able to feel at ease. Such gallantry was quite disinterested and a matter of course; he never flirted, and his respect was for 'Woman' in the abstract. Of course he was a centre of attraction for women, and was fully aware of it. Sometimes he would go so far as to comment 'She's beautiful' or 'A piquant little lady' but he never made any attempt to establish a closer relationship with any of these women. For all his courtesy and friendly manner, he was reserved.

— *A lot of his letters contain complaints about hotel food, or the kind of dishes served at banquets: 'I sit and starve through "lunch" and "dinner".' He liked Bavarian home cooking, prepared with skill: beef with a nice rim of fat to it, Steinpilze with dumplings, loin of pork with the kidneys still attached, kidneys in any form. He was also fond of the best French cuisine. He could not abide the sandwich, or what they like to serve as an evening meal in North Germany: cold cuts which the guest is expected to lay on a slice of bread, thinly buttered, if at all, and eat with a knife and fork.*

He was not a big eater, even of sweet things like the rosehip cheese mentioned in Intermezzo. *He inherited his sweet tooth from the Strauss family – it was obviously more of a psychological need than just greed.*

His wife watched over his eating with the precision of a dietician. At mealtimes, Anna laid the meat before her, which she would carve carefully and serve him his portion, together with vegetables. Only rarely did he get a second helping. If he entertained guests in a restaurant, he selected a good wine, though he usually drank mineral water himself. He hardly ever touched beer, but occasionally he took a glass of bordeaux with his midday meal.

Hans Hotter recalls an occasion when he and his wife visited the Strausses in 1943.
'Pauline said: "Times are hard but I have cooked a good meal." There was a wonderful soup. Pauline asked us: "Will you have some more?" and filled our bowls. He leant across the table: "I'd like some more, too, please." Pauline: "You're not having any – there's a war on!"'

— *The distinguished tenor Julius Patzak was sitting behind Strauss at a rehearsal of* Arabella. *On stage the Matteo was labouring. Strauss grew restless, finally turned round and whispered: 'Admit it yourself, Patzak – isn't a tenor like that a frightful object?'*

— *Leo Blech recalled a performance of the* Ring *in which Thila Plaichinger, a very temperamental Viennese soprano, failed to meet with Strauss's approval. Things came to a head during one of the intervals: 'I am fully aware, Herr Doktor, that you can't stand me.' 'Stand you or not, you can't sing Brünnhilde the way you do!' 'The way you conduct, I can't sing her. With your fast tempos a person can only bark!' 'So bark!' 'I was engaged to sing!' 'For that, I do better with the clarinets.'*

— *Viorica Ursuleac recalled a time she and Clemens Krauss spent in Paris, shortly before the Second World War, when the Strausses were also there. 'We saw each other every day, Strauss telephoned first thing every morning to draw up the day's programme, especially going to the Louvre with my husband.*

Because of currency restrictions in Germany, we had run out of money, but Strauss invited us to be his guests. He still had some francs from his French royalties. On the last evening he took us to Prunier's and ordered champagne. Krauss raised his glass and said in gratitude: "Look, Herr Doktor, this is exactly what champagne ought to be like: cold, sweet – and free." Strauss roared with laughter. I have seldom known him as happy and contented as in those days in Paris.'

The French man of letters, musicologist and Nobel Prize Winner Romain Rolland first met Strauss at Bayreuth in 1891, but their closer acquaintance began in 1898. Rolland left a record of their many meetings in his diary, and over the years the notes add up to a vivid portrait. He made a fresh observation about Strauss's physical appearance almost every time they met: 'A young man,' he wrote in 1898, 'tall and thin, curly hair . . . a fair moustache, pale eyes and face.' On later occasions: 'the moustache so fair as to be almost white'; 'his back rather round'; 'very tall and with broad shoulders, but his hands attract one's attention, delicate, long, well-kept, and with something rather . . . aristocratic about them . . . At table [he] sits by his plate with his knees crossed, lifts his plate near to his chin in order to eat, stuffs himself with sweets like a baby . . . Cordial and good-natured with us, he is curt with the others; he scarcely listens to them . . . "*Was?*" he says, "*Ach! so, so*"; and that's all.' At the piano: 'He has charming fingers, very gentle, caressing, light; but he does not play at all like a composer . . . he looks bored and indifferent.' After a performance of *Don Quixote*, 'an ovation in Roman style – trumpets, waving scarves, a rain of bouquets on Strauss . . . Not being able to persuade his friend Becker (the cello in *Don Quixote*) to come and take a call, he takes his instrument from him and presents that to the public.'

They spent a lot of time together in Paris in March 1900. 'He declares that he is absolutely indifferent to the Transvaal war. "I am very fond of the English," says he; "they are very agreeable when one is travelling. For example, when I was in Egypt I was very glad that the English were there, instead of the Egyptians; one is always sure of finding clean rooms, every comfort, etc. . . . The Boers are a barbarian people . . . The English are very civilised and very strong. It is an excellent thing that the strongest should prevail." But what about the weak? The Egyptians, the Boers, what if they suffer? "Oh! I don't know anything about it; I don't think about it; Egypt doesn't exist when I am not there." But what if the strong were only strong on the surface, if there was in the weak a moral force superior to that of their conquerors, and perhaps a source of genius, even of artistic genius, more alive than the English colossus, with its mediocre and moribund heart? "Perhaps you're right, I expect you're right; but I prefer to think what I think."'

They visited the Louvre together. 'He has real taste in painting, and a fashionable taste, what's more. He greatly admires Chardin, whose workmanship he compares to that of Velasquez, (the painter whom he most admires). Fragonard amuses him; Boucher disappoints him a little . . . The happiness and the talent for living which the eighteenth century exudes flatter him agreeably. He is clearly less attuned to our nineteenth-century painters . . .' (Rolland names Delacroix, Gérard and David.) 'I notice that everything which has a tendency to heroism, all painting which is tragic or

in the spirit of Corneille, leaves him cold or bored. From time to time he feels tired and sits down. He talks to me about Napoleon I, for whom he has a great affection, but whose features disappoint and displease him. He considers them to be those of an actor, that his expression is cold and displeasing . . . Drawings . . . give him more pleasure than paintings, because they are more sincere, more spontaneous.'

In March 1906 Strauss conducted *Symphonia domestica* in Paris, and Rolland compared his looks with a portrait he owned, which the composer had given him: 'Strauss, in real life, hasn't that vigour of expression; the impression he gives is pale, uncertain, eternally youngish, a little inconsistent. But when seeing him close to, at the concert, conducting his orchestra, I was struck by the *other* Strauss: his face is ageing, hardening, shrinking; it is acquiring and retaining an intense seriousness, which not the slightest

Quizzical.

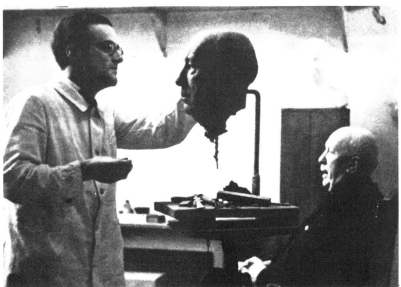

(Left, above) In the studio of Franz Mikorey, nephew of the tenor who sang Guntram in the one performance in Munich in 1895.

Absorbed in a game of chess with his grandson Richard.

gleam of gaiety illumines for an instant . . . he looks like a barbarian from Asia, one of those Huns who founded a family in Germany. But there is one thing which his portraits do not convey at all: that is the pale blondness of hair and complexion.'

Rolland went to fetch him from his hotel for a rehearsal. 'It is rather cold. Some snow fell last night. Strauss, who has come in a spring suit, is shivering; in spite of the icy wind he made, the day before, a fairly long trip to Versailles, travelling by car: naturally, he has a heavy cold. He is as rash as a child, and like a child he grizzles afterwards. . . . As we reach the stage, behind the curtain Mischa Elman can be heard playing the Andante from Beethoven's Violin Concerto. Strauss growls. I ask him, "What's the matter?" – "Oh, nothing! That piece. I would like to have written it."'

After the Fall

Strauss went to Antwerp in March 1936, to conduct a short season of his works at the Royal Flemish Opera. He wrote to Pauline:

> Anti-German feeling is so catastrophic that the management of the Flemish Theatre wanted to cancel my season altogether. They had already cancelled *Ariadne*, but it is going to be done today after all, since I scored a wild success on Monday with *Salome*, with every ticket sold. A fabulous dinner for fifty on Sunday, at the house of the richest man in Antwerp; the entire crème of the city came afterwards, I accompanied some of my songs. On Tuesday a formal reception at the city hall, with the mayor making a speech in *German*: an unheard-of event! It is not an exaggeration to say that I have *made* this success a German one entirely on my own, through my work, my conducting and my personal presence here. The newspapers are raving. I'd like to see any other German artist do what I have done – at a time like this, in a foreign country in a hostile mood. Really I deserve the Goldest Medal of the Propaganda Ministry. Here I am, after fifty years, still risking my neck as the pioneer of German music! (25 March 1936)

'I kill the boredom of the Advent season by composing an Olympic hymn for the proletarians – I, of all people, who hate and despise sports. Well, Idleness Is the Root of All Evil.' (To Stefan Zweig, 21 December 1934) He did not hide his opinion of sport from the President of the National Olympic Committee, Dr Lewald, either. Lewald replied with five sheets of outraged indignation: 'Your letter shocked me deeply. . . . You compare the Olympic Stadium to a recreation ground . . . and refer to our festival as an amateur orgy. . . .' The stadium, he declared, was a very artistic edifice, the opening ceremony, with dancing and people carrying banners and swinging Indian clubs, would be entrusted to choreographers of the first rank, and the music would be by Egk and Orff, no less! An abbreviated version of Schiller's *Ode to Joy* would be included, on account of the line '*Laufet*, Brüder, eure Bahn' – 'Brothers, *run* your course', an impeccable poetic injunction. With this letter (of 23 May 1935), Lewald enclosed Baron Coubertin's statement of the principle informing the modern Olympic Games: ideally they should comprise a single entity embracing the spirit as well as the body, with contests in architecture, sculpture, painting, music and literature as well as sports. Olympia was no mere recreation ground!

Joseph Gregor was born in Chernovtsy in the Ukraine in 1888, and began his academic career studying the history and theory of the theatre in Berlin, Vienna and Munich. After gaining his doctorate, he went to work in the Austrian National Library in Vienna, where he founded and ran the theatre collection. His career as an author began with short stories and poetry, but he also produced several scholarly works: *Weltgeschichte des*

With Joseph Gregor in a characteristic stance, at Garmisch.

The performance of the Olympic Hymn, in the stadium in Berlin, 1 August 1936.

Theaters, Shakespeare, Das Zeitalter des Films and others. His other works included new versions of classical plays. He died in Vienna in 1960.

He was an authority in his academic field, quick to take offence, painstaking and versatile. He spent most of his time on a high intellectual plane, and was unskilled in practical matters. He was no poet, however: scholarship and the taking of pains are no substitute if the flame of poetry does not burn.

His three librettos for Strauss are weak in construction and they lack the verbal flair necessary to strike a spark in the composer. Strauss took a lot of trouble over Gregor and hurt his feelings in the attempt to shake him out of his 'philosophical banalities' and 'bad imitations of Homeric jargon'. Everyone wondered why the mantle had fallen on Gregor; it did so because Strauss knew of no one else, and trusted Zweig's recommendation, hoping that Zweig would be able to work behind the scenes.

Adolf Mahnke's set for Friedenstag, *Dresden 1938. With the bells pealing out to proclaim the end of the war, the tower sank from view and the final chorus was sung against a background of brilliant light.*

Friedenstag, *24 July 1938, in Munich. Viorica Ursuleac (Maria), Hans Hotter (commandant of the fortress), Ludwig Weber (commander of the besieging force).*

The line-up after the performance: Weber, Ludwig Sievert (designer), Gregor, Strauss, Hotter, Krauss, Ursuleac, Rudolf Hartmann (producer).

Their first contact was in May 1935, not long before the premiere of *Die schweigsame Frau.* Gregor was thrilled to be working with Strauss but not interested in the subjects of either *Friedenstag* or *Capriccio,* and first of all sent a wordy and quite unusable scenario for a *Semiramis.* Strauss hauled him down to earth and explained that all he wanted was the dialogue for *Friedenstag,* which Gregor supplied quickly during July 1935.

Zweig had already drafted a scenario. The date of the action was 24 October 1648, the scene a German fortress held for the Austrian Emperor in the Thirty Years' War, under siege by a Swedish army and at the end of its strength. Hunger, despair – and heroic attitudes. The defenders prepare to use the last of the powder to blow the fort and themselves up. The fuse is lit – then extinguished as the enemy fire a cannon. They prepare to die fighting, but there is no second shot. Instead the sound of church bells is heard, at first distantly, then near at hand. The Peace of Westphalia has been concluded. Jubilation, curtain.

Why Strauss chose this subject, with its heroics and its military virtues, its overriding ethos of blind, suicidal obedience to a remote emperor is a mystery. (Rudolf Hartmann asked him straight out, and after a lot of rumbling and grumbling, Strauss gave him only an equivocal answer:

The intense expression is typical of Strauss in photographs of the late 1930s.

'Umm – military matters just do not excite me.') Following his theatrical instinct, he suggested a love-triangle to Zweig, with the commander's wife torn between her love for a young officer and her husband. Politely, Zweig dissuaded him from this, and the original scenario stood. But it was Gregor who wrote the dialogue, and spread himself in so doing. Strauss thundered:

> Action and character! No 'thoughts'! No poetry! Theatre!! The audience can only hear a third of the words, and if they can't follow the action, they get bored! You must permit me to accompany your first steps in the operatic classroom with the gentle strokes of the experienced, grey-haired schoolmaster's rod. No weighing of motives, no poetic self-indulgences. Headlines!

Zweig rewrote a few passages (the dialogue between the two commanders), declared the rest excellent, and withdrew from any further collaboration. In the meantime, Gregor had found the subject for *Daphne* on his own initiative, but it did not arouse any enthusiasm in Strauss to begin with.

There was music within him, demanding its release, so he composed *Friedenstag* in winter, exceptionally, between the autumn of 1935 and January 1936. For a time while he was doing so, he had Gregor to stay at Garmisch because 'I do not believe that I shall ever find the music for the second half: these are not real people, it's all so stilted, it's a kind of poetry which doesn't work at all in the theatre.' He demanded changes and cuts, which Gregor promptly executed in the tower room. The opera only lasts eighty minutes and Strauss's next wish was for another one-acter: his 'Cav' needed its own 'Pag', so *Daphne* it was.

The original intention was that the two one-act operas should have their premieres in Dresden on the same evening, in October 1938, but Strauss changed his mind. *Friedenstag* was dedicated to Clemens Krauss and Viorica Ursuleac and Krauss was allowed to give it its first performance during the Munich Festival on 24 July 1938. Both operas were then given together in Dresden in October, with the premiere of *Daphne* at the start of the evening. *Daphne* was dedicated to Karl Böhm. It was three years since *Die schweigsame Frau*. Goebbels was triumphant: Strauss did not need Zweig.

The Munich cast gave the first Viennese performance of *Friedenstag*, too, which was attended by Hitler, who gave a reception afterwards. He showed an astonishing array of musical knowledge, and was able, for example, to remind Hans Hotter of what he had been singing ten years previously: 'Isn't Scarpia too high for you? That G Flat in Act II?' He revealed his wish to give Munich a new opera house, and you would never have guessed from the way he spoke of Strauss that any cloud had ever settled on him.

Gregor lost no time in writing a fat book about his collaboration with Strauss, as well as producing copious articles and lectures. The name of Zweig was not mentioned in any of them: there could be no hint of his involvement with any of the new works under the Third Reich. Thus when Gregor writes that he had suggested six projects to Strauss at their very first meeting, and that Strauss had at once selected three of them – *Friedenstag*, *Daphne* and *Danae* – it is not true. The first was conceived by Zweig and the third went back to a scenario by Hofmannsthal, which Gregor laboured to develop with a great deal of assistance from Krauss and the composer. Later he made such heavy weather of *Capriccio* that Krauss and Strauss wrote the text themselves.

From his arrival in Munich in 1937 until the opera house was destroyed by bombing in 1943, Krauss systematically built up the Strauss repertory. He staged model productions of the operas with the help of the director Rudolf Hartmann and the designer Ludwig Sievert, and by the time of the premiere of *Capriccio* there were eleven of them permanently in the repertory. Looking back sadly and gratefully to that era, Strauss testified that the standards set in Munich under Krauss had not been equalled anywhere else. With *Daphne*, Krauss became increasingly valuable to him as an adviser and assistant in all practical and dramaturgical questions. He proved indefatigable in the search for perfection and the instigation of new projects.

Die Josephslegende needed a companion piece to make a full evening of ballet by Strauss. Krauss suggested that the Couperin suite composed in 1923 for the ballet of the Vienna Opera might be expanded. Strauss, who loved Couperin's ageless grace, adapted several of the keyboard pieces and achieved a successful synthesis of the old and the new. He described the process as 'supplying stuff for skipping to'. The new pieces were gathered together for concert performance under the title *Divertimento*, and received Strauss's last opus number, 86. In this form, Krauss conducted the first performance in Vienna in 1943.

In Ravenna, outside the church of S. Vitale.

Italy and Hellas

Illness in the late summer of 1937 prevented Strauss from taking part in the World Fair in Paris in September. In October he set off for Italy and did not return until April 1938. He spent Christmas in Taormina, where he finished *Daphne*.

This was the first time he had taken his family abroad with him for such a long period. He wanted to get out of Germany, where he now conducted only on special occasions. The warmer climate was good for his lungs. The emigration was only temporary, but they could wait and hope that circumstances would return to normal. The family had begun to steer a wary course through troubled waters.

Strauss had told Elisabeth Schumann during their American tour that he wanted enough money to be able to live in Italy. He rhapsodized about Greece, but he visited Italy more often. He had discovered the effect that the warmth and sunlight had on his creative energy and imagination during his first visit to Italy in 1886 at the age of twenty-two. He had gone back in the two following years, and *Aus Italien* had been the result.

In St Mark's Square, Venice.

The envelope and last page of Verdi's letter, 27 January 1895.

He spent some time there each year from 1892 to 1895, including his honeymoon. There was then an interval, until 1900, but from 1907 until 1913 (the year he travelled with Hofmannsthal) he again went each year. Altogether, he made twenty-two trips to Italy in his life. From 1936 onwards he spent whole winters in the south, for the sake of his lungs – and for the warmth he dreamed of in the north.

Berlioz and Mendelssohn, who had little enough in common, nevertheless agreed on the subject of the frivolity of Italian music. Italians knew a lot about singing, and not enough about composition, was the received opinion in Germany and France. For the compatriots of Rossini and Puccini, the German love of counterpoint was equally hard to take. The first performance of *Rosenkavalier* in Milan revealed some more curious preconceptions in the audience. The first act went very well, but turmoil broke out after the second: hissing, whistling, and a shower of Futurist pamphlets protesting against this self-degrading frivolity on the part of the composer of *Salome*. That gentleman was understandably puzzled when he was told that the cause of the objections was the waltz. At La Scala, it seemed, the Viennese waltz was tolerated only in ballet.

In 1895, Strauss sent a copy of the vocal score of *Guntram* to the eighty-two-year-old Verdi, with a letter in which he wrote of the powerful impression *Falstaff* had made on him. Verdi sent him a courteous reply, congratulating him on 'the expert hand' revealed by the cursory glance that was all he had so far had time for, and expressing regret that his ignorance of German prevented him from doing the work full justice. The letter was given a place of honour in the glass-fronted case at Garmisch, along with Strauss's medals, illuminated addresses, silver presentation batons, autograph letters of Beethoven and Mozart and the *Lohengrin* sketches given him by Winifred Wagner.

Strauss greatly admired Verdi as a melodist, but apart from *Otello* and above all, *Falstaff* he did not approve of Verdi's treatment of his literary sources.

Without the detailed psychological motivation provided by their poets, dramas like *Don Carlos* and *Macbeth* turn into cautionary tales, Gothic romances, with a handful of striking arias. The Italians read newspapers, or chat, between the arias. The conscientious German grows corns on his *derrière*. The most popular hits from Verdi's ten or twelve early operas ought to be combined in a sort of potpourri, to save the cultivated listener from the boredom of sitting through three-hour operas full of the most indifferent, often downright primitive note spinning for the sake of the arias.

Puccini admired Strauss, wrote him a respectful letter in 1900 and went to Graz specially to hear *Salome* in 1906. Strauss did not return his admiration. 'I've never been able to last through one of his operas to the end.' But he gave *Il Trittico* its Austrian premiere while director of the Vienna Opera.

He once outlined the following scenario to Hofmannsthal: two opera companies, travelling on the same ocean liner, are rehearsing the same opera by Puccini. The leader of one troupe bribes the ship's cook to poison their rivals. The other steals the first one's music and throws it into the sea. The farce would have given Strauss a lot of sardonic amusement, but Hofmannsthal did not rise to the proposal.

While working on *Capriccio*, his third 'anti-opera' (after *Feuersnot* and *Intermezzo*), he wrote to Krauss, who liked Puccini very much:

> Perhaps the anti-theatre ingredient will make my operas longer-lasting. If I compare Puccini to a delicate *Weisswurst* which must be eaten at 10 a.m. (within two hours of making) (then by 1 one is hungry again and wants something more substantial), while salami (more solidly made) lasts a little longer . . .

Viorica Ursuleac, however, heard him make an illuminating confession:

> Krauss sometimes said to him: 'Herr Doktor, *Bohème* is such a beautiful work', and he would answer ironically: '*Jaja*, very beautiful, all melody, all melody!' When we were doing *Arabella* in Amsterdam, we were out for a walk together and he was talking to me about so-called 'beautiful music': 'Everyone always thinks that I am hostile to Puccini. It isn't true. Only I cannot listen to his operas, because if I do I can't get the melodies out of my head afterwards. And I can't write Puccinian Strauss.

There are several parodies of Italian music in Strauss: the Italian Singer's aria in *Rosenkavalier*, the ironic but delicate numbers for the disguised Henry in *Die schweigsame Frau*, and the Metastasian duet in *Capriccio*, in which Krauss and Strauss smiled at bel canto and its practitioners. 'What a happy "Addio"! Indeed, words and music are not related.'

In 1932, Richard and Franz Strauss were received in audience by Mussolini. They talked about Verdi and Mozart, the Duce promised to use his influence to get '*La donna senza l'ombra*' produced in Italy, and asked for Strauss's advice in connection with his plan to rebuild the Rome Opera. Strauss recommended that it should not be left to the architects: musicians knew better what was needed. The very next day the architect appeared at their hotel for a consultation. 'A dictator's attention to detail', Strauss noted.

If he spent more time in Italy physically, his spirit dwelt longer in 'Hellas'. *Elektra* was ancient Greece under a psychologist's eye, *Ariadne* a *jeu l'esprit*, *Die ägyptische Helena* a literary paraphrase. *Daphne* was to be ancient Greece without the modern stance, and *Danae* a mixture of humour and pathos.

There are many dramas with great poetic virtues which do not work because the characters have no dramatic life. Others have interesting characters, but they are forced to drag themselves through limp plots.

The Italian publishers of this 'pin-up' postcard retouched the picture for the Italian taste: darkened eyebrows, flashing eyes, and highlighted hair.

A signed photograph of Benito Mussolini, 1924.

Daphne, *15 October 1938, in Dresden.*
The Dionysian feast.

There are only thirty-two basic situations in all drama and the craft o
putting any of them to effective use in the service of an original idea is hard
to learn. Dramaturgy is quite independent of literary standards, as a large
number of effective, well-constructed farces show. Few writers are as skilfu
as Shakespeare, Schiller, Wagner, Beaumarchais or da Ponte in construct
ing plot. Most opera librettos fail to provide either characters that arouse
and hold interest or the type of action that makes the audience eager to
know what will happen next.

Joseph Gregor knew a lot about the history and theory of the theatre
He was conscientious, diligent and eager to fulfil all Strauss's wishes
Lacking the skill to write his own librettos, Strauss had the experience and
the dramatic gifts to see where Gregor went wrong. Gregor wrote *Daphne* in
a flush of enthusiasm directly after *Friedenstag*, in August 1935. Straus
turned his attention to it in the following February, after finishing the other
one-acter.

You still allow yourself to be carried away by your own verses, of which
the audience in the opera house will understand about a fifth. They wil
be bored and instantly refuse to listen to any more if they are asked to
chew on 'thoughts' submerged in music, when they would prefer to hea
beautiful cantilenas resting on the bare minimum of text that i
necessary to help the action along. (4 March 1936)

That is the core of dramatic construction: whatever does not further th
action and keep it moving is wasted in the theatre. Gregor revised and wrot
more poetry, fell into despair and offered explanations of ethical and
psychological motives, but he remained wholly in the dark on questions c
structure, how to raise tension or arouse sympathy. Strauss enlisted Lotha
Wallerstein and Krauss to bring their practical experience to bear, and th
three harnessed themselves in front of their willing but earthbound Pegasus
He poured out an endless stream of new or revised text, which Strauss the
tautened, reformulated, cut and pasted, accepting whatever he could
Then after two months his letters to Gregor suddenly stopped. The spar

Margarete Teschemacher, the first
Daphne, in the transformation scene.

246

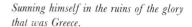

had been ignited, music began to flow – and he made any further minor alterations to the text himself.

There is a different inspiration at work in *Daphne* from that of *Friedenstag*. The beloved landscape of Greece moved Strauss as cardboard figures, divine or human, did not. He wrote bucolic chamber music for a large orchestra. His old skill of creating drama with tonalities resurged with Daphne's entrance, greeting the dying day in the most sensuous F sharp major, which is then not heard again until the end, in her transformation.

For Apollo's kiss he invented sounds that are without parallel in his entire output. Willi Schuh has called them an '*Ur-Einfall*' – a primal inspiration which does not evolve organically from the existing motivic material but rears up out of the polyphonic texture. There is nothing else in music quite like the terror that overcomes Daphne after the kiss, and the death of Leukippos, too, is a passage unprecedented in terms of musico-dramatic form.

To give Gregor his due, in places *Daphne* rises to poetic heights, especially towards the end. Strauss played him the ending on a bad hotel piano in Italy, and he went into ecstasies. Strauss, who was always irritated by extravagance, growled 'Get away, it's only the Magic Fire music with different notes'.

It was Krauss who made the decisive suggestion. The original plan was that after Daphne's transformation into a laurel tree the villagers should come back onstage and sing a hymn of praise. Krauss thought that the effect would be to turn the tree into a stage prop, whereas left alone, singing, it is a symbol of eternal nature.

Is it then quite impossible to have the transformation done kinematographically while the figure remains visible? People must be able to see how Daphne, as she runs after Apollo with outstretched arms, suddenly stops and branches and leaves start to grow out of her arms and hair and her feet turn into roots. All my music will be quite meaningless, if the audience is left to imagine everything! (Strauss to Krauss, 16 January 1940)

The first performance of the latest work of the 'time-honoured maestro' was broadcast by wireless all over Europe. The international press received

Visiting Greek ruins in Agrigento, Sicily. Pauline is wearing the latest fashion.

it in a respectful chorus, but the emotional shockwaves that *Salome* and *Rosenkavalier* had caused were a thing of the past. Strauss was now a 'classic', and for the first time in his life, according to Willi Schuh, he began to think about his place in the history of music.

The premiere of *Daphne* is overshadowed, in the history of 1938, by events that took place elsewhere in Germany – or 'Greater Germany': Austria was annexed in March; Neville Chamberlain went to Munich and flew home with a piece of paper that promised 'Peace in our time'; the Sudetenland was 'liberated' from Czech tyranny. The noise of military bands, political rallies and marching boots drowned the strains of a bucolic tragedy and a 'day of peace'.

Strauss was in Italy when his grandson Richard was threatened and then beaten up by other boys in his school in Garmisch. Both he and Christian were kept away from school for a while. When their grandfather heard of it he came home, wrote to people he trusted who had influence, and finally to Hitler. The party chancellery decreed that the two boys were to be treated as Aryans, but were not eligible for party membership, military service or public office (Richard was eleven years old at the time, Christian six.) As their mother said: 'We had to steer a course, somehow.'

In the years to come the old man had to pay dozens of calls to government offices to submit requests, spend hours in waiting rooms, and often have his business attended to in the end by arrogant minor officials. He who had been a citizen of the world bore the association with the national *plebs* stoically.

The title which Hofmannsthal gave to the scenario for an 'Offenbachiad' which he sent Strauss in 1920 was *Danae, or, The Marriage of Convenience*. Strauss had always claimed, after all, to possess the stuff for the Offenbach of the twentieth century, but he seems not to have felt any interest in a mythological operetta after '*Die FroSch*'. He read it and forgot it, until Willi Schuh recalled it to his memory in 1936.

Zweig had recently been lost to him, and the thought of a new subject emanating from Hofmannsthal appealed strongly to Strauss. But the libretto had to be written by Gregor. They were still working on *Daphne* when he started on *Danae*. It took longer than anything else Strauss ever wrote: four years and more. Strauss wanted verbal and dramatic grace, wit, humour, irony. He got Gregor.

He read and rejected the first draft in February 1937. Over the next eighteen months Gregor wrote and wrote, and still Strauss had nothing he could work with. He begged for a properly thought-through prose version, a light comedy, even just a detailed scenario – anything rather than the bombast he was getting. ('I do not want to read the word "Belovèd" once more!') He exhorted Gregor to listen to Caruso's recording of the aria from Donizetti's *L'elisir d'amore*: 'I love that piece. That is what *Danae* must be like!' He even tried setting scraps of the text, while neither the plot nor the text as a whole existed in a recognizable form.

Krauss, Wallerstein and Hartmann were enlisted again. Strauss wrote some text himself. Krauss suggested three acts, instead of the planned two Viorica Ursuleac came up with the title: *Die Liebe der Danae*. At last the firs act was finished, in Baden near Zurich, just after the outbreak of war, on 7 September 1939. Act III was completed on 28 June 1940, by which time Strauss had been working on the text of *Capriccio* with Krauss for a year.

After so difficult a birth, *Danae* was put away to be kept a secret and published as *opus posthumum*. But of course its existence was already known. The vocal score was published and then the work itself was heard before the war's end in moving circumstances.

The Second World War

Early in 1939 Strauss wrote a short piece for orchestra, a waltz he called *München* (*Munich*). The invitation to write it came from the city council, who wanted it for a brief film about Munich's cultural heritage. He used material from *Feuersnot*, it lasted only four minutes, and he subtitled it 'Occasional Waltz'. The film was shot and promptly banned by higher authority, though Strauss himself was informed of neither event.

His seventy-fifth birthday was celebrated with festival weeks in Dresden, Berlin and Munich; in Vienna, the Vienna Philharmonic Orchestra put on a birthday concert. Vienna, where he had built his fine town-house, had been his second home since 1919, and he spent more time there now that politics had become so oppressively present in every aspect of life in Germany. His association with the Vienna Philharmonic went back to 1892, when they had played *Don Juan* under Hans Richter. He conducted them himself for the first time in 1906, at a festival in Salzburg, with Mozart and Bruckner (Ninth Symphony) on the programme. In December 1906 he conducted them in Vienna for the first time: the *Oberon* Overture, Mozart's G minor Symphony and the *Eroica*. Thereafter he directed them with increasing frequency, until he became director of the Vienna Opera (for which the Philharmonic also play). He learnt to know them all well on the South American tours and took steps to have unsatisfactory players pensioned off and replaced by new blood. Standards rose as the grip of 'seniority' and routine was loosened.

Otto Strasser recalled the seventy-fifth birthday concert in his memoirs:

> It began with the suite from *Le bourgeois gentilhomme*. We had arranged for this music for chamber ensemble to be played by our youngest members, to demonstrate what would be lost if they were conscripted. During the interval I said how much this suite, in particular, impressed me. He remarked that he had 'written it with the left hand, so to speak'.
>
> Our colleague Swoboda had rehearsed an arrangement of the final duet from *Rosenkavalier* with young Richard, who played the flute. . . . After the presentation [of an early Italian painting] ten-year-old

The city of Vienna gave Strauss a bronze copy of the Beethoven monument in Heiligenstadt. He kept it in his study in Garmisch. The American soldiers who visited them in 1945 kept asking 'Who is that man?' After the twentieth time, Strauss muttered, exhausted, to Alice, 'If one more of them asks, I'll tell him it's Hitler's father.'

Richard played his little piece. Strauss was very amused and said when it was finished: 'Lovely, but no sense of rhythm, just like most flautists!'

Strauss entered the room to the strains of a fanfare he had written for the Vienna Philharmonic some years before, and he then conducted the *Bourgeois gentilhomme* suite himself. The concert ended with the *Symphonia domestica*:

> ... which was the real celebration so far as he was concerned. His family sat in the box, the grandsons wearing sailor suits, and while he conducted he kept turning to them and obviously lived through the familiar, familial course of the work with them.
>
> At the end he was stormily applauded, but when I met him at the exit from the platform, he suddenly threw the baton away, stumbled into the artists' room, sat down, visibly distressed, and murmured: 'Now it's all over', and began to cry bitterly. I was moved and at the same time had no idea what to do. He was a man who took such joy in life: was he thinking of the end at this moment of moments? After a short time his son arrived and put his arms around his father, who was growing calmer, and all was well again. The next morning Jerger [the manager of the Philharmonic] and I collected him from the Hotel Imperial, and as we strolled across the Ring together, he was fresh and cheerful and

The Vienna Philharmonic celebrated Strauss's 75th birthday: a speech by Wilhelm Jerger raises a laugh.

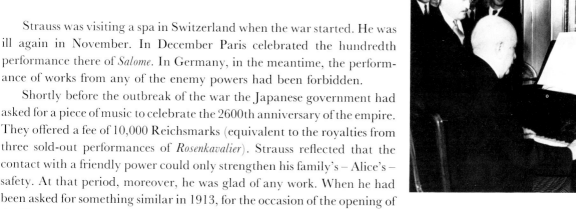

said that he would go to Dresden the same day, to conduct *Arabella*. He had overcome his depression, and turned his face to the world again.

Strauss was visiting a spa in Switzerland when the war started. He was ill again in November. In December Paris celebrated the hundredth performance there of *Salome*. In Germany, in the meantime, the performance of works from any of the enemy powers had been forbidden.

Shortly before the outbreak of the war the Japanese government had asked for a piece of music to celebrate the 2600th anniversary of the empire. They offered a fee of 10,000 Reichsmarks (equivalent to the royalties from three sold-out performances of *Rosenkavalier*). Strauss reflected that the contact with a friendly power could only strengthen his family's – Alice's – safety. At that period, moreover, he was glad of any work. When he had been asked for something similar in 1913, for the occasion of the opening of the Konzerthaus in Vienna, he had taken great pleasure in composing his *Festliches Präludium* and it had been a big success. The *Japanische Festmusik*

The librettists of Capriccio. *Strauss and Clemens Krauss.*

In 1943 Strauss participated as a guest in a course on opera production organized at Salzburg by the conductor Rudolf Hartmann, who directed the premier of Capriccio.

makes a strong impression – not least for its depiction of a volcanic eruption. Far-Eastern colouring is provided by certain modulations and the use of gongs: otherwise the fifteen-minute piece is pure Strauss. It was finished in Merano on 23 April 1940, and received the opus number 84. It uses material Strauss sketched in 1915, for a 'symphony on three subjects', which may be the reason why it does not sound like an occasional composition.

Since 1936 Strauss had taken to composing in wintertime as well as the summer, going straight from one opera to the next, producing music even before the libretto was ready. By the spring of 1939 he was ready to start on an idea that Zweig had first mentioned five years earlier. The title of a libretto by the Abbate Casti, *Prima la musica, poi le parole*, on the relative importance of words and music, was what appealed to Strauss, as Zweig had thought it would. Giambattista Casti (1721–1803) was poet to the court of Vienna under Joseph II. His text, a four-page intermezzo about the central issue in operatic composition, was set by Salieri and given at court on the same evening as the first performance of Mozart's *Impresario*. It was too out of date for Strauss to use, but perhaps Gregor could think up a new situation to fit the title.

He had a shot in May 1939 while the work on *Danae* continued, but without success. Strauss did not want an opera at all but an onstage discussion of taste, of art in general and the theatre in particular. Impatiently, he drafted scenes for himself, wrote pieces of dialogue and tried to outline a course for the action. He staked out the terrain. He spent long conversations and hours of letter-writing, trying to explain what he wanted to Gregor. Gregor experienced only dismay and perplexity, wrote verses in the only way he knew, and got steadily further away from the composer's intentions.

Strauss came to the conclusion that only another conductor with live theatrical experience could understand his wish for an anti-opera, and turned to Clemens Krauss. In September 1939 Krauss drafted a detailed scenario with opportunities for everything Strauss wanted: elegant language, witty, pointed, ironic and pithy dialogue. Strauss dismissed Gregor gratefully and started work on the text for *Capriccio* while he was still composing Act III of *Danae*. Rudolf Hartmann gave advice on design, the conductor Hans Swarowsky furnished the all-important sonnet, while Krauss revised Strauss's own drafts, invented new scenes and wrote new dialogue. He managed to draw musical history in as a natural constituent of the conversation; the prompter was his idea, he put flesh on the characters and their words and set them all within a flawless dramatic structure.

Wartime circumstances made his work at the head of the Munich Opera and the fulfilment of other conducting engagements more difficult, and he did not finish the text until January 1941. Elegant and ironic, it contains the essence of the experience of two professionals; it is 'full of grey cells and dry wit'. No longer did Strauss have to wrestle with bombast, unidiomatic phrasing, clumsy dramaturgy or inept metaphors. The people on the stage speak and act like real human beings, and are interesting in themselves. Strauss deployed all his compositional skills, up to and including a fugue. Once more, his composition flowed 'like the Loisach' and was enriched by all those graceful, original ideas that make his music unlike that of anyone else.

Krauss was on a working visit to Garmisch and Strauss played him something he had recently composed. Krauss suggested a change in the declamation at one point. They began to argue about it, and each played his own preferred version again. Frau Pauline came out of the small library and as she passed by on her way to the dining-room remarked, 'The way Krauss played it is better'. Strauss thought it over a moment longer then conceded the point. He even left the short score to Krauss, so that he could alter the vocal parts where it would help the declamation. It is the only work in his entire output that he allowed another person to amend. The subtitle, 'Conversation Piece for Music by Clemens Krauss and Richard Strauss', denominates their partnership. Strauss called it his musical testament.

Strauss wrote to Krauss when they were making plans for the first performance:

> . . . not a piece to put before an audience of 1,800 night after night. Perhaps a dainty morsel for cultural gourmets, not very substantial musically – at all events, not so succulent that the music will compensate for it, if the general public does not take a liking to the libretto. Your pleasure in the collaboration makes you overestimate the work out of the kindness of your heart, I believe. Libretto and music together (if they understand every word, if you conduct the Philharmonic and if your Pretorian Guard sings) may make it an agreeable evening for respectable people – I have no faith in its theatrical effectiveness in the usual sense. (12 October 1941)

Two months later he reported on Karl Böhm's disappointment at the news that Dresden was not to have the world premieres of either *Capriccio* or *Danae*. 'As he is a dear, good fellow he did not tell me our friendship was at an end (as some of his worthy colleagues would have done). Thank God that these will be the last world premieres of my life: they are enough to break one of the habit of composing!' (12 December 1941)

Krauss lectured the singers during rehearsal: 'Clarity! If they don't hear every single word, the opera is meaningless!' In the background, Strauss's voice was raised: 'Well, if they hear just a little of my music from time to time, I've nothing against that either.' He was purring after the dress rehearsal: 'I can do nothing better than this.'

The first performance, conducted by the librettist in Munich on 26 October 1942, was a success: the audience loved it. The war prevented the opera from becoming well known as quickly as it might otherwise have done. Only after 1948 was it possible for Krauss and Hartmann to take it to other houses and perform it with a rising generation of gifted singers.

Dr Goebbels was not satisfied with the degree of independence that he perceived German musicians still to enjoy. Strauss and some others were summoned to his office in Berlin at 10 a.m. on 10 February 1942. Werner Egk was of the party:

Frau Alice with her parents-in-law at the première *of* Capriccio.

The composer Flamand (Horst Taubmann) gets advice from another composer.

The composer (Taubmann) courts the Countess (Viorica Ursuleac).

Photos taken at the time of the first performance of Capriccio, *October 1942. Above right: Taubmann, Krauss and Strauss. Right centre: Krauss and Strauss.*

The theatre director La Roche (Georg Hann), the Countess (Ursuleac) and the poet Olivier (Hans Hotter).

Strauss saw the minister first, alone. Through the door we could hear Goebbels screaming. Then we were all ushered in. Goebbels ordered something that Strauss had written in a letter to be read aloud: 'In accordance with our agreed statute, we ourselves will decide questions concerning the distribution scheme. It is not for Dr Goebbels to interfere.'

Goebbels slapped the letter and screamed: 'Herr Strauss, did you write that?' 'Yes.' 'Be quiet! You have no conception of who you are, or of who I am! You dare refer to Lehár as a street musician?! I can have these outrageous statements of yours published in every newspaper in the world. Do you realize what would happen then? Lehár has the masses and you haven't! Stop your claptrap about the importance of serious music, once and for all. It will not serve to raise your own standing. Tomorrow's art is different from yesterday's! You, Herr Strauss, belong to yesterday!'

None of us said a word, then he threw us all out. Strauss was grey, ravaged and exhausted. He hid his face in his hands and murmured: 'If only I'd listened to my wife and stayed in Garmisch.' Tears were running down his cheeks. He could see that all his efforts on behalf of the protection of intellectual property were at an end.

'*That was how he looked when the name of Hitler was mentioned*', according to his son Franz.

Theodor Martin the chauffeur had become indispensable to the ageing couple. The threat of conscription hung over him constantly; each time his call-up papers came, Strauss took up his pen and asked for deferment, and each time it was granted – but only for a short period. Like everybody else in wartime, Strauss was for ever having to ask for things, fill in forms, seek permission to run a car, obtain a petrol ration, other rations. Rudolf Hartmann was present on one occasion when Martin came in with the news that something or other had been 'refused'. The word threw Strauss into a rage, he went very red and Hartmann thought he would have a stroke. Martin tried to soothe him, implored him to understand, it was the same for all Germans . . . 'I do not want to understand! I must be able to move around, for my work, for my commitments. Say that to those brown blockheads, as they drive about in limousines in their uniforms!' Softly Martin answered: 'Herr Doktor, I can't say that.' Strauss was silent. He did not know what to do. There was nothing he could do.

One day in 1943 Windeisen, the Kreisleiter (district commander) of Garmisch, presented himself at the house. He had been a member of the National Socialist party since 1923, and was the only person in the town on whom Hitler had paid a private social call during the Winter Olympics held in Garmisch in 1936. Windeisen refused to grant another deferment of Martin's call-up, and also declared that the Strauss family must provide accommodation for evacuees or other people made homeless. A heated argument broke out in Strauss's study. At one point, because Strauss continually referred to 'Herr Hitler', Windeisen shouted at him: 'Say "the Führer"!' 'I call people by their names. I say Herr Hitler.'

'Even you must make sacrifices for our people's heroic struggle. Think of the front, where thousands of the best Germans are falling . . .'.

'No soldier needs to fall on my account. I did not want this war, it is nothing to do with me.'

'Other heads than yours have already rolled, Herr Doktor Strauss!' Windeisen bawled, and marched out of the house. Strauss was beside himself with rage. Then he felt afraid. 'Other heads . . .'. What he had said was subversion, high treason. The penalty could be death. The family conferred: would this be the final drop that made the barrel run over?

Then the telephone rang. It was somebody Strauss had known for many years, a man who had attended every Strauss premiere when he was still a student, who had respectfully introduced himself during the 1920s when he practised law, and who had had a successful Party career since 1933. It was Dr Hans Frank, Reich Minister of Justice and Governor General of Poland for the last four years. 'I had some business in Munich. May I call on you for tea?' The chance guest was more than welcome.

Strauss made no secret of his fears. Frank telephoned Windeisen there and then, and told him he would be calling on his way back to Munich. Strauss never learned what Frank said to Windeisen, but Martin's deferment came without delay, and the question of billeting evacuees was postponed.

Windeisen never harassed the family again. At the end of the war he asked for but did not get written exoneration. Frank's fate is history; he was tried at Nuremberg and condemned to death. Gerhart Hauptmann and Hans Pfitzner were other artists whom he had helped when they were in difficulties with the Nazis. He always showed himself fair, friendly and helpful to Strauss.

The Gauleiter of Vienna, Baldur von Schirach, was the son of a theatre Intendant who had also composed. Strauss had performed a work of his in Berlin before the First World War. He was an early supporter of Hitler and ran the Hitler Youth. He appreciated and understood the arts, and as governor of Vienna during the war, with the assistance of his 'cultural deputy' Walter Thomas, did what he could to ensure that Strauss, Gerhart

Hauptmann and other artists of distinction who were regarded in Berlin as 'unreliable' were left in peace. It is not easy to see what the totalitarian régime feared from octogenarians. When Berlin ordered boycotts of their works Schirach found a way round the problem and prevented harassment of their families within the area of his responsibility. It was to him, above all, that Alice Strauss owed her own survival unscathed under the Third Reich. This humanity was probably the reason why the Nuremberg tribunal sentenced him to twenty years' imprisonment rather than to death.

> My life's work is at an end with *Capriccio*, and the music that I go on scribbling for the benefit of my heirs, exercises for my wrists (as Hermann Bahr used to say of his daily stints of dictation), has no significance whatever from the standpoint of musical history, any more than the scores of all the other symphonists and variationists. I only do it to dispel the boredom of idle hours, since one can't spend the entire day reading Wieland and playing skat. (To Willi Schuh, 8 October 1943)

Elsewhere he described these works of the war years as 'studies for singers and instrumentalists'. The more substantial examples are the Second Horn Concerto (November 1942), the Sonatina No. 1 for sixteen wind instruments: 'From the Studio of an Invalid' (February–July 1943), *An den Baum Daphne* for unaccompanied nine-part mixed choir (a setting of text by Gregor which was not used in the opera *Daphne*; November 1943), a potpourri from *Rosenkavalier* (October 1944; he commented: 'Because I have long been irritated by [Otto] Singer's terrible work with those dreadful transitions') and the Sonatina No. 2 (Symphony) for sixteen wind instruments: 'Cheerful Studio' (March–June 1945). After the end of the war he went on to write the second version of his 'Munich' waltz, *Metamorphosen*, the Oboe Concerto, symphonic fantasies on *Die Frau ohne Schatten* and *Die Josephslegende*, the Duett-Concertino and the Four Last Songs.

The Approaching End

Franz and Alice Strauss were visiting friends for a game of cards one evening, when at 10.30 the doorbell rang and eight Gestapo men with drawn revolvers pushed their way in, searched the flat, inspected the radio to see if it was tuned to a foreign station, gave no explanation for their intrusion and left after an hour. Franz and Alice went home to the Jacquingasse where they were arrested at 2 a.m., as were all the people with whom they had been playing cards. They were taken to Gestapo

> *The personal association of our leading men with Dr Strauss shall cease. However, the Führer, to whom Reichsminister Dr Goebbels referred the question, decided today that no obstacles should be put in the way of the performance of his works.*
> TEXT OF THE COMMUNIQUÉ 16/44, ISSUED BY THE NS PARTY HEADQUARTERS TO ALL REICHSLEITER AND GAULEITER, SIGNED BY MARTIN BORMANN,
> 24 JANUARY 1944.

headquarters and interrogated without being told what charges, if any, were made against them. In the morning Richard Strauss got on to Walter Thomas and Schirach, and representations were also made by the industrialist Manfred Mautner-Markhof, whom Strauss had helped to escape the clutches of the Gestapo in 1939. Franz and Alice were released after two days, without any explanation. The incident was a great shock to Strauss and Frau Pauline and affected their health both physically and psychologically.

The concert that the Vienna Philharmonic Orchestra gave to celebrate Strauss's eightieth birthday was on a grander scale than the one they had given for his seventy-fifth. Karl Böhm conducted the prelude to *Die Meistersinger*, then, as a surprise, the *Rosenkavalier* Waltz. The chairman of the orchestra board of management made a speech, then presented Strauss with an ornamental baton with which he directed the orchestra in *Till*

Eulenspiegel; he found it too heavy, however, and used a lighter stick for the *Symphonia domestica*.

During the war years Strauss went regularly to concerts and the theatre in Vienna. He no longer played as active a part in promoting contemporary music as in the past, but he went to hear it. Of Werner Egk, whose *Columbus* was given at the State Opera, he said 'He could have been a twentieth-century Meyerbeer'. He heard Orff's *Carmina Burana*, also in the State Opera, in February 1942. Although he liked the novelty of its medievalism he felt it was not really a piece for the stage at all. He corresponded with Orff on the topic of new paths whereby opera might return to the mimetic origins of theatrical art, an objective Orff explored in *Der Mond* and *Die Kluge*.

Strauss still conducted at the State Opera occasionally: *Salome* or *Idomeneo* for example. In 1930 he had made a performing edition of *Idomeneo*,

Conducting Till Eulenspiegel *with the heavy presentation baton.*

a work he loved, in the desire to see it staged more often than it was. He wrote a new ensemble finale, transitions, an orchestral interlude and all the recitatives. He made no attempt to imitate Mozartian idiom, and there can be no mistaking where Mozart ends and Strauss begins.

> I can take the accusation of stylistic vandalism with the same clear conscience as Richard Wagner when he embellished his youthful *Tannhäuser* with Tristanish sonorities – or the master-builders of the Franciscan Church [in Vienna] when they added a Gothic choir to the Romanesque nave, then later, without a second thought, incorporated the choir into a new Baroque building. If we succeed in putting this unique *opera seria* back on to the German stage, I will personally answer for my impiety to the divine Mozart if I ever actually get to Heaven.

The two masters complement each other splendidly, and the Mozartian

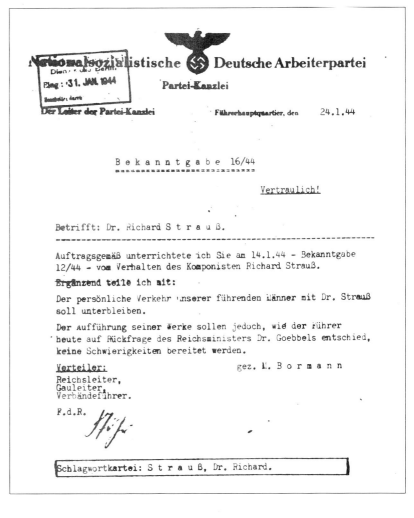

jewel shines all the more brightly for its Straussian setting. Aesthetic integrity is preserved more effectively for the absence of well-meant imitation.

> The day before yesterday I began to make a new copy of the score of *Eulenspiegel*. It is more sensible than continuing to turn out senile new works. *Don Juan* and *Tod und Verklärung* shall follow and ought to make a valuable Christmas present for you all. The work is giving me a lot of fun and at least it stops me thinking about other things, now that I don't even have an occasional game of skat to divert me and poor Mama needs a lot of comforting. (Strauss to his grandson Richard, 3 October 1944)

It was only a few weeks later that he began to write *Metamorphosen*.

Die Liebe der Danae had been printed. As artistic director of the Salzburg Festival, Krauss had long ago obtained the materials and fabrics for sets and costumes, going to Italy for what he could not find in Germany. He had a cast of outstanding singers to hand, Rudolf Hartmann to produce and the

Vienna Philharmonic to play. Travel restrictions made guest performances in distant places impossible, so all the artists were available and willing to take refuge on this island of art. Strauss let himself be persuaded to authorize a performance.

Hans Hotter was cast as Jupiter. He went to Garmisch to study the part with the composer. 'He played the opera to me on the piano. Pauline came through the room and said: "Watch out! He doesn't know anything about voices." Strauss said crossly, "Don't talk nonsense!" Pauline: "No, it's true. He expects too much. Don't let him write too many high passages into your part!"'

In 1943, a fire at the printers in Leipzig destroyed the parts and new ones had to be prepared. Some of the joinery, some columns intended for Act II and several hundred metres of cloth were destroyed in air-raids on Munich early in the summer of 1944.

There were great difficulties with transport from Munich to Salzburg. We had to try and move the finished sections of the set in furniture vans which ran on wood-gas.

The last act of Die Liebe der Danae *in rehearsal. Viorica Ursuleac (Danae), Hans Swarowsky (who was in political disgrace but allowed to act as Krauss's assistant), Franz and Richard Strauss, Hans Hotter (Jupiter).*

Jupiter's disembarkation at the end of Act 1 of Die Liebe der Danae.

The artists' work for the three sets of Act III was done in Prague and arrived here on schedule last week. The entire wardrobe department, who had to down needles in Munich because there were so many days without electricity or light, moved into temporary workshops in Salzburg last week, bringing with them all the costumes that had been started and the fabrics for the rest. I would very much like to telephone you, if only a connection was to be had for love or money. (Krauss to Strauss, 28 June 1944)

Whatever could be done in those difficult days, Krauss did. All the artists speak of a total dedication to the work. Nothing distracted them. While the world outside Salzburg went up in flames, they lived for Jupiter and Midas, Danae and Xanthe alone. But inevitably those flames began to lick round the last remaining islands of peace. On 1 August 1944 an order was published putting a stop to all festivals and closing all theatres. All males were to go into the armed forces, all females into munitions factories. There were some loopholes: radio and film work was allowed to continue. Lists of 'the blessed' were drawn up, bearing the names of artists whose lives were not to be put at risk. In Vienna there were poetry readings in the Burgtheater, in the hall of the Musikverein the Philharmonic gave concerts for the radio which were advertised only by word of mouth but were always packed out. The Gauleiter of Salzburg, Dr Scheel, took the responsibility on his own peaked cap: the work on *Danae* was allowed to proceed up to and including an unofficial premiere, a final dress rehearsal to be given behind closed doors on 16 August.

Rudolf Hartmann recalled a late rehearsal with the orchestra:

Towards the end of the second scene [of Act III] Strauss stood up and went down to the front row of the stalls. His unmistakable head stood out in lonely silhouette against the light rising from the pit. The Viennese were playing the wonderful interlude before the last scene ('Jupiter's renunciation', Strauss once called it) with an unsurpassably beautiful sound. Quite immobile, totally oblivious to all else, he stood listening to the performance of his glorious work.

And then something strange happened, which everyone present felt with the same intensity. As the last scene progressed the atmosphere became dense with a painful and melancholy seriousness. Out of the perfection of the scene, interpreted musically by Krauss with consummate mastery, out of the vocally and dramatically ideal performances of Ursuleac and Hotter, there grew and grew the undefiled purity of the highest artistic fulfilment. Profoundly moved and stirred to our depths, we sensed the almost physical presence of our divinity, art. We experienced one of those precious and very rare hours in which all trouble and effort sink into the darkness of the past, irradiated by the unique happiness of purest spiritual enjoyment.

Several moment of profound silence followed after the last notes died away. Then, clearly under the emotional impression of what we had all just experienced, Krauss spoke a few sentences outlining the significance of these last days in Salzburg. Strauss looked over the rail of the pit, raised his hands in a gesture of gratitude and spoke to the orchestra in a voice choked with tears: 'Perhaps we shall meet again in a better world.' He was unable to say any more. Silent and deeply moved, everyone present remained still as he left the auditorium, carefully guided by myself.

Slowly the eastern and the western fronts moved closer together. From the summer of 1944 onwards Strauss and his wife remained in Garmisch, while Franz and his family took care of the house in Vienna, as best they could. The hope that Austria would be spared proved illusory, and Vienna too suffered air-raids. The old couple in Garmisch were at least spared hours in the cellar, dirt and rubble in the house and delayed-action incendiary bombs.

Alice Strauss has a tale to tell of one wartime incident.

We knew that many members of my family had been taken to Theresienstadt and we thought there must be a labour camp there,

where they were collecting Jewish people before resettling them somewhere. We knew nothing of the extermination, and wouldn't have believed it. Now and then we received postcards with a few words of greeting. My old grandmother died there – we heard about that.

During the war Papa travelled from Vienna to Dresden. He stopped in Theresienstadt and wanted to visit my grandmother. He went to the camp-gate and said: 'My name is Richard Strauss, I want to see Frau Neumann.' The SS guards thought he was a lunatic and sent him packing.

We did not discover what went on in the camps until after the war. My Aunt Elli was a nurse in the typhus hut in Auschwitz. Twenty-six of my relatives died.

Anybody who had the chance went out into the countryside to barter valuables for food. This transaction required both parties to have been guilty of 'hoarding' (the Germans call it 'hamstering') but although that was illegal Franz and Alice made frequent sorties on their bicycles to get what they could. On one occasion, with a fur jacket and some bedclothes in their saddlebags, they arrived in Sindelsdorf, where there was a cooperative butcher, when it came under attack from low-flying aircraft. Strauss was beside himself when he heard about it and forbade any further excursions of the sort – but to no effect.

In Garmisch too, food and fuel were scarce, everyday articles of all kinds were unobtainable. If something broke, it could not be repaired, for want of materials and of skilled hands. It was a very cold winter and the snow fell metres thick. Strauss fell ill. Pauline spent months in bed with pneumonia (antibiotics were unknown), erysipelas and a severe eye infection. She was forbidden to read.

'It's dreadful for the poor woman. Day and night she thinks back over the good times. For me it's especially bad, having to talk about our misfortunes all the while.'

Every day the growing fear: would he and his family, like others, be bombed, driven away from their homes, killed? Every day some new ill

tidings came of friends who had lost all their possessions, died at the front or in an air-raid shelter, become refugees fleeing from unimaginable outrages. Strauss fell into ever deeper despair.

With hindsight it can be said that he was certainly lucky, when his fate is compared to that of millions of others. Yet the fact that others are worse off does not lessen one's own suffering. Strauss wrote to 'the children' in Vienna:

> Tomorrow is our golden wedding day, and we shall celebrate it with tears and sorrow after weeks of worry and troubles! Early on Tuesday our poor dear Anna left us (probably for ever!) Mama gave her a last farewell kiss in the kitchen at 5 in the morning, has cried every day since then and I generally join in and blubber too. Frau Martin went with her as far as Nuremberg where she promptly vanished into the nearest bunker with her niece. So far as we know she is now with her sister in Windsheim because there was still no bed free in the hospital in Erlangen. Neumaier gave her another jab on Sunday which gave her so much relief that on Monday she was able to hand over the entire housekeeping to Mama, keys and all, which was very moving. We have had no news since then, but Neumaier holds out scarcely any hope! The poor loyal soul, fifty-one years old, we are inconsolable. For poor Mama it is a catastrophe! (9 September 1944)

Anna Glossner died of cancer in November 1944. Anni Nitzl and her sister Resi moved into the house. Theodor Martin was now wholly indispensable to the old people.

The railway system, permanent way and rolling stock alike, suffered daily depredations from bombing. Special permits were required for travel. Passengers squeezed themselves into what space they could find in the corridors, in the toilets, or between the seats. They balanced on the buffers, on the carriage steps, on the roofs. The old and frail received hardly any consideration and Strauss would have been no exception. He and his wife wanted to go to Switzerland, to take a cure at Baden near Zurich, but Hitler personally forbade the journey.

Strauss was frantically worried by the bombing in Vienna and in mid-September ordered his family to come to Garmisch. Franz, Alice and Christian arrived in December and Franz went to work in the local hospital. Young Richard had to stay in Vienna, where he was sent to work in Manfred Mautner-Markhof's factory in Schwechat. He was staying with friends while the Serbian Government-in-Exile was billeted in the house in the Jacquingasse. Richard went over with a handcart every few days to get coal for his room from the cellar. The Schwechat factory was bombed on his second day at work and two giant fuel tanks exploded. He was unhurt but was not allowed to leave the city. His grandfather was not told of this: it would have distressed him too much.

An order for the arrest of Alice Strauss arrived at the NS district office in Garmisch, and a warning was sent by Franz Klarwein's sister. Franz and Alice turned for help to some acquaintances who had often boasted of their friendship with Himmler. They were embarrassed and evasive; the best they could suggest was that she ought to try to reach Switzerland secretly by way of the Bregenz Forest. Alice refused: 'Whether they shoot me from behind or arrest me from the front the outcome is the same. So I would rather stay with the old folk for as long as possible.' But there was a Herr

The Munich Opera after the bombing.

The sketch for the second version of the 'Munich', on a page of the Metamorphosen *sketchbook.*

Haas in the district office who made sure that the warrant for Alice Strauss stayed at the bottom of the in-tray, and in the end it was never served.

Munich experienced a total of sixty-six nights of bombing, until much of the old town lay in rubble around the ruins of the old Court Opera. In February 1945 Strauss took out the short waltz he had composed in homage to his birthplace in 1939 and began to expand it in the second of the notebooks containing the sketches for *Metamorphosen*. In his opera *Feuersnot* he had made Munich suffer the loss of fire: now it had suffered a horribly different form of 'Fire-Distress'. Following an opening section which is more densely polyphonic than in the original version of the waltz, Strauss wrote a new middle section in the minor which uses more material from *Feuersnot* and the dotted quavers from the *Eroica* funeral march which also went into *Metamorphosen*. With its cry of despair, its lamentation and its timidly hopeful conclusion it is a 'waltz-requiem', comparable in some ways to Ravel's nostalgic *La Valse*, composed during the First World War in memory of a lost civilization. Strauss had called the first version of the piece an 'occasional waltz'; this one he inscribed 'memorial waltz' and then put it away in a drawer.

He began to write the full score of *Metamorphosen*, his 'study for 23 solo strings', on 13 March 1945, the day after the destruction of the Vienna

Opera. The commission for a piece of this scale had come from Paul Sacher, founder and director of the Basle Collegium Musicum, in the previous September, through the mediation of Willi Schuh and Karl Böhm. It is a deeply moving expression of his emotions as he saw European culture in ruins: a sense of tragedy is relieved by surges of happier memories, then the music plunges back into even more profound sorrow. In the closing bars the basses play the opening of Beethoven's *Eroica* funeral march. The composer said later that the quotation flowed off the end of his pen. At the foot of the score he wrote 'In memoriam!'

He finished the score three weeks before the end of the war. He conducted the final rehearsal before its first performance himself, in Zurich on 25 January 1946. It made a deep impression on the players and all who heard it. Willi Schuh writes of the 'great developmental lines, the intensification of dynamics and tempos under his direction, even though it was also clear that his hearing was failing'. In that last respect, he was experiencing increasing difficulty with high pitches and with the interweaving of several conversations at once (what the doctors call the 'cocktail-party effect'). He told Böhm that he heard everything a semitone higher.

Some of the realities of the last months of the war seem not to have got through to Strauss: that emerges at times in the letters he sent his grandson Richard, unable to leave Vienna and confronted daily with air-raids and the difficulties of coming out alive.

I am very happy to think that you are practising the piano diligently and have resumed lessons in harmony. You will realize the benefit later when you find you can read a score as easily as Christian can read his Westerns. For before long it will be impossible to hear – let alone see – the *Ring*, *Salome*, *Daphne*, etc. I myself have a purer pleasure from *Meistersinger* and *Tristan* today, when I read the scores with all the right tempos, than from having to listen to a mediocre performance with the wrong tempos from one of my respected colleagues. Thank God, too, that you have your matriculation to crow about, so that you don't have to go out into life as a complete idiot and catch up later on things that are more difficult when you have passed twenty. There is not really any substitute for the degree of education that you achieve in your first youth.

My best wishes to your Professor Schmid. Have you got to *cantus firmus* yet? (30 October 1944)

The Vienna State Opera House, 12 March 1945.

Young Richard was yet again refused permission to leave Vienna on 1 April 1945. The Red Army was very close now, and everyone was needed to defend the home front. Richard left on his bicycle, riding at night along by-roads, expecting to be picked up at any moment by a military patrol as a deserter. He was caught once and escaped with a whole skin by pure luck. After a week he reached Garmisch.

By this time refugees had been billeted on the Strausses: there was no question of refusing now, in the face of palpable need. The Clemente family in the annexe were quiet, tried to be unobtrusive and were plainly not to blame for any trouble they caused. The father was a cabaret compère and the two children were so thin that Strauss repeatedly told his womenfolk to 'give them something to eat!' At the end of the war the conductor Kurt Overhoff moved into the main house – and so young Richard was able to continue his music lessons.

Liberation?

Germany 1945: 'Thus is the body dead, but the spirit is life.'

LUTHER

On 12 March the glorious Vienna Opera became one more victim of the bombs. But from 1 May onwards the most terrible period of human history came to an end, the twelve-year reign of bestiality, ignorance and anti-culture under the greatest criminals, during which Germany's 2000 years of cultural evolution met its doom and irreplaceable monuments of architecture and works or art were destroyed by a criminal soldiery. Accursed be technology!

STRAUSS, PRIVATE MEMORANDUM

Garmisch fell without a shot being fired. On the morning of 30 April American tanks appeared in the meadow beside the house, where a wood grows today. Young Richard saw them from his window: 'No one believes me, but I swear that there was a G.I. sitting on a tank, whistling the *Don Juan* theme!'

At about eleven o'clock some jeeps came up the drive. The army was commandeering villas for its use, and the inhabitants had fifteen minutes to vacate them. Anni and Richard went to break the news to Strauss, who had only just got up, Franz to soothe his mother, who was ill and in bed. Practical Alice started to pack food and valuables. Young Richard did not want to let his grandfather go out, but Strauss dressed, went out of the front door and said: 'I am Richard Strauss, the composer of *Rosenkavalier* and *Salome*'. A Major Kramer sat in the jeep, Dutch by descent and a music-lover. He at once ordered his men to show respect to this German. ('A complete victory of the spirit over matter', commented Strauss.) Strauss invited the soldiers into the house, showed them the scroll declaring him an honorary citizen of Morgantown, offered them wine and sent Anni to the kitchen to find something to eat. Eight officers crowded into the dining room, the men squatted on the stairs and they were all given venison stew. They left at midday and by that same evening the house was protected by the invaluable sign declaring it 'Off Limits', which forbade any further attempts to requisition it. This was for Strauss's sake, not because his daughter-in-law had been persecuted by the Nazis. (She spoke good English, Strauss only a few words: he was more at home in French and Greek.)

A few evenings later the American district commandant invited the family to dine in one of the requisitioned villas. Its owner had supported the Nazis, and now she had to work for the Americans as cook in her own kitchen. Strauss knew her and found the situation very painful.

A lot of the American soldiers wanted to make the acquaintance of the famous man, even though some of them, not surprisingly, thought he was the composer of the *Blue Danube*. They were all nice, decent young men and there was only one unhappy memory from those weeks, and that had to do with a Mr Brown.

Mr Brown made an irreproachable first impression. Young Richard admitted him and his friend, two good-looking, German-speaking journalists. Mr Brown spent several hours in the garden with Strauss, interviewing him, hearing about how he had steered Alice and the family safely through the Third Reich, taking careful notes about the help they had received from Baldur von Schirach and Hans Frank. He refused the invitation to stay for a meal and did not ask for a photograph or an autograph.

Soon afterwards the American soldiers' magazine *Stars and Stripes* published an exceptionally venomous article. 'Mr Brown' was revealed as

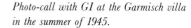

Photo-call with GI at the Garmisch villa in the summer of 1945.

John de Lancie, Alfred Mann (the Hamburg-born American musicologist, acting as interpreter), Christian, Richard, Pauline and Alice Strauss.

Klaus Mann (his companion had been the journalist Curt Riess). The article attracted a great deal of attention abroad and fuelled the legend of 'Strauss the Nazi'. Klaus Mann, the wayward son of Thomas, was full of prejudices, and made no attempt to understand Strauss's attitude and motives. He applied the standards of a person who had not been there at the time. Strauss wrote an angry letter to Thomas Mann but did not send it.

Another, bona fide, American visitor was John de Lancie, in peace-time an oboe player in the Pittsburgh Symphony Orchestra and later to be director of the Curtis Institute in Philadelphia. He wrote of the sorry circumstances in which he found the composer living: nothing to eat, no tobacco, no soap. The G.I.s did what they could to help and their assistance was much appreciated. De Lancie had many hours of conversation with Strauss, in French, about current affairs and literature and music. One

evening de Lancie's party included a photographer who made a comprehensive pictorial record of the occasion. It was while they were being
snapped together on the veranda that de Lancie asked Strauss if he had ever
thought of writing something for his own instrument. 'No', said Strauss, and
de Lancie let the subject drop. But later the composer thought over the
matter again, and the result was his lovely, tender Oboe Concerto, which he
composed that same autumn.

The dangers were over but the difficulties remained. It was as hard as
before to move around: travel was permitted only within a two-mile radius.
Within the devastated cities a few brave spirits stirred and tried to rekindle
the lamp of art. Many artists with great names were not allowed to work,
while others of the second and third rank were. Tribunals were set up to
investigate the activities of many individuals under the Third Reich.
Strauss, who had held an office, was among those charged. He gave the
appearance of taking no notice, but he was wounded by the charge.

He remained downcast, though at least he could now look forward to
the survival of his work. As after the First World War he had financial
worries. Without performances of his works his income had dried up. His
health and that of his wife were far from good. There was a shortage of
medicines, and all beds in hospitals and nursing homes were occupied by
the wounded and victims of bombing. It would be impossible to heat the
house in Garmisch during the next winter for there was no coal. (There was
not much of anything: if you were lucky enough to find a pound of butter on
the black market it cost 200 marks.) The people of Germany froze through
that winter. A revue artist joked: 'We all grew up believing that eternal fire
burns in Hell. Wrong! Hell is cold.' No one could run their central heating
systems. The chimneys of little cylindrical stoves poked through the
papered-over windows of every flat and house, and the inhabitants all
crowded into the one, stuffy, lukewarm room.

Strauss applied for permission to go to Switzerland. Christian should go
to a boarding school, Richard to a conservatory; educational facilities in
Germany were reduced to an absolute minimum. Bureaucracy, restrictions, suspicion and indifference stood in his way, but leave was finally
granted after American and Swiss friends had made certain guarantees.
Only Pauline and he were allowed out of the country, however; although
they were Austrian citizens the rest of the family had to stay.

A private tutorial in composition. Strauss loved to talk about his music with younger people, expounding and illustrating it on the piano.

Pauline listened in silence. Her health had been poor for many months.

Switzerland

Strauss had no money salted away outside Germany. Any he might now earn from performance royalties was appropriated by the Allied Property Control, the organ of an abstruse 'Washington Agreement'. His only negotiable 'currency' was in his luggage: manuscripts, some new, some of them autograph copies made during the war years, of the scores of *Ein Heldenleben*, *Symphonia domestica*, *Don Quixote*, *Also sprach Zarathustra*, the first Wind Sonatina, his suite of waltzes from *Rosenkavalier*, the 'Munich' Waltz, *An den Baum Daphne* and another *a cappella* piece *Die Göttin im Putzzimmer*, the Second Horn Concerto and the new Oboe Concerto, all found their way into the safe of the Hotel Verenahof in Baden as sureties against eventual payment of the bill.

Strauss's diary contains an account of his and Pauline's journey to Baden, near Zurich, which took a little longer than expected.

Tuesday 9 October. After having already said goodbye over the last few days to my dear little garden and the little wood, at 8.30 the last farewell to the dear children and grandsons. 3.30 safe arrival at Bregenz in very good weather. Turned back by the last French post before the Swiss frontier because we lacked last pass document. Nowhere to go. Put up by Prince Friedrich of Saxony (the rightful king) in his children's rooms, where his obliging daughters lit the stove themselves; we slept on two divans, under our green travelling rugs.

Wednesday 10 October. With the prince, who is touchingly obliging, to see Consul-General Bitz at 9. At 12 to the French commandant Comte d'Audibert, where I learnt that the scores which Alice had conveyed to the Hämmerle family in Dornbirn were unharmed and at my disposal. Overjoyed, I promised the French a manuscript for the Bibliothèque Nationale: the *Alpine* Symphony, which I inscribed there and then. The French enthusiastically carried the manuscripts from the cellar to the car themselves, we were invited to dinner at the Casino, they could not have been kinder. The scores were kept in the Bregenz command post overnight and taken to the American frontier the next morning by Martin escorted by a French orderly. Three stamp-albums, which were packed in only a leather suitcase, were – not to be found.

I gave the two Weinheber songs, which lay on top, to the amiable commandant and Major Moreau. They deserved them. Thanks to our 'passepartout' *none* of our baggage was opened and at 20 to 6 we were just looking forward to being in Baden by the evening when the equally very obliging Swiss told us that we would have to go to the Disinfection Unit in St Margareten; but that too went off very smoothly (with the aid of a dozen autographs). A good night's rest at the station hotel and at last –

11 October. 9 o'clock departure in a '*normal*' carriage, First Class, to Zurich. Pauline had an animated conversation with the Prussian Ambassador (formerly Minister) Kanitz, now resident in Lucerne. Met by Dr Schuh in Zurich at 11, 11.50 arrived in our haven, our 'Asyl', the Verenahof in Baden.

This is an earthly paradise! Exemplary, comfortable hotel with the best French cuisine (our 'menus' deserve to be perpetuated in writing), we have two beautiful, spotlessly clean south-east-facing rooms, attentively equipped to meet our every need, a big bath, as well as a large closet on the same corridor with wardrobes and chests of drawers. We are revelling in fruit again: grapes, pears, bananas, prunes. In short, for us two sad Germans, who have lived only for art, and have fled from chaos, misery, slavery and the shortage of coal, this is heaven; driven by the destruction of our poor ravaged homeland to leave our dear children and grandchildren and the beautiful things we have owned for decades, to come far away from the ruins of our burnt-out theatres and other seats of the Muses – we can pass the rest of our days in peace and quiet, in the company of good people and friends.

Two weeks later he finished the Oboe Concerto. The next question was: would the Zurich Opera, the last intact German-language house anywhere, put on any of his works – perhaps the banned *Schweigsame Frau*? Or would public opinion in even a neutral country turn against him? Without Strauss's knowledge the London publisher Boosey & Hawkes had acquired the rights to his works from Otto Fürstner in 1942 (Furtwängler's former secretary, Berta Geissmar, by then a refugee living in London, had acted as intermediary). The Austro-Czech Ernst Roth, once employed by Universal Edition in Vienna, was now the moving spirit of the English firm. He was a musician himself, had indeed just completed a concert suite drawn from *Die Frau ohne Schatten*. At the end of December 1945 he arrived in Baden and promised help to a Strauss who doubted if he was still a viable commodity. Though he did not have a Swiss franc to bless himself with, he refused £20,000 for the film rights to *Rosenkavalier* and *Salome* because Sir Alexander Korda would not guarantee that nothing would be cut or altered. As money continued not to arrive, the hotel-keeper Xaver Markwalder began to get nervous, and had the scores in his safe valued by the Swiss composer Heinrich Sutermeister, which offended Strauss.

The two old people's health was improving under the ministrations of excellent doctors. Once Pauline, the fresh-air fiend, had been persuaded not to sleep beneath an open window or go for walks without sufficient clothing on, the perpetual chills and colds became less severe, and eventually the new wonder-remedy penicillin gave them relief from various chronic ailments.

Old friends and skat-players came to see them or invited them to their homes: the loyal publisher Hürlimann, Schuh, the actress Käthe Gold, the poet John Knittel, conductors, aristocrats, pensioners, singers. Many brought them presents. Knittel gave them books and wine from his own vineyard, Schuh brought home-made pralines, others brought honey,

Lionel Barrymore in 'Key Largo'.

chocolate, cakes, marzipan and oranges. Strauss hoarded the sweets in order to send them to the children in Garmisch but communications with Germany were hindered by regulations and restrictions. A food-parcel for Garmisch, or for unfortunate friends like poor Gregor in Vienna, had to be sent by means of secret couriers using unofficial routes. Franz in Garmisch had learnt of his parents' safe arrival in Baden through Swiss Radio.

The world-famous actor Lionel Barrymore, who had been confined for years to a wheelchair in which he also played film roles, invited Strauss and Pauline to stay with him in Hollywood. He promised to overcome any difficulties with U.S. Immigration and to give his own affidavit as a guarantee. Strauss would have gone, Pauline was hesitant. Then, after a few weeks, Barrymore wrote to tell them that there had been so many hostile allegations in the American press about the role Strauss had played in the Nazi era that for the moment it would not be in Strauss's interests to come there, greatly though he himself would have wished it.

Public opinion in Switzerland too was turning against him. The protests of a Swiss soprano had nearly prevented a guest appearance by Maria Cebotari (Aminta in the Dresden *Schweigsame Frau*) when she came to sing in *Arabella*. ('Another glorious achievement of the Nazi régime, that artists are no longer judged by their abilities but by what Americans think of their political opinions', Strauss wrote in his diary on 5 January 1946.) A journalist called Maag fulminated in the Basle *Nationalzeitung* against Strauss's presence in the country. This kind of hostility had a debilitating effect, slowing his now intermittent creative activity and depressing him. He dared to express himself openly only to a few trusted friends. There was no question of the Zurich Opera undertaking a systematic programme of his works. It was a relatively small institution, and was subject to the same postwar difficulties as the rest of Europe. He had to be content with some isolated performances, few in new productions: the *Arabella* and, a year later, an *Ariadne*. His royalties were blocked by the Washington Agreement. What money his work was beginning to make again did not reach him and he was powerless to disperse the disapproval which hung over him as heavily as in the Nazi period.

Franz Lehár.

Because I am German? Wagner is another German. Lehár is Hungarian. The Hungarians also shot at the Russians and two of his operettas are being performed. The Italians fired on the Allies and they're doing three operas by Verdi. Must all the chauvinistic German-hatred of the entire Swiss nation come down on my head alone? Sure: Wagner and Verdi are dead, but Lehár is alive . . .' (To Schuh, 4 September 1946)

Strauss (like Schoenberg) had a hearty contempt for Lehár, on account of his hit-or-miss compositional technique. He owed his immense popularity to his melodic gift, but he longed for the approval of 'serious' composers, attended symphony concerts and the opera, admired Strauss and brooded over the latter's ignoring of him. 'If only he had listened to one of my operettas right through. I do make the most serious efforts.' But Strauss and other Titans could not forgive the likeable Hungarian for the fact that works like *The Tsarevich* and *Friederike* continued to make money even in times of real hardship, filling the Vienna Opera itself in the immediate aftermath of the First World War. Not until near the end of his life did Strauss remark to Alice: 'I was unjust to Lehár. I have always been too inconciliatory.'

The revolutionary of fifty years before cast a sceptical and jaundiced eye upon the dodecaphonists and the avant-garde and argued vehemently with loyal Willi Schuh, his chosen biographer, on the subject of 'post-musical atonality'. 'Melody from Bach to Wagner is the fire Prometheus stole from Olympus.' He knew western music was at an end and wanted Schuh to say so in print. He would not do so himself: 'When a man hasn't enough work to do, he becomes garrulous and doesn't reckon the consequences'; and he quoted Papageno with the padlock on his mouth (to Schuh, 22 November 1946).

His reading of Goethe turned up the following passage:

A turning-point often occurs in the life of a person. Where in his youth everything was to his advantage and everything gave him happiness, now one misfortune piles up upon another. I think he must be ruined again. Each man has a particular mission which he is called to carry out. When he has accomplished it he is no longer needed on the face of the earth in his present form and Providence turns him towards some other purpose. But since everything here on earth happens according to the natural course of things the daemons force him to go on setting down one foot after another until at last he succumbs.

He and Pauline continued to be plagued by minor illnesses, so he conscientiously noted their temperatures and blood pressures in his diary. Doctors called and sent the famous German inflated accounts. In April 1946 he underwent an operation on his appendix in Ouchy-Lausanne, which he called superfluous; he made a rapid recovery and brooded on the state of civilization.

'Two thousand years of cultural development found their apogee and their conclusion in Mozart's melody and Wagner's orchestra. Mozart's melody is the incarnation of the Platonic ideal, sought after by all the philosophers, the ideal of Eros hovering between earth and heaven.'

There would be no further evolution of opera. He himself had only contributed a few unimportant works at the end of the line. The function of the great opera houses now was custodial, to preserve the immortal works in their original form, exactly as museums preserved great paintings. At the same time the minor houses, the 'opéras comiques', could present a selection of new works as well as the classical repertory – if any were worth doing.

Mathis Piotrowski puts the finishing touches to a portrait bust.

The opera houses of smaller towns should form alliances, with three or four in each group. This would make it possible for them jointly to afford the cost of first-class soloists and orchestras as well as better standards of production and design. Common sense and coordination would thus help them to attain high quality even when money was short.

In a changing world he clung to art, and to eternal ethical values. He started to labour over an 'artistic testament', which he allowed friends he could trust to read but which he could not finish to his satisfaction. He was in a frame of mind where he would not accept contradiction, and would cite the classical maxims he had first learnt from his father, more convinced of their truth now than ever before. But his pessimism about the future of art was bottomless. He took refuge from his despair in a quiet cynicism. He had abandoned even the faint hope he had felt at the end of the war. He wrote to Schuh:

> All the historians of culture, the university professors, the Jewish press, as well as all the German patriots who look forward, following another war between America and Russia, to the resurgence of Germany as a 'world power' and the re-emergence of Barbarossa from the Kyffhäuser and of Hitler from the Reichskanzlei – there is a danger that all these will tear the author [i.e. himself] to pieces, quarter him, break him on the wheel, if he has the courage to write that political Germany had to be destroyed after it had fulfilled its mission to the world: the creation and the perfection of German music.

He was still scribbling music with 'no significance whatever for the history of music': the enchanting Duett-Concertino, for example, which is secretly another piece of programme music, for it was suggested by the fairy-tale of the Princess and the Swineherd.

Life in a hotel was irksome to Pauline. Sometimes she sent food back as uneatable, and got into arguments with the hotel staff. The hotelier Markwalder asked Ernst Roth to mediate. Pauline listened calmly to what he had to say and answered quietly: 'Where my husband has a table and manuscript paper, he is at home. But what about me, without my family, my house, my things? Nothing here belongs to me, I have nothing to do all day long. So I quarrel with people.' And so the atmosphere grew frostier. After ten months in Baden, on 26 August 1946, the Strausses moved to Vitznau.

In the autumn of 1945 Alice had made a hazardous journey across the 'green frontier' and reached Vienna to see how things were in the house in the Jacquingasse. A hundred Russians, with fifty police dogs and horses, had bivouacked there and had used the garage as a slaughter-house. Furniture had been damaged, small works of art and most of the carpets had disappeared. Since 20 June the house had been the British officers' mess. Alice approached the military authorities in the attempt to rescue what remained and recover what was missing. She was allowed to repossess the archive of documents and correspondence which had been stored in Schloss Eckartsau, and she carried it back to Garmisch in suitcases and rucksacks, crossing and recrossing the closed frontier countless times.

Visiting museums and art galleries was always a source of refreshment to Strauss's spirit.

Strauss in happier days, at his desk in his house in Vienna. The news that it had been plundered and that he would almost certainly never live there again so distressed him that he wrote out a detailed inventory, room by room, of all the beloved things pictures, furniture, objets d'art *– he had once had there, with notes of their exact positions and how he had acquired them. From his hotel room in Switzerland he yearned for his old home.*

In 1946 she managed to reach Lucerne, sleeping on railway-station benches, grazing her knuckles as she clambered over the wall of a churchyard on the way. She was reunited with her mother and sister, who had lived there in exile since 1938. And she saw her parents-in-law again too, who lived from one piece of news from home to the next. They yearned for their family, wrote letters, sent parcels of food and things to barter: sugar, coffee, tins of sardines, cigarettes, sewing needles. Later, when at last some money arrived for Strauss from London, Alice hid some dollars in a vacuum flask and smuggled them over the border, so as to have money in Garmisch for the bare necessities. By this time some theatres had managed to open again in Germany, and Strauss's works were being performed there, but the small income that came from the royalties was worthless: the Reichsmark was worthless.

Die schweigsame Frau found her voice again, and the neglected operas and the more recent, hitherto unperformed works were heard. Radio stations began to fill the gaps in their libraries of recordings. Germany did not bear Strauss a grudge. The de-Nazification tribunal in Garmisch regularly postponed hearing his case; there was a large number of testimonies which disputed the flimsy charges.

Austria was again an independent country. Manfred Mautner-Markhof invoked her past record in 'collecting' great composers and, with the thought of future plans for Salzburg and Vienna in people's minds, brought about an offer of Austrian citizenship to Strauss. On 31 January 1947 Strauss became an Austrian (he had been an honorary citizen of Vienna for twenty years). Eighteen months later, the tribunal in Garmisch cleared the new-baked foreigner of all charges. *E finita la commedia.*

After Vitznau Strauss and Pauline had stayed in Lugano, Pontresina, and eventually, from September onwards, when there was money from London and from the Swiss performing rights' organization, they spent twenty months in the Palace Hotel in Montreux. Their grandson Christian

A 1946 cutting from the New York
Herald Tribune.

RICHARD STRAUSS

Music lives on—the man forgotten

By ALVIN STEINKOPF

A T 83 Richard Strauss, the composer, who thinks that music
is all that counts, has gone to
London to earn some money. He
needs it to pay his rent.

If the world had kept a steady
course, he might have been able
to dream in some pleasant chim-
ney corner. But as it worked out,
there is no placid corner for him,
and in his ripe years life has become a succession of hotel rooms—
mostly in Switzerland.

The man who gave to the world
the music of "Rosenkavalier,"
"Don Quixote," "Salome," "Elektra," and "Don Juan" has troubles
with the landlord.

His old friend, Sir Thomas
Beecham, conductor of the Royal
Philharmonic Orchestra, has arranged a sort of Richard Strauss
season. Highlights will be concerts
of Strauss music, by the Philharmonic Orchestra for next Sunday,
and the B.B.C. Symphony Orchestra on October 29, conducted by

was sent to the boarding school run by the Benedictine monks of Ettal in
Upper Bavaria, until the family managed to get him into the Rosenberg
Internat in Switzerland. The rest of them had to be content with brief visits
to Switzerland.

Dr Roth and Sir Thomas Beecham decided to defy any political
objections and arranged a Strauss festival in London in 1947. A single
concert would have made no impact on London's busy and varied musical
scene, but a concerted programme of nine events of various kinds would
bring more than some urgently needed foreign currency: they would mark
the reinstatement of Strauss as an internationally important figure after the
years of distortion, misunderstanding and misrepresentation in the world's
press. (The most stupid thing a newspaper printed about him was the
statement that *Metamorphosen* had been composed as a requiem for Hitler.)

He flew in an aeroplane for the first time in his life ('From here the whole
world looks like a patched-up coat'), then, for four weeks in October 1947,
he enjoyed once more the excitement of a festive event arranged in his
honour. In the Savoy Hotel he courteously denied having written the *Blue
Danube* Waltz, discovered that the food upset his stomach (there was still
rationing) and took to a diet of gruel or bouillon, judicious helpings of
chicken or veal, and stewed apples with biscuits. Maria Cebotari selflessly
assumed the role of nurse.

Dr Schuh went with him to walk in St James's Park and visit the
National Gallery and the Wallace Collection. His interest was held by
paintings of mythological and historical subjects as well as portraits and
landscapes. He ranked Titian highest of all, comparing him to Wagner and
himself to Tintoretto and Correggio. He told Schuh about the idea he had
had fifty years before to write a 'Picture Symphony': he had made a lot of
sketches for it, and the slow movement would have been Veronese's *Helen of
Troy*. 'The only purpose of life is to make art possible', he said. 'Christianity
had to be invented in order, after Phidias, to make possible the Colmar

280

Altar, the Sistine Madonna, the *Missa solemnis* and *Parsifal*.' When a journalist asked him his plans for the future, he replied: 'Oh, just – die.'

After rehearsing for three hours in the morning before one of the big concerts he lay down for a short rest. Schuh wanted to put the light out, but Strauss asked him to leave it: 'I don't like being in semi-darkness, I like the light.' Then he sighed: 'These afternoons before a concert in a foreign town! Ah well, it won't last much longer.' On his way out to conduct he said: 'Well, the old horse leaves the stable again.'

An audience of 7500 gave him an ovation in the Royal Albert Hall. He had asked for the 45-minute-long *Symphonia domestica* to be placed first on the programme, so that he would get through the longest period of standing at an early stage. Broadcasting schedules made this impossible, unfortunately, and he lost his temper in one of those rages that terrified every witness: then he stood through the long evening like a man half his age. He later received no fewer than five proposals for tours in the United States.

London, 1947: with Beecham at a rehearsal.

Visiting his grandson Christian at his Swiss boarding-school.

The BBC broadcast the final scene of *Ariadne* with Cebotari and Karl Friedrich, and a complete studio performance of *Elektra* with Erna Schlüter and Elisabeth Höngen under Beecham. Strauss flew back to Pauline before the festival was over: the two old people embraced each other, sobbing with joy to be together again after four weeks' separation.

He wrote to Christian after his return to Montreux:

We flew at 2,500 metres above the clouds, just as calm as on the way there. From London to Geneva took two-and-a-half hours, on a straight line across France, nothing to worry about and comfortable seats. The flight is so calm that if you don't look down you are not aware of moving at all. There was a folding table in front of each seat, and we wrote letters, which is impossible on a jolting, swaying railway train. If those blasted bombers hadn't caused so much destruction, one could praise this speedy invention *nem. con.*.

He was approached by Father Schaller OSB with a request to write a short play with music for the boys at the monastery school at Ettal, not far from Garmisch, where Franz, Richard and Christian had all been pupils. Strauss chose the story of the Donkey's Shadow (*Des Esels Schatten*) from *Die Abderiten* by Wieland, one of his favourite authors. Joseph Gregor was asked to adapt Wieland's dialogue but wrote new verses of his own which Strauss called 'frog's droppings'; he was better served by Dr Hans Adler.

Strauss found out about the Greek modes for the project ('as I would never have passed an examination in musicology I am *homo ignotus* in this subject'); all he intended to do was heighten the text in a few places with melodrama, interpolate occasional short dashes of music, and begin and end each scene with a short verse in the style of Wilhelm Busch. He did not want to write an opera but hoped to give the boys something they would find fun to do. He lost interest, however, and abandoned it. He left enough sketches to make it possible for Karl Haussner later to finish and orchestrate them and in that form the piece was performed at Ettal in 1964.

He read even more than before in those last years: the classics, history, art history, philosophy, Confucius and Chinese civilization. He read Wagner's writings over and over again, above all *Opera and Drama*, which he thought should be on school reading-lists. Pauline immersed herself in volumes of memoirs.

Neither his English triumph nor the knowledge that his works were receiving more and more performances in the concert hall and the opera house could alleviate his moods of depression. He wrote letters to God and the world. He was told that his money could not be released until there was a peace treaty. Lawyers impeded every step. Everybody wanted to earn something before he got his share. His resignation deepened.

On one visit to Montreux in 1948 his son Franz tried to divert him: 'I said to him: "Papa, give over writing letters and brooding, it doesn't do any good. Write a few nice songs instead." He didn't answer me. The next time we were there, a few months later, he came into our room, put some scores down on the table and said to Alice: "Here are the songs your husband ordered." '

He had copied Eichendorff's poem *Im Abendrot* into his diary in 1947, beneath a newspaper cutting about the destruction of Dresden and the plundering of the city's treasures, on which he had written the caption 'The Mongols in Europe'. He had already sketched a version of *Im Abendrot* in 1947. He finished the song in May 1948, and then went on to complete the set of these Four Last Songs with three settings of poems by Hermann Hesse. The last to be finished, on 20 September 1948, was *September*. His last composition was another song, *Malven*, composed on 23 November, which lay unpublished for many years in the safe-keeping of Maria Jeritza.

Celebrating his 85th birthday: amusement.

Interest.

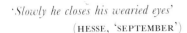

'Slowly he closes his wearied eyes'
(HESSE, 'SEPTEMBER')

Pleasure.

Attacks of bronchitis and fever – the ailments of old age – multiplied. In the Clinique Cécil in Lausanne on 15 December 1948 he underwent a major operation on his bladder, and had to have a catheter inserted. His recovery was slow and he had to dictate letters. He wrote to Schuh: 'I ask myself why they have fetched me back into an existence in which I have actually outlived myself.' (26 December 1948)

He read scores: *Tristan*, Beethoven's op. 127 quartet, Haydn's *Emperor* quartet, Mozart's Clarinet Quintet – and meditated on the asymmetry of the melodic structure in the Larghetto.

On one of Schuh's visits they were talking when he suddenly seized Schuh's hands and said, with tears in his eyes: 'Forgive me, let's not quarrel ever again. It's my eternal obstinacy.' He referred to their difference of opinion about new music. Schuh comments:

I never knew him anything other than kind, attentive, helpful, good-natured and soft-hearted. The implacability of his demands, the wilfulness which, as he was well aware, could become obstinacy, came from his father, his emotional warmth and tender-heartedness from his mother. There was deep involvement when he talked about music, above all when he talked about Mozart. A glow of transfiguration would spread across his features, originating in the brightness of his large blue and strangely moist eyes: 'The G minor quintet – that comes directly from above!'

Homecoming

In June 1948 the currency was reformed in the zones of Germany occupied by the three Western powers. Shortages, real need and barter disappeared. There was work to do and people willing to do it, to earn a wage with which to buy the things that were available again. Travel was a little easier. The economic reconstruction of 'West Germany' began, and with it a return to peacetime conditions.

Five months after his operation Strauss could no longer resist the longing to go home to Garmisch. Switzerland would renew his residence permit for only a short period at a time as if his presence was merely tolerated. The hand of occupation still lay heavily on Vienna; the house in the Jacquingasse was leased and what was left of its contents had been removed to Garmisch. After three-and-a-half years in Swiss hotels he wanted his own house and garden again.

So the old couple returned home on 10 May 1949. It was only a month to Strauss's eighty-fifth birthday. Numerous celebrations were planned, but he had to refuse the invitations. 'All my life I've been used to my body obeying me, and now I have to obey it – ?!' The fires were burning low.

But he was not allowed to rest. People from the radio and the press wanted to interview him. The population of Garmisch was delighted to see him home again. People arrived on the doorstep with their congratulations. The government of Bavaria and the town of Garmisch combined forces for a celebration on the morning of 11 June, in Garmisch town hall. The Violin Sonata and the Piano Quartet were played; newsreel cameras and radio (though not yet television) were present. What the occasion lacked in grandeur was more than made up by warmth of feeling

The state of Bavaria gave him a tanagra statuette. Garmisch made him an honorary citizen. The University of Munich made him an honorary Doctor of Law, and the deputy mayor of Munich announced the establishment of a Strauss Foundation. Strauss gave thanks, departing a little from his prepared speech. His hesitation and the occasional confusion in his words betrayed the effort the ceremony was costing him. He presented the manuscript of the original version of the 'Munich' Waltz to the Bavarian State Library. Later there was a small reception in the villa. That evening radio stations all over the world broadcast works by him: Paris, where a peace conference was due to open the next day, broadcast *Friedenstag*.

Two days later Strauss went into Munich to go to the theatre: a performance of Hofmannsthal's *Der Bürger als Edelmann* in the Gärtnerplatztheater, with Strauss's music. Ever since Ariadne had parted company with Monsieur Jourdain in 1916 he, at least in this version, had fared less well than she. But Strauss was fond of the work and well pleased to see it performed again.

In addition to these ceremonies, between May and July 1949 a short documentary film was made about Strauss, with the title *Ein Leben für die Musik (A Life for Music)*. He was filmed at home playing the piano (the last time he touched the instrument) and he went to the Prinzregententheater in Munich to conduct the conclusion of Act II of *Rosenkavalier*. The gestures

285

At home in Garmisch in 1949, in the old clothes most people in Germany wore in those days. (Below) With Sissy.

were as precise, the second beat in a 3/4 whipped out as swiftly, cues given by the same sharp glance, the refusal to sentimentalize a passage like the final bar of the waltz by rubato or overemphasis as dispassionate as ever. The last time he appeared before an orchestra was also in connection with the film, when he conducted the 'Moonlight' interlude from *Capriccio* in Munich Radio's Studio 1 to provide background music. The piece is marked 'alla breve': Strauss said 'In four, gentlemen, of course.' The first take was not satisfactory: 'Let's just do it again. I can do the piece better this time too.'

Then he went home to Garmisch again. From 13 August his bedroom became his sickroom. On 29 August he sent for Rudolf Hartmann and spoke with him urgently of the subjects nearest to his heart: the rebuilding of operatic life in Munich, repertory, productions, singers, the professional future of his grandson Richard, the conditions for the official premiere of *Danae* at Salzburg. In conclusion he said, 'Now we've made a good division of the world – our world. "Grüß mir die Welt" – what's that from?' Neither of them could recall for a moment. It is Wagner's Isolde in Act I: 'Now farewell Brangäne! Greet for me the world, greet my father and mother.'

Alice nursed him. 'I hear so much music', he said. She offered to bring him manuscript paper. 'I wrote it sixty years ago, in *Tod und Verklärung*. This is exactly like that.' Uraemia began to undermine his resistance. Angina and increasingly severe heart attacks weakened him further. He was given oxygen. The catheter inserted after his bladder operation had been hurting him for months. The last days were very painful, but then he died peacefully at 2.12 p.m. on 8 September 1949.

There had been bulletins on his condition for days in the international press. Now radio stations changed the scheduled programmes in order to pay tributes and play his music. A prince had died.

That evening Bernard Shaw, ninety-four years old, sat down at his piano and played and sang from *Ariadne*.

There were so many mourners at the funeral on 12 September that the ceremony was held in the open air outside the crematorium at the Ostfriedhof in Munich, for it was a mild early autumn morning. The orchestra of the State Opera, under its conductor Georg Solti, played the second movement of the *Eroica*. Among the speakers Egon Hilbert, director of the Vienna Opera, found the most beautiful words: 'Richard Strauss has entered eternity, and his music immortality.' A late butterfly fluttered over the flowers and the wreaths, settled on the pall for a while then flew up into the blue sky. At the end the concluding trio from *Der Rosenkavalier* was sung. The entire congregation was in tears. Pauline slipped from her chair sobbing, and her cry rang out in the silence: 'Richard! Richard!'

Alice said: 'I never realized that a person could weep so much. Her life was really over.' In October Pauline returned to the Palace Hotel in Montreux, as her husband, just before the end, had wished she would. Resi Nitzl went with her and she was never left alone; there was always a maid, a companion, a friend with her. She wept. She read. She scarcely ever went out; her passion for fresh air was gone. In March 1950 Alice fetched her home again.

Pictures taken during the filming of 'A Life for Music': Gerda Sommerschuh, who sang Sophie in the excerpt from Rosenkavalier, *presented a bouquet. The left hand rested on his knee, and he signalled new entries with his eyes. Afterwards, he was gently helped into a car by Antonio Mingotti, a music critic, and Kurt Pfister, who published a biography of Strauss.*

The musical director of the Munich Opera, Georg Solti, was in attendance during the recording of the Rosenkavalier *excerpt.*

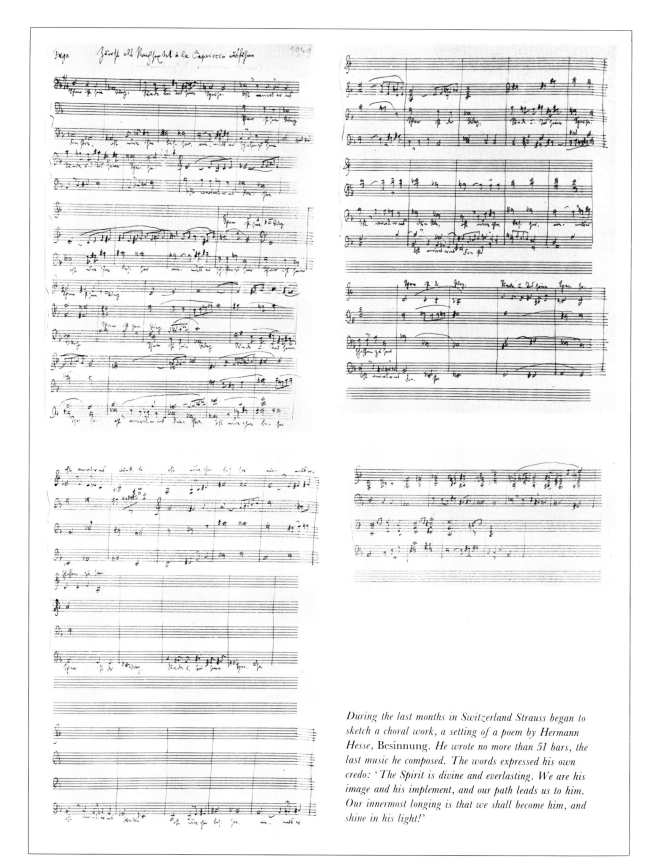

During the last months in Switzerland Strauss began to sketch a choral work, a setting of a poem by Hermann Hesse, Besinnung. *He wrote no more than 51 bars, the last music he composed. The words expressed his own credo: 'The Spirit is divine and everlasting. We are his image and his implement, and our path leads us to him. Our innermost longing is that we shall become him, and shine in his light!'*

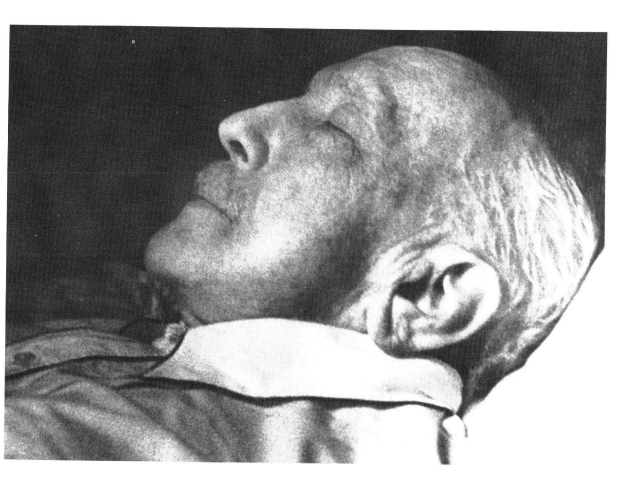

Taken after his death, 8 September 1949.

Her sight failed. 'Why have you put the light out?' Out in the garden she walked into the hedges, she could not get used to feeling her way with a stick, she would go to sit down and miss the chair. All her life she had refused to sit on the chairs in other people's houses if they did not meet her idea of cleanliness, but now she crouched on the stairs and on the floor. One night they found her in the room where her husband had died, weeping, half unconscious and very cold. Towards the end she spoke only French. After 247 days, on 13 May 1950, she followed her Richard.

Postlude

In the mid-1960s I did some research among young musicians, to find out what the music of Richard Strauss meant to them. In most cases the answer was a rather hesitant 'Nothing. Out-of-date. It's nice, but – no significance and no future.'

The general public thought differently. When I was young his music (even *Rosenkavalier*) was still regarded in many quarters as harmonically abstruse and ultra-modern, but audiences all over the world gradually discovered it and found that they liked it. Even the less well-known works were performed in foreign countries, led by Britain and America. Strauss's brand of *avant-gardisme* came to be accepted, like Mahler's and Stravinsky's. It was not necessary to wait for centenary celebrations in 1964.

The gramophone has certainly played a part in making Strauss's music familiar: virtually all the orchestral works, songs and stage works have been recorded. The choral works have not aroused the same interest, although there are some exquisite pieces among them. Nobody would have foreseen that, of all the symphonic poems, *Zarathustra* would be the one most often recorded, or that the *Alpine* Symphony, so much derided when it was new, would now be available in so many versions. Though there may be a question mark over the extent to which records are really listened to or studied, the sales figures are nonetheless impressive.

There were always those who said Strauss was a fad and would not last. He himself said that he was a person of no significance, who had merely made a few unimportant contributions to the last, post-Wagnerian phase of western music. He – and they – were wrong. Four decades or so after his death – a whole human generation – his work still lives and shines with an undiminished, even an enhanced, brightness.

A large number of books have been published about him. In as much as they refer to his life, most of them make it clear that every description of a historical personality is necessarily incomplete because it is not really possible to present the views, the values, the external circumstances and the fashions of a past epoch – to demonstrate what it felt like to be alive at that time – to a later generation. Every account contains obstinate, seemingly ineradicable misinterpretations, while factors that were essential and decisive at the time are forgotten (I need think only of the period since 1930, which I myself have consciously lived through).

For thirty years I never contemplated writing a book about the joy the music and the personality of Richard Strauss have given me. It was only when the idea of a substantial illustrated volume was mooted that it struck me that it held out the possibility of a form that might fit the bill. Facts, quotations and contemporary accounts, it seemed to me, could give thinking readers something to get their teeth into. Thus this book is constructed from reliable, well-authenticated material of that kind, with as little personal evaluation as possible. The selection and explanation of the material, as well as the unavoidable condensation, already introduce quite enough personal colouring.

I make no attempt to disguise my admiration for Strauss, even at a time when it is fashionable to be 'critical' and draw attention to the clay feet of great men. I get no joy from that kind of literature. I do not want to be lectured or lulled but I do want to find out about the possible motives for a person's actions and about the circumstances in which he performed them. Evaluating the past by today's standards is easy, and leaves the evaluator secure in his prejudices. I cannot understand authors who spend an entire

The bereaved Pauline and Franz.

(Above) The funeral ceremony at the Ostfriedhof in Munich, 12 September 1949. Frau Pauline pulled her chair into the shadow and sat alone.

(Below) In the front row of the mourners, from left to right: the Minister-President of Bavaria Hans Ehard and his wife, young Richard, Alice, Franz, Johanna von Rauchenberger, Christian, and the deputy mayor of Munich, Walter von Miller.

book doing a person down, in order to let readers bask in the sense of their own superiority.

Of course Strauss made mistakes in the course of his long life: he would have done better not to take either of the two appointments in Munich, he should not have wasted his energy and his time trying to run the Vienna Opera, leading to a creative stagnation that he was unable to overcome until the last decade of his life. Much as he loved Hellenic subject-matter it was no guarantee of real inspiration in the material he was given to work with. It was another mistake to accept Gregor instead of persisting in the search for a real dramatist.

The worst mistake of all, one may say with the benefit of hindsight, was the contempt for all political matters which led him, quite unsuspectingly, to allow the Nazis to use him as a figurehead. His eminence, they calculated, helped to make them look respectable in the eyes of the world. Quite apart from the vanity of hoping that anything could make such a crew look respectable, a far greater share of blame should be laid at the door of international diplomacy which in so many ways – treaties, exchanges of compliments, the unboycotted Olympic Games of 1936, congratulatory addresses to Hitler – flattered that murderous régime. The diplomats must have known what was brewing, but musicians, whose craft has a prior charge on their time and their energy, need not have done.

When I was a self-confident twenty-year-old I wrote an essay setting down my poetic interpretations of the symphonic poems of Strauss. I was in a Nazi prison at the time, for political reasons. In some wondrous way my little essay played a part in getting me released. In my newly-gained and still less than generous freedom I sent it to Strauss. The only thing giving me the courage to do so was the fact that in his youth the Grand Old Man of Garmisch had been acquainted with my family. I mentioned as much, but I did not dare hope for any reply.

One day in January 1945, however, as I lay low in a village, hoping to avoid being arrested again, the postman pushed his bike through the snow up to my retreat, bearing my self-addressed envelope with the sender's name on the back, in his own hand-writing: Dr Richard Strauss, Garmisch, Zoeppritzstr. 42. It contained my manuscript with his comments in the margin, and there was a personal letter too. Perhaps some people of my generation will understand what it meant to me, caught between flight, hunger and cold, and air-raids, as the world all around me disintegrated, to receive a letter from Mount Olympus.

In the autumn of 1945, three days before he left for Switzerland, I was able to visit Jupiter tonans in Garmisch. For years I had got as close a view of him as possible at concerts and at the opera in Vienna, so I already knew the sound of his voice and the penetrating gaze of his pale eyes. But during our conversation in his study these features riveted me. I had the opportunity to meet Hans Pfitzner on the same day and discovered that he came nowhere near exercising the same fascination.

I took note of Strauss's clear, precise reactions and turns of phrase – a budding author must train himself to be observant – and tried to grasp something of his essential nature. He was mistrustful of my questions, for it was not long since Klaus Mann had introduced himself under a false name and then published the article with such bad consequences for Strauss.

I paid another visit to Garmisch three days before his eighty-fifth birthday, three months before his death. His long illness had marked him, and he complained fretfully about his loss of physical strength. The light of his personality burned less brightly than before. Only when he came to talk about the first performance of *Ariadne* in 1912 did he briefly grow more animated. When my brother mentioned that he was studying music and also composed, his eyes flashed and he asked in that characteristically courteous, Bavarian tone that is like the up-stroke of a pen, 'Atonally?' No, said my brother, and he gave a satisfied nod.

After his death the family did their best to carry on doing the things he had done throughout his life: maintaining contacts with performers, impresarios and managements in order to prevent his works falling victim to the neglect the 'business of music' can so easily entail. In fact there was little real danger of that happening, for unlike some composers, he did not appeal solely to his own contemporaries, a dwindling band of elderly folk: young people discovered a need for his music, too.

Franz and Alice went on living in the house on Zoeppritzstrasse in Papa's style. Large numbers of guests, the famous and the enthusiasts, regularly sat down to lunch around the large dining table, where they were served with the dishes that Anni and Resi Nitzl prepared according to the long-established custom of the house. The house was placed under a conservation order and has been preserved, with its contents, as it was at the time of Strauss's death.

Tirelessly Franz and Alice dispensed information and made archival material available to institutions and other interested parties, for use in exhibitions and exhibition catalogues, programme notes, and other publications. Strauss's letters were sought out all over the world, copied and recorded in the archive.

In 1951 I began work cataloguing the contents of the letters and other writings. The task – no, the pleasure – held me in thrall for several years. In doing it, and in spending so many of my weekends in Garmisch, I felt I was getting to know Strauss better all the time. Through his family he was still a living presence in the house, and from their conversation and from the tales they told I learned much about that presence.

One thing in particular stands out in the letters, the memoranda and the spoken comments, and that is the sureness of his judgments in the field of art. There is no great figure that he failed to recognize, no development that he evaluated wrongly; reasonably and without prejudice, he saw to the heart of every passing fashion by the light of his sound common sense and his sense of proportion. Except in the cases of Mozart, Wagner and Beethoven he rarely went into the kind of raptures that cloud clear vision. In such matters his yea was yea and his nay nay, and nothing he ever said over and above that was malicious in origin.

I received a vivid impression of Strauss's childhood from his sister Johanna. Though her memories, at a distance of some seventy or more years, had grown stereotyped and anecdotal, her narration was always full

Franz Strauss with Tini and Konstantin, two of Christian's children.

In 1980 Anni Nitzl celebrated forty years with the family.

Johanna Rauchenberger-Strauss lived to be 99. This portrait by Annelies Trenner-Ehrlich was painted in 1965.

The younger Richard Strauss, 1982.

Gabriele Strauss-Hotter.

of life and interest. Her husband Otto Rauchenberger, a career officer in the King's Own Bavarian Infantry, had little interest in the arts, which created a degree of estrangement between Johanna and her brother, and it had been made worse when she and Pauline found they did not get on well together. They scored small points off each other: 'My son is already playing *The Merry Peasant* on the piano. How far has yours got? What? Still at five-finger exercises?' In the end the families met only rarely.

In 1944 Johanna, by then a widow, was bombed out of her home in Munich. Her son was at the front. She travelled to Garmisch which she reached at night, knocked at the door, was taken in, as a matter of course, and stayed for several months: another burden for the old people, bowed down as they were with infirmity, want and anxiety. After the war Johanna moved back to Munich where she settled down in her own room in a religious foundation in a mansion in Schwabing, surrounding herself with an atmosphere of comfort and good style. She died on 23 March 1966 in her ninety-ninth year. In spite of the estrangement she remained touchingly and sincerely devoted to her famous brother throughout her life. They wrote to each other from time to time, she wrote poems addressed to him and after his death she gave a warm welcome to every visitor who wanted to talk about him; she was generous with mementoes, letters and other little things. She remained alert into her biblical old age and her stories sparkled with humour and irony – the family tone.

Franz Strauss died on 14 February 1980. His parents' ashes had been kept in urns in the house, but they now lie with their son in the cemetery in Garmisch.

The younger Richard trained under Rudolf Hartmann to be an opera producer and directed productions of his grandfather's works in several theatres in the 1950s. The newspapers loved it: 'Richard Strauss produces Richard Strauss!' But he was criticized for lacking the genius of the works' progenitor, for taking an old-fashioned view of what constituted fidelity to the work, even for cashing in on the family business; he came to the conclusion that this kind of sniping would never cease and decided to branch out in a completely different direction. He made what had been his hobby his profession and became the managing director of a long-established Munich philatelic company.

His first wife was Annamarie Krug from the North Sea island of Norderney, but they were divorced amicably. In 1962 he married Gabriele, the daughter of Hans Hotter, the first 'Commandant', 'Olivier' and 'Jupiter'.

His brother Christian studied medicine and became head of the gynaecological department in the Garmisch hospital. He built himself a house two doors from the family house.

During the writing of this book it became clear to me that there are certain things that must be kept in mind if Richard Strauss is to be understood.

Where Beethoven and Wagner revolutionized music, Strauss enriched and refined it.

He did not take his yardsticks from what we call 'real' life, though he mastered that too, but from the laws of music, painting, literature and architecture. With their guidance, and by leading an orderly life with few distractions, he gained the strength for the logical concentration which is a hallmark of his works. His ethical and moral principles were not drawn from the workaday world.

He lived from the age of oil-lamps to the Atomic Age. The world was transformed with breathtaking speed during that span. As he entered his sixties after the First World War he stood back from the great social changes that took place and preferred to abide by the style and the standards of the prewar era. He was brought up in modest circumstances and was no spoilt prodigy. He owed his prosperity and world fame to hard work, talent and good luck: they bought him respect and envy; those who observe the axiom that rich equals bad and poor equals good found it easier to forgive Wagner his debts than Strauss his royalties.

He lost his savings twice. He was never really wealthy by comparison with princes of commerce, the aristocracy or industrialists. He never ceased to worry about whether he would be able to maintain his standard of living. But if that worry led him to make compromises his creative work was never touched by them. Everything he wrote served to develop his style and his ideas a step further.

His urge to create was compulsive and ultimately all his thought and all his actions were directed to that end. Setbacks depressed him but never succeeded in diminishing that inner drive. Even when he had crowned his life's work with *Capriccio*, he could not stop working.

Richard's daughters, Marie-Theres and Madeleine.

He translated impressions and emotions into logical musical fantasies, with subtlety and passion. He was an Impressionist who used the techniques of Expressionism.

He surpassed his contemporaries in harmonic versatility and poetic richness. His style dominated an epoch and many attempted to imitate it. His harmonic style deserves a book to itself.

Thanks to his stupendous command of all musical techniques and his powers of concentration his works possess a great density which is both intuitive and worked out. There are few pages indeed where he was content to let the music flow according to a familiar stereotype. He rarely used conventional musical forms and created new large forms instead in every work, according to the dictates of the central idea.

Christian Strauss, his wife Brigitte and son Alexander.

The thing he most admired about Mozart was the melodic inspiration. It was not given to him, nor to many composers, so generously as that. He had to apply himself with care and diligence to the development and shaping of his melodic ideas and the characterization of his thematic material but he had no equal in the craft of getting everything he needed from his initial ideas.

Many gifted composers have failed in the opera house because they used theatrically impossible librettos. He had a nose for fascinating subjects and the luck to find Hofmannsthal.

He was hypersensitive. He knew how to control his explosive temperament, while his inner restlessness demanded continual stimulation, the prime source of which was his wife Pauline. Frau Alice told me a tale which I

Alice Strauss.

Franz Strauss.

find characteristic: Papa had come to Vienna without Frau Pauline to spend a week with her and Franz. She spared no effort to make things agreeable for him, but after three days he heaved a big sigh: 'You are both kind and take such trouble, but – it is so boring! I must go home to Mama!'

His high spirits and his unvarnished speech are reflected in his letters in spontaneous, often mocking comments about disappointments, about people who failed to learn from experience, about narrowness of vision. He always took a large view. When he was the victim of intrigue or criticism he would often say: 'None of that is important. What happens over the large span is what matters.' He remarked unfavourably on the unimportant matters that got blown up into topics of the day, the idle boasts and empty postures – and on idealism when assumed as a cloak for egotism and ruthlessness.

His contempt for politics extended to politicking in the theatre and in the art world as a whole, and to all forms of ideological window-dressing. He had witnessed the cynical misuse of honourable motives and emotions like courage, patriotism, self-sacrifice and decency during the First World War, and the scorn which that experience taught him for the transience of 'burning issues' continued to grow for the rest of his life. Rationally and without prejudice, he lived according to a sense of order which kept his mental energy free for real work. He was a monomaniac and a pragmatist.

He took an active or judicious interest in the life of his friends and in everything that happened in his world, the world of music, right up to a great old age. He was ambitious, and resistance only stimulated him. Resignation or withdrawal was a very rare event, normally prevented by his indefatigable energy.

His family was the centre of his life. If they were well, then he was pleased and drew renewed strength from it.

I hope that through this mosaic of pictures, quotations and anecdotes this book has succeeded in its objective and has given the reader the feeling that he or she has come to know –

Richard Strauss.

Chronology

1864	Born 11 June at Altheimer Eck 2, Munich, son of the court musician Franz Strauss and his wife Josepha.
1867	Sister Johanna born.
1868	Begins to play piano.
1870	First compositions.
1871	Hears his first opers (*Freischütz*).
1871–2	Violin lessons from Benno Walter; family music-making.
1874	Attends Ludwig Grammar School.
1875	Composition lessons with Hofkapellmeister Meyer; piano lessons with Niest.
1876	Writes the Festmarsch, op. 1, the first work to be published.
1877	Begins correspondence with Ludwig Thuille.
1879	Plays chamber music regularly with schoolfriends. Public performance at Ludwig Grammar School of Beethoven's Trio op. 11.
1880–81	Festive Chorus and chorus from *Elektra* performed at the school; songs by Strauss sung in public by Cornelia Meysenheym of the Court Opera.
1881	First publications (opp. 1, 2, and 3).
1882	Leaves School. Attends Bayreuth Festival. Study at Munich University. Bülow hears the premiere of the Wind Senenade under Wüllner in Dresden. Strauss performs in Vienna with Benno Walter (arrangement of Violen Concerto op. 8 for violin and piano). Plays with the Wilde Gung'l (his father's orchestra).
1883	Visits Dresden and Berlin. Bülow performs the Serenade for wind in Meiningen (later in several German cities).
1884	Extended stay in Berlin (Leipziger Strasse 96). Artistic acquaintances include Menzel, Begas, Werner etc); Bülow inspires him to study Brahms. Conducting début in Munich with Suite for wind, op. 4.
1885–6	Appointments at court of Meiningen, first as Bülow's assistant then as chief conductor. Wins prize with Piano Quartet op. 13. Friendship with Ritter stimulates appreciation of Wagner, Liszt and Schopenhauer. Meets Brahms.
1886	Accepts post of assistant conductor at Court Theatre in Munich. Vacation tour takes him to Rome, Naples, Sorrento, Pompeii, Florence, Lake Como, Lake Lucerne, and the Bayreuth Festival (*Tristan* and *Parsifal*). Takes up conducting appointment at Munich alongside Levi and Fischer.
1887	Successful premieres of *Aus Italien* in Munich and *Wanderers Sturmlied* in Cologne. Meets Pauline de Ahna for first time in Feldafing. Concert tours to Leipzig and Milan.
1888	Concerts in Frankfurt, Mannheim and Bremen (visits Bülow in Hamburg). Visits Italy (Lake Garda, Verona and Bologna), Kempten and Neuschwanstein.
1889	Musical assistant at Bayreuth: rehearses *Parsifal*. Kapellmeister to the Grand Duke at Weimar, where he gives first performance of *Don Juan* and arranges Gluck's *Iphigénie en Tauride*.
1890	Guest conductor of Berlin Philharmonic. Congress of the Allgemeiner Deutscher Musikverein in Eisenach where Strauss gives first performances of *Burleske* (with Eugen d'Albert as soloist) and *Tod und Verklärung*. Conducts premiere of his *Macbeth* and accompanies Zeller in that of *Ständchen*.
1891	Pneumonia. Attends Bayreuth Festival.
1892	After conducting *Macbeth* in Berlin and *Tod und Verklärung* in Leipzig ill again. Convalesces in Greece.
1893	Egypt, Sicily and Corfu. Stays at General de Ahna's villa at Marquartstein. Conducts premiere of Humperdinck's *Hänsel und Gretel* in Weimar.
1894	Sees Bülow for last time in Hamburg and Berlin. Premiere of *Guntram* in Weimar. Conducting début at Bayreuth (*Tannhäuser*). Marries Pauline de Ahna. Kapellmeister in Munich, where he lives at Hildergardstr. 2 (later Herzog-Rudolf-Str. 2), but also conducts Berlin Philharmonic for season.
1895	*Guntram* under Strauss's direction in Munich. Conducts in Budapest, Berlin (Wagner Society), Leipzig (Liszt Society) and Munich (Musical Academy concerts).
1896	Holiday in Marquartstein. Takes Levi's place as General Musical Director in Munich. Concert tours to Moscow, Düsseldorf (Rhine Music Festival), Brussels, Liège, Leipzig (premiere of orchestral version of Violin Concerto), Frankfurt (premiere of *Also sprach Zarathustra*).

1897	Concert tours to Barcelona, Amsterdam, Brussels, London and Paris (*Tod und Verklärung* and *Till Eulenspiegel*). Son Franz born (12 Apr.).
1898	Concerts in Zurich and Madrid. Appointed first Kappelmeister at Court Opera in Berlin (10-year contract); lives at Knesebeckstr. 30. First assignment as colleague of Muck and Blech is *Tristan*. Foundation of the Genossenschaft Deutscher Tonsetzer (Strauss, Rösch and Sommer).
1899	Premiere of *Heldenleben* in Frankfurt. *Zarathustra* in Paris (Lamoureux Concert). Conducts *Ring* and *Die Fledermaus*, among others, in Berlin. Makes acquaintance of Hofmannsthal in Berlin.
1901	President of the Allgemeiner Deutscher Musikverein on the occasion of the Tonkünstler Festival in Heidelberg. Conducts Berlin Tonkünstler Orchestra; concert tours to Poznán, Hanover and Halle. Conducts *Guntram* in Prague.
1902	Concert tours to South Germany, Austria, Italy and Switzerland.
1903	Strauss week in London; premiere of *Hymnus* under Strauss. After mild illness, recuperates on Isle of Wight. Receives honorary doctorate from Heidelberg University (premiere of *Taillefer*). Moves to Joachimsthaler Str. 17, Berlin.
1904	Visits America; premiere of *Symphonia domestica* in New York. Total of 35 concerts and Lieder recitals (with Pauline Strauss). German premiere of *Symphonia domestica* in Frankfurt under Strauss (40th anniversary meeting of the Allgemeiner Deutscher Musikverein). Second Bavarian Music Festival in Regensburg. Honorary membership of the Vereinigung Schaffender Tonkünstler in Vienna.
1905	While Struass is attending a festival in Graz, his father dies. Travels to Marquartstein, then London where he conducts the *Domestica*. Receives Order of Austrian Crown, third class. Premiere of *Salome*. New edition of Berlioz's instrumentation treatise.
1906	*Salome* triumphs in Milan, Turin, Brussels, Amsterdam, Berlin. Big success with *Domestica* in Paris. Conducts Vienna Philharmonic in Salzburg for first time.
1907	Conducts six performances of *Salome* in Paris. Officer of the Legion of Honour. Extensive touring. Cure at Bad Nauheim.
1908	Concert tours to Rome and Paris. European tour with Berlin Philharmonic (to France, Spain, Portugal, Italy, South Germany). On Weingartner's departure, Strauss assumes responsibility for Berlin Philharmonic concerts; in autumn, accepts ten-year contract as General Music Director of Court Opera there. Strauss week in Wiesbaden. House in Garmisch (Zoeppritzstr. 42), built by Seidl, ready for occupation in September. One-year sabbatical from Berlin Opera.
1909	Premiere of *Elektra* under Schuch at Strauss week in Dresden. Work acclaimed in New York, Munich, Berlin, Vienna, Milan and Düsseldorf. Member of Berlin Academy of Arts. Resigns presidency of Allgemeiner Deutscher Musikverein (retains honorary positions).
1910	*Elektra* in London, Budapest, Prague, Brussels, The Hague (under Strauss); also Vienna (Strauss's début at the Vienna Opera). Strauss cycle in Frankfurt: *Guntram, Salome, Feuersnot, Elektra*. Death of mother. Strauss week in Munich. Relinquishes responsibility for Berlin Opera but concludes guest agreement (continues to conduct operas and concerts there until 1918). Knight of the Order of Maximilian. Moves to Hohenzollernstr. 7 in Berlin. Holiday in St. Moritz.
1911	Premiere of *Rosenkavalier* in Dresden (Reinhardt and Schuch), then in Nuremberg, Munich, Basel, Hamburg, Bremen, Frankfurt, Milan, Zurich, Prague, Leipzig, Vienna (Schalk, Wymetal), Budapest, Krefeld (Strauss festival), Düsseldorf, Berlin, Rome and at Strauss festival in The Hague under the composer. Conducts *Figaro* and *Tristan* at Munich festival. First Strauss biography (Steinitzer).
1912	Premiere of *Ariadne* (original version).
1913	Italian trip with Hofmannsthal (concert in Rome). Festival Prelude composed for the opening of the Vienna Konzerthaus.
1914	Premiere of *Josephslegende* in Paris. 50th birthday honours: plaque on house of birth. Honorary doctorate from Oxford.
1915	Memorial concert for Schuch in Dresden. Premiere of *Alpine* Symphony in Berlin (Dresden Court Orchestra).
1916	Premiere of *Ariadne* (revised version) in Vienna under Schalk. Honorary membership of the Gesellschaft der Musikfreunde in Vienna.
1917	With Reinhardt and Hofmannsthal lays foundations of Salzburg Festival. In Dresden, 100th performance of *Rosenkavalier* under Strauss.
1918	First Strauss week in Vienna. Honorary member of the Vienna Male Choral Society. Leaves post at Berlin Court Opera, but returns as Intendant of State

Opera for interregnum period of one year. *Salome* at the Vienna State Opera (Schalk). Opposition to Strauss.

1919   During 50th anniversary celebrations of Vienna Opera House, Strauss conducts *Magic Flute*, *Fidelio* and *Tristan*. Becomes joint director of Vienna Opera (with Schalk) and moves to house at Mozartplatz 4 there. Premiere of *Die Frau ohne Schatten* under Schalk.

1920   Conducts first performance of orchestral suite *Bürger als Edelmann*. With Schalk undertakes first trip to South America (*Salome*, *Elektra* etc.).

1921   German premiere of *Josephslegende* in Berlin under Strauss. Concert tour of USA. First recording for radio.

1922   New production of Wagner's *Fliegender Holländer* in Vienna. Mozart at Salzburg Festival, of whose Patrons Struass is made honorary member. In autumn to North America (New York PO and Philadelphia Orchestra).

1923   New production of *Tannhäuser*. Dance suite after Couperin (Redoutensaal, Vienna). Honorary member of the Vienna Philharmonic and Academy of Fine Arts. Second trip to South America (Vienna State Opera: *Salome*, *Elektra*, *Bürger als Edelmann*).

1924   Marriage of son Franz in Vienna. Italian trip. Vienna Strauss festival to celebrate his 60th birthday: premiere of *Schlagobers*. Honorary member of the Vienna Schubertbund. Strauss weeks in Berlin, Munich, Dresden and Breslau (first *Schlagobers* in Germany). Honorary doctorate from the Vienna Musikhochschule; freedom of the cities of Vienna and Salzburg. Honorary president of Salzburg Festival. With *Die Geschöpfe des Prometheus* (premiere) and *Bürger als Edelmann* in Redoutensaal, Strauss relinquishes directorship of Vienna Opera.

1925   Moves into house in Jacquingasse adjoining the Belvedere, newly built by Michael Rosenauer. Trip to Spain. Strauss week in Hamburg. Conducts *Così fan tutte* and *Tristan* at Munich festival. Trip to Italy.

1926   *Rosenkavalier* film. Premiere of *Intermezzo* in Dresden; Strauss week in Leipzig. Trip to Greece. Cure in Karlsbad. Salzburg Festival. Winter in Vienna.

1927   Grandson Richard born. Strauss weeks in Dresden and Frankfurt. Conducts Ninth Symphony in Dresden at celebrations marking centenary of Beethoven's death.

1928   Strauss week in Vienna: premiere of *Ägyptische Helena*. *Tageszeiten* (Vienna Schubertbund) and *Panathenäenzug*. Dresden Opera festival with *Rosenkavalier* under Strauss.

1929   Illness. Munich Festival: one concert, *Così* and *Tristan*.

1930   Premiere of *Österreichisches Lied* (Austria) in Vienna. Autumn in Paris.

1931   Conducts premiere of *Idomeneo* adaptation at Vienna State Opera. Trip to Switzerland. Munich Festival.

1932   Grandson Christian born. Strauss week in Munich. Conducts *Zarathustra*, *Fidelio* and two concerts at Salzburg Festival.

1933   50th anniversary of Wagner's death celebrated in Dresden with *Tristan* under Strauss. Conducts *Parsifal* at Bayreuth. President of Reich Music Chamber (until 1935).

1934   70th birthday celebrations in Dresden (*Rosenkavalier*); also Freeman of the City and honorary member of the Opera. Strauss weeks in Berlin, Vienna, Munich and Dresden. President of the Council permanent pour la coopération internationale des compositeurs.

1935   Dukas memorial concert in Vichy. Premiere of *Die schweigsame Frau* in Dresden (Böhm). Strauss week in Munich. Resigns presidency of Reich Music Chamber.

1936   *Die schweigsame Frau* in Graz, Milan and Zurich. Extended tours: Italy (*Arabella* in Genoa), France, Belgium. Munich festival. Cure in Baden, near Zurich. In London conducts guest performance of *Ariadne* by Dresden Opera and a concert of the Royal Philharmonic Society, who award him their gold medal.

1937   Trip to Sicily. Honorary member of Vienna Konzerthaus Society. Strauss week in Frankfurt. Munich festival (*Holländer* and a concert). Ends year in Taormina.

1938   Premieres of *Friedenstag* and *Daphne*.

1939   75th birthday. Strauss weeks in Vienna (Austrian premiere of *Friedenstag* and world premiere of choral work *Durch Einsamkeiten*), Berlin and Munich. Awarded gold ring by Garmisch-Partenkirchen. Celebrates golden wedding. Cure in Baden.

1940   Premiere of *Japanische Festmusik* in Tokyo.

1941   Premiere of *Verklungene Feste* in Munich.

1942	Beethoven Prize of the city of Vienna. Salzburg Festival (Mozart). Premiere of *Capriccio* in Munich. Wintertime in Vienna. Performance of *Daphne* marks final appearance as conductor at the National Theatre, Munich.
1943	Mild illness, early in year in Vienna. Returns to Garmisch. Premiere of Horn Concerto No. 2 in Salzburg (Böhm).
1944	Festival celebrations and Strauss week in Vienna to mark 80th birthday. *Liebe der Danae* in Salzburg. Tape recordings of orchestral works (nearly complete) under his direction.
1945	American forces take Garmisch. Strauss and Pauline travel to Baden, near Zurich. First German performance of a Strauss work after war is *Ariadne* in the Tonhalle, Dresden.
1946	Premieres of *Metamorphosen* (Sacher) and Oboe Concerto (Andreae) in Zurich; Sonatina No. 2 for 16 wind instruments in Winterthur (Scherchen). Journeys from Baden to Pontresina and Ouchy. April: appendix removed.
1947	Pontresina and Montreux. Concert tour of London: two concerts of the Royal Philharmonic and BBC Symphony Orchestras.
1948	Stay in Montreux: Four Last Songs.
1949	Having recovered from a major operation on his bladder, Strauss returns to Garmisch. 85th birthday celebrations: Strauss Foundation established in Munich, Freedom of Bayreuth, honorary doctorate from Munich University. Conducts for last time in Munich; last theatre visit (*Bürger als Edelmann*). After six weeks of illness, dies on 8 September in Garmisch.

Chronological list of works

Operas and ballets

YEAR	OPUS	
1889–90		Iphigénie en Tauride (Gluck, arrangement)
1892–3	25	Guntram (rev. version 1940)
1900–1	50	Feuersnot
1903–5	54	Salome
1906–8	58	Elektra
1909–10	59	Der Rosenkavalier
1911–12	and	
1916	60	Ariadne auf Naxos
1912–14	63	Josephslegende (ballet)
1917	60	Der Bürger als Edelmann (incidental music from 1912; rev. 1917)
1914–18	65	Die Frau ohne Schatten
1922–3	70	Schlagobers (ballet)
1918–23	72	Intermezzo
1923–4	—	Die Geschöpfe des Prometheus (melodrama after Beethoven's Ruins of Athens)
1923–7	75	Die ägyptische Helena
1930	—	Idomeneo (Mozart, arrangement)
1929–32	79	Arabella
1933–4	80	Die Schweigsame Frau
1935–6	81	Friedenstag
1936–7	82	Daphne
1938–40	83	Die Liebe der Danae
1940–41	—	Verklungene Feste (ballet, Tanzsuite of 1923 with six new numbers later incl. in Divertimento op. 86)
1940–41	—	Capriccio

Tone poems

1886	16	Aus Italien (symphonic fantasy)
1886–8	23	Macbeth (rev. 1888)
1888	20	Don Juan
1888–9	24	Tod und Verklärung
1894–5	28	Till Eulenspiegels lustige Streiche
1896	30	Also sprach Zarathustra

1897	38	Don Quixote
1898	40	Ein Heldenleben
1903	53	Symphonia domestica
1911–14	64	Alpine Symphony

Orchestral works (unprinted juvenilia not all indicated)

1872–3	—	Hochlands Treue Overture
1876	1	Festmarsch
1877	—	Serenade in G major
1878	—	Overture in E major
1879	—	Overture in A minor
	—	Romance for clarinet and orchestra
1880	—	Symphony in D minor
1882	8	Violin Concerto in D minor
1882–3	11	Horn Concerto No. 1 in E Flat major
1883	—	Concert Overture in C minor
	—	Romance for cello and orchestra
1883–4	12	Symphony in F minor
1885–6	—	Burleske in D minor for piano and orchestra
1888	—	Festmarsh in C major
1892	—	Festival Music for the Golden Wedding of the Grand Duke of Saxe-Weimar (3rd movement: 'Kampf und Sieg')
1905,		
1907	—	2 Parade Marches for the King's Huntsmen
1906	57	2 Military Marches, E flat major and C minor
1913	61	Festliches Präludium
1917	60B	Bürger als Edelmann Suite
1923	—	Tanzsuite (after keyboard pieces by Couperin)
1932	—	Schlagobers Suite
1938–9	—	'München' Waltz I
1940	84	Japanische Festmusik
1941	86	Divertimento (after Couperin)
1945	—	'München' II (memorial waltz)
1945	59	Rosenkavalier Suite
1946	—	Frau ohne Schatten Fantasia
1947	64A	Josephslegende (symphonic fragment)

Instrumental works

1881	7	Serenade for wind in E flat major (13 instruments)
1884	4	Suite for wind in B flat major (13 instruments)
	—	Cadenzas for Mozart's Piano Concerto in C minor K.491 (lost)
1909	—	Fanfare for the Solemn Procession of the Knights of the Order of St. John (brass and timpani, later rescored for full orchestra)
1924	—	Fanfare for the Vienna City Hall
	—	Fanfare for the Vienna Philharmonic
		Hochzeitspräludium (2 harmoniums)
1925	73	Parergon to Symphonia domestica (piano left hand and orchestra)
1927	74	Panathenäenzug (piano left hand and orchestra)
1942		Horn Concerto No. 2 in E flat major
1943	—	Sonatina No. 1 for 16 wind instruments ('From the Studio of an Invalid')
1944–5	—	Sonatina No. 2 (Symphony) for 16 wind instruments ('Cheerful Studio')
1945	—	Metamorphosen for 23 solo strings
1945–6	—	Oboe Concerto in D major
1947	—	Duett-Concertino (clarinet, bassoon, strings, harp)

Chamber works

1875	—	Concertante (2 violins, cello, piano)
1877	—	Piano Trio No. 1 in A major
1878	—	Introduction, Theme and Variations in E flat major (horn and piano)
1897	—	Introduction, Theme and Variations in G major (flute and piano)
1880	—	Piano Trio No. 2 in D major
1880	2	String Quartet in A major

1881	—	Ständchen (piano quartet)
1883	6	Cello Sonata in F major
1883	—	Variations on a dance tune by Cesare Negri (string quartet)
1883–4	13	Piano Quartet in C minor
1884	—	Festmarsch in D major (piano quartet)
1887–8	18	Violin Sonata in E flat major
1893	—	Arabian Dance in D minor (piano quartet)
		Liebesliedchen in G major (piano quartet)

Piano works

1870	—	Schneiderpolka
1872	—	Panzenburgpolka
1873	—	Sonata in E flat major
	—	Sonata in G minor
	—	Sonata in G major
	—	Sonata movement in D major
	—	5 Little Pieces
1873–4	—	6 Sonatinas
1874	—	Sonata in B flat major
	—	Sonata in E flat major
	—	Sonata in D major ('No. 6')
	—	Fantasie
1875	—	2 Little Pieces
1877	—	Sonata in E major ('No. 1')
1878	—	12 Variations
1879	—	Sonata in C minor ('No. 2': 'Grosse Sonate')
	—	Allegro, Andante and 3 Gavottes (Nos. 2–4: D, G, D)
1897(?)	—	Scherzo in B minor
1879–80	—	2 Little Pieces; I Andantino; II Gavotte
1880	—	Fugue on 4 themes
	—	Scherzando in G major
1880–81	5	Sonata in B minor
1881	3	5 Piano Pieces
1882	9	5 Stimmungsbilder (Mood Pictures): Auf stillem Waldespfad, An einsamer Quelle, Intermezzo, Träumerei, Heidebild
1884	—	Theme and 14 Improvisations with Fugue
1940	—	Kupelwieser Waltz (Schubert, noted down)
1946	—	Capriccio Suite for keyboard

Songs
*indicates orchestrated by Strauss

1870	—	Weihnachtslied (Schubart)
1871	—	Einkehr, Winterreise (Uhland)
1873(?)	—	Husarenlied, Der müde Wanderer (Fallersleben)
1877	—	Der Fischer, Lust und Qual (Goethe); Die Drossel (Uhland); Lass ruhn die Toten (Chamisso)
1878	—	Spielmann und Zither (Körner); Wiegenlied, Abend- und Morgenrot (Fallersleben); Im Walde (Geibel)
1878	—	Nebel (Lenau); Soldatenlied, Ein Röslein (Fallersleben)
1879	—	O schneller, mein Ross, Waldesgesang (Stieler); Es rauscht das Laub, Frühlingsanfang, Für Musik, Die Lilien glühn in Düften (Geibel); Die drei Lieder (Uhland); In Vaters Garten (Heine)
1880	—	Die erwachte Rose, Der Morgen (Sallet); Mutter, o sing mich zur Ruh (Felicia Hemans); Immer leiser wird mein Schlummer (Lingg); John Anderson (Burns)
1881	—	Geheiligte Stätte (Fischer)
1882	—	Ballade (Becker); Waldesgang (Stieler)
1883	—	Rote Rosen (Stieler)
1884	—	Aus den Hebräischen Melodien (Byron); Aus Mirza Schaffy (Bodenstedt)
1884–6	15	Madrigal (Michelangelo); Winternacht, Lob des Leidens, Dem Herzen ähnlich, Heimkehr (Schack)
1885	10	*Zueignung, Nichts, Die Nacht, Die Georgine, Geduld, Die Verschwiegenen, Die Zeitlose, Allerseelen (Gilm)

1885	—	Wer hat's gethan (Gilm)
1885–7	17	Seitdem dein Aug', Ständchen, Das Geheimnis, Aus den Liedern der Trauer, Nur Muth!, Barkarole (Schack)
	19	Wozu noch, Breit über mein Haupt, Schön sind, doch kalt die Himmelssterne, Wie sollten wir geheim sie halten, Hoffen, Mein Herz ist stumm (Schack)
	21	All' mein Gedanken, Du meines Herzens Krönelein, Ach Lieb, ich muss nun scheiden, Ach weh, mir unglückhaftem Mann, Die Frauen (Dahn)
1887	22	Kornblumen, Mohnblumen, Efeu, Wasserrose (Dahn)
1891	26	Frühlingsgedränge, O wärst du mein (Lenau)
1894	27	Ruhe, meine Seele (Henckell); *Cäcilie (Hart); *Heimliche Aufforderung, *Morgen (Mackay)
1895	29	Traum durch die Dämmerung, Schlagende Herzen, Nachtgang (Bierbaum)
1896	31	Blauer Sommer; Wenn . . ., Weisser Jasmin (Busse); Stiller Gang (Dehmel)
	32	Ich trage meine Minne, *Liebeshymnus, O süsser Mai (Henckell); Sehnsucht (Liliencron); Himmelsboten (Wunderhorn)
1898	36	*Das Rosenband (Klopstock); Für funfzehn Pfennige, Hat gesagt (Wunderhorn); Anbetung (Rückert)
	37	Glückes genug, Ich liebe dich (Liliencron): *Meinem Kinde (Falke); Mein Auge (Dehmel); Herr Lenz (Bodman); Hochzeitlich Lied (Lindner)
	39	Leises Lied, Der Arbeitsmann, *Befreit, Lied an meinen Sohn (Dehmel); Jung Hexenlied (Bierbaum)
1899	41	*Wiegenlied, Am Ufer (Dehmel); In der Campagna (Mackay); Bruder Liederlich (Liliencron); Leise Lieder (Morgenstern)
	43	An Sie (Klopstock); *Muttertändelei (Bürger); Die Ulme zu Hirsau (Uhland)
1900	46	Ein Obdach gegen Sturm und Regen, Gestern war ich Atlas, Die sieben Siegel, Morgenrot, Ich sehe wie in einem Spiegel (Rückert)
	47	Auf ein Kind, *Des Dichters Abendgang, Rückleben, Einkehr (2nd version), Von den sieben Zechbrüdern (Uhland)
	48	*Freundliche Vision (Bierbaum); Ich schwebe, Kling!, *Winterweihe, Winterliebe (Henckell)
1901	49	Waldseligkeit, Wiegenliedchen (Dehmel); In goldener Fülle (Remer); Lied des Steinklopfers (Henckell); Sie wissen's nicht (Panizza); Junggesellenschwur (Wunderhorn); Wer lieben will, Ach, was Kummer (Mündel)
1903–6	56	Gefunden (Goethe); Blindenklage (Henckell); Im Spätboot (Meyer); Mit deinen blauen Augen, *Frühlingsfeier, Weihnachtsidyll (Heine)
1918	66	Es war einmal ein Bock, Einst kam der Bock als Bote, Es liebte einst ein Hase, Drei Masken sah ich, Hast du ein Tongedicht vollbracht, O lieber Künstler, Unser Feind, Von Händlern wird die Kunst bedroht, Es war einmal eine Wanze, Die Künstler sind die Schöpfer, Die Händler und die Macher, O Schröpferschwarm (Kerr)
1919	67	Wie erkenn ich, Guten Morgen, Sie tragen ihn (Shakespeare); Wer wird von der Welt verlangen, Hab' ich euch denn je geraten, Übers Niederträchtige niemand sich beklage (Goethe)
	68	*An die Nacht, Ich wollt' ein Sträusslein binden, Säusle, liebe Myrte, Als mir dein Lied erklang, Amor, Lied der Frauen (Brentano)
	69	Der Stern, Der Pokal, Einerlei (Arnim); Waldesfahrt, Schlechtes Wetter (Heine)
1919	—	Sinnspruch (Goethe)
1922	—	Hans Adam war ein Erdenkloss (Goethe)
1925	—	Durch allen Schall und Klang (Goethe)
1928	77	Ihre Augen, Schwung, Liebesgeschenke, Die Allmächtige, Huldigung (translated by Von Bethge from the Persian and Chinese)
1930	—	Drei Lieder (Rückert)
1933	12	*Das Bächlein (Goethe)
1935	—	Zugemessne Rhythmen (Goethe)
1942	—	Distichon (Goethe); St. Michael, *Blick vom Oberen Belvedere (Weinheber)
1948	—	Malven

Songs with orchestra

1878	—	Der Spielmann und sein Kind (anon.)
	—	Alphorn (Kerner; voice, horn and piano)
1896–7	33	Verführung (Mackay); Gesang der Apollopriesterin (Bodmann); Hymnus (wrongly attrib. Schiller); Pilgers Morgenlied (Goethe)

1899	44	Notturno (Dehmel); Nächtlicher Gang (Rückert)
1902	51	Das Thal (Uhland)
1906	51	Der Einsame (Heine)
1921	71	Hymne an die Liebe, Rückkehr in die Heimat, Die Liebe (Hölderlin)
1948	—	Four Last Songs: Im Abendrot (Eichendorff); Frühling, Beim Schlafengehen, September (Hesse)

Melodramas

| 1899 | — | Das Schloss am Meere (Uhland) |
| 1897 | 38 | Enoch Arden (Tennyson) |

Choral works

1877	—	Kyrie, Sanctus (2-part unacc. mixed chorus)
1878	—	Auf aus der Ruhe (Goethe: Lila)
1880	—	Chorus from Elektra (Sophocles) (male voices and small orchestra)
	—	Songs (4-part unacc.): Winterlied (Eichendorff), Spielmannsweise, Käferlied (Reinick), Pfingsten, Waldessang, Schneeglöcklein, Trüb blinken nur die Sterne (Böttger), Frühlingsnacht
1881	—	Festchor (with piano acc.)
1884	—	Schwäbische Erbschaft (Löwe) (unacc. mixed chorus)
	14	Wandrers Sturmlied (Goethe) (6-part mixed chorus, large orchestra)
1889	—	Utan Svafel och fosfor (mixed chorus, unacc.)
1897	34	Der Abend (Schiller), Hymne (Rückert) (16-part mixed chorus, unacc.)
	—	Hymne (Licht, Du ewiglich Eines) (female chorus, brass band)
	42	Liebe, Altdeutsches Schlachtlied (Herder) (4-part male chorus, unacc.)
	45	Schlachtgesang, Lied der Freundschaft, Der Brauttanz (Herder) (male chorus, unacc.)
1903	52	Taillefer (Uhland) (soloists, 8-part mixed chorus, large orchestra)
1905	55	Bardengesang (Klopstock) (12 male voices, orchestra)
1905–6	—	6 Volkslieder (male chorus, unacc.): Geistlicher Maien, Misslungene Liebesjagd, Tummler, Hüt' du dich, Wächterlied, Kuckuck
1913	62	Deutsche Motette (Rückert) (4 soloists, 16-part mixed chorus, unacc.)
1914	—	Cantate (Hofmannsthal) (4-part male chorus, unacc.)
1928	76	Die Tageszeiten (Eichendorff) (4-part male chorus, orchestra)
1929	78	Austria (Wildgans) (male voices, orchestra)
1934	—	Olympic Hymn (Lubahn) (mixed chorus, large orchestra)
1935	—	Die Göttin im Putzzimmer (Rückert) (8-part mixed chorus, unacc.)
	—	3 choruses for unacc. male choir (Rückert): Von den Türen, Traumlicht, Frölich im Maien
1938	—	Durch Einsamkeiten (Wildgans) (male chorus, unacc.)
1943	—	An den Baum Daphne (Gregor) (9-part mixed chorus, unacc.)

Plans and sketches

Besinnung (Hesse). Choral work. Sketches
Bildersinfonie. Sketches for a symphony after pictures by Veronese and Hogarth
Coabbradibosimpur (Wolzogen). Plan for an opera
Donau. Tone poem with final chorus. Detailed sketches
Die Insel Kythere. Ballet. Libretto and detailed sketches
Ekke und Schnittlein (after Cervantes). Own opera text
Die Flöhe (Wedekind). Plan for a ballet
Das erhabene Leid der Könige. Plan for an opera. Sketch for own text
Letzte Metamorphose. Orchestral work. Sketch
Lila (Goethe). Sketches for Singspiel, with advice from Cosima Wagner
Peregrinus (Kerr). Plan for an opera
Rhapsody for piano and orchestra. Sketch
Des Esels Schatten (Adler, after Wieland). 'Children's opera', Singspiel
Semiramis (after Calderón). Plan for an opera
Symphony on 3 themes. Sketches
Symphony in E flat major. Sketches
Till Eulenspiegel bei den Schildbürgen. Own opera text (only Act I draft completed)
Ulrich von Liechtenstein (Hauptmann). Plan for an opera
Venus und Diana (Gregor). Plan for an opera

Index

Page numbers in italics indicate illustrations

Photographic acknowledgments

The great majority of the pictures are drawn from the Strauss-Archiv, Garmisch. These have been supplemented from the following sources:

Lustige Blätter, 1910
Suddeutsche Verlag
Bildarchiv Foto Marburg
Vereins- und Westbank, Hamburg
Spemann's goldenes buch der Musik, 1904
Humperdinck-Archiv, Frankfurt

Bibliographisches Institut, Leipzig
Kindler Verlag
Holinck
Mell and Füssli, Zurich
Schott, Mainz
Hadamowsky, Residenzverlag, Salzburg

Rogner und Bernhard
Bayreuth-Archiv
Krieg Verlag, Bad Bocklet
Unser Jahrhundert im Bild, Bertelsmann
Foto Sessner